Paths to Union Renewal

PATHS TO UNION RENEWAL

CANADIAN EXPERIENCES

edited by Pradeep Kumar and Christopher Schenk

 broadview press  Garamond Press

CCPA
CANADIAN CENTRE
for POLICY ALTERNATIVES
CENTRE CANADIEN
de POLITIQUES ALTERNATIVES

Library and Archives Canada Cataloguing in Publication

Paths to union renewal : Canadian experiences / edited by Pradeep Kumar and Christopher Schenk.

Includes bibliographical references and index.
ISBN 1-55193-058-7

1. Labor unions—Canada.   2. Organizational change—Canada.   3. Labor movement—Canada.   I. Kumar, Pradeep, 1940–   II. Schenk, Christopher Robert, 1942–

HD6524.P38 2005   331.88'0971   C2005-906247-9

Broadview Press, Ltd. is an independent, international publishing house, incorporated in 1985. Broadview believes in shared ownership, both with its employees and with the general public; since the year 2000 Broadview shares have traded publicly on the Toronto Venture Exchange under the symbol BDP.

We welcome any comments and suggestions regarding any aspect of our publications — please feel free to contact us at the addresses below, or at broadview@broadviewpress.com / www.broadviewpress.com

North America	*UK, Ireland, and*	*Australia and*
PO Box 1243,	*Continental Europe*	*New Zealand*
Peterborough, Ontario,	NBN Plymbridge	UNIREPS
Canada K9J 7H5	Estover Road	University of
Tel: (705) 743-8990	Plymouth PL6 7PY	New South Wales
Fax: (705) 743-8353	United Kingdom	Sydney, NSW, 2052
customerservice	Tel: +44 (0) 1752 202301	Tel: + 61 2 96640999
@broadviewpress.com	Fax: +44 (0) 1752 202333	Fax: + 61 2 96645420
	Customer Service:	info.press@unsw.edu.au
PO Box 1015	cservs@nbnplymbridge.com	
3576 California Road,	orders@nbnplymbridge.com	
Orchard Park, New York		
USA 14127		

Cover design and typeset by Zack Taylor, www.zacktaylor.com

Broadview Press Ltd. gratefully acknowledges the financial support of the Government of Canada through the Book Publishing Industry Development Program for our publishing activities.

Printed in Canada by Union Labour

This book is dedicated to the thousands of trade union activists across Canada who have worked tirelessly to defend their members and build their unions, often in the face of adversity. We hope this text helps make the link between your daily efforts and the better world that could be.

Contents

List of Figures and Tables   9
Contributors   11
Acknowledgements   13

Introduction   15
Pradeep Kumar and Christopher Schenk

Part I: Union Renewal and the State of Unions in Canada   27

Chapter 1:   Union Renewal and Organizational Change:
               A Review of the Literature   29
               Pradeep Kumar and Christopher Schenk

Chapter 2   Rowing Against the Tide: The Struggle to
               Raise Union Density in a Hostile Environment   61
               Andrew Jackson

Chapter 3   Innovation in Canadian Unions:
               Patterns, Causes and Consequences   79
               Pradeep Kumar and Gregor Murray

Chapter 4   Women are Key to Union Renewal:
               Lessons from the Canadian Labour Movement   103
               Charlotte Yates

Chapter 5   Globalization and Union Renewal:
               Perspectives from the Quebec Labour Movement   113
               Christian Lévesque and Gregor Murray

Part II: Case Studies on Union Renewal   127

Chapter 6   The BCGEU: The Road to Renewal   129
               Gary Steeves

Chapter 7   Union Renewal and CUPE   145
               Jane Stinson and Morna Ballantyne

Chapter 8   Union Resistance and Union Renewal in the CAW   161
               David Robertson and Bill Murninghan

Chapter 9   Rank-and-File Involvement in Policy-Making at the CEP   185
               Keith R. Newman

Chapter 10   Mobilizing Young People: A Case Study of
               UFCW Canada Youth Programs and Initiatives   191
               Anna Liu and Christopher O'Halloran

Chapter 11   Renewal from Different Directions:
               The Case of UNITE-HERE Local 75   201
               Steven Tufts

Chapter 12   Building Capacity for Global Action: Steelworkers'
               Humanity Fund   221
               Judith Marshall and Jorge Garcia-Orgales

Part III: Unions and Community: Campaigns and Organizing   235

Chapter 13   Community Unionism and Labour Movement Renewal:
               Organizing for Fair Employment   237
               Cynthia J. Cranford, Mary Gellatly, Deena Ladd, and Leah F. Vosko

Chapter 14   The Workers' Organizing and Resource Centre in Winnipeg   251
               Geoff Bickerton and Catherine Stearns

Chapter 15   A Community Coalition in Defense of Public Medicare   261
               Natalie Mehra

Chapter 16   Organizing Call Centres: The Steelworkers' Experience   277
               Julie Guard, Jorge Garcia-Orgales, Mercedes Steedman, and D'Arcy Martin

Part IV: Leadership Development and Education   293

Chapter 17   Increasing Inter-Union Co-operation and Co-ordination:
               The BC Federation of Labour Organizing Institute   295
               John Weir

Chapter 18   Union Education, Union Leadership and Union Renewal:
               The Role of PEL   307
               Johanna Weststar

               Index   323

List of Figures and Tables

Introduction
Table 1: Membership of Major Canadian Unions, 1985-2004   21

Chapter 2
Table 1: Union Members as % of Wage and Salary Earners   62
Table 2: Union Membership in Canada (as reported by trade unions)   62
Table 3: The Union Wage Advantage in 2003   63
Table 4: Trends in Unionization Rate   67
Table 5: Employment by Broad Occupation   70
Table 6: Changes in Union Density, 1997 to 2003   72
Table 7: Where Can We Find New Members? A Profile of Non-Union
    Employees – Private Sector Only – in 2003   77

Chapter 3
Table 1: Areas of Change   89
Table 2: Use of New Technologies and Communications Techniques   90
Table 3: Implementation of Activist Servicing Strategies   91
Table 4: Changes in Inclusiveness Strategies   93
Table 5: Distribution by Sector of New Certification and/or Bargaining Units
    Organized by Canadian Unions in the Past Three Years   94
Table 6: Innovations in Organizing   96

Chapter 4
Table 1: Organizing Outcome (Win/Loss) by Gender Majority Bargaining
    Unit   106
Table 2: Organizing in Public vs. Private Sector by Male and Female
    Majority   107

Chapter 5
Figure 1: Local Union Power Resources   120

Chapter 7
Table 1: CUPE Membership, 1963-2004   146

Chapter 8
Figure 1: Composition of CAW Membership, 1987 and 2005   162
Figure 2: Strategic Determinants of Union Strength   164

9

Chapter 11
Figure 1: Downtown Toronto Hotels by Size and Bargaining Agent   204
Figure 2: Room Attendant Hourly Wage Rates, Selected Toronto Hotels, 1994–
    2005   210

Table 1: Selected Toronto CMA Labour Force Characteristics, all Occupations, all
    Industries and Hotels, Motels and Tourist Courts Industry (Standard Industrial
    Classification 911), 2001   202
Table 2: Selected Greater Toronto Area Labour Force Characteristics, all
    Occupations, all Industries, and all Selected Occupations in Hotels, Motels and
    Tourist Courts Industry (Standard Industrial Classification 911), 1996   203
Table 3: Major Provisions of Neutrality Agreement for a New Hotel   214

Chapter 12
Figure 1: Total Membership over the Years   224
Figure 2: Membership by Sectors—2005   226

Chapter 18
Table 1: Activity Levels Before and After PEL   311
Table 2: The Impact of PEL on Feelings of Solidarity toward Various
    Groups   313

Figure 1: Percentage of PEL Participants more likely to Question the Decisions
    made by Various Sources   312
Figure 2: The Impact of PEL on Awareness Regarding Diversity in the
    CAW   314
Figure 3: PEL Coverage by Bargaining Unit Size   315
Figure 4: PEL Coverage by Sector   316
Figure 5: PEL Coverage by Region   316

Contributors

Morna Ballantyne works as Managing Director of Union Development for the Canadian Union of Public Employees (CUPE) in Ottawa.

Geoff Bickerton is the Research Director of the Canadian Union of Postal Employees (CUPW) in Ottawa.

Cynthia J. Cranford teaches in the Department of Sociology, University of Toronto, in Toronto, Ontario.

Jorge Garcia-Orgales works in th Research Department of the United Steelworkers (USW) union in Toronto, Ontario.

Mary Gellatly is a community legal worker in the Workers' Rights Division at Parkdale Community Legal Services in Toronto, Ontario.

Julie Guard teaches Labour Studies and coordinates the Labour and Workplace Studies Program at the University of Manitoba, Winnipeg, Manitoba.

Andrew Jackson is the National Director of Social and Economic Policy at the Canadian Labour Congress in Ottawa.

Pradeep Kumar teaches labour relations and is the Director of the MIR program in the School of Policy Studies at Queen's University, Kingston, Ontario.

Deena Ladd is the Coordinator of the Toronto Organizing For Fair Employment (TOFFE), now called the Workers' Action Centre, in Toronto, Ontario.

Christian Lévesque teaches in the École des Haute Études Commerciales (HEC) in Montreal, Quebec and is the Co-Director of the Interuniversity Research Centre on Globalization and Work (CRIMT).

Anna Liu is a graduate of the United Food and Commercial Worker's youth internship program. She currently works as an organizer for UFCW Canada, based in Toronto, Ontario.

Judith Marshall works for the Humanity Fund of the United Steelworkers in Toronto, Ontario.

D'Arcy Martin is the coordinator of the Centre for the Study of Education and Work, OISE/University of Toronto.

Natalie Mehra is the Provincial Coordinator of the Ontario Health Coalition (OHC).

Bill Murninghan works in the Research Department of the Canadian Auto Workers (CAW) union in Toronto, Ontario.

Gregor Murray teaches in the School of Industrial Relations and is the Director of the Interuniversity Research Centre on Globalization and Work (CRIMT) at the Universite de Montreal in Montreal, Quebec.

Keith R. Newman is the Research Director of the Communications, Energy and Paperworkers Union of Canada (CEP), in Ottawa.

Christopher O'Halloran is a graduate of the United Food and Commercial Worker's youth internship program. He currently works as the National Youth Co-ordinator for UFCW Canada, in Toronto, Ontario.

David Robertson is the Director of the Work Organization and Training Department of the Canadian Auto Workers (CAW) union based in Toronto, Ontario.

Christopher Schenk is the Research Director of the Ontario Federation of Labour (OFL) based in Toronto, Ontario.

Catherine Stearns is the co-ordinator of the Winnipeg-based Workers' Organizing Resource Centre (WORC) and an activist with the Canadian Union of Postal Workers (CUPW).

Mercedes Steedman coordinates and teaches in the Labour and Trade Union Studies program at Laurentian University, Sudbury, Ontario.

Gary Steeves is the former Director of Organizing and Field Studies of the British Columbia Government and Services Employees Union (BCGEU) in Vancouver, B.C.

Jane Stinson is an Education Officer with the Canadian Union of Public Employees (CUPE) in Ottawa.

Steven Tufts teaches in the Department of Geography at Trent University in Peterborough, Ontario.

Leah F. Vosko is Canada Research Chair in Feminist Political Economy and teaches in the Political Science, Sociology, and Women's Studies departments at York University, Toronto, Ontario.

John Weir is Director of the Organizing Institute at the British Columbia Federation of Labour in Vancouver, B.C.

Johanna Weststar is a doctoral candidate at the Centre for Industrial Relations at the University of Toronto in Toronto, Ontario.

Charlotte Yates teaches in and is the Director of the Labour Studies Program at McMaster University in Hamilton, Ontario.

Acknowledgements

The preparation and production of this volume would not have been possible without the enthusiastic cooperation and constant encouragement of many individuals in the labour movement and academia. The editors particularly wish to express their deep appreciation to the contributors for taking time from their hectic schedules to prepare papers for this volume under tight deadlines.

The editors would also like to acknowledge the generous financial assistance towards the publication of the volume from a number of organizations. We were highly encouraged by the promise of assistance and support from the Canadian Labour Congress (CLC) and the Ontario Federation of Labour (OFL) in advance of the publication. This generosity was extended by unions, specifically the Canadian Union of Public Employees (CUPE), the Canadian Auto Workers (CAW), the United Steelworkers (USW), the United Food and Commercial Workers (UFCW Canada), the Communications, Energy and Paperworkers (CEP), the British Columbia Government and General Employees (BCGEU) and the Canadian Union of Postal Workers (CUPW).

We wish to thank Wayne Samuelson, President of the OFL, for his support and for enabling co-editor Chris Schenk the time to work on this volume. Our thanks also go to Jill Michalko of the OFL for keeping track of the progress of the papers and her skill in pulling together text and charts in a readable format. We also acknowledge and appreciate the efforts of our publishers, Broadview Press, Garamond Press and the Canadian Centre for Policy Alternatives (CCPA) for their hard work in bringing this book to publication in a timely manner.

The editors are also grateful to the Interuniversity Research Centre on Globalization and Work (CRIMT) and its Director Gregory Murray, for facilitating presentation and discussion of the preliminary drafts of papers in this volume at the International Colloquium on Union Renewal in Montreal. The Colloquium, organized by CRIMT within the framework of its project, Rethinking Institutions of Work and Employment in Global Era, funded by the Social Science and Humanities Research Council, was attended by nearly 200 trade unionists and academics from North and South America, Europe, and Australia, providing a unique opportunity to exchange ideas and experiences of union renewal in diverse settings. CRIMT also provided generous financial assistance towards this publication.

The Editors

Introduction

PRADEEP KUMAR AND CHRISTOPHER SCHENK

Unions in Canada and elsewhere are at a crossroads, facing difficult challenges of adaptation, adjustment, and confrontation with a substantively different external and internal environment. Globalization, free trade, and neo-liberal policies of employers and governments constitute formidable challenges. Corporate restructuring, downsizing, employers' increased demand for "concessions" from workers, and the rising precarious and contingent workforce remain a day-to-day experience for many workers, causing significant anxiety and insecurities. In the current environment, unions cannot afford to be complacent.

This is particularly the case in countries where unions have experienced a substantive decrease in their membership. A range of academic books, union policy papers, and commentaries have examined the process of change and have exchanged ideas on how to reverse the decline of union strength and influence, reinvigorate membership participation and democratic decision-making, increase union visibility in communities, and expand unionization rates through increased organizing and closer links with social movement groups.

In contrast to other countries, the debate on union renewal in Canada has been slower to surface. In significant part this is because unions in Canada have not undergone the same dramatic losses as unions in some other countries. While the unionized percentage of the workforce from Australia to Britain to the United States and even parts of continental Europe has experienced significant decline, union density in Canada has slipped only marginally. Another reason may be that union renewal in Canada has been an ongoing process for more than two decades, reflected in various mergers, an uneven though significant pace of new organizing, modifications in organizational structures and strategies and resistance to concession bargaining. Nonetheless, unionization rates are lower today than they were in the 1980s. More aggressive approaches and initiatives are needed to halt this slippage, however small, and thereby widely diffuse the process of change.

To say that discussion and debate on union renewal in Canada has been limited, in comparison to more extensive debates in countries such as United States, Britain and Australia, is not to say it is non-existent. Unions in Canada have been concerned about the growing threat to their organizational and bargaining strength since the early 1980s, and have been reassessing their strategies, organizational structures, and methods and approaches to more effectively organize the unorganized and provide better services to their members. Past conventions of the Canadian Labour Congress (CLC), the Ontario Federation of Labour (OFL) and other provincial federations have discussed ways and means of rebuilding labour's strength. The British Columbia Federation of Labour (B.C. Fed) established an Organizing Institute nearly ten years ago. Federations of labour on the prairies have been exploring the feasibility of such an initiative for themselves. The CLC and OFL have also passed resolutions urging these central labour bodies to explore the desirability of organizing institutes to train a new generation of organizers. The CLC also hosted a conference in Ottawa on union organizing in October 2003, where a number of ideas to speed the process of change and renewal were debated. Key presentations and commentary from this conference were later documented in the journal *Studies in Political Economy* (2004). The Canadian Auto Workers (CAW) has produced a discussion paper on union renewal which was debated at their constitutional convention in August 2003. A national survey of innovation and change in Canadian unions was conducted by Pradeep Kumar and Gregor Murray in 2001. It revealed that unions in Canada have been engaged in organizational change for several years, focusing on organizational reviews, implementation of new technologies, and modifications in their bargaining and organizing strategies, structures, and processes. Other examples of union renewal proposals and initiatives can be found in the resolutions, convention policy papers, and other writings and activities within unions and union central labour bodies themselves.

The purpose of this book is to document and analyze Canadian experiences with union renewal. We assess the vast and growing literature on union renewal to derive lessons for accelerating the process of change in Canada. The book includes studies of trends and patterns of union density in Canada, together with an analysis of the potential for organizing in the private sector, incidence of organizational change in unions, the role of women in union renewal, initiatives for leadership development through education and training, the union revival in Quebec through capacity and power-building, and inter-union competition and case studies of innovations currently underway in unions and communities across the country. The case studies are particularly valuable, as there exists no single model of union renewal. Change is often a slower and more uneven process embedded in particular contexts than one might have first expected. It is therefore important to examine various paths to union renewal and learn from them. In this text we provide a series of case studies constituting what might be termed "best practices" to inform and assist the change.

With this publication we hope to create a better understanding of the dynamics of change in union organizations and thus initiate further debate and discussions within the labour movement on the need for diffusing the process of change more widely and deeply. To our knowledge, this is the first text of its kind in Canada. Many books are written about unions by people outside labour's ranks. This volume includes contributions from unionists and selected academics working in association with them. It is written for union activists as a guide to action, for students of labour studies and other disciplines, and more generally for those who have an interest in unions and their positive role in social and economic change.

Why unions matter

This volume is not designed as an introduction to unions (see Black and Silver 2001; Jackson 2005); rather, its focus is on the adaptation and change initiatives undertaken by unions to restore their strength and influence. However, unions are so often maligned in the press—creating the misleading perception that unions are no longer necessary or capable of protecting working people—that a word on their role and purpose may well be of value. "In the dominant discourse," notes Beynon in the context of Britain (2003, 272), "trade unions are seen either as villains or as outdated." In the United States, Ruth Milkman and Kim Voss state that "organized labor's obituary appears regularly in the news as well as in scholarly commentary..." (2004, 1). In Canada, there are frequent references in the media that unions are a special interest group, are "inflexible," are always demanding more, cause inefficiencies, and are undemocratic and autocratic with self-serving leadership. Yet, for all their shortcomings, unions are major institutions in almost all countries, where they play an important role in determining wages and working conditions, promoting progressive social and economic change, and advancing the immediate interests of workers through legislative and political activities. In developed capitalist societies, where a vast majority of their populations are engaged in paid work for their livelihood, unions are a central institution of work and society and have been associated with significant improvements in worker and societal well-being.

The basic terms of the modern employment relationship consist of workers agreeing to work for an employer for a certain number of hours, in a specific location, to conduct particular tasks for a certain wage or salary. This employment relationship also involves a power relationship, albeit unequal, in which employers have the right to hire, organize and direct the work, and terminate workers not wanted or needed. Without unions, individual workers would have to negotiate the terms and conditions of their work arrangements, such as their hours of work, their wages, their benefits and working conditions in this highly unequal relationship. Workers would also be left to their own devices when it came to arbitrary and unfair treatment by employers, such as unjust dismissal, discrimination, favouritism, and so on (Jackson 2005, 143-145).

This is not to say that all employers are personally vengeful or grossly unfair, but rather to recognize that a conflict of interest exists between their desire and need to produce goods or services at least cost and maximum profit and the aspirations of working people for a better quality of life that comes in substantial part with higher compensation, shorter hours, and improved working conditions. The introduction of a collective organization by workers to improve their situation creates an improved balance of power for employees in the workplace. This enables the development of protective rules and procedures, negotiations over terms and conditions of employment codified in a legal collective agreement, and due process regarding worker complaints known as a grievance arbitration procedure. "What a union does is give workers a "voice" in their workplaces, a way to put themselves on a more equal footing with their employers" (Yates 1998, 20). In short, unions add an element of democracy in the workplace as workers have a say over wages, working conditions, benefits, schedules, and arbitrary employer behaviour.

For unionized workers, this system has proved remarkably successful. Not only have unions fought for dignity and respect in the workplace (one of the key reasons why workers support a union, for women's equality, against racial discrimination and more), but they have also substantially improved wages and working conditions.

A policy document adopted at the recent convention of the Canadian Labour Congress proclaimed:

> We are proud of the profound difference the labour movement has made at the workplace and society. Better wages, more job security, pensions and benefits, protection against racism and discrimination, same-sex benefits, pay equity, health and safety measures—these are just some of the advantages unions have fought for and won. (CLC 2005)

The proponents of a global economy have asserted that in the new economy, where workers are considered to be empowered, unions are not needed, they are anachronisms. However, as Yates has noted (2001, 40), "unions are needed now more than ever." As he puts it:

> How are workers to protect themselves from the negative effects of lean production? How are workers to combat the corporate-state alliance that has created havoc on their living standards through trade agreements, anti-labour legislation, refusal to enforce labour laws, the destruction of the welfare state, and the privatization of public services? How are workers, including specially those who are contingent, going to make themselves more secure, guarantee safe workplaces, and ensure their future?

Rather than viewing unions as relics of the past, we need to see them as organizations with a future: basic collectivities with a proven track record of defending and improving the lives of millions of working people across Canada and around the globe.

Yet, despite all the improvements unions have championed and won, they are currently faced with a hostile environment that demands new innovations, strategies and ideas if it is to be successfully confronted.

Contents of this volume

This book has been organized in four parts. Part I, titled *Union Renewal and the State of Unions in Canada,* includes five contributions on the assessment of the various dimensions of the union renewal process and the general nature and scope of organizational change in Canadian unions.

Chapter 1, by the editors, is an extensive review of recent academic and union literature, highlighting the varying experience and approaches to union renewal in differing institutional and environmental contexts and its general lessons for Canada. The chapter discusses the meaning and concepts of union renewal, its rational and major thesis, key renewal strategies, comparative experience, obstacles to change, and facilitating factors and the challenges of union renewal in the Canadian setting. This chapter, necessarily more theoretical than others, is key to understanding the "big picture," particularly the economic and political context within which unions find themselves embedded and the various strategies advocated for union renewal.

Chapter 2, by Andrew Jackson, provides an overview of the trends and patterns of union density in Canada and its implications for union renewal. Of particular interest is his analysis of the opportunities for new organizing in various industries and occupations. He makes two major points. First, the "highly gendered pattern of union growth and decline merits careful reflection," a theme discussed more fully in Yates's paper in this volume. Second, "the challenge of reversing a slow union density decline through new organizing is formidable, but recent breakthroughs in both private services and the broader public sector give hope that union renewal can begin to reverse union decline."

Chapter 3, by Pradeep Kumar and Gregor Murray, highlights some of the innovations in structures, policies, and practices underway in union organizations in Canada, and the factors underlying the patterns of change. The paper draws on an extensive survey of innovations and change conducted by the authors in 2001 in partnership with Human Resources and Skills Development Canada and major unions and federations. The paper notes that the innovations are a product of "an interplay between organizational characteristics, environment, and union culture and philosophy." The authors also point out that, while unions in Canada have pursued a wide variety of organizational changes, "the implementation of so-called best practices is highly uneven." They emphasize the need for a discussion and debate on the form of unionism before making changes in structures, policies and practices. They find that the unions that are pursuing larger social visions and enlarged solidarities are most likely to be associated with innovations in such key areas as membership involvement, politics, implementation of new technologies, activist servicing, and new methods and targets for organizing.

Chapter 4, by Charlotte Yates, examines the ways in which union organizing is gender-biased and highlights possible union strategies to overcome the bias and improve organizing success. She argues that "women are critical to the revitalization of unions, but they must undo the gender-bias in their approach to organizing if they are going to build on this potential." The paper draws on the survey of union organizers in Ontario and British Columbia conducted by the author in 2000 and 2001. Based on her data, Yates finds that, in both Ontario and British Columbia, organizing drives were more likely to be successful in workplaces where women were a majority compared to the male-dominated workplaces. The differences in success rates for female- and male-dominated workplaces were particularly notable in the private sector, where there is a significant concentration of women workers and where unions are weak. She argues that union strategies need to take into account women's experiences if unions are serious about organizing the large and growing non-union private service sector. Yates also cautions unions that they need to do more than simply add women in their decision-making structures. "Rather, unions need to shift the lens with which they see the workforce so that they reveal the complex ways in which gender shapes workforce experiences, relations with co-workers and employers, and labour market needs and concerns."

Chapter 5, by Christian Levesque and Gregor Murray, analyzes the Quebec experience with union renewal, focusing on the critical role of power resources, that is "resources that a union can access and mobilize in order to influence the process of change." They emphasize the significance of three resources for the development of union power: 1) the strategic capacity to develop a vision or an agenda; 2) internal solidarity or democracy; and 3) external solidarity or the capacity to embed the local unions in networks through alliances with the larger union movement, other unions, and the community. They believe, based on their research, that the Quebec labour movement has been relatively successful in developing these resources effectively. Many unions in other regions of Canada are also engaged in a similar power building process. "The challenge for trade unionists is to think more systemically about the kind of power resources likely to enhance worker voice in globalized workplaces," according to Levesque and Murray.

Part II of the volume includes case studies of renewal in two public sector and five predominantly private sector unions. The two public sector unions are the Canadian Union Of Public Employees (CUPE), the union with the largest membership in Canada, and the British Columbia Government and Service Employees Union (BCGEU), a component of the National Union of Public and General Employees Union (NUPGE), Canada's second largest union. Among the private sector unions are the Canadian Auto Workers (CAW), the United Steelworkers Union (USW), United Food and Commercial Workers Union (UFCW), Communications, Energy and Paperworkers' Union (CEP), and the UNITE-HERE, a new union formed in 2004 with the merger of the Union of Needletrades, Industrial and Textile Employees' Union (UNITE) and the Hotel Employees and Restaurant Employees (HERE). All of these unions, with the exception of UNITE-HERE, have been successful in increasing their membership through mergers and aggressive organizing (See Table 1). The seven union case study chapters form the core of this text. They have been written primarily by trade unionists for unionists, as well as labour studies students and others interested in what unions are doing that activates and empowers their members. The case studies provide a menu of best practices that, with the necessary modifications, could be adapted by other unions or union locals to develop more fully their democratic potential and increase their membership.

Of the seven union case studies, three describe the process of union renewal as an evolutionary strategic exercise. In the case of CUPE (Chapter 7), the renewal began 16 years ago with the establishment of a Commission on Structure and Services in 1989 to review the effectiveness of the union and has been an ongoing process ever since. The consultative process of the Commission stimulated a fundamental discussion on "what the union is, what it does, what it should be, and what it should do," according to Jane Stinson and Morna Ballantyne, the authors of the study.

Over time, the union has been involved in a number of initiatives and programs aimed at increasing the power of the union through increased membership involvement and greater solidarity among members. It has also been able to build a shared vision of "a progressive, forward-looking, active union, responsive to the needs of both members and working people generally." The authors note that CUPE's renewal program has been profoundly influenced by the belief that "a union is only as strong as it is democratic; only as strong as it is active; and only as strong as it is ready

Table 1: Membership of Major* Canadian Unions, 1985–2004

	Membership (1000)		
Unions	1985	1995	2004
Private Sector Unions:			
Canadian Auto Workers (CAW)	136	205	260
United Steelworkers (USW)	148	161	235
United Food and Commercial Workers (UFCW)	146	185	230
Communication, Energy and Paperworkers (CEP)	134	125	150
International Brotherhood of Teamsters (IBT)	92	95	125
UNITE–HERE	77	68	55
Laborers' International Union (LIUNA)	51	55	85
International Brotherhood of Electrical Workers (IBEW)	69	67	55
United Brotherhood of Carpenters and Joiners (UBC)	73	56	52
Public Sector Unions:			
Canadian Union of Public Employees (CUPE)	296	445	540
National Union of Public and General Employees (NUPGE)	245	300	337
Public Service Alliance of Canada (PSAC)	182	168	157
Social Affairs Federation (FAS/CSN)	93	97	101
Service Employees International Union (SEIU)	70	80	78
Quebec Teaching Congress (CEQ)	90	112	126
Elementary Teachers Federation of Ontario (ETFO)	46	72	65
Canadian Union of Postal Workers (CUPW)	24	51	55
Ontario Secondary School Teachers Federations (OSSTF)	36	49	53
Ontario Nurses' Assn (ONA)	39	50	50

Source: HR SDC Workplace Information Directorate, Directory of Labour Organizations
* Unions with a membership of 50,000 and over.

and able to exercise collective action in defence of workers' rights in the workplace and citizens' rights in the community."

In Chapter 8, David Robertson and Bill Murnighan of the CAW state that the renewal in their union has been an ongoing process. "In many respects, the very formation of the CAW represents a large scale renewal project." The theme of the union's first collective bargaining convention in 1985 was: "We're Building a Future Together." Robertson and Murnighan maintain that, twenty years later, "we are still building that future together." The union has grown dramatically over the past 20 years, both in numbers and in the scope of its activities. From a largely auto workers' union, with a concentration of membership in Ontario, it has transformed into a truly national union with a diverse membership in almost all sectors of the economy. The CAW has been credited with many innovations at the bargaining table and in politics. The case study by Robertson and Murnighan not only describes the various initiatives taken by the union over the past two decades, but also includes parts of a policy paper, *Union Resistance and Union Renewal*, debated and adopted at the union's constitutional convention in August 2003. The paper discusses the determinants of a strong union movement, the evolution of the union, and the challenges of union resistance and union renewal. These include making gains in bargaining, expanding democracy, organizing, deepening membership involvement and participation, generational renewal, strengthening social unionism, building alliances with social movements, international solidarity, strengthening our capacity to mobilize, and defining ourselves by what we do. The paper asserts that one of the union's greatest strengths is its culture. The case study ends with excerpts from interviews with key staff and elected leaders of the union, including the CAW President Buzz Hargrove.

The BCGEU case study by Gary Steeves (Chapter 6) similarly describes union renewal as an ongoing process in his union over the past two decades. It started with the union's participation in Operation Solidarity in 1983 when it "saw itself clearly as a social union rejecting the more traditional role of 'business unionism'." The following year it adopted a policy paper entitled *Building for the Future,* emphasizing aggressive organizing with a high degree of membership involvement. A more formal strategic exercise in 1998 to review the union's approach to servicing led to the adoption of five objectives as pilot projects. These included reinforcing members' ownership of the union, expanding local activists' sense of responsibility for their own collective agreements, expanding the skills and experience of stewards and local officers, more effective utilization of union staff's time and expertise, and increasing the authority and accountability of locals. The union continues to monitor the progress of these projects. In 2001, it adopted 22 recommendations to more effectively implement the pilot projects. Among them were more resources for education programs and other support measures to promote the vision of union renewal. The case study discusses the implementation of methods to meet major challenges and outlines lessons from the process of renewal and change within the union. Steeves concludes his study by stating that "renewal is a democratic, membership-driven belief in the possibility of engaging more effectively in the world around us. Its failure is a failure of people to seize an opportunity to shape their own future."

Another three case studies (USW, UFCW, and CEP) focus on specific renewal initiatives. The focus of the USW case study (Chapter 12) is the Humanities Fund, an initiative to build international exchanges and solidarity and alliances in response to growing power of multinationals through capital mobility. The paper by Judith Marshall and Jorge Garcia-Orgales first describes the working of the Humanities Fund and then assesses how the global connections with Chile and Peru in the mining sector have contributed to the union renewal in the USW. According to Marshall and Garcia-Orgales, the Humanities Fund has helped build international union solidarity through the support of long-term development projects in association with labour and community organizations in 14 countries, through education programs and worker exchanges and through lobby activities and policy development. They believe that the worker exchanges and alliances forged through the Humanities Fund have become "a powerful force for revitalizing the union and equipping our members to better contend with corporate globalization."

The UFCW case study in Chapter 10 by Anna Liu and Chris O'Halloran, examines the development of youth programs and initiatives within UFCW Canada to increase youth involvement and participation in the union. Of interest are the union's national youth internship program, designed to train young union activists by providing them with basic labour education and training, local union youth committees, and youth conferences for exchange of experiences and views on union strategies and campaigns. The authors believe that the youth initiative has led to the integration of young workers into every level of the union and increased their participation in decision-making structures, servicing, and organizing. They note that the success of the program can be attributed to the union leadership's commitment to the promotion of youth involvement and their understanding of its value for building an inclusive social unionism that moves away from service unionism.

The CEP study (Chapter 9) by Keith Newman outlines the process of decision-making in the union on major policies, emphasizing the involvement of rank-and-file membership. The case study describes how the union formulated the energy policy in 2001 and the benefits of rank-and-file member participation in policy-making. Newman asserts that the new process not only builds the confidence of members to debate issues with other members and industry spokespeople, but also ensures that policy is well grounded in the union and reflects the democratic input and views of members.

The UNITE–HERE case study in Chapter 11 by Steve Tufts is distinct in that it relates to renewal in one of the union's locals (Local 75), using multiple strategies, integrated to reinforce one another. The study is important for many reasons. It relates to a large local of workers in major hotels in Toronto, owned by multinational firms. The workforce consists largely of immigrant and visible minority women with poor wages and working conditions. As Tufts points out, the gender, ethnic and income segmentation of the hotel labour market creates difficult challenges for building union solidarity and for new organizing and effective bargaining. In this context, Local 75's experience with organizing and pattern bargaining is instructive.

Part III, *Unions and Community: Campaigns and Organizing,* includes four papers. Three relate to union-community alliances to defend and advance worker rights and build worker confidence and solidarity, and one focuses on innovative organizing with rank-and-file worker participation.

Cynthia Cranford, Mary Gellatly, Deena Ladd and Leah Vosko, in their paper (Chapter 13), discuss the concept and practice of community unionism and demonstrate the potential for building a union-community alliance for labour movement renewal through an analysis of the working of the Workers' Action Centre (WAC) in Toronto. The WAC, a product of the merger of Toronto Organizing for Fair Employment (TOFFE) and the Workers' Information Centre, is a "community union" working with people in precarious employment—workers (largely new immigrant women and men of colour) with very low wages and few benefits, who are routinely denied basic rights and employment security. The Centre outreaches these workers to foster "self-organizing" against precarious employment through specific campaigns, targeting employers who contravene basic employment standards and pressuring government to enforce and improve labour and employment legislation. The Centre, according to the authors, has had considerable success in terms of the number of people involved, the response by employers, and the concrete gains for individual workers. They point out, however, that community-union initiatives like the WAC face two major challenges. First is the difficulty of organizing workers who move in between multiple sectors. Second is the "arduous task of balancing individual advocacy and collective mobilization." Both these challenges are made more difficult by the tenuous funding of such initiatives. The authors suggest that "one of the logical sources of funding for workers' centres is the union movement, since this aid would allow for more community-based innovative programming."

The paper by Geoff Bickerton and Catherine Stearns (Chapter 14) evaluates the experience of the Winnipeg based Workers' Organizing and Resource Centre (WORC), an initiative of the Canadian Union of Postal Workers (CUPW) and community activists drawn from several communities. "The importance of WORC" according to Bickerton and Stearns, "extends beyond the city limits of Winnipeg. Within CUPW, WORC represents a tangible symbol of the union's belief in community unionism." The mandate of the Centre is "1) to help establish, maintain, and facilitate community organizations that represent and enforce people's rights within our community; 2) to advocate on behalf of the unorganized workers for protection of their rights in the workplace and beyond; and 3) to organize the unorganized." The WORC has been a successful venture. "In seven years of operation, WORC has provided assistance to thousands of workers, assisted in the development of new and existing working class institutions, and gained the respect of organized labour and the progressive community ..." It "continues as a vibrant centre of progressive working class activity. With continued support it will serve and grow as a model of union-community solidarity and cooperation."

Natalie Mehra's paper (Chapter 15) on the Ontario Health Coalition (OHC) campaign to defend public Medicare is another example of the potential of union-community alliances. The campaign came about in 2001 when a Royal Commission headed by former Saskatchewan Premier Roy Romanow was appointed by the federal government to assess public Medicare in Canada and recommend policies and measures to ensure the long-term sustainability of a universally accessible, publicly-funded health care system. The community outreach campaign was launched to counteract the intense private health care lobby's efforts to make Canadians believe that public health care was inadequate, inefficient, and unsustainable. It involved all major public and private sector unions, ethnic and cultural groups, diverse faith community organizations, seniors' organizations, community social service organizations, and the Council of Canadians. While the campaign was not able to achieve all its goals, it was highly successful in mounting an effective opposition to forces that were campaigning to dismantle the public health insurance system. Mehra points out that the study of the health coalition campaign is important for the union renewal discussions for several reasons. It was forged in response to a public policy issue that had serious implications for social and economic equality—the cherished goal of labour movements everywhere. The campaign was able to mobilize a massive community response reaching millions of workers and households. It involved both public and private sector unions, working collectively, internally, and externally. The campaign was a "true partnership between unions and community groups" that are not a part of the labour movement. The massive mobilization was "successful in forcing into retreat—at least temporarily—the forces working to privatize the public health insurance system."

The paper by Julie Guard, Jorge Garcia–Orgales, Mercedes Steedman and D'Arcy Martin (Chapter 16) relates to organizing call centres with a case example of efforts to organize Omega Direct Response, a call centre in Sudbury, Ontario.

The case study shows that, by working together, rank-and-file workers as inside organizers and experienced professional organizers can develop winning strategies that can enable unions to organize hard to organize workplaces. The paper also includes perspectives from a conference on organizing call centres held in Toronto in September 2003. The conference brought together rank-and-file organizers, union staff, and academic researchers from Canada, the United States, and the United Kingdom to share experiences and develop strategies for successful organizing of workers in the fast-growing call centres sector.

Part IV on *Leadership Development and Education* has two papers, one on the experience with the British Columbia Organizing Institute, the only such academy in Canada for training union organizers, and the other on union education as a source of union renewal through programs such as the CAW's Paid Education Leave Program.

The evaluation of the B.C. Organizing Institute (Chapter 17), an initiative of the British Columbia Federation of Labour, by its current Director, John Weir, provides valuable insights into the problems that have to be overcome in developing coordinated education and training programs for leadership development, promoting inter-union cooperation, and creating a culture of organizing. As Weir notes, the Institute was designed not only to train organizers, but also to build a network of organizers through inter-union cooperation, educating leaders of the affiliated unions, providing help in union campaigns, and to be a focal point for information to non-union workers about the process of forming a union. Weir's critical assessment of the impact of the Institute shows that, despite many ups and downs, the Institute has been able to foster a culture of organizing, and has contributed "to developing a new generation of organizers with a greater commitment to solidarity." According to Weir, the Institute has especially helped smaller organizations which lack sufficient internal resources to support and monitor the progress of organizers. Weir's analysis may be useful for other central bodies contemplating the establishment of similar institutes.

The final paper (Chapter 18), by Johanna Weststar, examines the Paid Education Leave (PEL) program, a negotiated employer-funded worker education program administered by the Canadian Auto Workers Union (CAW). The primary purpose of her study is to evaluate the ability of the PEL to develop membership knowledge, activism and leadership to facilitate union renewal. Weststar's paper, based on survey research and interviews, maintains that the PEL program does contribute to leadership development and to the union renewal process by serving to alter the perceptions and attitudes of its participants. "PEL graduates return to their workplaces with an increased awareness of their role as workers in society, an increased desire to become active in their union and community, strengthened feelings of solidarity toward other workers and community groups, a broader understanding and appreciation of the diverse composition of their union, and with tangible strategies for workplace change." She feels, however, that, in the absence of a clearer union agenda on the use and purposes of the program, the seeds of activism and solidarity planted during the training are not adequately supported following graduates' return to the workplace. Weststar's study could be useful for other unions in evaluating their PEL programs.

As rich in detail and ideas as these chapters are, they are written at what the editors hope is just the beginning of a long-needed debate on the state and direction of the labour movement. Given the outset of such a discussion, there are necessarily more questions than definitive answers. Far from being able to document and assess patterns of a renewal process or precisely detail its current state across the country, at this time one is faced with uneven and partial material. Admittedly, there is more evidence to be gathered, further initiatives to be located, documented and assessed, yet our findings suggest that there has yet to appear a generalized state of union revitalization and growth across Canada. Despite continued union vitality and energy, the various "paths to union renewal" have yet to be clearly defined, formulated, or acted upon. The intention of this book is to provide a stimulus and inspiration for this process.

References

Beynon, Hew. 2003. Globalization, Trade Union Organization and Workers' Rights. In *Trade Unions in Renewal: A Comparative Study*, ed. Peter Fairbrother and Charlotte Yates. London, U.K.: Continuum.

Black, Errol, and Jim Silver. 2001. *Building a Better World: An Introduction to Trade Unionism In Canada*. Halifax: Fernwood Publishing.

Canadian Labour Congress (CLC). 2005. *Unions Make a Difference at the Workplace*. Committee Report, Document No. 1, 24th CLC Constitutional Convention, June 13-17, 2005. Ottawa: Canadian Labour Congress.

Jackson, Andrew. 2005. *Work and Labour In Canada: Critical Issues*. Toronto: Canadian Scholar's Press.

Milkman, Ruth, and Kim Voss. 2004. Introduction to *Rebuilding Labour: Organizing and Organizers in the New Union Movement*. Ithaca, NY: Cornell University Press.

Studies in Political Economy. 2004. Forum: Reorganizing Unions. *Studies in Political Economy* 74 (Fall): 124-190.

Yates, Michael. 1998. *Why Unions Matter*. New York: Monthly Review Press.

———. 2001. The 'New' Economy and the Labour Movement. *Monthly Review* 52 (11): 28-42.

PART I
Union Renewal and the State of Unions in Canada

Chapter 1
Union Renewal and Organizational Change: A Review of the Literature

PRADEEP KUMAR AND CHRISTOPHER SCHENK

Introduction

Union renewal has been a subject of intense debate and discussion among academics and unions over the past few years. There is a growing volume of literature in the form of books, journal articles, symposium and colloquium reports, surveys, policy discussion papers, and commentaries. The writings provide a wide variety of views on challenges facing unions, their relative performance over time and across countries, and suggestions on how they can adapt to the changing external and internal environment. The literature is based on the assumption that "unions have an important degree of control over their own destiny" (Jarley, Fiorito, and Delaney 1998, 277). To be effective as an institution of, for and by the workers, they have to continually take stock of their situation, identify the challenges, and adapt and modify their approaches, strategies and structures.

The increasing precariousness of the trade union movement around the world, reflected in its declining strength and influence, is the primary reason for the burgeoning literature and the growing sense of urgency among unions to devise ways and means to rebuild and restructure. The various analyses of the trends and patterns of unionism across countries confirm that, although the pace and scope of change differ, the decline in unionization rates has been pervasive over the past two decades, impacting organized labour's workplace and political influence (Visser 2003; Eiro-online 2004). A recent ILO study of the national federations in major industrialized countries concluded that "trade unions are facing a time of enormous structural and attitudinal change which is threatening their viability ... necessitating renewal and reorientation" (Olney 1996, 1). The need to adapt and adjust, according to the study, is related to a host of interrelated changes in economic, political, social, and labour market factors, including the far-reaching impacts of globalization and associated neo-liberal market emphasis in public policy. The study emphasized that "the role of trade unions at this juncture cannot be passive; they must respond to the challenge presented to them, and thus be instrumental in directing their own fate" (Onley 1996, 1).

The key questions before unions are: What can unions do to halt their declining strength and influence? And how can unions revitalize themselves and grow in their particular institutional and environmental context? There is growing body of research that documents and analyzes the initiatives taken by labour movements in a diverse range of countries to rebuild and re-strengthen themselves. Their success, and in some cases failure, provides valuable lessons. Perhaps the most important lesson is that "even in most adverse settings, union action of some kind is still possible and can often make an important difference to the lives of working people" (Kelly 2002, 18).

This chapter examines the diverse—and at times complex—conceptual and institutional perspectives on union renewal, based on a review of both academic and union literature. The purpose is to highlight the varying experience and approaches to union renewal in differing institutional and environmental contexts and to derive general lessons for an effective program of action for rebuilding the Canadian labour movement. The examination provides an analytical framework for assessing the various case studies and analyses of union revival presented in the volume. The discussion has been organized under eight headings: 1) meaning and concept of union renewal, 2) rationale of union renewal, 3) thesis of union renewal, 4) major union renewal strategies, 5) obstacles to change, 6) factors facilitating change, 7) experience with renewal in a comparative context, and 8) the challenge of union renewal in the Canadian setting.

Meaning and concepts of union renewal

Union renewal is the term[1] used to describe the process of change, underway or desired, to "put new life and vigour" in the labour movement to rebuild its organizational and institutional strength. It refers to the variety of actions/initiatives taken or needed by labour organizations to strengthen themselves in the face of their declining role and influence in the workplace and society. The range of these actions differ among unions, depending on their institutional and environment context. There is a general consensus, however, that: "labour organizations strengthen themselves by resonating more deeply and broadly with current and prospective union members ... labour revitalization itself consists of initiatives conceived, developed and taken by labour organizations to redefine their relations with workers, employers, and the state" (Cornfield and McCammon 2003, 16). These could include changes in organizational culture to promote rank-and-file activism and greater participation and involvement of members in union activities, new leadership, increased resources and new strategies for organizing, collective bargaining and political action, developing competencies to participate in workplace change, broadening the range of services, and building coalitions and networks with social and community groups for wide spread mobilization of workers to effect progressive social, economic and legislative change.

In general, union renewal is seen as organizational change within unions in response to a fundamentally different external and internal environment. It entails developing a culture of learning and change to undertake innovations and modifications in organizational structures, leadership, policies and practices, with a view to becoming a more effective organization for advancing membership interests. As Peter Fairbrother sees it (2000, 18), "Union renewal refers to the way unions organize and compose themselves in the circumstances of restructuring and reorganization at the workplace level and beyond so as to lay the foundations for active, engaged and participative forms of unionism in the context of the flux and flow of labour-capital relations."

Union renewal is reflected in one or more measures of union effectiveness: membership density, bargaining power, political power, and institutional vitality or "union innovation and openness to substantial change" (Hurd and Behrens 2003, 144). While priorities on organizing, bargaining, and political action vary from union to union, depending on environmental pressures, institutional vitality is considered a prerequisite to union renewal. Hurd and Behren (2003, 16) emphasize that, while environmental pressures are an important factor in determining the level of urgency for restructuring, they are not sufficient to cause change. "Unions need a clearly articulated mission (or vision) that provides the basis for strategic priorities."

A variety of perspectives are presented in the literature on the innovative efforts underway in unions and the desired nature and scope of change. This literature has become increasingly complex and varied over the last decade. The academic literature in particular has been shaped by differing perceptions of worker interests and how they are best represented by unions. Heery (2003) examines three currents of this literature. The first, "the evolutionary theories of trade unionism," consists of perspectives based on the claim that the changing structure of work and employment requires a new unionism. However there are sharp differences over what form this new unionism should take due to varying perceptions of environmental pressures on union adaptations. For example, those who believe that high performance work systems provide increased scope for shared interest with employers with opportunities for skills development, greater worker involvement and satisfaction of workers' intrinsic needs, advocate partnerships or mutual gains form of unionism. On the other hand, the critics of high performance work systems, concerned over growing insecurities, increased stress, and greater management control under these systems, stress the need for a militant form of unionism to facilitate worker mobilization to counter injustice. Similarly, academics convinced of a marked shift in worker attitudes towards individualism support expansion of union services through mutual aid or consumer unionism. Another stream espouses a form of unionism that is sensitive to the diverse needs and aspirations of the new worker identities grounded in ethnicity, gender, age, sexuality, and disability. The diversity thesis emphasizes the need for adaptations in union structures and bargaining priorities.

The second current of academic theorizing on union renewal rests on the assumption that there is a wide gulf between the interests of rank-and-file membership and leadership or union officials. Two perspectives of union renewal emerge from this theme. One stresses the need for grassroots-led change, based on rank-and-file activism and militancy, to challenge "not just the employers, but accommodative and ineffective forms of worker representation." The other, termed "managerial theory of union renewal," focuses on "more effective management of unions, to ensure coordination and cross-subsidy of union activities." The third category of literature, called agency theories by Heery (2003), assumes that worker interests are multiple and ambiguous and subject to varying interpretations. Unions face a range of strategic choices on the form that renewal could take, depending on their orientation. It could be the development of partnerships with employers, expanded servicing, or a focus on worker mobilization and activism. Each of these choices has constrains originating from worker and employer behaviour and attitudes. Consequently, revitalization implies strategic innovations and renewal of leadership.

In the North American context, particularly with respect to Canada and the United States, it is useful to distinguish between two alternate schools of thought. One, generally referred to as a "value-added" or "mutual gains" model of unionism, looks at union renewal in terms of creating value-added networks or organizations or developing partnerships that offer positive gains to both workers and employers. The second, known as social movement unionism,[2] emphasizes building working class solidarity and rank-and-file activism through organizational and political change within unions for widespread worker mobilization and democratic participatory decision-making with a broader community or societal focus (Nissen 2003). While both perspectives seek renewed influence of organized labour at the workplace and in civil society, they differ radically in their approach and strategies to achieve this goal.

The value-added school believes that unions can survive only if they work closely with employers to enable them to compete effectively in the current rapidly changing environment, "thereby reducing managerial opposition, increasing demand for unionization from labour, and promoting the public interest." As one advocate to this approach argues:

> Unions that can add value to firm performance while at the same time fulfilling their responsibilities to represent the collective and individual interests of their membership have greater appeal to potential members seeking opportunities for both representation and participation. Since they add value to firms, they may also reduce the level of managerial resistance that we have seen in recent history ... This value-added approach offers one strategy to preserve and expand union employment in firms where it is already established, thus slowing or reversing the decline. (Rubinstein 2002, 144)

Unions are counseled to make labour-management cooperation the foundation of their renewal strategies. Adversarial relations are considered outmoded. Such perspectives are not new, of course; one only has to recall the growth of company unionism in Canada in the early part of 20th century, influenced by Prime Minister Mackenzie King's ideas as expressed in his book *Industry and Humanity* (see MacDowell 2000) or in the United States the work of John R. Commons and other scholars of the "Wisconsin School" towards the development of labour-management cooperation. By contrast, social movement unionism is based on membership activism, involvement, and militancy. The essence of social movement unionism, according to Turner and Hurd (2001, 11), is "rank-and-file mobilization in organizing, grassroots politics and elsewhere," with emphasis on community and societal issues and working with various social and community activists.

Both of these current perspectives seek to transcend the 1990s debate, originating in the United States, which counterposed a "servicing" or "business unionism" model to an "organizing model" of unionism (Russo and Banks 1996; Diamond 1988; Banks and Metzger 1989; Masters and Atkin 1999; in Canada, Schenk 2003; Eaton 2004). The servicing or business unionism approach, widely regarded as a key characteristic of American unions historically, is associated with maintaining the "status quo," with a focus on meeting the immediate economic needs of union members through collective bargaining, partnerships with employers, or legislative lobbying. Under the servicing approach, union leaders make decisions for members, membership is passive or limited to responses to leaders' requests for cooperation, and union structures are centralized with heavy input from specialists, experts, and union staff. The organizing model, on the other hand, advocates rank-and-file involvement and participation in union decision-making, decentralized structures, emphasis on education and communication, and independence from management (Schenk 2003).

"Social movement unionism," says Moody (1997, 4), "goes beyond the 'organizing model' of unionism used in the U.S. in opposition to the older 'service model' of American business unionism by asserting the centrality of union democracy as a source of power and broader social visions and outreach as a means of enhancing that power." Thus, social movement unionism aims to strengthen unions through membership activism and empowerment for purposes of social change in both the workplace and in society at large. As Eisenscher (2002, 97) sees it, social movement unionism envisions a labour movement that is inclusive, egalitarian, acts as an "agency of worker empowerment based on democratic member participation," "fosters solidarity and unity across gender, race, ethnicity, nationality, and craft line through expanding class consciousness," "struggles for broad class and social demands as well as workplace interests," and "have leaders inspired by a vision of a more democratic humane social and economic order." He emphasizes that union renewal must go beyond greater activism, militancy and involvement. There has to be a genuine and meaningful membership participation and control. "Achieving greater union democracy is an integral part of the effort to rebuild labour's rank and influence," according to Eisenscher (2000, 114).

While the distinction between servicing/business/value-added unionism and organizing model/social movement unionism is important, the two perspectives are not always mutually exclusive. To understand the significance of servicing for union revival, it is necessary to disentangle the perspectives of business unionism and servicing. Membership servicing is part of the necessary representational work of a union and, as such, should not be misrepresented, caricatured, or necessarily equated with business unionism. The essence of business unionism is the assumption that the interests of workers and management are fundamentally non-antagonistic and that a harmonious relationship, if not an actual partnership, between the company and the union is the best way for the union to obtain improvements for the membership. On the other hand, even the most democratic and participatory unions that have clearly broken with this view and recognize a conflictual dynamic between the interests of labour and management, need to provide some services to their membership. The logic of servicing can also be interpreted as mutual aid logic, where the union is seen as "an extended family, a corporate entity whose members have multiple obligations to one another and share a collective responsibility for the well-being of one another," rather than like an insurance agent with "obligation to provide members with excellent benefits for a small cost" (Bacharach et al. 2001, 7).

A similar idea, called social capital unionism, seeks to enhance the value of a union through building interpersonal and community networks of workers. From this perspective of servicing, there does not appear to be a contradiction between servicing and organizing and social movement unionism. Indeed, using this logic, "unions may come to be viewed as community-building organizations worthy of support from national governments and full partnership status with employers" (Jarley 2005, 19). However, the mutual aids / social capital view is incompatible with value-added unionism, which advocates labour-management partnerships for meeting the employer goals. The value-added approach, grounded in the corporate agenda of competitiveness, is in our view misguided, undermining basic union values and the unions' independent role in workplace and society. We concur with Gindin (1998, 193), that "nothing is more naïve, more disorienting or more debilitating of an independent labour movement than the acceptance of the competitive framework."

Although the mutual aids /social capital perspectives have been criticized for their bias towards avoiding conflict with employers (Banks and Metzgar 2005; Clawson 2005), there appears to be a broad agreement that, at least in the American case and perhaps more generally, "no single model of unionism may lead to organized labour's resurgence, but rather a portfolio approach" may be necessary (Jarley 2005, 21). As the report of the Task Force on Reconstructing America's Labour Market Institutions notes:

> We see the "next generation unions" as coalition partners offering po-
> litical voice, direct participation, collective bargaining, strategic partner-
> ships, mobility, and occupational community. To adapt to the changing
> industrial structure and varied circumstances and needs of workers, we
> envision them as extended networks that represent and serve workers'
> interests in a variety of ways inside firms, in local areas and labour
> markets, in professional communities, and in political affairs... Linking
> together unions and coalition partners at the community level will take
> on particular significance in future than in the recent past. (Osterman
> et al. 2001, 98–99)

Rationale of union renewal

The growing importance of union renewal, as indicated in the introduction, is related to the increasing precariousness of the trade union movement around the world as reflected in its declining strength and influence. While union decline is "notoriously difficult to define" in the comparative context, due to its different meaning in different industrial relations environment (Frege and Kelly 2003),[3] unions everywhere over the past two decades have faced unprecedented and interrelated changes in economic, labour market, and public policy environment, adversely affecting their capacity to protect and advance workers' interests. As noted by a recent ILO study, "the last quarter of the 20th century was a period of profound social and economic transformation which has profound implications for organized labour" (Jose 2002, 1).

The key changes in internal and external environment shaping union power and influence include: 1) globalization,[4] taken to mean the gradual integration of economies and societies driven by the neo-liberal philosophy, adoption of new technologies,[5] and the increasing role of multinational corporations, resulting in intense competitive pressures and widespread corporate restructuring involving outsourcing, downsizing, and the emphasis on flexibility and cost efficiency; 2) the increasingly precarious nature of non-standard employment through temporary, contingent, and part-time work and consequent polarizations of incomes and jobs; 3) growing workforce diversity by age, gender, ethnicity, and disability with varying needs and aspirations; 4) the changing orientation of public policy favouring deregulation, privatization and other market-oriented solutions; and 5) the regional integration of economies in both North America and Europe with increasing employer demands for lower wages, benefits and reduction in social safety standards to create a "level playing field."

In addition to the changes in external environment, the unions also face pressures from members' rising expectations, poor union image, and worker resistance to unionize due to either unsatisfactory union performance or a lack of awareness of union instrumentality (Penny 2004; Lopez 2004). Union solidarity has become more precarious as traditional manufacturing and resource industries employ a declining percentage of the workforce, as inequality has increased, and as newer service industries have grown with different workplace experiences and traditions. New ethnic, gender, and sexual identities have also added to the weakening of the notions of solidarity (Jackson 2005; Mantsios 1998). These trends, coupled with a highly decentralized industrial relations system of mainly workplace-by-workplace organizing, enterprise bargaining, and the lack of a coherent worker-centred vision, continue to hinder union strength and influence.

The result, while uneven from country to country, has been declining union density and bargaining power, membership passivity, and reduced influence on public policy. At the same time, the changed environment has strengthened employers' power and their relentless pursuit of efficiency and flexibility. As if stunned by these developments and caught up in a web of industrial rules, regulations and anti-union labour legislation, unions have found themselves ill-equipped to mobilize their members in political protest or otherwise take the necessary steps to ensure their growth, strength, and solidarity.

In short, the challenges confronting unions today are substantial. It appears that such challenges will continue to plague them in the near future. To meet these challenges, unions have to adapt and adjust, and revive themselves to become an effective institution of workers again. The success of labour movements everywhere will depend on their ability to reach unorganized workers, engage in creative bargaining to effect positive outcomes for workers, offer an alternate vision of economic and social change, modify their structures and practices to become more inclusive and democratic, build political alliances and community networks, and mobilize workers to overcome the insecurities and inequities created by globalization. The task of renewal is indeed formidable.

Thesis of union renewal

There is general consensus in both the academic and union literature that the notion of union renewal or labour revitalization focuses on those *changes over which the union has some direct control and therefore ability to change and act in new ways.* Indeed, it is precisely these changes that the recent literature has demonstrated to have the most explanatory value. Union renewal therefore concerns organizational and political change to:

1. rebuild and expand union capacity to respond to the strategic challenge of organizing;
2. engage in creative bargaining to meet "unfilled needs" of an increasingly diverse workforce and to influence the nature and direction of workplace change;
3. devise new ways to shape public policy through strategic mobilization, lobbying and public engagement;
4. initiate structural change to build local activism and encourage greater participation of rank and file in union decision making;
5. build solidarity and a worker-centred view of the world so as to become a catalyst of progressive social and economic change; and
6. strengthen and expand community links both nationally and internationally.

Major renewal strategies

Studies of union renewal have identified a number of initiatives/strategies that have been used or discussed by unions to rebuild themselves. Among the key strategies are: 1) organizational restructuring through mergers or/and internal reorganization; 2) organizing the unorganized workers through innovative tactics and approaches; 3) grassroots political action and campaigns to expand rank-and-file activism and worker mobilization; 4) coalition-building and alliances with social and community groups to acquire power resources for progressive social and economic change; 5) inter-union cooperation and related solidarity networks at both the national and international levels; 6) "partnerships" with employers and governments in areas of mutual interests or/and to engage in workplace change to advance and protect worker interests; and 7) expanded programs of education, training, and research for leadership development and better rank-and-file awareness of the changing environment in which they live.

The menu of strategies varies from union to union, and is shaped by both the organizational culture and leadership, the nature and scope of the challenges to union legitimacy, as well as employer and state actions and behaviour. There is also the recognition in the literature that no single strategy is sufficient to restore the union influence. An integrated set of interactive strategies are needed for effective change. In the United States, for example, strategic coordination of politics, organizing, bargaining and coalition-building with community-based organizations has been the common theme for unions engaged in a rebuilding process.

Among the various strategies, **organizational restructuring** through mergers, modification of structures, and rationalization and modernization of services has been the most widespread union response. Mergers have been increasingly popular in almost all developed countries, and have been aggressively supported by national centrals to increase resources, create economies of scale, and build mobilization capacity (Chaison 2001; Ebbinghaus 2003). However, as one academic who has re-searched mergers for over two decades comments, the efficacy of mergers for union renewal is far from certain (Chaison 2001). He questions whether union mergers contribute to union revival and states that "in many ways we ask too much of union mergers." Chaison finds mixed evidence on such anticipated outcomes as increased provision of resources for organizing, stronger strength in bargaining, increased political activity, alone or through community coalitions, or greater participation and involvement of the rank and file in organizing, negotiations, and union deci-sion-making structures. Ebbinghaus, in a study of union mergers in Europe (2003), maintains that the growing concentration of membership in a few super-unions contains the potential for increased competition between these large players and threatens to weaken national confederations.

The modification of union structures, on the other hand, to provide representation to women, youth, and ethnic minorities, constitutes a positive organizational change and has the potential for transformation to social movement unionism through greater rank-and-file involvement and participation in the union decision-making process. Similarly, the widespread use of information technology such as the Internet, cell-phones, and global satellites has not only made servicing more cost-effective and efficient, but has also led to greater rank-and-file communication, easier ac-cess to workers to boost organizing, staff development, and inter-union alliances and networking. While computerization offers many creative possibilities, there are also concerns about the unrestrained use of computer power. Among the key concerns are the potential erosion of personal contact, loss of control over medium, increased generational rift, loss of confidentiality, and work overload on staff.[6]

Organizing the unorganized, through increased resource allocation and in-novative tactics and approaches emphasizing greater rank-and-file involvement and participation, is another strategy that has been widely used by unions, especially in Anglo Saxon countries where the decline in union density has been pronounced (Fairbrother and Yates 2003; Heery and Adler 2004). These countries are also char-acterized by decentralized bargaining structures and low bargaining coverage, single channel of employee voice, and in many cases by the legislative requirement of majority vote to gain worker representation. Each of these characteristics provides high incentive to organize and influence the form and direction of organizing tactics and methods. The prioritization of organizing strategy, according to Heery and Adler, is also influenced by employer strategies, public policy and legislative framework, and the nature of unionism. The high priority given to organizing in Anglo Saxon countries reflects their institutional context, employer hostility to unionism, increasingly market-oriented public policy unfavourable to organ-ized labour, and the perceived need for internal change within unions to broaden their appeal and promote rank-and-file activism. All of these countries, including Canada, the United States, the United Kingdom, Australia, and New Zealand, have committed themselves, in varying degree, to a change from purely servicing to an organizing model of unionism, emphasizing both "internal organizing to mobilize members, and external organizing that promotes grassroots activism as a way to build support for union representation" (Hurd 2004, 8).

The United States provides the best example of the use of organizing strategy for union renewal. While organizing has been at the heart of union strategy discussions in the U.S. labour movement for nearly two decades, it moved to the front and centre in 1995 with the election of John Sweeny to the presidency of the AFL-CIO and the precipitous decline in union membership and density. Sweeny, in his "New Voice" campaign, declared that "the most important critical challenge facing unions today is organizing," and called upon unions to "organize at a pace and scale that is unprecedented" (Hurd 2004, 8). He pushed unions to devote more resources to organizing, develop a strong organizing staff, devise and implement a strategic plan, and mobilize membership around organizing. The organizing priority has entailed increased investment in organizing efforts by many unions, establishment of an Organizing Institute to train organizers, a Union Summer Program to involve students in organizing, a Union Cities Program to energize local labour councils, negotiations of neutrality and card-check agreements with employers, an emphasis on political action to rejuvenate activism to elect politicians willing to back workers' issues and help bring about organizing-friendly labour legislation reforms, as well as coalition building with non-labour community groups in support of local organizing and bargaining campaigns.

A vast volume of literature has been produced assessing the organizing activity to reverse the decline of union membership in the United States. Two volumes, based on conference proceedings, are particularly noteworthy: *Organizing to Win; New Research on Union Strategies,* edited by Bronfenbrenner et al. (1998), and *Rebuilding Labour: Organizing and Organizers in the New Union Movement,* edited by Milkman and Voss (2004). They contain insightful contributions of prominent academics and labour activists. A report by Cornell University academics Kate Bronfenbenner and Robert Hickey (2003, 41), also published in Milkman and Voss (2004), provides the most comprehensive assessment of organizing strategies used for union revival in the American context. Their report includes a sombre evaluation of the changing climate for organizing and key organizing strategies and tactics employed by unions. They find that union gains depend on a multi-faceted campaign utilizing comprehensive union-building strategies. The core elements of a comprehensive strategy include adequate and appropriate staff and financial resources, an active representation committee in the workplace and community, and benchmarks and assessments. The unions that have brought in the most new members through organizing, both inside and outside the legal process, are those that have followed a more comprehensive organizing strategy.

Based on their assessment of organizing activity over the period 1997-2002, the authors conclude that, "despite all the new initiatives and resources being devoted to organizing and all the talk of 'changing to organize,' American unions are at best standing still." The report outlines a ten-point plan for organizing success: 1) unions need to commit greater staff and financial resources; 2) organizing should be strategically targeted based on research and power analysis; 3) unions need to take a hard look at the nature and intensity of the campaigns they are losing and determine what they could do differently to win; 4) unions need to establish clear benchmarks to determine what they need to accomplish and where they need to go before moving forward with the campaign, and an effective assessment system to honestly evaluate worker support and commitment to the union campaign at every stage of the process; 5) unions have to build alliance with other unions, community groups, political leaders, clergy, and other non-governmental organizations before the organizing campaign begins; 6) membership education and leadership development are central to building capacity for organizing; 7) new workers from diverse ethnic, racial, and gender backgrounds offer an opportunity to jump-start a more inspired, committed and effective grass roots movement; 8) unions have to seek the support of unions and non-governmental organizations around the world and become more engaged in supporting organizing and bargaining efforts by unions in other countries by contributing resources, using their bargaining leverage, and engaging in cross-border resources; 9) effective organizing strategies require greater coordination of unions' traditional core of activities—collective bargaining, political action and organizing; and 10) the task of organizing in manufacturing, high tech, and other mobile sectors of the economy must become the responsibility of the entire labour movement. The authors of the report are convinced that "making these changes will require major changes in resource allocation, institutional structures, organizational culture and leadership."

The "mixed" outcomes of intense organizing efforts has created serious tensions within the American labour movement. A number of large unions, under the banner "New Unity Partnership" (NUP), expressed dissatisfaction with the AFL-CIO leadership for not aggressively pursuing the organizing agenda (Hurd 2004). Except for a marginal increase in 1999, the overall membership and union density continues to decline, albeit at a slower rate than in the 1980s and early 1990s. These unions, some of whom have now withdrawn from the central federation, have called for a "massive shift in resources and focus to organizing and growth in unions' core industries and sectors," restructuring of unions through mergers, and redefinition of the role of the AFL-CIO. However, some commentators have argued that organizing is not enough, that unions have to embrace organizational change, and articulate a unifying vision of a different world to inspire workers and challenge the status quo: "a coherent vision about how our economy and our society would be different with a more vibrant labor movement" (Hurd 2004, 23; see also Day 2004; Lerner 2002).

While **political action** has always been one of the key union activities every where, its significance as a revitalization strategy has increased in recent years. Grassroots political action is regarded as essential to expand rank and file activism and promote worker mobilization both to defend worker rights and to press for public policy reforms to achieve progressive economic and social change. Political action is also inextricably linked to effective organizing and collective bargaining as well as such renewal strategies as coalition building and inter-union solidarity. Hamann and Kelly (2003, 2004) in their review of political action as a union revitalization strategy in comparative context distinguish between six forms of political action; links with a political party, electoral activity, particularly voter mobilization, lobbying for progressive legislation and its effective implementation, social pacts with governments to influence policy formation, political strikes, and legal challenges. The cross-national patterns of political action are influenced by a multitude of factors, including the nature of economic and industrial relations institutions, the electoral system (first-past-the-post versus proportional representation), union leadership and union culture, the role of unions in community and society, and the attitudes of government and employers. The forms of political action have also changed over time. For example, union links with political parties have weakened in the past two decades, leading to a greater emphasis on direct worker mobilization. As Baccaro, Hamann, and Turner (2003, 119-120) have noted:

> Labour movement politics today go well beyond traditional links with labour-friendly political parties and negotiations with governments, to involve grassroot politics and local campaigns. The exact forms taken by such political strategies are shaped differently in each country according to the challenges faced, existing institutions and opportunity structures. But in all cases, the shift towards a fuller political subject orientation lies at the center of contemporary strategic adaptation and revitalization.

This shift is most pronounced in the United States, where unions have recognized that their survival depends on substantial labour law reforms which, "no matter how badly it was needed or how well it is justified, could not be achieved without first significantly expanding labor's political power" (Day 2004, 31). Over the past decade, the American labour movement has mounted a massive political action program to support politicians sympathetic to labour legislation reforms, influence law makers, and mobilizes voters (Masters 2004). Despite the disappointing outcomes of their efforts to elect labour-friendly law makers and extensive lobbying for changes in labour legislation, most labour leaders are convinced that political action has to remain a top priority "to build our ability to win crucial elections ... to impact health care, trade, or the right to organize ... and to preserve collective bargaining rights" (AFL-CIO 2005a; see also AFL-CIO 2005b). While supporting political action as a high priority, we should also note that a key reason for disappointing outcomes to date relates to the difficulties the American trade union movement has experienced in breaking from the established parties (Democratic and Republican) and creating a new labour-based formation as occurred in other advanced industrial-cum-neoliberal-capitalist societies.

Coalition-building is regarded as one of the most innovative strategies for union revitalization.[7] Frege, Heery, and Turner (2003, 123; 2004, 138) define coalitions as "involving discreet, intermittent, or continuous joint activity in pursuit of shared or common goals between trade unions and other non-labour institutions in civil society, including community, faith, identity, welfare, and campaigning organizations." According to the authors, while coalition-building is a supporting activity, undertaken by unions to win certifications /recognition from employers, help organize minority or difficult-to-organize workers, provide additional pressures on employers in high-profile negotiations, or mobilize wider community for legislative change, it also provides legitimacy for unions' broader social and economic goals. They state that "advocates of social movement unionism tend to offer it as a universal solution to labour's ills, appropriate to the general context of globalization or the triumph of neoliberal political economy" (Frege, Heery and

Turner 2004, 155). Whatever the objective of coalition-building, coalition partners provide unions with valuable resources in the form of a network of activists, material support in organizing efforts or protracted work stoppages, expertise, access to new groups, legitimacy and capacity to mobilize on a wider scale. Based on their comparative research, Frege, Heery and Turner are convinced that the upward trend in coalition activity is likely to increase in future, partly because of growing pressures on unions to broaden their policy and social agenda, and partly because of such issues as globalization, environmentalism, labour standards, gender equality, and work-family balance. Indeed, reflecting the significance of coalition-building, Clawson (2003, 194) believes that "Labour must do more than building alliances; it must fuse with these movements such that it is no longer clear what is a 'labour' issue and what is a 'women's' issue or an 'immigrant' issue."

Related to coalition-building is the strategy for joint action or common front between unions, both nationally and internationally. The various forms of international structures and inter-union initiatives that have promoted transnational cooperation include the expanded role of the International Confederation of Free Trade Unions, international trade secretariats, transnational trade union bodies such as the European Trade Union Confederation and its program to form European Works Councils, inter-union cooperation and collaboration in organizing, bargaining, and education and training, and campaigns such as the anti-sweatshop movement for minimum global labour standards and worker rights, involving unions and community groups.

While there is voluminous literature on the internationalization of labour or **transnational networking** of unions (Gordon and Turner 2000; Nissen 2002; Wells 1998), research on inter-union cooperation has been lacking. As Lillie and Martinez Lucio (2004, 163) point out, "Labour internationalism does not occur in some abstract global space, but is rather the interaction between unions which exist within different union spaces. The form of labour internationalism depends on the strength and character of national unions in their national institutions." In the same vein, Gindin (1998, 202) has remarked:

> International labour bodies ... are useful vehicles for exchanging information and analysis and mobilizing modest acts of solidarity and support. Strategic international coordination depends on the strength of national movements.... The key to international solidarity isn't international institutions, but internationalizing the struggle, carrying on the fight (for example, over work time) in each country and thereby reinforcing and creating the space for working class struggles in other countries.

The various analyses of international collaboration among unions suggest that cross-border solidarity as a revitalization strategy has proven to be the weakest to date. "The key stumbling block to attaining stronger ties of solidarity with unions and workers abroad is the organizational dynamics inherited from the past, which make genuine cross-border organizing and solidarity out of the ordinary" (Nissen 2002, 265).

Labour-management partnerships, or social partnerships as they are called in continental Europe, have also been discussed as a strategy for union renewal. While the partnerships with employers, and in some countries social pacts with governments, are common in Western Europe and Scandinavian countries through such institutional arrangements as co-determination, works councils, and "solidaristic welfare and labour market re-integration programs," they are looked at with considerable suspicion and cynicism in North America. Based on evidence from the United States, the United Kingdom, Germany, Italy and Spain, Fichter and Greer (2004, 7) find that "social partnership contributes to revitalization, when it is institutionally integrated with other union strategies, and, most importantly, when it is pursued in the interests of a broader social agenda." They define partnership as "a kind of interaction between unions and employers" and distinguish between partnership and cooperation. According to them "cooperation occurs in nearly every workplace and bargaining relationship, even where it is not formalized as a partnership or shaped by a union capable of wielding countervailing power"(Fichter and Greer 2004, 88).

In the context of Anglo-Saxon countries, Fichter and Greer provide many reasons why, despite their growing use, skepticism abounds regarding the postulated link between partnership and union revitalization. First, there is "only a sparse evidence" connecting partnership to outcomes such as enhanced wages, job security, or union membership levels. Second, partnerships have not been found to curtail the unilateral management actions or management prerogatives over outsourcing, restructuring and downsizing initiatives. Third, unions are usually excluded from decisions over investment, training, and broader human resource planning and management. Fourth, partnerships tend to emphasize the contribution of employees to the enterprise more than employee welfare or vigorous representation. Therefore, partnerships have little to offer in fulfilling the union agenda. The authors conclude that, "despite the proliferation of literature about labour-management partnerships and the widespread belief that they ensure better outcomes for workers when unions are strong, there is still little understanding of how they can help unions revive themselves" (Fichter and Greer 2004, 87-88). Their findings are corroborated by a recent study of union-management partnerships in the United States which also finds that, in the absence of public policy that would mandate or encourage such arrangements, strategic partnerships between unions and management are "exceedingly unlikely" (Appelbaum and Hunter 2005).

An expanded program of **education, training and research** is also a key element in effective union revitalization strategies. Although a neglected area of academic and union research, there is a widely-held perception that an accelerated program of education and training of rank-and-file members and activists is needed to facilitate internal reforms and, perhaps more importantly, leadership development. As Eisenscher (2002, 121) has noted:

> The labour movement needs a dramatically expanded approach to education. However valuable and necessary skills training is, unions should go further. While skills building such as grievance handling teaches people how to do, union education should affect how members think

to develop their capacities for critical thinking and strategic analysis over the entire range of concerns of working people.

Fletcher (1998) makes a similar argument. He believes that labour education should be woven through the fabric of the work of organized labour. He suggests four areas where labour education can be both timely and useful 1) leadership development aimed at developing and consolidating a new echelon of labour union leadership as well as opening up accessible pathways for women and people of colour to enter the leadership of organized labour; 2) organizing; 3) class consciousness-raising; and 4) relationship between college-based and union-based labour education. In the case of Canada, where there has been a long tradition of labour education, Taylor (2001) argues that "a new emphasis on broad-based and activist education today promises to rekindle the sense of an education movement that was present in the labour movement in the 1930s and 1940s."

Obstacles to change

Unions face formidable challenges in their quest to reverse their declining influence and transform themselves into a social movement. Obstacles to change are both internal and external. Among the external barriers to change—or what might better be termed inhibitors to growth that unions face—can broadly be explored in four categories: *Economic*, i.e., capital mobility, corporate restructuring and downsizing, outsourcing, industrial and occupational shifts in the economy such as the relative decline in manufacturing employment versus the growth of the commercial service sector, an increasingly contingent and precarious workforce; *Legal*, i.e., restrictive employment and labour legislation including legal restrictions on organizing nonunion workers; *Social*, i.e., employer hostility towards unions, worker resistance to unionization due to fear of job loss or employer reprisal, very conservative ideologies of individualism, or negative union instrumentality perceptions; and *Political*, i.e., the emergence of an unfriendly political climate, lax enforcement of basic employment and labour rights, inadequate penalties for violations, and back-to-work orders against striking workers (Day 2004).

Canada's labour relations system, favouring workplace-by-workplace organizing and bargaining, is another key external barrier to expanding union coverage. As Day (2004) has noted, countries with higher union densities tend to have more centralized labour relations systems. Indeed, he emphasizes that "centralized labour markets are actually a cause—perhaps the most important cause—of whether a country's union density will grow, decline, or remain stable." Reasons cited include fewer incentives for employers to oppose union organizing, powerful national confederations, and their involvement in economic policy-making. In Canada, the industrial relations system is dominated by workplace-by-workplace bargaining and divided for all but 10% of the workforce into various provincial jurisdictions with distinct, though broadly similar, laws and regulations. Virtually all bargaining bypasses central labour bodies and, with the notable exceptions of the construction sector, direct government employees and some hospitals, there is little broader-based or sector-wide negotiations. True, in the auto sector there is pattern bargaining, but this only pertains to the big assembly plants of the major companies. excluding most auto parts and other suppliers. With the dramatic growth of the service sector with its thousands of small- to medium-workplaces, the need for more centralized bargaining mechanisms is becoming more and more apparent and remains a challenge for the future of unions across Canada.

There is a general consensus in the literature that the rise of neoliberalism, combined with the forces of globalization, new technology and related dramatic shifts in the labour market, have promoted an environment of insecurity and vulnerability leading to increasing employer hostility, state antipathy, and worker ambivalence towards unionization. Unions everywhere find themselves on the defensive, less able to make gains at the bargaining table and in the political sphere, and facing worker resistance to expand employee voice and mobilization for progressive social and economic change (Turner 2003). As Kelly and Frege (2004) note, "although there are exceptions, unions' major successes these days often consist in slowing down or modifying neoliberal reforms." Similarly, while there is a hard core of workers opposed to unionization, a substantial minority of employees, particularly youth, women, and ethnic minorities, want to join unions.[8] However, unions have found it difficult to attract these potential members.

Thus, although the external factors—in particular, the anti-union attitudes and behaviour of employers and governments—are significant constraints on the ability of unions to reverse their declining influence, the more serious obstacles to union revival are internal, particularly the institutional inertia, established bureaucratic structures of the past, the mis-match between union leadership and the changing gender and ethnicity of the workforce, inter-union divisions, and, most importantly, the lack of an inspiring vision. Internal obstacles to change include a range of issues that can be grouped around the following headings (Milkman and Voss 2004; Day 2004; Hurd 2004):

Lack of crisis and bureaucratic inertia

The absence of a sense of urgency for change is cited as one of the most important reasons why union renewal has been "timid or non-existent" in most countries. This is true of both the Anglo-Saxon countries, where union density decline has been serious, and the European countries, where union decline has been moderated by a high and stable collective bargaining coverage and social partnerships. For different reasons, union officials appear complacent about the "crisis" in their labour movement. There has been little incentive for radical reforms in European Unions because of their established close relationships with employers and the state reflected in such institutions as co-determination and works councils. As Turner (2003, 40) has pointed out in the case of Germany, "unions, in solid institutional position, are simply not desperate enough to move towards risky and potentially de-stabilizing new strategy—even if that strategy may be necessary in the long run." In Anglo-Saxon countries, especially in Canada and the United States, the lived experience of this crisis has been fragmented because of the decentralized structure of the labour movement. While some unions have experienced a serious decline in their membership and faced intense pressures from employers for wage and benefit concessions, others have been able to maintain their membership and withstand demands for concessions, either through their involvement in workplace change or by mobilizing their rank and file. In these situations, leaders are reluctant to undertake radical organizational reforms for the fear of upsetting the status quo.

In Canada, since many unions have continued to grow numerically and maintain a social union perspective, albeit limited, there exists little sense of crisis in unions across the various provincial jurisdictions of Canada. Union activities such as bargaining and organizing are conducted more or less as usual. The commitment to change on the part of leadership, staff, and even members, is far too circumscribed and fragmented. Bureaucratic inertia often dominates innovation and stymies bold action. Education, debate, and consequent action by all concerned about the state of unions and union density can begin to overcome these obstacles.

Fear of change

There are risks to change in every situation. For example, moving from a business unionism perspective to a social movement perspective involves a profound internal organizational change, some new prioritization to everyday work assignments, and participatory work practices. Unsettling perceptions of change—steps into the unknown—can easily be perceived and experienced as threatening for leaders as well as staff and members. Changed union priorities towards organizing, for example, can legitimately be perceived as the end of adequate servicing to members and a significant workload increase by staff. Such fears dissipate, however, as change becomes fully explored and understood and a consensus on new priorities and practices are agreed upon. Union strategic planning of resources, education and training further eases fears (Weil 1997).

Inter-union tensions

Lack of union unity and inter-union tensions are another obstacle to union renewal. While inter-union conflicts, based on ideological differences or approaches to dealing with employers and governments are common, they have become problematic and a matter of serious concern in countries where unions have been looking for growth through mergers and amalgamations. Recent trends in Canada and the United States towards general unionism—unions which are no longer occupationally based but rather include a multitude of occupations and sectors—and the creation of larger unions with increased capacity and power sources, are also causing inter-union tensions. The "raiding" of members of other unions to compensate for reduced membership levels and the general competition for increased members is a further and related problem. According to Milkman and Voos (2004, 6):

> This boosts the membership of the raiding union (and may even be presented as an 'organizing victory'), it has no impact whatsoever on the overall union density problem. And of course raiding involves unions expending valuable resources fighting one another rather than focusing on the challenges facing the movement as a whole.

In Canada, these tensions between union affiliates have had perverse implications for central labour bodies from local labour councils, to provincial federations of labour and the Canadian Labour Congress. In decentralized labour movements such as Canada's, wherein central labour bodies function at the behest of key unions, inter-union conflicts render them less effective, if not at times powerless. The internal divisions and mistrust between unions, or between locals and their parent bodies, seriously limit opportunities for coordinated multi-union bargaining and organizing and common political action in the form of lobbying and demonstrations. In the exceptional cases when such efforts have been launched they are usually limited to single issue and regional campaigns. "They have proven difficult to sustain because of the internal tensions within labour's ranks" (Milkman and Voss 2004, 6).

On the other hand, Gindin (1998), citing the example of divisions within the International Union of Auto Workers (UAW), leading to a breakaway of the Canadian district in 1985, argues that, while painful and dangerous, divisions within unions do not necessarily paralyze the labour movement. They can, as the CAW example shows, "even lead to the discovery of new energies." He points out that the CAW, following the breakaway, was energized and strengthened through a greater share of resources committed to organizing and education, creative bargaining, coalition-building, and radical changes in organizational structure and leadership. He maintains that unity among unions has to be built on a unifying theme of democratization and social movement unionism.

Demographic makeup of union leadership

Over the last several decades, demographic change has created a gender and ethnic mis-match in unions between leaders, staff, members, and the unorganized sector of the workforce. In the United States at least, there is a widely held perception that, "despite the Sweeney administration's efforts to increase diversity at the highest level of labour's officialdom, the majority of union officials are still older, native-born white males, who often have difficulty appealing to the nation's increasingly female, foreign-born and relatively youthful workforce" (Milkman and Voss 2004, 6). While information on demographic characteristics of union leaders is unavailable for other countries, the U.S. does not appear to be an exception in this regard. Certainly the mismatch is also a problem in Canada, although not to such a serious extent as in the United States. Part of the reason for this difference is that the Canadian Labour Congress, provincial federations of labour, and many affiliated unions have made systematic efforts to include women, people of colour, disabled and aboriginals in leadership and staff positions. Statistics Canada recently (2004) reported that the women's rate of unionization of 30.6% surpassed that of men's (30.3%), whereas back in 1981 unionization rates were 42.1% for men and 31.4% for women (Morissette, Schellenberg, and Johnson 2005).

Yet, while more and more women are playing a leadership role in unions, most unions, even where women members form the majority, are still led by men. As several hundred thousand immigrants continue to locate in the major cities across Canada every year, the mis-match between union leaders, staff and members continues despite efforts to be more inclusive. The need for further change has not gone unnoticed, as union convention policy documents and concomitant debates over a considerable period of time have returned to these themes many times and af-firmative action positions for women, minorities and people with disabilities have been established within key union structures (OFL 1982, 1986). Nonetheless, since progress on these issues has been limited, the perceived mis-match continues to be a major obstacle to the substantive changes necessary for solidarity and union renewal. As a CLC (1998, 10) discussion paper on diversity notes: "[Unions] clearly need to take a hard look at the many facets of union structures and understand that barriers are stopping the growth and development of leadership within the rank and file."

Facilitating factors in the change process

While it is easy to be overwhelmed by the many challenges confronting change, there are also a number of facilitating factors for union renewal that should not be overlooked or discounted. As Clawson (2003, 34) notes in his book *The Next Labour Upsurge*, "The labour movement's power ... depends on the ability to involve and give voice to the concerns, hopes, and fears of millions of ordinary workers." In short, the power of labour rests not primarily on monetary or technical resources, facilitating institutions, nor even on progressive labour legislation, as important as that is. Rather, it depends on large numbers of people acting collectively—in solidarity—for their needs and aspirations. It is for this reason—the building of solidarity, of power—that most analysts have stressed the importance of unions building a new organizational culture: one focused on a more inclusive and partici-patory democracy, on membership involvement and empowerment, on traditions of struggle—for change in the workplace and society as a whole.

Here also one can see the importance of education, research, training, and com-munication networks in raising awareness and participation in the renewal process.

While these factors are not optimal in the Canadian labour movement, they are far from absent. Indeed, there is considerable evidence of solidaristic perspectives and activities, despite a very decentralized industrial relations system. To the extent such activities exist, they constitute factors facilitating union renewal.

Further factors facilitating change include: effective union leadership; strategic planning; proper resource allocation; and successes at the bargaining table and in union campaigns. The latter can serve to both improve workers' lot in life and to inspire and further activate members. The recent union victories in Los Angeles and Las Vegas are examples of social movement campaigns that hold the promise of rebuilding a vibrant labour movement (Fantasia and Voss 2004).

While we have emphasized the importance of solidarity and its development and expansion, this does not mean that new and favourable labour legislation is unimportant. On the contrary, legislation that expands workers' rights, which facilitates organizing and union functioning (or the opposite), is a significant factor in union growth or decline. Labour legislation is uneven across Canada, with some provinces, such as Quebec, Manitoba and Saskatchewan, maintaining a card certification system, while others, such as Nova Scotia, Ontario and British Columbia, have imposed a vote system in addition to a card check. This enables companies to campaign against certification between card signing and the vote, thereby making it more difficult for workers to join the union of their choice. Thus, whether labour legislation is a facilitating factor or not may well depend upon where in the country one lives, as well as one's critical assessment.

Finally, a high level of union density, reflecting the strength and power of the labour movement, is in itself a facilitating factor in union renewal. In the case of Canada, while there has been a slippage of union membership as a percentage of the workforce, the unionization level remains over twice that of the United States, and the absolute number of union members continues to grow. While the proportional slippage has not yet created a crisis upon which to galvanize change on the desired scale, the level of union density continues to reflect a residual strength of the Canadian labour movement that can (and is) being utilized in collective bargaining, in union and community campaigns, as well as imparting added leverage in organizing efforts.

Experience with renewal in a comparative context

Over the past few years, there has been a flurry of research on union renewal in the comparative context, covering both developed and developing countries. Four edited volumes are noteworthy. The volume titled *Varieties of Unionism: Strategies for Union Revitalization* (2004), edited by Carola Frege and John Kelly, assesses the strategies for union renewal based on the experience of the U.S., U.K., Germany, Italy, and Spain. The book *Labour Revitalization: Global Perspectives and New Initiatives* (2003), edited by Daniel Cornfield and Holly McCammon, provides a sociological perspective on union revival in a global context, highlighting union adaptation to a changed environment in a wide range of countries, including the U.S., U.K., Netherlands, Brazil, Korea, Australia, Mexico and Venezuela. A chapter discusses the union revival from a comparative perspective. The experience of five Anglo-Saxon countries (U.S., U.K. Australia, New Zealand and Canada) with similar cultural norms is examined in *Trade Unions In Renewal: A Comparative Perspective*, (2003) edited by Peter Fairbrother and Charlotte Yates. An ILO publication, *Organized Labour in the 21ˢᵗ Century* (2002), edited by A.V. Jose, includes case studies of trade union responses to globalization in the U.S., Japan, Sweden, Chile, Israel, Korea, Lithuania, India, Ghana, Niger, and South Africa. In addition, there is a voluminous literature in the form of books and articles on the American experience. The recent contributions include Milkman and Voss (2004), Turner, Katz, and Hurd (2001), Bacharach et al. (2001), Bennett and Kauffman (2002), Clawson (2003), and Lopez (2004). Developments in union membership and union density since 1985 are examined in Visser (2003) covering 103 countries. Eiro-line (2005), a web site of the Dublin-based European Foundation for Improvement in Living and Working Conditions, annually updates industrial relations developments, including union membership and density trends, in Europe, the United States, and Japan. Together, these publications provide an insightful perspective on challenges facing unions around the world, and their responses in the form of adaptations and innovations to meet these challenges.

A key conclusion of these studies is that labour movements everywhere are under attack in the face of pervasive market-oriented neoliberal ideology and in varying degrees losing their strength and influence at both the societal and workplace level. This is evident from the trends in union density and collective bargaining coverage, a measure of the "effectiveness of unions in defending or regulating minimum standards of income and related terms of employment for employees," analyzed by Visser (2003). His figures point out that except for a few countries (notably Finland, Belgium, Sweden, Spain, Turkey, South Africa, Zambia, Zimbabwe, and Chile), union density over the period 1985-2000 declined in every country. While collective bargaining coverage has remained steady in most European countries (with the exception of Denmark and Switzerland, where it has been negatively affected) it too has shown reduction in many countries. The decline has been particularly marked in United Kingdom, United States, Australia, New Zealand, and Japan.

It is also evident from these studies that there is a heightened awareness in labour movements around the world to change their structures to accommodate the "new" workforce and promote greater membership involvement and participation in decision-making, develop innovative strategies and approaches to servicing, bargaining, organizing, and political action. Coalition-building with non-labour groups has been a common vehicle for expanding the sphere of action, with encouraging examples from such diverse countries as the United States, South Africa, Mexico and India. The future of such coalitions is nonetheless uncertain due to their fragile nature.

While union renewal efforts appear to be underway on a wide scale, union strategies, approaches and priorities vary markedly, shaped by the severity of the "crisis" and the institutional and political context. As Kelly and Frege (2004, 182) note in their concluding chapter, "there is no single strategy that works well for all union movements, irrespective of national context; the same strategy is likely to produce different results in different countries." As pointed out earlier, organizing has been the main focus of union revival efforts in Anglo-Saxon countries which have faced serious decline in their membership and where unions are the only channel of employee voice. On the other hand, strengthening partnerships between labour, business, and the state has been the major preoccupation in the European countries on account of their centralized structures, high collective bargaining coverage, and a tradition of corporatist industrial relations, together with the pressing employer and employee needs for "flexibility." Alternatively, unions in developing countries have focused their energies on economic development, democratization of institutions and human rights, and on safeguarding and advancing the social wage, safety nets, and equal access to opportunities (Jose 2002). No union movement has used a single strategy for revival, but have experimented with a complex mix of strategies, including organizational restructuring, political action for worker mobilization, forging community and other social alliances, and collaborating with other unions, nationally or internationally.

Although the union revival has been shaped by differing institutional and political contexts, social movement unionism—with its emphasis on labour activism, expanded opportunities for rank-and-file participation, and involvement in union activities through democratization of union structures, and coalition-building—appears to be the main inspiration in union revitalization across countries. Turner (2003, 24) concludes his comparative analysis by asserting that "widespread mobilization is an important force for institutional change" because of its powerful effects on both individual and organizational behaviour. However, as a critic of social movement unionism in the American context has noted, in a climate of worker conservatism, bureaucratic rigidities within unions, and a host of internal and external barriers to change, "union revitalization will be an extremely difficult uphill struggle" (Katz 2001, 349). To be successful, unions will have to be creative and innovative to meet the diverse and often conflicting needs of workers, and to overcome the power advantage employers have from globalization and related developments. Turner (2004, 5) describes the daunting task of union renewal in the comparative context quite succinctly:

> [Unions] must take responsibility for both internal reforms and in-
> novative external strategies to promote revitalization in today's ex-
> traordinarily difficult context. It will not do labour any good (beyond
> catharsis) to blame employers or governments—for everything from
> union decline to massive economic and social inequality (although
> employers and governments are very much responsible)—unless labour
> is also confronting the reality that new strategies and organizational
> reforms, new linkages and coalitions, are what unions require if present
> circumstances are to be turned around. The desired transformation is
> a task for mobilization, strategic participation, and a greatly broadened
> field of solidarity (from politics to local coalitions to international col-
> laboration).

Challenge of union renewal in the Canadian context

Although unions in Canada have weathered the past two decades better than many other labour movements and have long been favourably contrasted with the dra-matic declines noted in other countries,[9] they too have undergone slippage. While numerically union membership has been increasing steadily, albeit at a slower place over the past two decades, the unionized percentage of the workforce has gradually declined from a high point of nearly 40% in the mid-1980s to 30.6% in 2004 (HRDC 2004; Morissette, Schellenberg, and Johnson 2005). Unless decisive steps are taken by unions to change their external and internal environment, the union density rate is likely to slip further. Provincial differences in unionization rates are significant, with Quebec and Newfoundland and Labrador being at the high end with close to 40% in each province, and Alberta with the lowest density of about 22%. Most disconcerting is Ontario, with 38% of the Canadian workforce and the country's industrial heartland, undergoing a decline in unionization from 33.7% in 1981 to 27.3% in 2004 (Morissette, Schellenberg, and Johnson 2005). Even more significant is the declining level of unionization in the private sector, from nearly 30% in 1981 to 20% in 2004. However, union density has continued to grow or hold its own in the public sector. Even in provinces where the unionization rate in the private sector has declined to under 20%, the public sector unionization rate remains stable in the range of 70-80%.

A balanced picture of unionization across Canada reveals a labour movement that, while declining in strength as a percentage of the workforce, has nonetheless been growing in terms of total membership, adding over half a million workers to its ranks since 1997 (Akyeampong 2004). With absolute membership rising, most major unions appear to be relatively healthy, which can easily breed a degree of complacency—what Murray (2004, 158) refers to as "membership illusion."

In summary, while the Canadian labour movement is not facing a crisis similar to that in the United States and has continued to show vitality and dynamism in many spheres of activity, it confronts many of the same serious challenges that other labour movements are experiencing, highlighting the need for strategic thinking and bold action to overcome them.

The challenge across Canada of reversing the gradual and uneven fall in unionization rates is a formidable one. Indeed, the seriousness of the challenges becomes particularly apparent when measured against the growing anti-union attitude and conduct of employers encouraged by both the increasing North American economic integration and related neoliberal public policies undermining Canada's social programs, and by regressive amendments to labour laws that thwart union growth. Recent research has indicated that it is not only anti-labour legislation that impedes union organizing and activities, but also a hostile political and economic climate created by market-oriented public policy and corporate anti-unionism that has led to a decline in union influence (Martinello 2000; OFL 2002). As noted above, however, studies of union renewal also demonstrate that integrated union strategies with a strategic focus within this cold climate can and do make a difference (Kumar and Murray 2002; Yates 2003).

Strategic opportunities for mobilization of workers and union organizing exist in both particular union campaigns and on broader community and social issues. This holds true even in a decentralized industrial relations regime and one without the institutional supports to be found in countries with high unionization rates.[10]

Challenge of democratization

Just as unions have long stood for democratic rights, such as freedom of speech and freedom of association, including the right to join the union of one's choice, they must also champion democracy within their own ranks.

Unions affiliated to the Canadian Labour Congress do contain formally democratic constitutions and hold regular conventions to elect their leaders and take positions on the key issues facing them. Meaningful democracy, however, is about more than elections every two years; it is also about regularly engaging members in decision-making on the issues that affect their daily lives and thereby expanding their political education, developing their capacities, and thus their confidence in themselves and their collective power as workers.

Challenge of leadership and alternative visions

Largely absent from the debate on union renewal so far is a meaningful discussion of what the labour movement actually believes in. Shared worker-centred perspectives are central to the development of cohesive strategies, innovative tactics, and the related membership motivation necessary for union growth and mobilization.

Most unions in Canada have a vision of themselves as social unions. Unions affiliated with the Canadian Labour Congress and the various provincial federations of labour across the country have long held views in support of universal public health care, quality public education, women's equality, full employment and the like, but it is also fair to say that these visions often lack articulation and are only rarely combined into a clear alternative vision of social change. Yet the work by Levesque, Kumar and Murray (2003) in examining polling results demonstrates that there is considerable support for "the extension of the traditional social union agenda to a larger set of citizenship issues" (see also Canadian Labour Congress 2003). This suggests that there is support for alternative visions being clarified and concretized into an independent workers' agenda for both workplace and societal change.

Linked to the issue of vision is the critical role of union leaders. Leaders play a key role in articulating the environment in which a union operates and in translating goals into strategic choices. In the American context, Voss and Sherman (2000) stress the need for leadership change in union revitalization, while Fiorito (2004), in the context of the United Kingdom, documents how "leaders' commitments to organizing and organizational change are keys to their optimism about their union." Fiorito also finds that, "where pessimism about union futures lurks, it is almost invariably tied to a view that leaders have 'given up,' adopted a very short-term view, and in other ways resigned themselves to managing decline." Together, these findings further confirm our view as to the importance of leadership. At the same time, they connote a changing role for union leaders. Leadership in a more democratic participatory union culture is about the ability to engage members in broad-ranging discussions, to problem solve and to articulate and operationalize the unions' vision. Kumar (2004, 152) has stressed that "union values and mission are not always clear to members and the public at large," and hence the need to articulate a clear vision and specify its links with the needs and aspirations of communities.

Challenge of expanding organizing

Central to the concept of union renewal is the issue of union growth. Organizing both current members to participate in union activities and decision-making rather than being dependent upon union staff, and gaining new members through organizing the unorganized comprise the central task of unions. When Fiorito (2004, 28) asked survey respondents in Britain, "What does the term 'union renewal' mean to your union?" he found that a substantial majority (68%) saw "membership growth as key to union renewal."

More debate is needed on precisely what resources, human and financial, should be allocated to organizing, on what strategies and tactics are the most appropriate to utilize and how, when, and under what circumstances. Stepped-up organizing efforts through coordinated drives, increased resources, and more innovative approaches are needed if unions are going to grow and prosper. There are times when multi-union organizing drives with innovative tactics may be called for against certain national and trans-national corporations. In other cases, union growth may well be assisted by the creation and functioning of an organizing institute similar to the initiative taken in the United Kingdom, Australia, the United States, and in Canada by the British Columbia Federation of Labour.

It has to be kept in mind, however, that expanding membership through intensified organizing efforts and devoting more resources to organizing is not synonymous with union renewal. The U.S. experience suggests that organizing new members is closely related to effective bargaining, a capacity to mobilize workers through political action and community alliances, and developing a participatory union culture.

Challenge of organizing and bargaining in small workplaces

Employment growth in small workplaces continues to be higher than in large workplaces. Small workplaces (employing fewer than 20 employees) have very low levels of unionization (12.6% compared to 54.1% in workplaces with over 500 employees in 2003) and are characterized by low wages and virtually non-existent benefits. However, the number of organizing drives and their success rate is much higher in small workplaces than in large ones. The challenge for the trade union movement is to not only to continue to organize small workplaces, but to engage in meaningful collective bargaining.

Bargaining and servicing small units is costly, and significant collective agreement improvements are difficult to obtain, given weak bargaining leverage. New efforts are needed in order to achieve greater bargaining strength. Broader-based structures of bargaining may be necessary to secure and maintain such improvements. Sectoral bargaining mechanisms may be one answer. Outside of the unique construction sector, such mechanisms are largely found in British Columbia with community health care units and chains such as the White Spot restaurants, Starbucks, and Kentucky Fried Chicken. More widespread are union trusteed or jointly trusteed pension plans and union delivery of other non-wage benefits to reduce the costs of providing workplace-by-workplace benefits. Sooner or later, unions in their organizing campaigns and collective bargaining negotiations in the small workplace sector will have to confront the inefficiencies and ineffectiveness of separate workplace-by-workplace bargaining and consider the need to establish appropriate forms of more centralized bargaining structures, either through joint union action or legislative provision.

Challenge of contingent workers and growing precariousness

As in all too many countries, there is a growing polarization of the labour market across Canada, with implications on a number of levels such as hours of work, income levels, and changes in forms of work. More Canadians than ever are part of a "flexible" workforce working in "non-standard" jobs, i.e., work that is neither permanent nor full-time. Today, about 34% of the workforce work in jobs that are precarious, such as irregular part-time, casual, contract, temporary, and self employed (Vosko, Cranford, and Zukewich 2003). These jobs are also precarious in terms of quality of employment, providing poor job security, generally low income, few if any benefits, and are overwhelmingly non-union. This workforce is "over-represented" by women—precariousness is gendered—but it also includes a disproportionate number of youth, minorities, and disadvantaged workers. Ironically, it is these very workers that are most open to unionization. Yet the industrial relations system, its rules and regulations and concomitant union practices, were designed and developed in the post-World War II period when standard employment relationships were the norm and have yet to adapt to the reality of a contingent and precarious work force (Fudge and Vosko 2001; Chaykowski 2005; Vallee 2005). The challenge for unions in many provincial jurisdictions is to begin to find ways of protecting these largely marginalized precarious workers on the same scale as permanent full-time core workers.

Challenge of organizational innovation

While perhaps surprising to the uninitiated, recent surveys and academic studies find that a significant number of unions across Canada are engaged in a critical assessment of their goals, strategies, and ways of operating. Approaches and priorities relating to collective bargaining, membership services, organizing and community alliances are in the process of change and rethinking. Organization structures, for example, are undergoing modification so as to encompass women, workers of colour, youth, people with disabilities, and aboriginals to reflect both changing demographics and the necessary inclusiveness for union solidarity.

Many of these changes are shown in the 2000-01 Human Resources Development Canada survey conducted by Kumar and Murray (2002). The survey found an increased emphasis on organizational change that enabled membership involvement, participation and communication. It further found a high priority being placed on education and training for purposes of increased awareness, activism, and solidarity. At the same time, the authors warn that:

> Slow and incremental change is unlikely to bring about revival, nor even restoration of the strength unions enjoyed twenty years ago. Labour leaders have to think strategically and proactively to accelerate the speed of change, and to widely diffuse the process of innovation.

The issue of diffusion is most important, given the labour movement's decentralized framework. Locals will have to be catalysts for change, aided by appropriate vertical and horizontal networks of support in their union. Innovation will also need to be inter-union and extend to labour's community allies, confirming the important co-ordinating role of labour councils, provincial federations of labour, and the Canadian Labour Congress.

Challenge of inclusion and diversity

An important challenge facing unions is to recognize and adapt to increased workforce diversity due to the growing immigration from Asia and Africa. This is particularly true in the major cities across the country such as Toronto, Montreal and Vancouver, where most immigrants tend to locate. Unions in every part of the country need to champion the fight against all forms of intolerance, such as racism, sexism and homophobia. By so doing, unions promote a culture of inclusiveness and solidarity within their ranks and a positive outreach in the broader society. This in turn fosters a growing willingness of immigrants, people of colour, women, youth, and disadvantaged workers to join unions and support union renewal. It also enables new alliances with community coalitions and support for community unionism.

Challenge of union education

It is presumptuous to think that working people, whether unionized or not, will blindly follow or somehow come to identify with a particular viewpoint or ideology. In addition to concrete experience in collective actions to defend or gain membership improvements, members need to have the opportunity to participate in union educational programs. Some of these will no doubt need to be "tool courses" such as steward training or basic health and safety programs, but other programs will need to critically discuss societal issues and alternative solutions. Education can help link members' own experience to relevant issues and new ways of interpreting them. This form of education promotes dialogue and debate, respect for each other's views, and has the potential to both invigorate and empower participants.

Activism without education, in the absence of a coherent conceptual framework by which to comprehend the world around one (and without participation in democratic decision-making) is most often dis-empowering, despite the best of intentions. Many unions have yet to confront the challenge of developing and operationalizing a substantial and progressive educational program. As Taylor (2001, 249) in his history of labour education has noted, unions have to develop learning strategies for their organizations consistent with their strategic plan for union renewal. According to him, "[what] is needed are new approaches that meet the needs of labour organizations for trained and critically engaged workplace representatives, that provide union members a thorough understanding of the labour movement and its agenda, and that allow trade unionists to gain access to a range of educational opportunities from basic skills to university-level courses." He believes that the labour movement has to build close and enduring relationships with external allies and providers to accomplish this task.

Conclusion

The foregoing has been a rather extensive review and critical assessment of the literature on union renewal. We have engaged in a discussion of the key concepts and rationale of union renewal, union strategies, the formidable obstacles as well as facilitating factors of change. We have also referenced union renewal in a global context before focusing on the particular challenges in Canada.

The following chapters in this volume provide a series of case studies on how unions across Canada are confronting at least some of the challenges outlined above.

The intention is to thereby assist in opening up various "paths to union renewal," to develop alternatives to the traditional politics, to explore ways of halting the decline of unions as a percentage of the workforce—indeed, to foster their expansion. While at this time we don't see a generalized advance by unions across the county that would merit the description union renewal or labour revitalization, we do see, as the following pages attest, considerable innovation, a certain increase in discussion and debate concerning today's reality and the future of unions, plus actual initiatives arising out of particular circumstances.

Notes

1. A variety of terms have been used in the literature to analyze the change process. Among the common terms are union renewal, labour revitalization, restructuring, rebuilding, rebirth, revival, resurgence, reinventing, rekindling and transformation. While their intent is the same, that is rebuilding union strength and power, they differ in their prescriptions. A major distinction is made between structural change in structures and processes to regain unions' organizational, bargaining and political strength, and institutional or cultural change with a clearly articulated mission or vision to facilitate capacity building for rank and file mobilization and participation (Hurd and Behren 2003).

2. Turner and Hurd (2001, 11) note that "[There] is a difference between social movements and social movement unionism. Social movements are broad society-wide phenomena that rise and fall in unpredictable historical waves. Social movement unionism, by contrast, is a type of unionism based on member involvement and activism. "Social movement unionism is another, albeit "more powerful," version of social unionism, "a unionism that considers workers as more than just sellers of labour, that is sensitive to broader concerns, and that contributes to those in need in the community and internationally" (Gindin 1995, 266). The purpose of social movement unionism, according to Gindin, is make the unions centres of "working class life and culture." "It means making the union into a vehicle through which its members can not only address their bargaining demands but actively lead the fight for everything that affects working people in their communities and the country." More precisely, social movement unionism is a type of unionism "that is workplace based, community rooted, democratic, ideological, and committed to building a the kind of movement that is a precondition for any sustained resistance and fundamental change" (Gindin 1998, 197). Social movement unionism has also been described by some union activists as a form of community unionism. See Banks (1992) and Clawson (2003).

3. According to Frege and Kelly (2003, 8), "the literature has usually focused on quantitative measures such as membership density or collective bargaining coverage." However, while the loss of membership may be a strong indicator of union decline in Anglo-Saxon Countries (i.e. United States, United Kingdom, Canada, Australia, and New Zealand), it is not necessarily so in countries such as France or Germany where although the union density has declined, the collective bargaining coverage remains high and stable.

4. See Gunter and Hoeven (2004) for a review of literature on economic characteristics of globalization and its social dimensions. The review draws on over 1200 articles and books listed in Gunter (2004) prepared for the report of the World Commission On the Social Dimensions of Globalization.

5. By neo-liberal philosophy we mean an ideology and practices that stress the private market, competitiveness, entrepreneurship and individualism over collective needs and aspirations, such as universal social programs, public ownership and intervention in the economy, and the rights of trade unions.

6. See the special Spring 2002 issue of the *Journal of Labor Research* for the threats and opportunities created by cyber space, in particular papers by Shostak and Chaison.

7. The Canadian Labour Congress in 1992 revised its constitution to include coalition building as one of its main purposes, following the recommendation of the Task Force On the Role and Structure of the Congress, appointed in 1990 to undertake "a comprehensive review of mandate, role and functions of the CLC." The preamble of the Constitution was amended to include that "When action is required on behalf of working people, the congress shall mobilize its resources, coordinate the efforts of its affiliates, and join with other progressive organizations in mounting national campaigns to achieve worth while goals." Similarly Article II (PURPOSES) was revised to include Section 6 which reads that among the purposes of the congress is "To help create and participate in coalitions with groups which share our aims and principles in the pursuit of social and economic justice" (Canadian Labour Congress 1992).

8. See Lipset and Meltz (2003), and the Canadian Labour Congress (2003) for evidence on Canada and the United States.

9. See Fairbrother and Yates (2003:23) and Jose (2002:4). According to Fairbrother and Yates "In some ways the Canadian case stands out as exceptional when compared with other four countries [United States, United Kingdom, Australia and New Zealand], in that trade union membership levels were maintained for a far longer time than elsewhere." Jose notes that "Sweden, Canada, and Singapore stand out among the countries that followed new approaches with positive results."

10. The many challenges facing trade unionists in Canada are further noted in *Studies in Political Economy* (2004).

References

AFL-CIO. 2005a. *A More Effective and Unified Force.* Washington, D.C.: AFL-CIO. A joint statement by the presidents of CWA, IAM, APWU, USWA, AFL, AFSCME, IAFF, IUPAT, and ALPA.

———. 2005b. *Winning for Working Families: A Call For Change.* Washington, D.C.: AFL-CIO.

Akyeampong, Ernest B. 2004. The Union Movement in Transition. *Perspectives on Labor and Income.* August.

Appelbaum, Eileen, and Larry W. Hunter. 2005. Union Participation in Strategic Decisions of Corporations. In *Emerging Labor Market Institutions for the Twenty-First Century*, ed. Richard Freeman, Joni Hersch and Lawrence Mishel. Chicago: University of Chicago Press.

Baccaro, Lucio, Kerstin Hamann, and Lowell Turner. 2003. The Politics of Labour Movement Revitalization: The Need for a Revitalized Perspective. *European Journal of Industrial Relations* 9 (1): 119-133.

Bacharach, Samuel, et al. 2001. *Mutual Aid and Union Renewal: Cycles of Logics of Action.* Ithaca, NY: Cornell University Press.

Banks, Andy. 1992. The Power and Promise of Community Unionism. *Labor Research Review* 18:17-31.

Banks, Andy, and Jack Metzgar. 1989. Participating in Management: Union Organizing on a New Terrain. *Labor Research Review* 14:1-55.

———. 2005. Response to "Unions as Social Capital." *Labor Studies Journal* 29 (4): 27-35.

Bennett, James, and Bruce Kaufman. 2002. *The Future of Private Sector Unionism in the United States.* Armonk, NY: M. E. Sharpe.

Brofenbrenner, Kate, and Robert Hickey. 2003. *Blueprint For Change: A National Assessment of Winning Union Organizing Strategies.* Ithaca, NY: School of Industrial and Labor Relations, Cornell University.

———. 2004. Changing to Organize: A National Assessment of Union Strategies. In *Rebuilding Labor*, ed. Ruth Milkman and Kim Voss. Ithaca, NY: Cornell University Press.

Bronfenbrenner, Kate, S. Friedman, R. Hurd, R. Oswald, and R. Seeber, eds. 1998. *Organizing to Win: New Research on Union Strategies.* Ithaca, NY: Cornell University Press.

Canadian Labour Congress (CLC). 1998. *No Easy Recipe: Building the Diversity and Strength of the Labour Movement.* Ottawa: CLC.

———. 2002. *Building the Congress of Tomorrow: Report of the Task Force on the Role and Structure of the CLC.* Ottawa: CLC.

———. 2003. *Canadians Talk About Unions.* Ottawa: CLC.

Chaison, Gary. 2001. Union Mergers and Union Revival: Are We Asking Too Much or Too Little? In Turner, Katz, and Hurd 2001.

Chaykowski, Richard P. 2005. *Non-Standard Work and Economic Vulnerability.* Ottawa: Canadian Policy Research Networks.

Clawson, Dan. 2003. *The Next Upsurge: Labor and New Social Movements.* Ithaca, NY: Cornell University Press.

———. 2005. Response: Organizing, Movements, and Social Capital. *Labor Studies Journal* 29 (4): 37-44.

Cornfield, Daniel, and Holly McCammon. 2003. *Labor Revitalization: Global Perspectives and New Initiatives.* Research in the Sociology of Work, vol. 11. Danvers, MA: Elsevier.

Day, Benjamin. 2004. Organizing For (Spare) Change: A Radical Politics for American Labor. *Working USA: The Journal of Labor and Society* 8 (September): 27-43.

Diamond, V. 1988. *Numbers That Count: A Manual on Internal Organizing.* Washington, DC: AFL-CIO.

Eaton, Jonathon. 2004. Union Renewal in Canada: Strategies, Tactics, and Public Perception. PhD thesis, University of Toronto.

Ebbinghaus, Bernhard. 2003. Ever Larger Unions: Organizational Restructuring and Its Impact on Union Confederations. *Industrial Relations Journal* 34 (5): 446-460.

Eiro-online. 2004. *Trade Union Membership 1993-2003*. Dublin, Ireland: European Foundation for the Improvement of Living and Working Conditions. Available at www.eiro.eurofound.eu.int/2004/03/update.

————. 2005. *Industrial Relations in the EU, Japan, and the United States*. Dublin, Ireland: European Foundation for the Improvement of Living and Working Conditions. Available at www.eiro.eurofound.eu.int/2005/02/feature.

Eisenscher, Michael. 2002. Is the Secret to Labor's Future in The Past? *Working USA: The Journal of Labor and Society* 5 (4): 95-122.

Fairbrother, Peter. 2000. *Unions at the Crossroads*. London: Mansell Publishing.

Fairbrother, Peter, and Charlotte Yates, eds. 2003. *Trade Unions in Renewal: A Comparative Study*. London, U.K.: Continuum.

Fantasia, Rick, and Kim Voss. 2004. *Hard Work: Remaking the American Labor Movement*. Berkley, CA: University of California Press.

Fichter, Michael, and Ian Green. 2004. Analyzing Social Partnership: A Tool of Union Revitalization. In Frege and Kelly 2004.

Fiorito, Jack. 2004. Union Renewal and the Organizing Model in the United Kingdom. *Labor Studies Journal* 29 (2): 21-53.

Fletcher, Bill, Jr. 1998. Labor Education in the Maelstrom of Class Struggle. In *Rising from the Ashes? Labor in the Age of "Global" Capitalism*, ed. Ellen Melksins Wood, Peter Melksins, and Michael Yates. New York, NY: Monthy Review Press.

Frege, Carola, Edmund Heery, and Lowell Turner. 2003. Comparative Coalition Building and the Revitalization of the Labor Movement. In *Proceedings of the 55th Annual Meeting*, ed. Adrienne E. Eaton. Champaigne, IL: Industrial Relations Research Association.

————. 2004. The New Solidarity: Trade Union Coalition Building in Five Countries. In Frege and Kelly 2004.

Frege, Carola, and John Kelly. 2003. Union Revitalization Strategies in Comparative Perspectives. Special issue on union revitalization, *European Journal of Industrial Relation* 9 (1).

————. 2004. *Varieties of Unionism: Strategies for Union Revitalization in a Globalizing Economy*. Oxford, U.K.: Oxford University Press.

Fudge, Judy, and Leah Vosko. 2001. By Whose Standards? Re-regulating the Canadian Labour Market. *Economic and Industrial Democracy* 22 (3): 327-356.

Gindin, Sam. 1995. *The Canadian Auto Workers: The Birth and Transformation of a Union*. Toronto: James Lorimer.

————. 1998, Notes on Labor at the End of the Century: Starting Over. In *Rising From the Ashes? Labor in the Age of "Global" Capitalism*, ed. Ellen Melksins Wood, Peter Melksins, and Michael Yates. New York, NY: Monthly Review Press.

Gordon, Michael, and Lowell Turner. 2000. *Transnational Cooperation Among Labor Unions*. Ithaca, NY: Cornell University Press.

Gunter, Bernhard. 2004. *A Comprehensive Collection of the Recent Literature on the Social Impacts of Globalization*. Geneva: International Labour Organization.

Gunter, Bernhard G., and Rolph van der Hoeven. 2004. The Social Dimension of Globalization: A Review of the Literature. *International Labour Review* 143 (1-2): 7-43.

Hamann, Kerstin, and John Kelly. 2003. Union Revitalization Through Political Action: Evidence From Five Countries. In *Proceedings of the 55th Annual Meeting*, ed. Adrienne E. Eaton. Champaigne, IL: Industrial Relations Research Association.

————. 2004. Unions As Political Actors: A Recipe for Revitalization. In Frege and Kelly 2004.

Heery, Edmund. 2003. Trade Unions and Industrial Relations. In *Understanding Work and Employment*, ed. Peter Ackers and Adrian Wilkinson. Oxford, U.K.: Oxford University Press.

Heery, Edmund, and Lee Adler. 2004. Organizing the Unorganized. In Frege and Kelly 2004.

Human Resources Development Canada (HRDC). 2004. Union Membership In Canada, 2004. *Workplace Gazette* 7 (3).

Hurd, Richard. 2004. The Failure of Organizing, The New Unity Partnership and the Future of The Labor Movement. *Working USA: The Journal of Labor and Society* 8 (September): 5-25.

Hurd, Richard, and Martin Behrens. 2003. Structural Change and Union Transformation. In *Proceedings of the 55th Annual Meeting*, ed. Adrienne E. Eaton. Champaigne, IL: Industrial Relations Research Association.

Jackson, Andrew. 2005. *Work and Labour in Canada: Critical Issues.* Toronto: Canadian Scholars' Press.

Jarley, Paul. 2005. Unions as Social Capital: Renewal Through a Return to the Logic of Mutual Aid? *Labor Studies Journal* 29 (4): 1-26.

Jarley, Paul, Jack Fiorito, and John T. Delaney. 1998. Do Unions Control Their Density? *Proceedings of the Fiftieth Annual Meeting.* Madison, WI: Industrial Relations Research Association.

Jose, A.V. 2002. *Organized Labour in the 21st Century.* Geneva: International Labour Organization.

Journal of Labor Research. 2002. Special Issue on Information Technology and Unions. *Journal of Labor Research* 23 (2).

Katz, Harry C. 2001. Afterword to Whither the American Labor Movement? In Turner, Katz, and Hurd 2001.

Kelly, John. 2002. *Union Revival: Organizing Around the World.* London, U.K.: Trade Union Congress.

Kelly, John, and Carola Frege. 2004. Conclusions: Varieties of Unionism. In Frege and Kelly 2004.

Kumar, Pradeep. 2004. Diffusing Innovations and Articulating Labour's Vision. *Studies in Political Economy* 74 (Autumn): 147-155.

Kumar, Pradeep, and Gregor Murray. 2002. *Innovation and Change in Labour Organizations in Canada: Results of the National 2000-2001 HRDC Survey.* Available at www.crimt.org.

Lerner, Stephen. 2002. Three Steps to Reorganizing and Rebuilding the Labor Movement. *Labor Notes,* December.

Levesque, C., P. Kumar, and Gregor Murray. 2003. Is Social Unionism the Way to the Future? Explaining Member and Non-member Perceptions. A Paper presented to the Annual Conference of the Canadian Industrial Relations Conference, Halifax, June.

Lillie, Nathan, and Migue Martinez Lucio. 2004. International Trade Union Revitalization: The Role of National Union Approaches. In Frege and Kelly 2004.

Lipset, Seymour M., and Noah M. Meltz. 2004. *The Paradox of American Unionism: Why Americans Like Unions More than Canadians Do But Join Much Less?* Ithaca, NY: Cornell University Press.

Lopez, Steven Henry. 2004. *Reorganizing the Rust Belt: An Inside Study of the American Labor Movement.* Berkley, CA: University of California Press.

MacDowell, Laurel Sefton. 2000. Company Unionism in Canada. In *Nonunion Employee Representation: History, Contemporary Practice, and Policy*, ed. Bruce E. Kaufman and Daphne Gottlieb Taras. Armonk, NY: M. E. Sharpe.

Mantsios, Gregory. 1998. *A New Labor Movement for the New Century.* New York, NY: Monthly Review Press.

Martinello, F. 2002. Mr. Harris, Mr. Rae, and Union Activity in Ontario. *Canadian Public Policy* 26 (1): 17-33.

Masters, Marick. 2004. Unions in the 2000 Election: A Strategic Choice Perspective. *Journal of Labour Research* 25 (1): 139-182.

Masters, Marick, and Robert Atkin. 1999. Union Strategies for Revival: A Conceptual Framework and Literature Review. *Research in Personnel and Human Resource Management* 27.

Milkman, Ruth, and Kim Voss. 2004. *Rebuilding Labor: Organizing and Organizers in the New Union Movement.* Ithaca, NY: Cornell University Press.

Moody, Kim. 1997. *Workers in a Lean World: Unions in the International Economy.* New York, NY: Verso.

Morisette, René, Grant Schellenberg, and Anick Johnson. 2005. Diverging Trends in Unionization. *Perspectives on Labour and Income* 17 (2).

Murray, Gregor. 2004. Union Myths, Enigmas, and Other Tales: Five Challenges for Union Renewal. *Studies in Political Economy* 74 (Autumn): 57-169.

Nissen, Bruce. 2002. *Unions in a Globalized Environment.* Armonk, NY: M. E. Sharpe.

———. 2003. Alternative Strategic Directions for the U.S. Labor Movement: Recent Scholarship. *Labor Studies Journal* 28 (1): 133-135.

Ontario Federation of Labour. 1982. *Statement on Women and Affirmative Action.* Toronto: Ontario Federation of Labour.

———. 1986. *Racism and Discrimination: 30th Annual Convention Document.* Toronto: Ontario Federation of Labour.

———. 2003. *Organizing in a Cold Climate.* Toronto: Ontario Federation of Labour.

Olney, Shauna. 1996. *Unions in a Changing World: Problems and Prospects in Selected Industrialized Countries.* Geneva: International Labour Organization.

Osterman, Paul, Thomas Kochan, Richard Locke, and Michael Piore. 2001. *Working in America: A Blueprint for the New Labor Market.* Cambridge, MA: The MIT Press.

Penny, Robert A. 2004. Workers Against Unions: Unions Organizing and Anti-Union Counter Mobilization. In Milkman and Voss 2004.

Rubinstein, Saul. 2002. Unions As Value-Adding Networks: Possibilities for the Future of U.S. Unionism. In Bennett and Kaufman 2002.

Russo, J., and A. Banks. 1996. Teaching the Organizing Model of Unionism and Campaign-Based Education: National and International Trends. A paper presented at the AFL-CIO/Cornell University Research Conference on Unions Organizing, Washington DC, April.

Schenk, Christopher. 2003. Social Movement Unionism: Beyond the Organizing Model. In Fairbrother and Yates 2003.

Statistics Canada. 2004. Fact Sheet on Unionization. *Perspectives on Labour and Income,* August.

Studies in Political Economy. 2004. Forum: Reorganizing Unions. *Studies in Political Economy* 74 (Fall): 124–190.

Taylor, Jeff. 2001. *Union Learning: Canadian Labour Education in the Twentieth Century.* Toronto: Thompson Publishing House.

Turner, Lowell. 2003. Reviving the Labor Movement: A Comparative Perspective. In Cornfield and McCammon 2003.

——. 2004, Why Revitalize? Labour's Urgent Mission in a Contested Global Economy. In Frege and Kelly 2004, 1–10.

Turner, Lowell, and Richard Hurd. 2001. Building Social Movement Unionism. In Turner, Katz, and Hurd 2001.

Turner, Lowell, Harry Katz, and Richard Hurd, eds. 2001. *Rekindling the Movement: Labor's Quest for Relevance in the 21st Century.* Ithaca, NY: Cornell University Press.

Vallée, Guylaine. 2005. *Toward Enhancing the Employment Conditions of Vulnerable Workers: A Public Policy Perspective.* Ottawa: Canadian Policy Research Networks.

Vasser, Jelle. 2003. Unions and Unionism Around the World. In *International Handbook of Trade Unions,* ed. John T. Addison and Claus Schnabel. Northampton, MA: Edward Elgar.

Vosko, L., C. Cranford, and N. Zukewich. 2003. Precarious Jobs? A New Typology of Employment. *Perspectives on Labour and Income* 15 (4): 16–26.

Voss, Kim, and Rachel Sherman. 2000. Breaking the Iron Law of Oligarchy: Union Revitalization in the American Labor Movement. *American Journal of Sociology* 106 (September): 327–33.

Weil, David. 1997. *Turning the Tide: Strategic Planning for Labor Unions.* London, U.K.: Macmillan.

Wells, Don. 1998. Building Transnational Coordinative Unionism. In *Confronting Change: Auto Labor and Lean Production in North America,* ed. Huberto Juarez Nunez and Steve Babson. Detroit, MI: Wayne State University Labor Studies Centre.

Yates, Charlotte A. B. 2003. The Revival of Industrial Unions in Canada: The Extension and Adaptation of Industrial Union Practices in the New Economy. In Fairbrother and Yates 2003.

Chapter 2
Rowing Against the Tide: The Struggle to Raise Union Density in a Hostile Environment

ANDREW JACKSON

Introduction

Canada is one of very few advanced industrial countries in which union density is not in sharp decline, and in which union membership is still growing in terms of absolute numbers. Canadian unions continue to make gains for their members and for all workers, and remain an important force in the workplace, in society and in politics. Set against the background of sharp union decline in the United States, Great Britain, Australia, New Zealand, and many other broadly comparable countries, this performance by Canadian unions is quite impressive (Fairbrother and Yates 2003).

Despite continental economic integration, one in every three Canadian workers is still covered by a collective agreement, more than double the proportion in the United States, and union membership as a share of the workforce is now not far below the level of many continental European countries and exceeds that in the United Kingdom. As shown in Table 1, union membership as a proportion of all wage and salary earners has held up relatively much better than in most other advanced industrial countries since 1980, with the exception of Sweden. However, the proportion of workers covered by collective bargaining arrangements is still much higher in most of the larger European countries because of the formal and informal extension of union-negotiated agreements to non-union workers.

As shown in Table 2, total Canadian union membership has continued to gradually rise to well over 4 million workers today, including from 2000 to 2004. However, union density—the proportion of all workers who belong to a union—has slipped from the high point of 37.2% in 1984 to just above 30% today. Less than one-in-five private-sector workers now belong to a union. (For a detailed statistical analysis see Jackson and Schetagne 2003; Akyeampong 2004; Morissette, Schellenberg, and Johnson 2005). Note that there are different estimates of union density from different surveys, and that union membership as a proportion of all workers is somewhat less than collective bargaining coverage since some non-union workers, such as lower level supervisors, are covered even though they are not union members.) New union organizing is taking place, especially among women and minority workers in services jobs. But it is not enough to counter the ongoing loss of union jobs from economic restructuring and the fact that job growth in the private sector is concentrated in mainly non-union sectors and occupations.

Table 1: Union Members as % of Wage and Salary Earners

	1980 (%)	2000 (%)
Canada	35 (37)	28 (32)
United States	22	13
United Kingdom	51	31
Germany	35 (80)	25 (68)
Italy	50 (80)	35 (80)
Sweden	80 (80)	90 (80)
Japan	31	22
New Zealand	69	23
Australia	48	25

(Figure in brackets is % Employees Covered by Collective Bargaining Arrangements.)
Source: OECD Employment Outlook, 2004. Table 3.3, p.145.

Table 2: Union Membership in Canada (as reported by trade unions)

	Union Membership (000s)	Union Membership as % of non-agricultural paid workers (%)
1980	3,397	35.7
1984	3,651	37.2★
1988	3,841	34.8
1992	4,089	35.8
1996	4,033	34.3
2000	4,058	31.9
2004	4,261	30.4

Source: *Workplace Gazette*, Vol. 2, #3, 1999, and Vol. 7, #3, 2004.
Labour Program, Human Resources and Skills Development Canada (HRSDC).
★   peak year

The bad news is that Canadian unions risk marginalization if the ongoing process of union renewal does not eventually begin to reverse the slow decline of union density. The good news is that unions are increasingly aware of this challenge, and are doing something about it.

This paper provides background factual information of broad trends in the job market and is organized as follows. Part Two very briefly summarizes the reasons why union density is important. Part Three describes some of the key forces driving density. Part Four surveys the broad historical trends in Canadian union density. Part Five sets union density and organizing in the context of the changing structure of the Canadian labour market. Finally, Part Six provides an overview of recent trends and describes the context for organizing strategies and union renewal.

Why union density is important

Union representation provides access to rights and protections, and has an important positive impact upon wages, benefits, and working conditions. (For a longer

Table 3: The Union Wage Advantage in 2003

	Union	Non-Union	Union Advantage	Union Advantage as % of Non-Union
Median Hourly Wage				
All	$20.00	$14.00	$6.00	42.9%
Men	$21.00	$15.98	$5.02	31.4%
Women	$18.75	$12.02	$6.73	56.0%
Average Hourly Wage				
All	$21.01	$16.65	$4.36	26.2%
Men	$22.00	$18.69	$3.31	17.7%
Women	$19.94	$14.55	$5.39	37.1%
Age 15–24	$12.66	$9.88	$2.78	28.1%
Public Sector	$23.10	$22.09	$1.01	4.6%
Private Sector	$18.70	$16.17	$2.53	15.6%
Sales and Service Occupations	$13.16	$11.28	$1.88	16.7%
Processing and Manufacturing Occupations	$18.11	$14.76	$3.35	22.7%

Source: Statistics Canada. *Labour Force Survey*. Data from "Gender and Work" database.

discussion of the "union advantage" see Jackson 2003.) As shown in Table 3, the union wage advantage is particularly high for women, younger workers, and workers in lower-paid sales and services jobs. The union wage advantage does reflect factors other than belonging to a union, such as working in the public sector. However, holding all other relevant factors such as age, education, industry and occupation constant, union workers in Canada earn 7% to 14% more per hour than non-union workers, are about three times more likely to be covered by an employer-sponsored pension plan, and are twice as likely to be covered by a medical or dental plan (Fang and Verma 2002; Lipsett and Reesor 1997).

The union advantage is greatest for workers who are otherwise disadvantaged in the job market, notably women, workers of colour, young workers, and the relatively unskilled. As a result, unions help equalize outcomes and opportunities between different groups of workers and disproportionately improve conditions for low-wage and precarious workers.

Achieving high union density is important since it extends the union advantage to more workers, and since it can change the way in which the job market operates on a community, sector-by-sector, and even national basis. If union density is low and is confined to workers with a lot of bargaining power, there is a risk that unionized workers will become a privileged labour aristocracy rather than a broad, inclusive, and equalizing social movement. If union density is high, as in the Scandinavian countries, collective bargaining can produce a job market marked by quite small wage differences and by low levels of low-paid and insecure work. It should be noted that union impacts in Sweden and some other European countries are amplified by centralized or industry-wide collective bargaining, and by the ability of unions to influence or dominate statutory works councils.

High union density gives the labour movement potential power in the work-place, in the labour market, and in politics. While undercut to some degree by growing international competition, high union density can provide the power to take wages, benefits, and working conditions out of the competitive equation faced by employers, and the ability to set decent wage floors and to promote good work-ing conditions across whole sectors. For example, high union density in Sweden means that hotel, retail, child care and elder care workers are paid much closer to average wages than is the case in Canada, benefiting mainly women and minority workers who would otherwise be low paid. About one-in-four full-time workers in Canada in the mid-1990s (23.7%) were low paid—defined as earning less than two-thirds of the median national full-time wage—compared to just one-in-twenty (5.2%) in Sweden. One-third of women in Canada were low paid, compared to just 8.4% in Sweden (OECD 1996).

Even in a North American context, high union density in an economically relevant sector in a local labour market can make a big difference for workers. For example, high union density in Las Vegas has significantly raised wages, benefits, and access to good jobs for hotel and hospitality industry workers and made it very difficult for employers to resist unionization (Meyerson 2004). City-wide *Justice for Janitors* campaigns and agreements have raised wages and benefits for U.S. build-ing cleaners. In Canada, sector-wide union organization and sectoral bargaining have underpinned significant gains for groups such as security guards in Quebec, and (under an NDP government) B.C. community services workers. In the final analysis, density is about power.

Key forces driving union density

In most advanced capitalist countries, including Canada, the two historical bas-tions of union strength have been the male industrial working-class and, more recently, mainly women workers in public and social services. In Canada, the two historically large waves of union organization came in the 1940s with the rise of mass industrial unions, and in the 1960s and 1970s with the rise of public services unions. Union strength, from at least the 1980s, has been challenged by de-indus-trialization, deregulation, privatization, and the increased importance of the private services sector of the economy. It is important to note that the latter includes both low-paid and insecure jobs, and well-paid and fairly secure professional and techni-cal "knowledge-based" jobs. Union coverage typically extends to only a minority of both kinds of private services workers, particularly when they are employed in small firms.

The two key differences between low-union-density countries like Canada and high-union-density European countries like Sweden is the size of the broader pub-lic services sector compared to the private services sector, and the extent of union coverage of private service sector workers. In a "post-industrial" economy, unions will live or die less by their ability to hang onto traditional areas of strength than by their ability to expand into growing areas of employment.

Unions have been forced to confront major changes, not just in the economy, but also in the wider society. The emergence of a more diverse and more highly educated workforce, which is now almost equally divided between women and men and includes many workers of colour, has posed challenges for labour movements that were once made up mainly of white, male, manual workers. Unions were once a powerful expression of tightly knit working-class communities, but old solidarities and forms of class consciousness have declined. What workers expect of unions has also changed, with quality of work, equality, and work-life-balance issues becoming as important as the "bread and butter" issues of wages and benefits.

Most union members become members by being hired into a job in an already unionized workplace, rather than by actively joining or supporting a union campaign to organize a non-union workplace. Most non-union members stay that way simply because there is no active union campaign to certify the workplace in which they work. Changing union density is thus a function of three trends: 1) net changes in employment in already-unionized workplaces as a result of closures, layoffs and new hirings; 2) net changes in employment in non-union workplaces and predominantly non-union sectors and occupations; and 3) the rate at which non-union workers are organized into unions.

Changes in employment in both union and non-union workplaces are mainly driven by employers and are outside the direct control of unions. The gradual ongoing rise of private services and of a "knowledge-based economy" strongly influences changes of employment by industry, occupation, firm size, form of employment (i.e., part-time *vs* full-time, permanent *vs* temporary, employee *vs* self-employed), and level of education and skills. Sheer inertia and the slow decline of union membership in traditional areas of strength can slow union decline, but ultimately unions must organize in sectors of the job market which are expanding if they are to achieve success.

Union density will also be influenced by the changing composition of the workforce, especially by age, gender and race, which is overlaid upon the changing industrial and occupational mix. Unlike the big structural economic shifts which have often tended to work against unions, the increased participation of women and workers of colour in the workforce has been positive. Women, minorities and youth are now significantly more likely to support new organizing efforts than are white older men.

A Vector Poll commissioned for the 2003 CLC conference on union renewal found that one-in-seven non-union workers (14%) would "very likely" vote for a union tomorrow if they had the chance. Another 19% would be "somewhat likely" to vote yes, indicating potential one-third support even before any union campaign for certification. Forty-three per cent of non-union workers would be "very or somewhat likely" to join a union if there were no grounds for fear of employer reprisal. This underlying support for unions is even higher among young workers aged 18-29 (52%), visible minorities (54%) and women (50% *vs* 37% for men). This does not mean that workers are beating down the doors to join unions, but it does show that many workers are aware of the union advantage and could be persuaded to join an organizing drive.

Despite adverse structural changes and an often very hostile public policy environment, unions remain potential authors of their own fate. The process of union renewal, which is the subject of this book, is about changing unions to meet new realities, about how to increase bargaining strength, and about how to reach out to unorganized workers. Canadian unions have changed quite profoundly since the late-1980s as a result of mergers, internal organizational changes, and the ongoing shift of members to new sectors and occupations. The changing face of the labour movement is underscored by the fact that membership is now almost equally divided between women and men (though women lag in terms of equal representation among leaders and staff), by the increased participation of workers of colour, and by the greater weight being given to new bargaining issues and to union organizing.

The fragmentary evidence on new organizing shows that Canadian unions have been less complacent than some other labour movements. From the mid-1970s to the late-1990s, anywhere between 60,000 and 100,000 workers, or as many as 2% of all non-union workers, have been organized into unions through new certifications (minus decertifications) each year (Katz-Rosene 2003; Johnson 2002; Martinello 1996). There has been a downward trend since the high point of the mid-1980s, with some ups and downs, and by the late-1990s just under 1% of all non-union paid workers were joining unions each year. The organization rate has been consistently much higher than average in Quebec and, until recently, in British Columbia. The content and administration of labour laws clearly make a major difference. In Ontario, more than 30,000 workers were organized into unions in 1994-95, after the passage of new labour laws by the NDP government, but the total had fallen back to just 14,000 by 2002-03.

Unions as social and political actors can shape the broad terrain of new organizing in several key respects. At the most basic level, union-friendly labour law is both reflective of, and a key cause of, union success. At a wider level, a vital and active labour movement can reach out to and attract non-union workers, and engage the community as a whole in causes and campaigns which lay the basis for organizing and bargaining success. The success of unions is, for example, intimately bound up in increasing the size and scope of the public sector and community-based social services, as opposed to competitive and privatized delivery.

The key point is that unions are able to row against (or even with) the tides of economic and social change and help steer their own destiny. In Canada, new organizing has not been enough to prevent gradual density decline. But it has been enough to make a difference, particularly in private services and in the broader public sector.

Longer-term trends in union coverage

Table Four provides data on union coverage in 1981 and 2004. Union density (union members as a percentage of employees) has fallen by about seven percentage points, from 37.6% to 30.6%, over this period. The decline mainly took place in the recession and slow recovery period of the late-1980s through the mid-1990s when

Table 4: Trends in Unionization Rate

	1981	2004
Total	37.6	30.6
Men	42.1	30.4
Women	31.4	30.8
Non-Commercial Sector	61.4	61.4
Commercial Sector	29.8	20.0
Age		
17–24	26.4	13.6
25–34	39.8	26.1
35–44	42.0	32.8
45–54	41.7	41.2
55 and over	41.9	38.2
Province		
Newfoundland and Labrador	45.2	39.1
Prince Edward Island	38.0	30.1
Nova Scotia	33.8	27.4
New Brunswick	39.8	28.8
Quebec	44.2	37.4
Ontario	33.7	27.3
Manitoba	37.9	35.4
Saskatchewan	37.9	35.2
Alberta	28.4	21.7
British Columbia	43.3	33.1
Selected Industry	*1981*	*1998*
Manufacturing	43.9	31.3
Construction	39.9	27.0
Distributive Services	43.0	33.1
Business Services	5.7	6.9
Consumer Services	13.7	11.0

Source: Morissette, Rene, Grant Schellenberg and Anick Johnson.
"Diverging Trends in Unionization." Statistics Canada Cat. 75-001-XPE.
Perspectives on Labour and Income. Summer, 2005. Pp. 1-8.

many jobs were lost in unionized workplaces due to industrial restructuring, and overall density has been stable since 1997.

The decline in union coverage since the early 1980s has been much more pronounced among younger than older workers. This is likely the result of low rates of hiring into larger, already unionized workplaces in sectors like public services and manufacturing, and higher rates of hiring into smaller non-union workplaces in private services.

Density decline has also been far greater among men than among women. Between 1981 and 2004, the unionization rate for men fell sharply, from 42.1% to

30.4%, while it remained quite stable for women, slipping only slightly from 31.4% to 30.8%. The historically large difference in union coverage between women and men (more than 10 percentage points in 1981) has now almost completely disappeared. This is mainly because women are much more likely than men to work in highly unionized public and social services than in the private sector, where union density is now under 20%. Two-thirds of union women work in the public sector (defined as direct government employment, plus employment in directly government-funded institutions, such as schools, universities, colleges, and hospitals) and just one-third work in the private sector. By contrast, more than 60% of unionized men work in the private sector. (Note that the data in Table 4 for non-commercial services include all health, social services and education workers, even though some of these workers are not public sector workers.)

Union coverage is very high, above 70%, in both education and public adminis-tration, and well above average in health and social services (which has a significant not-for-profit and private-for-profit sector as opposed to public sector component parts, such as doctors' offices and long-term care homes). These three sectors alone now account for more than half of all union members. The public and social serv-ices labour force, which is made up mainly of women workers, has continued to be a key source of union strength, despite privatization, contracting-out, and attacks on the bargaining rights of public sector workers. As will be noted below, this reflects significant recent organizing successes in the broader public sector.

Meanwhile, private-sector union density has fallen from about almost 30% in 1981 to under 20% today (18.2% in 2003). Private-sector density is much more variable than public sector density, ranging from a low of just 9.5% in Prince Edward Island and 12.6% in Alberta to 17.4% in Ontario, to highs of 21.4% in British Columbia and 27.4% in Quebec (Jackson and Schetagne 2003. Data for 2002). The process of private-sector density decline has slowed, but has not been completely halted since 1997. New private-sector hiring, especially of younger workers and new immigrants, seems to have taken place more in non-union than in union workplaces, and new organizing has fallen far short of job growth. Between 1997 and 2003, the number of private-sector employees grew by 1,569,000, while the number of unionized private-sector workers rose by just 210,000 (Akyeampong 2004).

The fall in private-sector density partly reflects the loss of unionized jobs in the traditional bastions of male blue-collar unionism. Between 1981 and 1998, density fell from 43.9% to 31.3% in manufacturing, from 43.0% to 33.1% in distribu-tive services (transportation, utilities, warehousing), and from 39.9% to 27.0% in construction (see Table 4). The big negative forces of free trade, globalization, tech-nological change and deregulation have clearly had a negative impact. Increased competitive pressures have almost certainly increased employer hostility to unions, especially where new non-union firms have undercut established unionized firms.

Union coverage has always been very low in private consumer services like stores, hotels and restaurants, as well as in financial and business services. However, density slipped only modestly in consumer services, from 13.7% to 11.0%, between 1981 and 1998. This probably reflects a combination of stable employment in some traditionally unionized sectors, and some successful new organizing, more or less matching job growth.

Turning to geographical trends in union coverage, Ontario and Alberta, where job growth has been most rapid, have experienced somewhat greater-than-average declines in density from already well below-average levels. The highest union density provinces—Newfoundland and Labrador, Manitoba and Saskatchewan, and, to a lesser extent, Quebec—have, by contrast, experienced below-average declines in density. This suggests that relative union strength is self-reinforcing to a degree because of the ability of stronger labour movements to influence party politics, governments, and thus legal rules affecting new organizing. Disturbingly, union density is much lower than the national average in two fast-growing cities, the huge Toronto Census Metropolitan Area (22.4%) and Calgary (21.5%). (For detailed data see Jackson and Schetagne 2003.)

A labour market framework for analyzing union organizing and union renewal

Table 5 provides a very broad framework for looking at union representation and organizing in relation to the changing occupational structure of the job market, which is divided along overlapping lines of gender and education/skill level.

Four key points can be noted.

First, about one-third of both women and men are employed in professional or highly skilled occupations, and this proportion has been increasing since the late-1980s. However, there is a very gendered division of labour between professional/highly skilled men and women. Men are relatively much more concentrated in management, professional occupations in business and finance, and professional jobs in natural and applied sciences (mainly to be found in the private sector), while professional and highly skilled women are much more likely than men to be found in health care, social services, and education (jobs which are mainly in the public sector). Further, women predominate in technical, assisting jobs in health. About one-in-five of all women work in health, education, and social services jobs.

Second, the proportion of men working in blue-collar jobs has been falling, from 45% to 41% since 1989, but remains high, while very few women are employed in such jobs. This "blue-collar" category includes processing and assembly jobs in primary industries and manufacturing, as well as labourers, the construction trades, and transport and equipment operators.

Third, the proportion of women in administrative, secretarial and clerical "pink-collar" jobs has been falling, from 30% to 24%, but remains fairly high. These kinds of jobs are divided between the public and private sector.

Fourth, one-in-five men and one-in-three women work in generally low-paid sales and service jobs, overwhelmingly to be found in the private services sector. This is the area of the job market dominated by smaller firms, by non-standard part-time and temporary contract jobs, by young workers and recent immigrants. It has been growing somewhat as a share of the total job market over time.

To summarize, there has been a modest shift from traditional male blue-collar and traditionally female pink-collar jobs to both higher paid and higher skilled jobs, and, to a lesser extent, to low-paid private-service jobs with the upward movement

Table 5: Employment by Broad Occupation

	Men		Women	
	1989	2003	1989	2003
Management	10.6%	10.6%	6.3%	6.7%
Professional Occupations in Business and Finance	2.3%	2.8%	2.0%	3.0%
Natural and Applied Sciences	7.2%	9.6%	1.9%	3.1%
Professional Occupations in Health	1.1%	1.2%	4.6%	4.5%
Social Science, Government, Religion	1.9%	2.1%	2.5%	4.2%
Teachers and Professors	2.6%	2.7%	4.1%	5.2%
Art, Culture, Recreation and Sport	2.1%	2.5%	2.8%	3.3%
Sub-Total Professional / Highly Skilled	17.2%	20.9%	17.9%	23.3%
Technical, Assisting Occupations in Health	0.8%	0.8%	4.3%	5.1%
Financial, Secretarial, Clerical, Administrative	7.8%	7.0%	30.2%	24.1%
Sales and Service Occupations	18.2%	19.8%	31.1%	32.2%
Blue Collar	45.3%	40.9%	10.1%	8.5%
Sub-Total Blue-Collar and Pink-Collar	72.1%	68.5%	75.7%	69.9%

Source: Statistics Canada. *Labour Force Historical Review.* 2003.
Sub-total categories are not from original source.

of women on the occupational ladder being strongly associated with the growth of public and social services.

Unions and professional/managerial jobs

Almost one-in-four men (23%) work as managers, in professional jobs in the natural and applied sciences, and in professional jobs in business and finance, compared to 13% of women. This group of jobs includes managers, engineers, accountants, systems analysts, consultants, and so on. These kinds of jobs have been growing modestly since the late-1980s with the rise of the so-called "new economy" and "knowledge-based economy," though there is no evidence that this ongoing shift is any greater than it was in earlier periods. In terms of industrial sectors, many of these jobs are to be found in financial services, and in services to business, but also in government employment. While a small layer of women has shared in professional/managerial job growth in the private sector, the great majority of professional/managerial women are to be found in public and social services, especially in social sciences occupations.

Union coverage is very low in these kinds of jobs unless they are to be found in the public sector, and few union organizing efforts appear to have taken place. This is not unusual in a comparative context, though unions of salaried private-sector professionals and among bank workers are strong in a few countries, like Sweden. If there is to be success here in the future, it is most likely to come from small unions of professionals (likely to be found in the public or quasi-public sector) expanding into the private sector by reaching out to workers in similar kinds of occupations.

Union and public and social services jobs

One-in-five women work in professional and technical and assisting jobs in health, education and social services, three times the proportion of men. This group includes nurses, teachers, social workers, and health and community social services workers with technical skills. Most of these jobs are to be found either directly in the public sector, or in the broader public sector of community and social services which are largely financed by governments. This group of jobs is both significant in size and growing.

Union coverage is high in these kinds of jobs, and union density has been stable or increasing despite the pressures of privatization and contracting-out to non-governmental organizations and commercial providers. It is notable that union coverage is quite high, at 28% in 2002, even in the private/not-for-profit part of health care and social services. Union density (measured by the proportion of workers who are union members) rose from 69.7% to 72.0% in the direct public sector between 1997 and 2003, and also rose from 52.6% to 53.4% in health and social services, and from 68.2% to 69.0% in educational services (Table 6. For further detail see Akyeampong 2004. Table 4).

The large public and social services labour force has continued to be a key bastion of union strength. The direct public sector was cut in the first half of the 1990s, but has since been growing in numbers. Between 1997 and 2004, the direct public sector added almost 400,000 new jobs, mainly in health care and social services, and public-sector union membership grew proportionately more as density rose slightly. Moreover, unions have actively organized workers in private and non-profit, often contracted-out services, such as long-term care, child care and home care, as well as in academic-support positions. There has been a significant concentration of new certifications in this area of the job market (Katz-Rosene 2003). Some of this organizing has been among workers with technical skills, such as child care and health-support workers, while other workers (such as cleaners) would be classified as service workers.

Public services unions such as the Canadian Union of Public Employees (CUPE) and provincial government workers' unions (united at the national level in the National Union of Public and General Employees—NUPGE) have actively organized not just within but also around the boundaries of the formal public sector, and have had some notable successes. Some formerly private-sector industrial unions have also actively organized in this area. It should be noted that the unionization rate is also very high, at 73%, among part-time workers in public services, contrasting sharply with a unionization rate of just 13.5% among part-time workers in the private sector.

As shown in Table 6, the occupational groups which showed the largest increase in union density between 1997 and 2003 include child care and home support workers, support staff in health, nurses, health professionals, and teachers.

Unions and male blue-collar workers

Looking at longer term changes within the private sector, there has been a marked decline in union density in the traditional bastions of male blue-collar unionism,

Table 6: Changes in Union Density, 1997 to 2003
(Union Density is Members as % of Employees)

	Union Density (%)	
	1997	2003
Total	30.8	30.3
Sex		
Women	29.3	30.0
Men	32.1	30.5
Public Sector	69.7	72.0
Private Sector	19.0	18.2
Age		
15 to 24	10.8	13.5
25 to 44	35.2	36.3
45 to 54	31.5	30.1
55 and over	43.6	40.8
Province		
Newfoundland and Labrador	39.1	38.2
Prince Edward Island	26.9	28.3
Nova Scotia	28.4	27.4
New Brunswick	27.9	26.4
Quebec	36.9	37.6
Ontario	27.7	26.8
Manitoba	35.1	34.9
Saskatchewan	33.0	34.3
Alberta	22.4	22.4
British Columbia	34.0	32.4
Work status		
Part-time	21.4	23.3
Full-time	32.9	31.8
Job status		
Non-permanent	22.7	25.1
Permanent	31.8	31.0
Job tenure		
1 to 12 months	12.9	14.7
1 to 5 years	19.8	23.1
5 to 9 years	35.7	30.8
9 to 14 years	41.9	40.2
Over 14 years	57.1	53.9
Workplace size		
Under 20 employees	11.9	12.6
20 to 99 employees	30.8	30.9
100 to 500 employees	46.4	42.9
Over 500 employees	58.0	54.1
Occupation (ranked by increase in density)		
Childcare and home support	31.4	38.6
Support staff (health)	50.8	54.1
Nursing	78.1	81.0
Construction trades	37.7	40.6
Culture and recreation	24.5	26.7

	Union Density (%)	
	1997	2003
Health professionals	39.9	42.0
Legal, social and religious	38.6	40.0
Secondary/elementary teachers	87.4	88.6
Retail	12.0	12.8
Travel and accommodation	26.1	26.8
Protective services	52.8	53.2
Wholesale	6.1	5.8
Contractors and supervisors	31.4	31.0
Teachers and professors	75.4	75.0
Helpers and labourers	34.7	34.2
Financial and administrative	22.4	21.8
Unique to primary industry	16.9	16.1
Other teachers	47.0	46.1
Transport equipment operators	37.8	36.9
Food and beverage	9.9	8.9
Professional	18.0	16.9
Labourers	39.5	38.3
Machine operators and assemblers	39.3	38.0
Natural and applied sciences	26.9	24.8
Management	11.3	9.1
Clerical	29.5	27.0
Other trades	42.3	39.2
Technical (health)	61.6	57.5
Major industry groups (by descending order of density change)		
Local administration	59.4	64.9
Federal administration	66.0	69.2
Construction	29.9	32.7
Finance and insurance	8.1	9.0
Educational services	68.2	69.0
Health care and social assistance	52.6	53.4
Retail trade	13.6	14.2
Professional, scientific and technical	4.1	4.5
Utilities	67.4	67.7
Provincial administration	70.7	71.0
Agriculture	3.3	3.5
Other services	9.0	9.2
Real estate and leasing	7.6	7.6
Business, building and other support services	12.9	12.9
Accommodation and food services	7.9	7.4
Wholesale trade	10.4	9.4
Transportation and warehousing	43.0	41.7
Non-durable manufacturing	33.2	30.9
Information, culture and recreation	28.1	25.4
Natural resources	28.2	24.9
Durable manufacturing	33.3	29.8

Source: Ernest Akyeampong "The Union Movement in Transition."
Statistics Canada. Cat. 75-001-XIE. *Perspectives on Labour and Income.* August, 2004.

from manufacturing to the resource industries to transportation (trucking, airlines, railways and ports) and utilities.

Density has fallen from almost one-half to under one-third of all workers in manufacturing since the early-1980s. This is a big enough sector for the drop to have had a major impact on overall union density in the total private sector. About one-third of the fall of private-sector union density since the peak is explained by the fall within manufacturing alone. It is important to note that this slippage is due more to the decline of density within manufacturing than to the loss of manufacturing jobs as such. Similarly, the rate of unionization among male blue-collar workers has been falling more rapidly than the slow decline in the proportion of blue-collar workers in the male work force.

The density decline in manufacturing has been pervasive across most sub-sectors and occupations, and is almost certainly closely linked to a huge turnover in establishments since the mid-1980s and the shift of jobs to small and non-union plants. For example, a lot of the job growth in the auto industry has been in non-union Japanese assembly plants, and in non-union parts suppliers, rather than in the unionized Big Three and closely associated unionized suppliers. Widespread industrial restructuring in response to free trade with the U.S. after 1988 and increased trade with developing countries likely drives down union density through a combination of large job losses in union plants because of plant closures and layoffs, and much greater employer hostility to new organizing in a highly competitive environment. Under free trade, workers in Canadian manufacturing have been more directly exposed to competition from mainly non-union U.S. and Mexican manufacturing operations.

There has been a marked decline of union density in other industries which have undergone similar restructuring: primary industries, transportation and, to a lesser extent, communications and utilities. Deregulation saw the rise of non-union airlines and telecommunications companies, forcing unions at union airlines and telephone companies on the defensive. The rise of non-union construction, particularly in the institutional and commercial sector, has been similarly destabilizing, though construction-union density has actually reversed direction and increased since 1997. The industrial construction sector remains highly unionized in some provinces, and construction union employment has benefited from the housing and commercial building boom in some cities.

Since 1997, union density has continued to slip in manufacturing, resources, and transportation industries and most blue-collar occupations such as machine operators, transport-equipment operators and labourers (see Table 6). New union certifications in these kinds of industries have been few and far between, and largely confined to smaller operations. It is interesting to note that, while union density continues to be much higher in large than small plants and operations, it has fallen much more in large industrial operations and actually increased a bit in small operations. As noted, support for unions is currently weaker among men than among women, perhaps reflecting the fact that the wages of unionized male workers have barely kept pace with inflation in recent years.

Unions and low-wage private services

Union coverage has always been very low in private consumer services like stores, hotels, and restaurants, but seems to have held up relatively much better than in the traditional high-union-density blue-collar industries since the late-1980s. As shown in Table 6, coverage is low (14.2%) in retail trade, but has been on the rise since 1997. Many workers in grocery stores and a few department stores are represented by unions, and new certifications are not uncommon in the retail trade. Coverage is very low, but has always been very low, in accommodation and food services (i.e., restaurants and hotels).

Unions remain a presence in big city hotels. Coverage is extremely low in business services, though unions have successfully organized some groups of workers like security guards and building cleaners in recent years. Union organizing is especially difficult in high-worker-turnover sectors dominated by part-time jobs. Control of hours gives employers an important extra lever in fighting unions, and low density in highly competitive industries makes it very difficult, not just to organize, but also to make gains for workers after certification.

Statistics Canada occupational data (see Table 6) suggest that the union presence in low-wage private services has been stable between 1997 and 2003, rising from 12.0% to 12.8% among retail workers, from 52.8% to 53.2% in protective services (i.e., security guards) and slipping a bit from 9.9% to 8.9% among food and beverage workers. It is worth noting that union success in these areas of the job market, once gained, makes a big difference for workers. In 2003, just 14.4% of sales and services workers were unionized. They earned an average $15.41 per hour, or 34% more than the average of $11.47 earned by non-union workers (Jackson 2004, Table 3).

Overview of recent trends and some implications for union renewal

The traditional bases of Canadian union strength were among male blue-collar workers in large industrial workplaces and among women public and social services workers, many in professional and technical jobs. The former base has been undercut by structural economic change, strong employer resistance to unions, and perhaps by a growing dissonance between unions and the values, attitudes, and perceived interests of male blue-collar workers. The latter base has remained strong, partly because of continued occupational shifts, and partly because it has been well-defended. The labour movement can learn a lot from the reasons for relative success, which seem to owe a lot to a fit between what unions are saying and doing and what women workers expect from their unions. The highly gendered pattern of union growth and decline merits careful reflection.

Since 1997, union density has been remarkably stable, rising slightly among women and falling a bit among men, rising in the public sector while falling a bit in the private sector. At the margins, the recent growth of unions seems to have been in sectors and occupations where unions have been traditionally weak: among youth and workers of colour, in non-standard jobs, and in smaller workplaces. Union density among workers of colour is rising, albeit from below average levels. It rose from 19.7% to 21.3% between 1996 and 2001 (Jackson and Schetagne 2003,

Table 25). As shown in Table 6, which provides data on changes from 1997 to 2003, union density has risen significantly among young workers (10.8% to 13.5%). It has increased in part-time jobs (from 21.4% to 23.3%) while falling in full-time jobs; has risen in non-permanent jobs (from 22.7% to 25.1%) while slipping slightly in permanent jobs; and has risen significantly among low-job-tenure workers while falling among high-tenure workers. Among workers with less than five years job tenure, density rose from 19.8% to 23.1%, while falling from 57.1% to 53.9% among workers with more than 14 years job tenure. Density has also increased in very small workplaces, while falling in larger workplaces.

In sum, density has been rising among precarious, probably lower-paid workers, reflecting new organizing in private services and among less secure workers in the broader public sector. As indicated in recent certification data, most new bargaining units are in smaller workplaces. It seems that conscious union efforts to reach out to, and to organize, vulnerable workers have begun to pay off. To this considerable extent, unions can cite some success in dealing with the downside of the new economy—much more insecure forms of work, and a high incidence of low pay, especially among women, youth and workers of colour.

At the same time, a note of caution is in order. Since 1997, a lot of jobs have also been created in relatively highly skilled and well-paid jobs, including in larger workplaces. Since 1997, there has actually been stronger growth in full-time than in part-time jobs, and in very large as opposed to very small workplaces. As noted above, the long-term trend is toward the creation of more professional and skilled jobs, and blue-collar work remains important as a share of all private-sector jobs. Unions cannot confine their organizing efforts to just the most precarious parts of the private sector.

In a new economy marked by increased polarization of the work force, unions must work harder than ever to build labour unity and solidarity across lines of gender and skill. It is good news that labour's efforts to organize the most vulnerable seem to be paying off, in significant part because of the ongoing and still incomplete process of union renewal. But the wider challenge of building a strong labour movement in a changing job market and a changing society remains very much with us.

Table 7 provides a broad context to frame some of the organizing challenges and opportunities facing the labour movement. Of the 8.3 million non-union private sector workers in Canada, almost 1.5 million are to be found in manufacturing, one-in-three of whom are women workers. Many of these unorganized workers, especially women and recent immigrants who are more attracted to unions than white male workers, are employed in small plants and are not well paid. There are also more than 400,000 non-union construction workers. In short, there is still at lot of organizing potential among blue-collar workers.

But the biggest opportunities lie in private services, especially among women workers. There are more 1.8 million trade (mainly retail trade) workers, the majority of whom are women. More than one-quarter of trade sector workers work part-time, and almost one-third are younger workers, who are more attracted to unions than are older workers. Similarly, there are 846,000 non-union workers in accommodation and food services, predominantly women and young workers, many of whom are in part-time jobs.

Table 7: Where Can We Find New Members?
A Profile of Non-Union Employees – Private Sector Only – in 2003

	Union Coverage in 2003	Number of Non-Union Workers (000s)	Percentage of Non-Union Private-Sector Workers Who Are:		
			Women	Part-Time	Age 15-25
All Industries	19.9%	8,282	48.5%	20.3%	22.2%
Agriculture	3.9%	115	34.8%	21.3%	33.6%
Forestry, Fishing, Mining, Oil and Gas	24.8%	172	20.0%	3.8%	13.6%
Utilities	49.8%	17	31.1%	0.0%	10.1%
Construction	33.0%	417	16.8%	7.8%	20.6%
Manufacturing	32.6%	1,483	33.7%	4.4%	11.6%
Trade	14.1%	1,839	50.9%	28.6%	30.3%
Transportation and Warehousing	32.0%	337	28.6%	12.5%	10.7%
Finance, Insurance, Real Estate and Leasing	7.2%	693	63.4%	14.0%	11.6%
Professional, Scientific and Technical Services	4.9%	613	50.0%	10.5%	11.4%
Management, Administrative and Other Support	14.2%	397	49.4%	18.1%	23.5%
Educational Services	14.8%	65	63.8%	41.7%	20.6%
Health Care and Social Assistance	28.2%	475	88.0%	32.1%	13.3%
Information, Culture and Recreation	23.2%	384	49.4%	27.5%	31.4%
Accommodation and Food services	8.1%	846	61.7%	44.2%	47.5%

Source: Statistics Canada Labour Force Survey Data from the Gender and Work Database.

Finally, there are 475,000 non-union workers in the private sector part of health care and social assistance, overwhelmingly women, many of whom also work part-time.

The key concluding point is that the challenge of reversing a slow union density decline through new organizing is formidable, but recent breakthroughs in both private services and the broader public sector give hope that union renewal can begin to reverse union decline.

References

Akyeampong, Ernest. 2004. The Union Movement in Transition. *Perspectives on Labour and Income.* Statistics Canada, Cat. 75-001-XIE. August, 5-13.

Fairbrother, Peter, and Charlotte A. B. Yates, eds. 2003. *Unions in Renewal: A Comparative Study.* New York: Continuum.

Fang, Tony, and Anil Verma. 2002. The Union Wage Premium. *Perspectives on Labour and Income*. Statistics Canada. September.

Jackson, Andrew. 2003. The Union Advantage. Research Paper 27. Ottawa: Canadian Labour Congress. Available from http://www.clc-ctc.ca.

———. 2004. Gender Inequality and Precarious Work: Exploring the Impact of Unions. Research Paper 31. Ottawa: Canadian Labour Congress. Available from http://www.clc-ctc.ca.

Jackson, Andrew, and Sylvain Schetagne. 2003. Solidarity Forever? Trends in Union Density. Research Paper 25. Ottawa: Canadian Labour Congress. Available from http://www.clc-ctc.ca.

Johnson, Susan. 2002. Canadian Union Density 1980 to 1998 and Prospects for the Future. *Canadian Public Policy* 28 (3).

Katz-Rosene, Ryan. 2003. Union Organizing: A Look at Recent Organizing Activity Through an Analysis of Certification Across Canadian Jurisdictions. Research Paper 26. Ottawa: Canadian Labour Congress. Available from http://www.clc-ctc.ca.

Lipsett, Brenda, and Mark Reesor. 1997. *Employer-Sponsored Pension Plans: Who Benefits?* Ottawa: Applied Research Branch of Human Resources Development Canada.

Martinello, Felice. 1996. *Certification and Decertification Activity in Canadian Jurisdictions*. Kingston: Industrial Relations Centre, Queen's University.

Meyerson, Harold. 2004. Las Vegas as a Workers' Paradise. *The American Prospect*, January.

Morissette, Rene, Grant Schellenberg, and Anick Johnson. 2005. Diverging Trends in Unionization. *Perspectives on Labour and Income*. Statistics Canada, Cat. 75-001-XPE. Summer, 1-8.

Organisation for Economic Cooperation and Development (OECD). 1996. Earnings Inequality, Low-Paid Employment and Earnings Mobility. *OECD Employment Outlook*.

Chapter 3
Innovation in Canadian Unions: Patterns, Causes and Consequences

PRADEEP KUMAR AND GREGOR MURRAY[1]

The expressions "renewal" and "revitalization" evoke the challenges faced by labour organizations in the context of deep structural change. While the pursuit of dignity at work through actions in the workplace and beyond remains the core mission of the labour movement, it is argued that existing structures and policies must change, that the status quo is not a viable option to secure the future. This impetus to change arises, among other factors, from the globalization of economic relations, modifications in the way that production and services are organized, the shifting contours of the employment contract, and the changing nature and aspirations of the labour force. In essence, the difficult nature of the environment unions face compels them to innovate. This same message has spread to unions in most developed countries, and it is argued that they ignore this imperative at their peril.

Innovation, of course, refers to change, or altering the established ways of doing things. There are arguably many forms of innovation being adopted (or being talked about) by different union organizations. Moreover, there is a proliferation of writing on this theme as analysts and practitioners offer their diagnoses and prognoses for a labour movement in search of its future. Indeed, the purpose of this collection of essays is not to serve as an instrument of self-reflection on the paths already travelled, but to explore new avenues and the lessons they offer for the future.

All organizations—be they commercial firms, public sector organizations, or unions—are commonly concerned with their purpose and their governance. They make changes to better accomplish their objectives as they engage in the politics of their governance. They also make changes to reflect the mobilization of interests inside and outside the organization. The pioneering scholars of the early history of British trade unions, Beatrice and Sidney Webb (1897), referred to this as the dynamic between democracy and efficiency. In order to accomplish this trade-off between democratic politics and organizational purpose, organizations develop structures, policies, and practices. The debates on union renewal largely concern these changes in structures, policies, and practices, but they must also be related to the purposes and governance of the organizations concerned.

There are different ways of interpreting these changes currently taking place. Some observers and practitioners point to a process of experiential organizational learning in which experience is a guide for the progressive improvement of labour's organizational responses to its new environment. The labour organizations best able to innovate on the basis of the lessons that they can draw from their experience and then to diffuse those innovations within their organizations are likely to prosper. Thus, we can identify sets of "best practices" that should be implemented and, through strategic learning, improved thereafter. A compelling example is that of the union organizing literature in the United States where Kate Bronfenbrenner and colleagues have made considerable strides in identifying clusters of organizing practices that definitely appear to work better (see, for example, Brofenbrenner and Hickey 2004, and, for a Canadian example, the chapter by Yates in this volume). On this basis, it can be argued that union leaders, staff, and activists know what needs to be done and the question then becomes how to structure their efforts in order to implement these practices.

Alternatively, and more pessimistically, unions facing a hostile environment and deeply uncertain about the best course of action are likely to make similar types of change. Two American sociologists, DiMaggio and Powell (1983), offer the somewhat obscure but ultimately insightful expression, "institutional isomorphism," to label what they perceive as happening in most organizations. Institutional isomorphism refers to how organizations copy each other in an attempt to legitimize their practice and, arguably, be seen to be doing something. This does not necessarily translate into better performance because performance is never the ultimate measure. Rather, it is through the political process that participants make judgments about what is taking place. Most people in workplaces in Canada have experience of this kind of change; where change is made for change's sake because those governing the organization have to be seen to be doing something and the risk of not making these changes when other organizations make them is too great, even if the consequences of these changes remain open to debate. Thus, organizational circumstances dictate change, and this is all the more so in periods of deep structural uncertainty such as the current context.

We can draw several lessons from this sociology of organizational change. First, in a period of uncertainty about the future of the labour movement, innovation, renewal, and revitalization are likely to be important themes. Second, organizations are likely to be making changes as a response to uncertainty, and their leaders are probably very uncertain about the validity of these changes, however compellingly they make the political case for change. Third, it is important to try to disentangle which organizations are making which changes. Finally, we must ask how these changes relate to the purposes and governance of the organizations concerned. Are they merely window dressing? Or are they a reflection of their environment? Or, again, are they related to a larger change in the conception of union purpose and governance?

Such is the purpose of this chapter: to give an overview of some of the innovations taking shape in union organizations in Canada. In order to do this, we draw on an extensive survey that we conducted on change and innovation in unions in Canada in partnership with Human Resources and Skills Development Canada and the major unions and labour federations. We hope that the results from this study will help to test some of the ideas about emerging "best practice" in unions, as well as the factors underlying the patterns of change observed. We first present the study and then some of its key findings as regards the nature and goals of unions in Canada and the innovations they are pursuing. Indeed, there are many areas of so-called union best practice where we would expect unions to be making changes. In order to understand the nature of these changes, we queried about the use of a variety of practices, including the use of new technologies and other techniques, the recourse to forms of activist servicing, changes in inclusiveness practices, and innovations in organizing. After examining the patterns of change in each of these areas, we offer an explanation of some of the trends observed and seek to relate them to larger shifts in union culture and philosophy.

The HRSDC union survey

Over the winter, spring and summer of 2001, on behalf of the Workplace Information Directorate of HRSDC and in cooperation with a broad range of union organizations, the authors conducted a survey of innovation and change in labour organizations in Canada. The purpose of this survey was threefold: first, to document the extent of organizational change taking place and benchmark the state of union renewal in Canada; second, to explore the nature of particular unions as regards their culture, goals, and objectives, and the extent of innovations and change in union structures, strategies, policies and priorities; and finally, to examine the role of key characteristics that favour innovation and renewal.

The population surveyed was all national or international unions of 500 or more members in Canada. With the cooperation of the Human Resources and Skills Development Canada, the Canadian Labour Congress, and other central labour bodies in Quebec such as the CSN and the CSQ, the survey was sent to heads of 205 unions representing 3.8 million members. After many efforts to secure the cooperation of different union bodies, we received responses from 120 unions representing 2.9 million members. The response rate was therefore 58.5% of unions covering 76.5% of union members in Canada. The typical respondent was a senior officer or staff person with strategic overview of union activities. The responding unions were both large and small national and international unions, provincial public sector unions (such as teachers and nurses), and other unions in Quebec. There was a slight bias in the response rate of large unions, with more than 68% of unions with 10,000 members and more participating in the study. The survey therefore gives a credible portrait of some of the key trends in unions in Canada. It has the benefit of both an excellent response rate for this kind of postal survey and the participation of key observers of change within unions who can share their in-depth knowledge of internal union change processes.

What kind of unionism?

Types of unionism

In a society characterized by rapid social and political change, unions' ability to express and influence political and civic discourse is undoubtedly a key dimension of their renewal. What are the main union approaches observed to economic and political change? Three prototypical configurations of union character and/or ideology are generally prevalent in North America: business unionism, social unionism, and social movement unionism.[2]

Business unionism tends to privilege a narrow conception of the extent of solidarity that a union should pursue. In particular, it favours the defence of the worker as wage earner as opposed to the worker as citizen (Murray and Verge 1999); hence, its narrower, economic instrumentality, or what has often been prosaically labelled a kind of "*bread and butterism.*" Business unionism is more likely to work within the confines of existing market relations. Moreover, it is more likely to focus on the workplace than on the market, unless the particular occupation or job territory it represents is characterized by such a high degree of mobility that the interests of the worker as wage earner cannot be adequately pursued at the level of the workplace. There is no fixed ideological space for business unionism as regards conflict and cooperation, although, in the highly decentralized Canadian bargaining regime, it has historically tended to be more conflictual than cooperative in the pursuit of its primarily economic objectives.

This business unionism model is by and large predicated on job control in the workplace. This is often pursued with a high degree of militancy, in which political action is less important except when it impinges on the organizational possibility of defending members' interests at the place of work. Thus it tends to favour economic as opposed to political means of action but there is no rule that excludes the use of political pressures, particularly through lobbying, to defend the worker as wage earner. The creation of the Canadian Federation of Labour in the 1980s, a breakaway of the construction trades from the Canadian Labour Congress, represented a certain triumph for this business unionism approach. Disillusioned with the increasingly political and social orientations that they felt drove the industrial and public sector unions in the Canadian Labour Congress, these union leaders sought to found a labour central that did not engage in partisan politics nor seek to transform the social order.[3] Such an approach has also been the underlying ideological orientation of many of the new professional public sector unions, notably some of the professionalized union groupings in parts of the health sector.

Social unionism is predicated on a broader definition of solidarity and job territory because it purports to represent the interests of the worker as citizen as well as the interests of the worker as wage earner. Social unionism tends to work within the confines of existing market relations, but it also seeks to transform these market relations. It focuses on both workplace and market and engages in political as well as economic action. Relations with political parties are therefore important and, almost by definition, organic inasmuch as they have historically represented an extension of industrial action. Social unionism might be conflictual or cooperative at the level of the workplace, but its partially transformative character tends to leave a more conflictual imprint. Social unionism, particularly as represented by industrial unions, has certainly been the dominant union mode in Canada (Kumar 1995). The notion of fighting for the improvement of working conditions and wages has historically entailed a twofold agenda of collective bargaining and political action. The former typically involved some combination of contractually-based job control and pattern bargaining for semi-skilled and unskilled workers, while the latter involved the pursuit of a social and political agenda which addressed the conditions of workers in general, as both wage-earners and citizens, notably through support for a social democratic party and its policies. Many of the new public sector unions organizing in these same pools of less skilled workers also fit this political space, except that their members demonstrated much greater ambivalence about a political role and these unions therefore often avoided any direct involvement in partisan politics.

Social movement unionism closely resembles social unionism but there are significant differences of degree. In particular, the emphasis on the social transformation of the market as the only way of truly advancing worker interests, both as wage earner and as citizen, tends to differentiate social and social movement unionism. Moreover, traditional social democratic parties are seen from this perspective to have made too cosy an accommodation with the market. Extra-parliamentary politics are therefore a vital dimension of union action, not least to maintain an independent source of pressure on the state. Another important difference between social and social movement unionism concerns the transformative potential of conflict as a method of action. Social movement unionism is predicated on this latter: it is only from struggle that the politics of renewal can emerge. Such an approach to union practice is present in many unions, but has rarely been entirely dominant. However, it has played an important role as an ideological counterpoint to the prevailing social union philosophy and has been an important part of a continuing debate between and within labour organizations.

At the risk of oversimplification, it has generally been difficult for unions in Canada to adopt a purely "business unionism" approach. The state has been so important in the development of the Canadian political economy that there has simply been less ideological space for this kind of union practice. Canadian unions have always had a social orientation and a tradition of social activism. The dominant strands of social unionism in industrial unions in Canada have long been very innovative on social wage issues such as unemployment assistance, health care, public education, and other public services. However, the distance of the social unions' political preference, the New Democratic Party, from parliamentary political power in most jurisdictions has meant that the economic and workplace voice dimensions of social unionism, such as health and safety in the workplace, have also been very prevalent. Indeed, social unionism has rarely had to contend with the paradoxes of proximity to power, particularly at the federal level. Rare examples have been the sometimes tempestuous relationship between Quebec unions and the Parti Québécois governments of the last three decades, as well as in British Columbia, Saskatchewan, Manitoba, and Ontario, when the NDP has been in power in these provinces. However, as in many other political formations, even where political parties linked to the union movement were in power, it was not so much their presence in government as the direction of their policies which tended to reflect a prevailing neo-liberal drift, generally in opposition to many of organized labour's public positions.

It could be thus argued that the union movement in Canada, despite some notable exceptions, has exercised a declining influence on the direction of overall political agenda in most jurisdictions over the past two decades. This has occurred within the context of an increasing embrace of continental free-trade agreements, which have reduced at least some of the scope for autonomous policy initiative. Moreover, the administrative decentralization of the legislative regimes in a federal system like that of Canada has increasingly highlighted the vulnerability of the basic coherence of the collective labour relations regime as individual provinces go their own way to embrace liberalization.

This declining influence on state policies has certainly prompted Canadian unions to become much more involved in civil society coalitions designed to affect the terms of political and social debates. A number of unions began to engage in increased political dialogue with their members over trade issues. It was also apparent from the results of successive federal elections that these debates were unlikely to be won in the traditional political arena. Rather, unions had to seek to influence public opinion, and it was thus that a number of traditional social unions increasingly began to embrace aspects of social movement unionism in an attempt to build extra-parliamentary coalitions and to frame the terms of debates about economic and social justice issues.

Working conditions are currently under pressure, but it seems that workplace actions cannot suffice to ensure basic dignity at work. The strategic importance of occupying a favourable political space therefore becomes much more important, but it has also increased conflict over what that space should be. This has given rise to increasingly bitter divisions within the labour movement over appropriate political strategies: between unions that have sought to retreat into forms of business unionism; unions that emphasize their traditional social union roots, including the importance of links with the parliamentary labour party; and unions that tend to emphasize civil society strategies.

Patterns of organizational cultures and philosophies

In order to better assess the types of unionism in play, we asked our Canadian union respondents a series of questions concerning their organizational cultures and philosophies. What can generally be described as social unionism and social movement unionism appear to be an important motivating philosophy for unions in Canada. This can be seen in the extent to which union respondents identify with different types of actions and priorities, ranging from political action to building coalitions and educating their membership.

Political action is clearly a very important dimension of Canadian union activity, but this does not necessarily translate into support for particular political parties. For example, 65.0% of union respondents either strongly agree or agree that their union engages in political action to change public policy and bring about social and economic change, while only 17.5% indicate that their union does not engage in such action. However, when asked if their union supports a political party to protect and advance the interests of its members, only 15% agree or strongly agree with this statement, whereas 69.2% disagree. This certainly reflects the prevailing trend among public sector unions, which make up the majority of unions in Canada.

As for their tendency to reach out to community and social groups in order to build coalitions with what has come to be known as the "civil society," 47.5% of unions agree or strongly agree that they work in coalition with community groups to pursue their goals, and a further 33.7% agree or strongly agree that they work in coalition with women's groups. At the opposite end of this spectrum, 31.2% of unions indicate that they do not work in coalition with women's groups, and 23.3% that they do not work in coalition with community groups.

Other forms of community involvement also concern the relative importance of welfare and charity activities: 45% of union respondents indicate that such activities are very important for their union, whereas 22.5% disagree that such activities are important. In order that their organizations reflect better the sexual and racial composition of Canadian society as a whole, the promotion of gender and racial equality also appears to be a significant goal. As regards such policies, 66.6% of respondents indicate that their union has taken specific action to promote racial and gender equality; while only 9.2% of union respondents disagree that their union has taken specific action on this front, and a further 24.2% neither agree nor disagree that their union has sought to promote racial and gender equality.

Another important social dimension concerns the degree to which unions seek to promote and encourage membership participation in their union. Half of unions in Canada (50 %) either agree or strongly agree that promoting members' understanding of union history, goals, and activities is a high priority in their union; and 25.4% of unions disagree that this is a high priority. Similarly, 50.4% of union respondents agree or strongly agree that member education and organizing in their union is just as important as collective bargaining; 21% disagree that this is the case.

To what degree do unions in Canada seek to construct broader forms of solidarity as opposed to the particular goals associated with the profession or industry of their main membership groupings? Many union leaders certainly feel that they play a role for all workers, not just for their members. Half of union respondents either agree or strongly agree that advancing the interests of all workers is as important as representing current members in their union; 23.3% disagree or strongly disagree that this is the case, and 26.7% neither agree nor disagree. Unions in Canada are fairly divided as regards the relative importance of solidarity in the labour movement as a whole, as opposed to the promotion of their union's particular policies. When asked if promoting solidarity between different unions in the wider labour movement is as important as promoting their unions' particular policies, 38.3% of respondents either agree or strongly agree that this is the case, and 30% either disagree or strongly disagree.

In the context of globalization, the construction of forms of international solidarity between unions in different countries is likely to be increasingly important. To what degree are unions in Canada engaged in such forms of solidarity? Keeping in mind that international unions with members in both Canada and the U.S. are naturally involved in some forms of cross-border coordination, respondents were asked to what degree unions in Canada are involved in solidarity work with unions outside of Canada and the U.S.? Almost half of unions in Canada (48.3 %) agree or strongly agree that they are involved in such work, whereas 34.1% disagree or strongly disagree. As for actual cross-border coordination with other unions to pursue their goals, be it with unions in the U.S. or beyond, 44.1% of unions in Canada agree or strongly agree that their union is engaged in cross-border coordination activity with other unions to pursue its goals; 33.3% disagree or strongly disagree that this is the case.

For some, the so-called new industrial relations imply greater cooperation be-tween unions and employers. To what degree can we discern such a trend among the major Canadian unions? It appears that the evidence is quite mixed. In terms of a trend towards increased workplace cooperation, 39.8% of union respondents agree or strongly agree that their union cooperates with employers in order to secure new investment and promote workplace modernization, whereas 22.9% disagree that this is the case, and 37.3% neither agree nor disagree. The high proportion in this latter category would tend to suggest that it is naturally difficult for some union respondents to generalize the varied experiences of particular workplaces to their union as a whole.

Another indicator of a more proactive approach to workplace change is the use of worker investment funds such as the Fonds de solidarité (FTQ), Fondaction (CSN), Working Ventures, etc. When asked if their union promotes the use of such funds in order to encourage new employment opportunities, 37.9% of respondents agree or strongly agree that this is the case, and 37% disagree or strongly disagree.

Another form of engagement with the employer concerns the spread of bipar-tite and tripartite industry committees with employers and governments on issues such as training and industry development. When asked if their union is involved with such committees, 51.3% of respondents agree or strongly agree that this is the case, and 32.8% disagree or strongly disagree.

Shifting terrain for types of unionism

What do these results tell us about the different union goals and philosophies? First, the environmental pressures to restructure workplaces reinforce the intuitive understanding that firms need to be competitive and this leads many unions in a search to alleviate the worst aspects of market restructuring through workplace cooperation. This kind of broad philosophy of "jointness" represents an often com-plex terrain for business unions, because the extent of possible cooperation can bring them into conflict with their own members. In particular, the employer quest for greater organizational flexibility means that traditions of tight union job con-trol that characterize business unionism are often directly challenged. Indeed, the reaction against the problems associated with strategic engagement in workplace change sometimes pushes such unions in the direction of more traditional forms of wage militancy. Yet it is especially difficult for unions to be purely instrumental when they become deeply enmeshed in the complexities of ensuring the survival for firms and the jobs in which they have invested (for example, through worker investment funds). Moreover, whatever these micro-corporatist temptations, an exclusive focus on the workplace is not always sufficient to ensure the survival of members' jobs. In this sense, the increasing experimentation with different kinds of sectoral mechanisms concerned with worker investment funds, skill development, and workplace change marks a significant shift in focus and this sparks yet further changes in the labour and social policy agenda of business unionism. There are thus greater pressures to engage in political action, so much so that some unions traditionally representative of business unionism have increasingly found themselves on the terrain of social unionism.

The changed environment certainly offers more space for *social unionism*. First, as industrial unions in Canada have evolved into general unions, there is a much greater emphasis on the need to defend the worker as citizen in this new environment. Second, in the context of diminishing bargaining power and an ability to influence state policy in the context of globalization, the question of the extent to which the union should seek to transform or to regulate the market is at the core of strategic thinking. Some unions have sought to espouse new forms of institutional regulation. These include worker investment funds, such as the Solidarity Fund initiated by unions in Quebec, and new parity mechanisms that promote dialogue between business and labour, or sectoral initiatives on training and restructuring. Third, public sector cutbacks have greatly reduced the ambivalence of many unions in the public sector about engaging in political action. Indeed, a number of education and health sector unions have recently affiliated with the Canadian Labour Congress. Fourth, the question that divides social unions in Canada, particularly between public and private sectors, concerns the limits of social democratic politics. While some of the older private sector social unions tend to emphasize the importance of traditional links with the NDP, a number of the public sector unions are embittered by their experience of cutbacks at the behest of NDP governments in power at the provincial level. Finally, this cleavage has also spilled over to accentuate the differences between unions as regards the scope for strategic engagement in workplace change.

Social movement unionism is clearly invigorated by this new environment. Its orientation towards a broader definition of collectivity, its emphasis on the worker as citizen as well as wage earner, its dedication to the transformation rather than the regulation of the market, its focus on both the workplace and society, the importance of political action, and its emphasis on the transformative character of conflict are all reinforced by adverse changes in the environment. Political action has been largely transformed by the development of larger coalitions of community groups around issues such as globalization and free trade, privatization and the quality of public services, the protection of the environment, etc. In this context, the philosophy of social movement unionism is much less isolated and indeed more likely to work within many of the traditional social unions. Indeed, Gindin (1998) has argued that social movement unionism is in this sense a natural development from social unionism. In practical terms, its emphasis is on the development of rank-and-file activism, workplace struggle as a form of membership education, and coalition-building and community outreach as opposed to a narrower service-oriented unionism.

In practice, however, such a social unionism approach also encounters a number of problems. First, it can be vulnerable to cross-cutting political contingencies, in particular increased manifestations of worker support for right-wing political parties within the very unions most associated with social movement unionism. Second, in some unions at least, social unionism, typified by community solidarity activities, remains a luxury item, above and beyond the basic defensive activity of unions in the workplace. In other words, the ability of many unions to pursue pro-active policies in the civic and political realm is crucially dependent on their ability to make gains for their members at the level of the workplace. Some unions have developed political alliances, only to have to cut back on such activity, sometimes because of membership revolt over the allocation of union resources and sometimes simply because of a diminishing resource base. For other unions, this type of community solidarity has been a deeply transformative experience.

Not only has the last decade placed increasing pressures on Canadian labour's social and political agenda, but it has also contributed to a sharpening of differences between the major strategic approaches. The realities of economic restructuring have meant that business unionism is increasingly compelled to engage the terrain of social unionism in the often elusive search for appropriate industry and state policies to support its positions on issues such as training and investment. Given its lack of impact on the evolution of public policy, and sometimes even on the policies of its parliamentary allies, social unionism has also increasingly pursued innovations in civil society coalitions in order to effect the terms of social and po-litical debates. Social movement unionism has placed even greater emphasis on this same trend towards civil society actions, to the point of questioning the relevance of traditional links with a social democratic party, but also at the risk of demonstrating the relevance and efficacy of these actions to a membership fully engaged with defensive struggles in the workplace when it appears that such civil society strate-gies are not likely to exert much short-term impact on the direction of employer and state policies.

Patterns of organizational innovations

Extent of change

Faced with a period of profound change, to what degree are unions in Canada effecting organizational innovations? In terms of the extent of changes made by their union, respondents were asked to assess their union's performance from little or no change on particular items to a very high degree of change. When we looked at the many areas in which unions report a high or very high degree of change over the past three years, the innovations tended to be grouped around three sets of considerations: membership engagement, political action, and new agenda items.

First, it is clear from the results reported by the unions that they are involved in a significant battle to win the hearts and minds of their members, for it is in the area of membership engagement that they report the highest levels of organizational in-novation (see Table 1). Half or more of unions report a high or very high degree of change in rank-and-file communication and the education and training of mem-bers, and 45% of unions report a high degree of change in methods of servicing and bargaining approaches and strategies. Moreover, about four unions out of ten report a high degree of change in membership participation and involvement in organizational structures.

A second area of change identified by union respondents is in the realm of political action. Many observers believe that unions must be more fully engaged in political action. It is argued that a more active engagement in politics and coali-tion building are key avenues to protecting workers as workers. In other words, to protect workers as workers, unions must also seek to represent workers as citizens

Table 1: Areas of Change

Percentage of unions in Canada reporting a high or very high degree of change
on each item over the last three years:

Membership engagement	
52%	Rank and file communication
50%	Education and training of members
45%	Methods of servicing
45%	Bargaining approaches and strategies
41%	Membership participation and involvement
38%	Organizational structures
Political action	
36%	Political action
32%	Coalition-building
16%	Cross-border or international coordination
New Agenda	
36%	Organizing and recruitment
21%	Workplace change agenda

Source: Kumar and Murray 2003, HRDC Union Innovation Survey

and engage other citizens in their communities in their struggles. The evidence is
somewhat mixed on this front: 36% of unions report a high degree of change on
political action, 32% on coalition-building, and just 16% note a high degree of
change in terms of cross-border and international coordination. It is important
to emphasize, however, that this increased political activity was more likely to be
changing among public sector than private sector unions.

A third area of change that emerged from our analysis concerns what we label
new agenda items. Thus, unions that are making significant changes in organizing
and recruitment (36 % of respondents) are also among those most likely to be making changes to their workplace change agenda (21%). Once again, these are areas
where less change is taking place, even though they are areas that are trumpeted as
critical to the future of the labour movement in Canada.

New technologies

In the information age, the use of new technologies is increasingly important. The
survey asked respondents to assess the frequency of use of different techniques,
ranging from never to systematically (see Table 2). In terms of their relative frequency, the use of websites or the Internet to communicate with members (61.8%
either often or systematically) and the use of computer networks to communicate
between union officers, staff and activists (54.6%) appear to be the technological
innovations with the highest rate of diffusion. Educational conferences on special
themes (45.4%), surveys or polls of members (39.5%), formal programs to train staff
in the use of new technologies (34.4%), the use of advertising in the mass media to
promote campaigns (32.8%), and computer data analysis to aid bargaining and/or
recruitment (31.1%) are among some of the other major initiatives in the area of

Table 2: Use of New Technologies and Communications Techniques

Percentage of unions in Canada reporting frequent or systematic use of the following:

62% use websites to communicate with members
55% staff computer networks
45% educational conferences
40% polls of members
34% staff training on new technologies
33% mass media advertising on campaigns
31% data analysis for bargaining/recruitment
13% videos to communicate with members

Source: Kumar and Murray 2003, HRDC Union Innovation Survey

communications and new technologies. Few unions (12.6 %) appear to produce videos to communicate with their members.

Servicing

Unionism in Canada has largely been constructed on the assumption that workplace size is relatively large, that services provided by the union are focused on contract administration, and that the wages earned are sufficient to pay for professional servicing. Many unions have also been able to secure complementary resources for financing through the negotiation of time-off-with-pay provisions (paid release) for some union activities in their collective agreement. While this picture of the basic mechanics of union servicing remains true for many workplaces, the picture has altered in the newly organized workplaces. New units are smaller, often much smaller, and workers are often paid less, especially in the indirect or semi-privatized public sector and in private services. Moreover, the growing impact of complex legislative provisions on work and other issues increases the need for an array of specialist services linked to workers' compensation and work-related health issues, the enforcement of human rights, the reorganization of workplaces, and the need to defend the quality of working life and job security. Faced with acute pressures on cost structures, employers are also often less willing to grant paid release. In other words, there are real pressures on the traditional servicing model.

These pressures have prompted a number of unions to rethink their servicing model. In particular, it has been argued that there is a need to shift the burden from staff to activist servicing. These pressures have been more acute where there is a move to increase dramatically the resources going to new organizing. Indeed, much of the argument around so-called organizing models are concerned with the degree to which it is possible to shift part of the burden of union servicing over to activists, both in existing units in order to free up resources or new organizing initiatives, and in new units because the underlying cost structure of small unit size and low wages means that it would be difficult to replicate existing models of servicing for these newly organized groups.

Table 3: Implementation of Activist Servicing Strategies

Percentage of unions in Canada reporting frequent or systematic use of the following methods of activist servicing:

84% offer education programs or courses to train local activists

32% encourage the merger or amalgamation of locals

32% use activists on paid release in organizing

19% use activists on paid release in contract administration

16% shifted the primary responsibility for contract administration from staff to local stewards/officers

9% shifted emphasis from general to specialist servicing

Source: Kumar and Murray 2003, HRDC Union Innovation Survey

There appears to be a fairly high degree of stability as regards the general approach to servicing in Canadian unions (see Table 3). One idea that is frequently mentioned in some of the union renewal literature is the need to re-allocate resources to new areas of activity by shifting the primary burden of servicing from staff to activists. For example, this has been a point of contention within some unions about the organizing model. However, only 16.3 % of respondents agree or strongly agree that their union has shifted the primary responsibility for contract administration from staff to local union stewards and/or officers, and 57.2% of respondents disagree or strongly disagree with this statement. Similarly, only 19.2% of respondents agree or strongly agree that their union frequently draws on a substantial group of activists on paid release to carry out servicing activities such as contract administration. Indeed, only 8.5% of union respondents agree or strongly agree that their union has had to cut back on general servicing because of the need to devote more resources to specialized services such as organizing, recruitment, training, education, and political action.

There are, however, some areas of change in the organization of servicing, especially relating to attempts to involve members in the life of the union, to train activists to take on new roles and to change basic union structures to facilitate servicing. Undoubtedly the most significant area of change concerns rank-and-file communication as 84.9% of union respondents agree or strongly agree that their union has sought to increase communication with its rank-and-file membership. This relates as much to the argument about winning hearts and minds as it does to servicing. Most unions (83.8%) also offer education programs or courses to train local leadership. On average, according to estimates provided by the respondents, roughly 55,000 members annually participated in these courses in each of the three years preceding the survey. Just under one-third of unions (32.2%) also report that they encourage the merger or amalgamation of locals.

Another notion is that the future of unions is tied to their ability to respond to new needs in the labour market and to develop new services for their members. The origins of unions as "friendly" or mutual assurance societies (ensuring that working families did not become destitute because of the costs associated with periods of unemployment and catastrophic family events such as funerals) are tied to the whole notion of unions offering relevant services not otherwise available on the labour market. The rise of the welfare state and universal access to many forms of social benefits, as well as the high-end collective agreements with elaborate fringe and supplementary benefits, has of course reduced the importance of such services. It has been a continuing argument that many in the labour market do not have access to such benefits and that unions are in a good position to offer them. Indeed, there are many sectors such as retail food, trucking, and construction where it is more typically the union rather than the employer that organizes pensions and other supplementary benefits. Indeed, in a pamphlet issued in a union renewal debate of the late 1980s in the United Kingdom, Bassett and Cave (1993) polemically argued that the future of unions would be more like the automobile associations where workers could get information on workplace rights and have them enforced through a well-placed telephone call. Some Canadian unions have also recently sought to upgrade their capacity to offer individualized services to members in a timely manner. One of the most innovative is that of the Manitoba Government Employees Union, since emulated by a number of other NUPGE components, to use a general-purpose call centre for both supplementary servicing and offering some special benefits.

It is clear that some unions in Canada are pursuing such complementary forms of servicing: 57.1% of the participating unions offer special insurance programs; 41.2% legal service programs; 37.8% supplementary medical or dental programs; and 28% low-cost travel and/or affinity credit cards. A substantial proportion of unions (38.7%) also offers the possibility for those not in a certified bargaining unit to be associate members of their union.

Identities and inclusiveness

A common criticism of the labour movement in Canada is that it better represents how the labour force used to look than how it actually is. In other words, that unions in Canada have not sufficiently reached out to new groups of workers (Yates 2004). On the other hand, many have argued that, despite gender and racial gaps, unions in Canada have probably been more innovative on this front than many other union movements (Murray 1994).

It is clear from the survey results that a number of unions have sought to improve the access of specific target groups to the life of the union (see Table 4), but that the importance of such programs varies from one union to another and does not reach the majority of unions in the country. To what degree can we observe the presence of specific identity structures and programs in unions in Canada? The most common manifestation of such structures are for women members (43.2% of unions), retired members (31.4%), young members (26.9%), workers of colour or visible minorities (23.5%), gay or lesbian members (20.2%), and members with disabilities (15.1%). Only 29.1% of unions indicate that they are able to report the number of persons of colour who are members of their union.

A second concern is the degree to which the public face of unions reflects the people that they might aspire to have join their ranks. In terms of staff profile, 35% of unions indicate that they have sought to change the composition of their staff in order to better reflect the demographics of the labour market. That said, only 17.8%

Table 4: Changes in Inclusiveness Strategies

Percentage of unions in Canada reporting the presence of specific identity programs or structures for the following groups:
43% for women
31% for the retired
27% for the young
24% for people of colour
20% for gays and lesbians
15% for people with disabilities

Percentage of unions in Canada reporting changes in staff profile:
35% change composition of staff to reflect realities of labour market
18% able to service members in languages other than French or English

Source: Kumar and Murray 2003, HRDC Union Innovation Survey

of respondents agree or strongly agree that their union is able to service members in languages other than English or French.

Organizing

A key aspect of the union renewal debate concerns organizing and recruitment strategies. The unions participating in this survey report a total of 242 staff working full-time on organizing and recruitment, of which 26.9% are women. Less than half of unions (44.8%) report the presence of a person who has overall responsibility for establishing policy and targets for organizing and recruiting new members. Over two-fifths (42%) indicate that they have specific organizing or recruitment targets.

What is the portrait of new organizing activity reported by the participating units over the three years preceding the survey? Respondents were asked to detail the sectoral distribution of their newly organized certification/bargaining units over this period (see Table 5). The unions participating in the survey indicated that they organized 2,399 new units covering a total of 190,051 members during this period. In terms of the distribution of the number of members organized, 21.2% were in goods producing, 22.4% were in private services, 16.6% in direct public services, and 39.9% in indirect public services. While considerable new organizing is taking place, it would seem readily apparent that the extent of organizing in private services does not reflect the huge concentration of non-unionized workplaces in this sector. Moreover, the extent of organizing in indirect public services is quite remarkable—the single largest concentration of members. This seems to suggest that one of the key drivers in recent union organizing is the attempt to keep pace with the restructuring of the public sector.

In terms of recruitment targets, union respondents were asked to indicate which sectors had the highest priority in current attempts by their union to organize new members. By order or relative importance, these are in the public services (45.8% indicate that this is a high or very high priority), private services (30.8%), newly privatized or reorganized former public services (27.2%) and goods production (23.9%). In other words, despite the high degree of union penetration in public services, a very

Table 5: Distribution by Sector of New Certification and/or Bargaining Units Organized by Canadian Unions in the Past Three Years

Economic Sector	New Units (%)	New Members (%)
Goods Producing	11.2	21.2
Private Services	11.5	22.4
Direct Public Services	61.3	16.6
Indirect Public Services (not-for-profit)	16.0	39.9
Total Number	2,399	190,051

Source: Kumar and Murray 2003, HRDC Union Innovation Survey

high priority continues to be attached to new organizing and the consolidation of existing organizing in this sector. Not surprisingly, perhaps, union respondents also indicate that their union is likely to attach a high or very high priority to organizing in existing areas of membership concentration (59.1%) and in large units (41.9%), as opposed to new areas where their union has fewer members (24%) and in small units (27.6%). Thus, the highest priorities for the recruitment of new members tend to reflect existing areas of membership strength and presence, as opposed to areas where there are the most significant numbers of non-unionized workers. Indeed, two-thirds of respondents (66.6%) agreed that the primary organizing/recruitment effort of their union is focused on traditional areas of membership strength, and only 7.3% of respondents disagreed that this was the case.

Most unions (78.5%) do appear to have a minimum number of potential members below which they would be unlikely to organize or recruit a group of non-unionized workers into a new bargaining unit. Among the 23 unions that do report having such a threshold, the average minimum is 40 workers, but that threshold varies from just 3 to 200 workers.

Newly organized units can be integrated into various types of structures, depending on both the structure of the recruiting union and its policy choices. In particular, it is sometimes argued that unions need to favour more encompassing structures in order to ensure that smaller units are economically viable. Among the respondent unions in the survey that favour one or the other of independent locals or composite local structures for their newly organized units, 33.3% favoured mainly independent locals, 27% favoured mainly composite or amalgamated locals, and 27% favoured both types of local structure. A further 12.7% of unions indicate that they did not favour either one or the other type of structure.

Most unions do not have a set target to spend on organizing and recruitment. Only 12.5% of unions indicate that they have such a target. In the twelve cases where they do have such a target, the average target is 17% of resources. In fact, when asked roughly what percentage of their revenue was currently spent on recruitment, the average percentage was 6.8%. In terms of the overall profile of their resources dedicated to organizing and recruitment, 21% of unions report that they do not spend any money on organizing; 48.1% of unions spend from 1% to 5% of their expenditure; 11% of unions spend from 6% to 10%; 13.5% of unions spend from 11% to 20%; and 6.2% of unions spend more than 20% of their expenditure on organizing.

When asked to assess the current degree of responsibility of general servicing staff for organizing/recruiting new members, more than half of the respondent unions (54.6%) indicated that organizing/recruitment is just one of the many tasks for which general servicing staff are responsible, and just under one-quarter (22.2%) reported that organizing/recruitment is not really an integral part of their job. In 13% of unions, the role of general servicing staff is limited to identifying potential targets. Only 10.2% of unions indicate that organizing/recruitment is currently one of the highest priorities among the tasks assigned to general servicing staff. Indeed, respondents were sharply divided as to the potential role for general servicing staff in organizing: 37.5% of respondents disagree with the statement that general servicing staff feel so overworked that they are unlikely to make a substantial contribution to organizing/recruiting new members; whereas 30.2% of respondents agreed that this is the case and a further 32.3% neither agreed nor disagreed.

One way of overcoming lack of staff resources to deal with organizing is to involve local activists in new organizing. Over half of the unions participating in the survey (56.4%) report some form of training for local officers and/or activists to participate in organizing/recruitment campaigns. Furthermore, 41.4% of respondents agree that unpaid activists play a major role in organizing/recruitment campaigns, and 38.9% of unions report that the training of activists is an integral part of their approach to organizing and recruitment.

In terms of general approaches to organizing, there does appear to be considerable emphasis on this activity. More than half of union respondents disagree that organizing and recruitment has not really been a priority for their union over the past few years (60%) and that there is a strong possibility of membership backlash when their union puts too much emphasis on organizing/recruitment (50.6%).

With regard to more specific approaches to organizing, 19.6% of unions indicate that their organizing campaigns tend to highlight social justice and worker voice issues; 19.3% report that the gender, age, and ethnic profile of their staff reflect the kinds of workers they are seeking to recruit; and 15.1% note that they emphasize a community approach to organizing. When asked about the relative influence of recent efforts by a number of U.S. unions to renew their approach to organizing and recruitment, 61.5% of respondents indicated that they have not been influenced by these efforts, and 16.7% of respondents reported that their union has been influenced by these efforts. Many, but certainly not all, of the unions that have been influenced by the U.S. experience are international unions with their headquarters in the U.S.

Just over half of the respondent unions (50.6%) report that they have met a high degree of success in their organizing efforts, and only 14% of respondents disagree that this is the case. When asked to evaluate the relative importance of various obstacles to new organizing and unionization, the survey respondents indicated that saturation of their existing jurisdiction (an important or extremely important obstacle for 49.5% of unions), too many other pressing issues to deal with (45.6%), inter-union competition (39.6%), employer opposition (31.7%), the small size of potential bargaining units (31.4%), and unfavourable public policy (23.2%) were

Table 6: Innovations in Organizing

Percentage of unions in Canada reporting the adoption of the following organizing practices:
56% train local officers/activists to organize new units
45% one person with overall responsibility for organizing
42% have specific organizing targets
33% have full-time staff working exclusively on organizing
13% have a percentage target of overall revenues to spend on organizing and recruitment

Percentage of unions in Canada reporting that their focus on organizing:
66% focused on traditional areas where membership is concentrated
42% organizing is a response to restructuring of core

Source: Kumar and Murray 2003, HRDC Union Innovation Survey

among the most significant obstacles to new organizing activity. Apart from the inevitable question of work overload, internal obstacles do not appear to be very significant. Only 11% of respondents identify the lack of staff support as an important or extremely important obstacle, and only 13% see the lack of specialist staff as a problem. Similarly, only 14% identify the lack of financial resources, 14.2% the lack of support from union leadership, and 18.1% the lack of support from existing members. More significant, however, are the relatively low organizational priority for organizing (28.2%), and the absence of a strategic plan (22.3%).

Financial pressures

It is clear that the union respondents do not feel a great deal of financial pressure to effect organizational change. For example, 71.8% disagree or strongly disagree that their union has had to reduce the number of staff and increase staff servicing loads because of financial constraints; only 18.8% of respondents agree or strongly agree that this is the case. Similarly, only 13.7% agree or strongly agree that their union has reduced the frequency of representative delegate meetings such as conventions, congresses and councils. Indeed, more than half of respondents (52.6%) reported that their union has an accumulated surplus and properties on which it can draw to finance current expenditures, and only 12.2% indicated that their union has an accumulated debt which must be serviced from current revenues. In other words, however acute the environmental pressures, unions in Canada do not appear to be facing severe financial constraints.

Factors influencing innovation

If unions in Canada are engaged in varying degrees of change, what is behind the adoption of some practices rather than others? For example, does adversity foster innovation? Do unions facing more difficult external challenges or unions with faltering financial resources tend to make changes more than others? Or are the changes being implemented merely a question of a union's size, its sectoral location, or type of bargaining structure? Or, again, do union philosophies about the way the world should be and the types of solidarity to be promoted affect their internal practices? In other words, are the fairly fluid frontiers between business, social and social movement unionism shifting, and how do such movements translate into union structures, policies, and practices? In order to shed some light on these questions, we have sought to assess the influence of different types of organizational factor and union culture, goals, and philosophies on union innovation.

In terms of organizational factors, we consider the impact of six different union characteristics. First, what is the importance of size when a third of unions participating in the survey have fewer than 2,600 members and another third have 12,500 members or more? Second, the members of 70% of the unions participating in the survey were primarily in the public sector, whereas 30% of the unions had members primarily in the private sector. Is innovation or certain types of innovations more prevalent in the private than the public sector, or vice versa? Third, are innovations in union structures and practices merely a reflection of existing servicing models? For example, organizing, bargaining, grievance arbitration, and workers' compensation tended to be the responsibility of mainly their locals for 37% of unions in Canada, and more centralized for 63% of unions. Fourth, what is the impact of financial pressures or the absence thereof (60% of unions report increased revenues, whereas 40% have experienced decreasing revenues)? Fifth, and closely related, do trends in numbers of full-time staff make a difference? For example, 70% of unions report an increase in the number of full-time staff, whereas 30% have experienced a decline in numbers of staff. Finally, what is the impact of the external environment on the trends observed? For example, on the basis of the detailed reporting of environmental trends, we were able to distinguish between unions for which the bargaining, organizing, and political environment were fairly favourable (37%) from those where it was only the bargaining environment (29%) and those where it was only the political environment (34%).

In terms of union culture and philosophies, three types of factors seemed to distinguish the unions participating in the survey, according to the data that they provided to us. For each of these factors, the responses provided by unions tended to resemble each other, both positively and negatively. First, there emerged a fairly coherent set of social union practices among the roughly 41% of the unions participating in the study which scored strongly on this factor. These unions tended to score higher than other unions on the following items: working in coalition with women's and community groups; engaging in political action to change public policy and effect social and economic change; prioritizing an involvement in the community; taking specific action to promote gender and racial equality; and promoting membership understanding of their union.

A second factor concerned the promotion of broader forms of solidarity. In this much smaller groups of unions (just 11% of unions scored strongly on this factor), advancing the interests of all workers is as important as those of their particular members; education and organizing are as important as collective bargaining; the promotion of solidarity between unions is an important priority; as is support for a particular political party.

Finally, a third factor concerns the degree to which particular unions are involved in jointness strategies. These unions—and 20% of the participating unions scored strongly on this factor—tend to cooperate with employers to secure new investments and promote workplace modernization; they also promote works investment funds, and they also tend to be involved in bipartite and tripartite industry committees.

While these three factors are not exact equivalencies of our business, social, and social movement union types, they do cover some of the same terrain. In particular, the articulation of the social union practices is very close to the evolution of social unions, while the enlarged solidarities tend to straddle social and social movement unionism and the jointness strategies are closer to the evolution of business unionism, as described above.

The question, therefore, is how do these organizational and cultural factors affect the patterns of innovation observed? In order to respond to this question, we used a series of statistical analyses (logistic regressions) to distinguish how the different types of factors are related to the pursuit of different patterns of innovation in Canadian unions.

The first pattern observed above concerned the degree to which unions were experiencing a high or very high degree of change in three key areas of endeavour which emerged from the analysis: more membership involvement in the union through innovations in communication, education, servicing, and structures; the pursuit of new forms of political action such as coalitions and cross-border solidarities; and a new agenda in terms of organizing and workplace change. A first intriguing result is that more membership involvement is associated with favourable organizational factors, notably a more favourable environment and increased resources. In other words, adversity is not driving internal organizational innovations; rather, unions seem to need a secure and expanding resource base to undertake such changes. Second, the unions undertaking new forms of political action tend to espouse a set of social union practices in terms of their goals and priorities. These include community work, emphasis on political action, equality within the union, and membership involvement. The unions undergoing change in their workplace and organizing agenda also tend to espouse social union practices, but they are also unions more extensively engaged in jointness practices such as cooperation to secure investment, worker investment funds, and presence in bipartite and tripartite structures.

A second pattern concerns the use of new technologies. What are the factors associated with unions undertaking more extensive implementation of new technologies such as websites to communicate with members, staff training on technologies, membership polling, etc.? These unions are more likely to be large unions in the public sector, unions with increased resources, and unions with decentralized servicing structures. In other words, a resource base is necessary to make such changes, which are also a way of using technology to contend with decentralization. It should also be emphasized that the unions experimenting with new technologies were also more likely to espouse social unionism, and it is plausible that the new technologies offer an avenue for empowering members.

A third pattern concerns the unions implementing new forms of activist servicing, such as the greater use of activists to undertake organizing and contract administration, as well as the restructuring of locals into composite locals in order to facilitate servicing. The unions pursuing this type of innovation tended to be large and facing less favourable environments. They also tended to advocate a broader agenda of solidarity, with a mission to represent all workers to engage in education and organizing, as well as collective bargaining, to promote solidarity between unions and to support particular political parties.

A fourth pattern concerns inclusiveness structures. The unions implementing changes to staff profiles in order to better reflect the contemporary labour market were large unions in the private sector. The unions that had implemented more extensive inclusiveness structures in their forms of representation and their policy forums are large unions and unions with a set of social union practices, including attaching a priority to inclusiveness.

Finally, the implementation of changes in organizing, both in terms of the adoption of new techniques and organizing beyond the union's traditional core, is related to a vision of broader solidarities.

What drives union innovation?

To summarize, there appears to be an interplay between organizational characteristics, environment, and union culture and philosophy. A first path of analysis is that certain key organizational characteristics such as size, resources, sector and existing servicing models matter. Large unions are more likely to be implementing new technologies, experimenting with activist servicing, and developing representativeness policies and structures. It is also important to highlight how unions with increasing resources are more likely to engage in formal assessments of their strategies, to implement new technologies, and to be experiencing greater change in the area of membership involvement. Sector has a more limited impact, since there is more likely to be experiments in the public sector with new technologies, and more attempts in the private sector to modify staff profiles to reflect labour market change and to be making changes in types of political action. A pattern of decentralized servicing also tends to be associated with efforts to develop new technologies.

A second insight is that the impact of the external environment on the union is probably less important and certainly more equivocal than one might expect. Unions faced with an unfavourable environment are more likely to pursue activist servicing, but unions facing a favourable environment are more likely to be engaged in change to enhance membership involvement in the union. External environment does not therefore appear to be a driving factor (except when activist servicing is developed in response to unfavourable circumstances). Indeed, the ability to engage in more extensive change in the area of greater membership involvement in the union is linked to a more favourable environment and to increased resources. Similarly, increased resources are also related to formal assessments of union strategy and greater recourse to new technologies. In other words, it would appear that unions have a window of opportunity to make change through a combination of environmental circumstances and an adequate resource base. Innovation is therefore more likely to be stimulated by both enhanced resources and a favourable environment, and not the contrary.

Third, and perhaps most importantly, the kinds of innovation being analyzed here are closely tied to union culture and philosophy. Moral vision and union philosophy seem to matter. Unions that are more engaged in a social vision of their mandate are more likely to undertake a formal assessment of their strategies, to implement new technologies, to develop inclusiveness policies and structures, and to be making change in terms of their methods of political action and their organizing and workplace agenda. Similarly, unions exhibiting a vision of the need for enlarged labour market solidarities are more likely to be experimenting with activist servicing, changing their staff profile to reflect labour market identities, using new techniques in organizing, and seeking to organize members beyond their traditional core of membership. Thus, innovations in workplace change and organizing, both in terms of the development of more sophisticated organizing techniques and a focus on organizing beyond traditional areas of membership strength, are linked to the practice of social unionism and to a vision of the importance of broader solidarities. This importance of union culture and philosophy is compelling inasmuch as it suggests that the pursuit of innovation cannot simply be a technical or modernizing question of getting the right blend of techniques. Instead, the pursuit of different kinds of innovation in union structures, policies, and practices is closely related to the vision of the role of the union in society. This result also underscores the importance of engaging in debates about vision and purpose as a prelude to other types of change within the union.

Conclusion

This chapter has highlighted some of the complex patterns of change being pursued by unions in Canada. While there are many changes being implemented by the unions covered in this study, it is important to note that the implementation of so-called union best practices is highly uneven. The good news is that Canadian unions report considerable efforts to communicate with and educate their members, to engage activists in the life of the union, and to enhance the representation of certain social identity groups within their structures. However, these same unions are less likely to engage in political change, to implement activist servicing, and to change their organizing strategies and targets.

A second major conclusion links these patterns of change to certain organizational characteristics. The kinds of innovation trumpeted in the literature about where union practice should be heading are more likely to be taking place in large unions with increased resources and a more favourable environment.

The final and undoubtedly the most important conclusion is that the innovations observed in Canadian unions need to be seen as an integral part of a larger discussion about the nature of the union organization. It is, in fact, the unions that are pursuing larger social visions and enlarged solidarities that are most likely to be associated with innovations in the degree of change in membership involvement, politics and agenda, as well as in the implementation of new technologies, activist servicing, and new methods and targets for organizing. In other words, innovation in structures, policies, and practices cannot be understood in isolation from larger debates over the purposes and governance of unions. In the absence of such discussions about the kind of unionism required, technical changes in structures, policies, and practices are likely to have much less traction in the continuing debate about union futures. On the other hand, unions able to foster such debates about their fundamental purposes also appear more likely to implement the range of innovations purported to yield better union performance.

Notes

1. Some of the materials presented in this chapter are the result of a research partnership on innovation and change in labour organizations between the Workplace Information Directorate of Human Resources and Skills Development Canada and the authors of this chapter. Of course, the views expressed here do not necessarily reflect those of the Government of Canada. The authors wish to acknowledge the collaboration of a number of individuals and organizations in the gathering and analysis of the data presented in this chapter: the many trade unionists who assisted with and participated in the HRSDC survey of innovation and change in Canadian labour organizations; Suzanne Payette at the Workplace Information Directorate of HRSDC in the conception and development of the project; Bruce Aldridge, also at HRSDC, Herbert Law (Queen's University), and Lucie Morissette (Université de Montréal) in the administration of the survey; and Nicolas Roby (Université de Montréal) for his assistance in the analysis of the survey results. The pursuit of this particular study is part of the larger CRIMT (Interuniversity Researcher Centre on Globalization and Work) project on Rethinking Institutions for Work and Employment in a Global Era, financed by the Social Sciences and Humanities Research Council of Canada's Major Collaborative Research Initiatives Programme.

2. For more general discussions of these prototypes, see Kumar (1993), Pupo and White (1994), Robinson (1994), and Schenk (2003). This particular discussion draws on Murray (2002).

3. The subsequent demise of the Canadian Labour Federation, of course, also highlighted the limits of such an approach.

References

Bassett, Philip, and Alan Caves. 1993. *All For One: The Future of the Unions*. Fabian Society Pamphlet 559. London, U.K.: Fabian Society.

Bronfenbrenner, Kate, and Robert Hickey. 2004. Changing to Organize: A National Assessment of Union Strategies. In *Rebuilding Labor: Organizers and Organizing in the New Union Movement*, ed. Ruth Milkman and Kim Voss, 17-61. Ithaca, NY: Cornell University Press.

DiMaggio, Paul J., and Walter W. Powell. 1983. The Iron Cage Revisited: Institutional Isomorphism and Collective Rationality in Organizational Fields. *American Sociological Review* 48:147-160.

Gindin, Sam. 1998. Notes on Labor at the End of the Century: Starting Over. In *Rising From the Ashes? Labor in the Age of "Global" Capitalism*, ed. Ellen Meiksins Wood, Peter Meiksins, and Michael Yates, 190-202. New York: Monthly Review Press.

Kumar, Pradeep. 1993. *From Uniformity to Divergence: Industrial Relations in Canada and the United States*. Kingston: IRC Press, Queen's University.

———. 1995. *Unions and Workplace Change in Canada*. Kingston: IRC Press, Queen's University.

Kumar, Pradeep, and Gregor Murray. 2003. *Innovation and Change in Labour Organizations in Canada: Results of the National 2000-2001 HRDC Survey*. Available at http://www.crimt.org.

Murray, Gregor. 1994. Structure and Identity: The Impact of Union Structure in Comparative Perspective. *Employee Relations* 16 (2): 24-40.

———. 2002. Unions in Canada: Strategic Renewal, Strategic Conundrums. In *Changing Prospects for Trade Unionism*, ed. Peter Fairbrother and Gerard Griffin, 93-136. London, U.K.: Continuum.

Murray, Gregor, and Pierre Verge. 1999. *La représentation syndicale*. Québec: Presses de l'Université Laval.

Pupo, Noreen, and Jerry White. 1994. Union Leaders and the Economic Crisis: Responses to Restructuring. *Relations industrielles/Industrial Relations* 49 (4): 821-845.

Robinson, Ian. 1994. NAFTA, Social Unionism and Labour Movement Power in Canada and the United States. *Relations industrielles/Industrial Relations* 49 (4): 657-695.

Schenk, Chris. 2003. Social Movement Unionism: Beyond the Organizing Model. In *Trade Unions in Renewal: A Comparative Study*, Peter Fairbrother and Charlotte Yates, 244-262. London, U.K.: Continuum.

Webb, Sidney, and Beatrice Webb. 1897. *Industrial Democracy*. London: Longmans, Green and Co.

Yates, Charlotte. 2004. Rebuilding the Labour Movement By Organizing the Unorganized: Strategic Considerations. *Studies in Political Economy* 74:171-180.

Chapter 4
Women are Key to Union Renewal: Lessons from the Canadian Labour Movement

CHARLOTTE YATES

> In 1983, anything to do with women was the last item on the agenda at the (Australian Council of Trade Unions) congress.... You can see that it was very marginal. It was seen like a social-welfare type issue [rather] than like a mainstream industrial matter. So we've come a long way in 12 years.
>
> > Quote from Jennie George, on the eve of her becoming the first female president of the Australian Council of Trade Unions (*The Weekend Australian*, August 19-20, 1995, 28).

> I worked at Westinghouse for 30 years. I started when I was 16. When the union changed the seniority rules, they did me out of a job. Girls who had just two years kept their jobs, and I was laid off. That job was everything to me.
>
> > Quote from female worker at Westinghouse laid off in 1990. She now works looking after children and cleaning houses.

> We'd like a union. I called five unions and none of them wanted to organize us. There are too few of us.
>
> > Woman who worked at a women's shelter in Toronto with eight employees. 2000.

These three quotes are testament to the tensions inherent in unions' relationships to women workers. Unions *have* come a long way in their organization and representation of women workers. At the same time, unions often fail women, leaving them without union representation at all or with collective agreements that lead women to question the value of a union card and contract. Yet in today's labour market, unions cannot afford to fail women. Women not only constitute a growing proportion of the labour force, but they also constitute the most likely source of new union membership in Canada. As will be argued below, however, union organizing practices are deeply gender-biased, often reflecting the segmented and differentiated conditions under which women engage in the labour market. This limits the "supply" of unions to women, thereby reducing women's chances of benefiting from union membership while preventing unions from building on women's potential contribution to union revitalization.

In this paper, I examine the ways in which union organizing is gender-biased. In so doing, I also highlight possible strategies that unions could employ to increase their chances of organizing success. The data upon which this paper is based come from a survey of union organizers I conducted in Ontario and British Columbia (B.C.) The survey is discussed briefly in the next section before I proceed with my analysis of union organizing. Overall, the argument presented in this paper is that women are critical to the revitalization of unions, but that unions must undo the gender-bias in their approach to organizing if they are going to build on this potential.

The survey of organizers

This article bases much of its analysis on the results of a mass survey of union organizers operating in Ontario and British Columbia. A nine-page survey was sent to union organizers involved in all applications for certification in Ontario and British Columbia for a two-year period. This part of the study was modeled on work undertaken by Kate Bronfenbrenner at Cornell University (Bronfenbrenner and Juravich 1998), although in this instance I sent surveys to the entire population of organizing drives, rather than a sample of the population. The questionnaire asked questions about the organizers themselves, the nature of the workforce and workplace they were trying to organize, and the union and employer strategies used during the organizing drive. In places, the survey data were supplemented with information gathered from attending meetings of several unions, as well as both the Ontario Federation of Labour (OFL) and the B.C. Federation of Labour (BCFL), and interviewing unionists involved in organizing.

Surveys for 1,281 certification applications in Ontario in the period from September 1, 1996 to August 31, 1998 were sent to union organizers who were primarily responsible for the organizing drives resulting in the certification applications, and 677 surveys or 52.8% of the total population were returned completed. Of those surveys returned, 39 organizing campaigns, or 5.8% of the population, were raids. There was a slight non-reporting bias among employee associations and small, non-affiliated unions, most of which were recorded as having one or two applications for certification. In B.C., surveys for 978 certification applications in the period from January 1, 1997 to December 31, 1999 were sent to the union organizers who were primarily responsible for the organizing drives resulting in the certification applications, and 439 surveys, or 44.9% of the total population, were returned completed. There was a non-reporting bias among the construction trades, as well as small, non-affiliated unions.

For my analysis of the differences between men and women in the bargaining units under investigation, I separate the data into Female Majority Workplaces (FMW) where more than 50% of the workforce are women, and Male Majority Workplaces (MMW) where more than 50% of the workforce are men. This reflects labour market segmentation experienced by women and men generally, and captured in my survey of organizers. The depth of gender segregation of workplaces captured in the survey can be discerned from the number of bargaining units in which the workforce is either exclusively male or female. In Ontario, 36.4% of the bargaining units in the survey had a workforce that was 100% male, compared to 9% with a workforce of only women. In B.C., 16.3% of the bargaining units where unions attempted to organize employed only men, compared to 31% that employed only women. Therefore, a large number of workplaces studied through my survey were either exclusively male or exclusively female, with limited numbers of mixed-gender workplaces.

Women and the labour market

Over several years, women's rate of labour force participation has increased more than men's. At the same time, women's rate of unionization has also been growing. All or most of the annual increases in union membership reported by Statistics Canada over the last few years have been made up of women. Yet it is still remarkable that, in 2004, women's rate of unionization exceeded slightly the rate for men for the first time in history, with women's rate at 30.6% compared to men's at 30.3%.

Many analysts argue that this higher rate of unionization reflects women's concentration in the public sector, where unionization is higher overall in Canada. Figures on current rates of unionization support this conclusion. In 2003, the unionization rate of women in the public sector stood at 73.9%, compared to 69% for men, whereas unionization rates in the private sector stood at 13% for women compared to 22.5% for men. Statistics Canada concludes that "the lower rate among women reflected their predominance in sales and several service occupations" (Statistics Canada 2004).

Women's growing rates of unionization reflect many factors, not just their concentration in the public sector. Women tend to be employed in sectors where unionization is low and potential for union membership is high, in part due to women's poorer wages and working conditions. Not surprisingly, then, unions have made growing attempts at organizing the private service sector, with some degree of success (Yates 2000). As Statistics Canada reported in 2004, unionization rose in only five of the 16 industry groups (Statistics Canada 2004, 59). Included among these were information, culture and recreation, finance and insurance and other miscellaneous services that have high numbers of women. Finally, and most germane to our argument about organizing, women have demonstrated a greater interest in joining unions, a phenomenon evident in many countries, including Canada (Milkman 1992; Bronfenbrenner and Juravich 1998; Yates 2000; Vector Polling 1999).

Women's greater propensity to join unions

For decades, many industrial relations experts, as well as unions, insisted that women are less interested in joining unions, with the possible exception of the public sector. Explanations for women's lack of interest in unions have varied. Some have argued that women's status as secondary wage-earners in the family, and repeated interruptions in their labour market participation, reflected a weaker commitment among women to their jobs, the result of which was an unwillingness to unionize. Others identified innate characteristics of women, such as their passive nature and desire to avoid conflict, as the key barrier to their unionization. More recently, analysts have turned to work-based explanations for women's lower rate of unionization in the private sector, including the difficulty of organizing small workplaces and the

Table 1: Organizing Outcome (Win/Loss) by Gender Majority Bargaining Unit

	Bargaining Unit by Gender Majority			
	Ontario		British Columbia	
	Majority Female	Majority Male	Majority Female	Majority Male
Loss	22.8% (57)	36.3% (144)	17.4% (43)	26% (38)
Win	77.2% (193)	63.7% (253)	82.6% (204)	74% (108)
Total	100% (250)	100% (397)	100% (247)	100% (146)

lack of time available to women to get involved in a union. Although some of these barriers are important, evidence from my survey of organizers demonstrates that women are more likely to support unionization than are men.

Comparing organizing success in FMW and MMW in both Ontario and B.C., I found that organizing drives in FMW were 13% more likely than MMW to result in the winning of union certification in Ontario, and 9% more likely to result in union certification in B.C. (See Table 1). Further analysis reveals that this is not the result of women's employment in the public sector. Rates of success in organizing in FMW and MMW in the public sector are virtually the same in both provinces. Similar success rates also exist in FMW and MMW in the manufacturing sector. The most important difference in success rates for FMW and MMW is in workplaces in the private sector—and this is the very sector where non-union women are concentrated. This suggests that there is tremendous potential for increases in union membership among women employed in the private sector, but that unions need to figure out why they are not organizing them in greater numbers, and how to overcome these problems.

Who are unions trying to organize?

After almost forty years with little or no attention paid to organizing, unions across Canada, and in Anglo-American liberal democracies more broadly, began in the 1990s to ask the question of how to organize the unorganized into unions. This renewed concern with organizing was driven by stagnant or declining union memberships, as well as a more generalized crisis in labour movements. In Canada, the United States, Australia, New Zealand and Great Britain, unions sought to recruit new members. Ensuing debates over how best to increase union memberships and influence fed into broader debates about the need for reform of union organizations and structures, democratic practices, political alliances, and orientations to the state (Fairbrother and Yates 2003). Consequently, labour movements were launched into a struggle over union renewal.

Within Canada, unions varied in their responses to the challenge of organizing. Many of the larger industrial unions shifted resources into their organizing departments and adopted policies committed to expanding their membership outside of traditional sectors. Some small unions, most notably HERE, relied upon creative innovation to get the most for their limited resources, developing strategies that

Table 2: Organizing in Public vs Private Sector
by Male and Female Majority

	Bargaining Unit by Gender Majority			
	Ontario		British Columbia	
	Majority Female	Majority Male	Majority Female	Majority Male
Public Sector	43.1% (107)	14% (55)	47.7% (116)	10.3% (15)
Private Sector	56.9% (141)	86% (338)	52.3% (127)	89.7% (130)

built on membership activism, community outreach, and getting results within targeted sectors. Some of the construction unions borrowed from the IBEW in the U.S., emphasizing education and training through which they developed a large cadre of member organizers. Public sector unions sought to hold on to their bargaining power by organizing in response to government restructuring initiatives, often chasing members forced into the private sector through privatization or contracting-out.

In general, however, unions have committed fewer hard resources to organizing than their public promises would suggest. Worse still, many unions have recently retrenched their financial commitments to organizing, shifting these resources to other priorities. In this context, it is perhaps not surprising to discover that the numbers of workers organized in both B.C. and Ontario have declined since 1999 and 2000, respectively, reaching all-time lows since the early 1980s (Katz-Rosene 2003).

With the exception of young workers, organizing strategies designed to address the needs of particular constituencies of workers are uncommon. All workers, regardless of race, ethnicity, gender, or sexual orientation, are assumed to experience common problems related to work and the employer-employee relationship that form the basis for union appeals. Although unions often acknowledge the growth in the female labour force in their analysis of organizing strategies, this recognition is usually limited to the different sectors and jobs in which women are employed. There is limited acknowledgment of other differences between women and men. Considerations of women, and how they might figure in union renewal strategies, have therefore been few and far between.

If we break down bargaining units that unions have attempted to organize into female majority (FMW) and male majority workplaces (MMW), we find that B.C. unions have a far better record of attempting to organize FMW workplaces than do Ontario unions. Whereas 63% of workplaces where B.C. unions tried to organize were FMW, this contrasts to 39% of workplaces in Ontario. This can in part be explained by the differences between the provinces in organizing intensity in the private and public sectors. In B.C., in the period covered by the survey, there was a higher proportion of organizing going on in the public sector than in Ontario, where organizing was concentrated in the private sector (Table 2). This in part reflects the distinct constellation of activist unions in the different provinces. In B.C., the B.C. Government and General Employees Union (BCGEU) and the B.C. Nurses' Union (BCNU) have been much more committed to organizing than any equivalent public sector union in Ontario, whereas large industrial unions such as the USWA, CAW, and UFCW have a much weaker organizing presence in B.C.

than in Ontario, where they account for a considerable proportion of organizing drives each year.

But these differences in the propensity to organize FMW and MMW also reflect choices made by unions. In general, white men in the private sector remain the focus of many organizing efforts of unions in both provinces. Although more organizing in B.C. takes place in public than private sector workplaces compared to Ontario, where the reverse is true, private sector workplaces in which unions attempted to organize were predominantly male in both provinces. This poses a particular challenge for long-term union renewal, as it is in the private sector where union density rates are lowest and where union renewal is most needed.

A large proportion of organizing drives in both provinces are initiated in response to workers' calling the union. This trend is more pronounced among FMW in both provinces than MMW, a trend that suggests that women have to take tremendous initiative in order to get organized. The survey data also indicate that unions have difficulty translating many of their organizing goals into practice. Whereas in both provinces organizers reported that a larger number of organizing drives in female-dominated workplaces than male dominated workplaces were pursued because they had been identified as a target for organizing by their union, organizers also reported a very low incidence of having been able to initiate contact with targeted workplaces. In other words, organizers lack the necessary avenues of contact into many female-dominated workplaces that have been targeted by their union for organizing. This corresponds to another trend in Ontario, where organizers are more likely to initiate an organizing drive through their own contacts, and in workplaces that are disproportionately MMW. Both of these trends suggest a gender bias towards organizing in MMW.

Part of the answer to these trends lies in who the organizers are. Organizing strategists have long understood that reaching out to diverse constituencies of workers means that the organizer her/himself has to reflect the constituency of workers they are trying to organize. In organizing women, this has most often meant ensuring that more organizers are women and addressing the particular concerns of women workers. Although most unions recognize the importance of this commitment, they have been unable to translate this commitment into practice. In both B.C. and Ontario, the majority of organizers are white and male, although B.C. has a considerably higher proportion of women organizers at 42% of organizers, compared to Ontario where only 22% of lead organizers surveyed were women. Gender composition of organizing departments has a direct effect on who gets organized: women organizers in both B.C. and Ontario are more likely than male organizers to organize FMW. The influence of organizers over who is organized is even greater when they have large degrees of discretion in deciding which workplaces get organized. As men tend to have networks that are male-dominated, just as women have female-dominated networks, this reinforces the bias towards organizing MMW, especially in Ontario where a large number of organizing drives are initiated on the basis of the organizer's personal contacts.

The first step towards increasing the rate of organizing among women would therefore appear to be a fairly simple one of increasing the number of women organizers. Unions, however, have found that it is hard to attract women into organizing. The barriers into this job include long, unpredictable hours, the need to travel and often re-locate, albeit temporarily, to another community, and the lack of an available pool of trained women activists from which to hire organizers. B.C.'s greater success at securing women organizers than Ontario's probably lies in two factors. First, public sector unions, which have a larger proportion of women members and therefore activists, are more actively engaged in organizing in B.C. than in Ontario, resulting in a larger available pool of women organizers. Second, B.C.'s Organizing Institute (BCOI), run out of the office of the B.C. Federation of Labour, has played a considerable role in recruiting and training a pool of organizers with a greater emphasis on diversity than many individual unions have been able to deliver. In many instances, unions that do not have women organizers from their own ranks can look to the B.C.O.I. for support.

The success of the B.C.O.I. speaks to the importance of coordination between unions and pooled resources, something that other labour groups have tried to emulate. Unfortunately, the Alberta Federation of Labour's proposal for a western Organizing Institute is still struggling against leadership inertia and early growing pains. The jury is still out on the success of the Toronto Labour Council's Organizing Institute that was established in 2001.

Training of organizers by gender was also quite different in the two provinces. Approximately 35% of all organizers in each of the provinces reported that they received no training. Surprisingly, in B.C. a much larger proportion of female organizers reported having received no training, than did female organizers in Ontario. Of those female organizers who did receive training in the two provinces, a much higher proportion of Ontario female organizers received their training from outside the labour movement—from other social movements or community groups—whereas female organizers in B.C. tended to have been trained through the labour movement. The latter is another possible effect of the training offered by the B.C.O.I., although the high proportion of untrained female organizers in B.C. suggests that more unions should and could use the training opportunities offered by the B.C.O.I.

Gender differences in organizing campaigns

Organizers emphasized different issues when organizing FMW and MMW, although these results were not especially strong. In both Ontario and B.C., wages were a slightly more important issue in FMW in the public sector than either MMW in the public sector or all private sector workplaces. Job security was a more important issue in FMW in both the private and public sectors in both provinces. Interestingly, the so-called "new age" organizing issues of dignity, fairness, and voice in the workplace were more important in organizing FMW in both the private and public sectors in Ontario, whereas no such clearly gendered pattern was evident in B.C.. Although these findings were not especially strong, they suggest that unions are in some way responding to women's structurally disadvantaged position in the labour market.

Yet, in B.C., where there were more women organizers, there were some distinctly gendered patterns to the tactics used by organizers when organizing a workplace. In B.C., women organizers were more likely to rely on tactics that involved face-to-face interaction with workers being organized, more likely to hold meetings with workers (both small group and large group meetings), and more likely to do house-calls. Conversely, they were less likely than men to use leaflets at work, send letters to workers' homes, or use newsletters to communicate. The one exception to this pattern was in contacting workers by phone, which was used similarly by both male and female organizers. No such similarly gendered patterns in strategy were evident in Ontario (Eaton 2004). In Ontario, Martinello and Yates (2004) found that there were distinct clusters of union strategies by sector, and in one cluster by union. In public sector workplaces, unions used fewer tactics, whereas in private sector workplaces unions tended to use several tactics, especially in the manufacturing sector where organizing drives were the most highly contested.

Overall, organizers in both provinces reported that women tended to take longer to make a decision to join a union, but, once they decided to support the union, they were less likely than men to change their mind. This is indirectly supported by evidence on the effect of anti-union employer strategies on rates of organizing success. Employer strategies have a profoundly negative effect on organizing both FMW and MMW. Employers tended to be more aggressive in Ontario and less aggressive in B.C., where a more union-friendly labour law regime at the time of the survey reduced the effect and changed the type of employer strategy.

In Ontario, employers were especially aggressive and had greater opportunities to influence the outcome of an organizing drive, due to the legal regime's reliance on a vote to determine certification. Employers tended to use fewer tactics when faced with an organizing drive in a FMW. Yet, when one compares organizing drives in FMW and MMW where the same number of employer strategies were used, unions continue to have a higher rate of success in certifying FMW than MMW. This would tend to support the view expressed by organizers that women are harder to dissuade from joining a union once they have made up their mind.

Implications for union strategy

Why does the gendering of organizing strategies matter? The most important reason is that organizing drives in FMW in both provinces are much more likely to be successful than those in MMW. In short, when women are given the opportunity to join a union, they are more likely to join unions than men. If unions want to reverse the waning of union membership and influence, they need to pay heed to the challenge of women workers. What does this mean when we think about organizing the unorganized?

The first thing that unions need to do is recognize that they are not just organizing workers, but that they are organizing women whose work experience and structural position in the labour market are different from those of men. Unions have long recognized the maleness of their membership and incorporated this into their organizational structures and practices. Moreover, since the 1970s, they have undergone a series of changes in response to pressure from growing women memberships, including affirmative action leadership structures for most labour federations, recognition of women's committees, women's leadership training, and the elimination of sexist language in public proceedings and union documents. The first step towards changing organizing practices therefore entails a deepening and broadening of existing internal transformations, especially empowering women activists to take on these organizational and leadership challenges. HERE has been especially adept at involving newly organized women in union and broader labour movement affairs, encouraging them to become leaders in their own workplaces and agents of change within their union as a whole. As unions engage in this process, they need to remember and remind others that the labour movement is way ahead of employers in addressing the structural inequalities and discrimination experienced by women workers.

Second, unions need to recognize that women have fewer opportunities to join a union than men, especially women employed in the private sector. From this recognition they need to systematically break down the barriers that prevent women from having access to unions. This involves many changes, including: using the knowledge of women's greater support for unions to develop strategic organizing targets in heavily female-dominated workplaces, such as non-profit agencies (where union certification success rates are exceptionally high), hiring more women organizers, and increasing the investment in organizing departments and reducing their ghettoization within union organizations.

Third, unions need to educate organizers and other union activists about women's segregated position in the labour market, thereby arming them with the information needed to understand and respond to women's workplace demands. From this, organizers can map out more effective strategies. First and foremost, this entails recognizing that women need union protection on the most fundamental of workplace concerns, namely wages and job security, two issues in which unions have a wealth of experience.

There are dangers here, however. In today's labour market, unions have found it increasingly difficult to deliver wage increases and enhanced job security. This difficulty is likely to be greater in private sector workplaces, where many women are employed. Alongside learning to organize women, therefore, unions need to be engaged in strategic thinking about how to deliver wages, benefits, and enhanced job security in small workplaces with low profit margins. Many unions have successfully addressed these challenges, including, to name a few, the United Steelworkers of America in its organization and bargaining for security guards, the B.C. branch of the Canadian Auto Workers with Kentucky Fried Chicken outlets, and the B.C. Government Employees Union in its organization and bargaining for health care units in the interior of the province (Yates 2001). But learning from these union experiences is next to impossible, given the growing hostility and mounting barriers to inter-union cooperation evident in Canada, but especially in Ontario.

Which brings me to my fourth and final suggestion for strategic change. Although unions have always been internally competitive, it is imperative that this be tempered by the building of means for information sharing and strategic collaboration. To date, the seemingly most successful examples of this in Canada are the B.C. Organizing Institute, as well as the practice of many B.C. unions of entering into bilateral "peace" agreements wherein two unions agree to rules of competition in organizing the unorganized, substituting arbitration for all-out war in the event of growing conflict. The attempts by other labour organizations to establish organizing institutes are important innovations that need to be supported. But the question remains: how does such collaboration play a role in dismantling gender bias in organizing? As discussed above, in very practical terms, central organizing institutes have a better track record than many individual unions of drawing into the labour movement diverse constituencies of organizers, including more women. Institutions such as the B.C.O.I. encourage information sharing and other forms of collaboration among unions, thus increasing the chances that unions will learn from their successes as well as their mistakes, hopefully translating this into success in organizing women.

Moreover, many of the large corporate chains that employ a large number of women, such as Wal-Mart, will not be organized by one union alone. Teams of unions need to pool their resources and creative energies to win these battles. To successfully engage in such collaboration, unions need to rebuild institutions where dialogue and cooperation are fostered. At the very least, institutions such as the B.C.O.I. draw women activists from different unions together and open the door to women-initiated strategies for change that have at their heart the recognition that more women need and want unions.

If unions in Canada are serious about reversing their declining memberships and political-economic marginalization, they must grapple with how to draw more women into the labour movement. But to do this successfully and tap into the potential revitalization offered by organizing women, unions need to do more than add women into their activities as one more group of workers. Rather, unions need to shift the lens with which they see the workforce, so that they reveal the complex ways in which gender shapes workplace experience, relations with co-workers and employers, and labour market needs and concerns.

References

Bronfenbrenner, Kate, and Tom Juravich. 1998. It Takes More Than House Calls: Organizing to Win With a Comprehensive Union Building Strategy. In Organizing to Win, ed. Kate Bronfenbrenner, Sheldon Friedman, Richard Hurd, Rudolph A. Oswald, and Ronald Seeber, 19-36. Ithaca, NY: Cornell University Press.

Eaton, Jonathon. 2004. Union Renewal in Canada: Strategies, Tactics, and Public Perception. PhD thesis, University of Toronto.

Fairbrother, Peter, and Charlotte Yates, eds. 2003. Trade Unions in Renewal. London, U.K.: Continuum.

Katz-Rosene, Ryan. 2003. Union Organizing: A Look at Recent Organizing Activity Through Analysis of Certification Across Canadian Jurisdictions. Research Paper 26. Ottawa: Canadian Labour Congress.

Martinello, Felice, and Charlotte Yates. 2004. Unions Employer Tactics in Ontario Organizing Campaigns. In Advances in Industrial and Labor Relations, ed. David Lewin and Bruce Kaufman. Boston, MA: Elsevier.

Milkman, Ruth. 1992. Union Responses to Workforce Feminization in the U.S. In The Challenge of Restructuring: North American Labor Movements Respond, ed. Jane Jenson and Rianne Mahon. Philadelphia, PA: Temple University Press.

Statistics Canada. 2004. Fact-Sheet on Unionization. Perspectives on Labour and Income, Autumn, 58-65.

Vector Polling. 1999. Organizing: A Lagging Factor. Vector Research and Development National Polls, November.

Yates, Charlotte. 2000. Staying the Decline in Union Membership: Union Organizing in Ontario, 1985-1999. Relations industrielles/Industrial Relations 55 (4): 640-674.

———. 2001. Making it Your Economy: Unions and Economic Justice. Toronto: Centre for Social Justice and Ontario Federation of Labour.

Chapter 5
Globalization and Union Renewal: Perspectives from the Quebec Labour Movement

CHRISTIAN LÉVESQUE AND GREGOR MURRAY

Globalization is changing the rules of the game between workers, their employers, and the union organizations that represent workers. It is commonly believed that these new rules tilt the playing field in favour of employers because workers and unions appear less able to effect change in the workplace and protect their terms and conditions of employment. Collective bargaining concessions, rationalization and downsizing, privatization and outsourcing, the proliferation of precarious forms of work and employment, greater flexibility in the organization and execution of work, work intensification and the associated decline in the quality of life at work are just a few of the many familiar faces of this new environment in unionized workplaces across the country. Thus, or at least so goes the argument, workers and their unions have little choice but to accept the new global realities and to do the best they can in their globalized workplaces over which unions will have either less or little influence. This narrative certainly depicts current trends in many work-places, irrespective of industry or nation, and its hold on the collective imagination underscores to what degree globalization can be advanced as an all-encompassing explanation of social change. It is also, however, a discourse of collective incapacity, paralyzing the ability to understand and the will to act.

It is our contention that globalization is an altogether more nuanced and con-tradictory process than this overly simplistic interpretation would have us believe. Our objective in this chapter is to offer a different narrative. Drawing on a wide range of empirical research conducted in partnership with Québec unions over the past decade,[1] we outline what we believe are some of the key conditions for union renewal in a global context. Our reading of union renewal developed in this chapter intertwines three core strands that run through the entire analysis. First, globalization is not a juggernaut, demolishing everything in its path. Rather, it is an inherently contradictory process, creating constraints but also many opportunities for union action. Second, globalization highlights the importance of power for all actors, especially unions. If globalization is an open-ended process, then organiza-tional capacity or the ability of social actors to mobilize their power becomes that much more important, but it does not mean that the sources of power used by unions in the past are adapted to this new context. Finally, following on the first two strands of the argument, it is evident why reinforcing power resources is at the very heart of debates about union renewal (see, for example, Murray, Lévesque, and Vallée 2000; Lévesque and Murray 2002), and why it is so important to turn our analytical attention to the sources and mechanisms of union power. We argue here the idea that union power is constructed from complementary but different resources that must be cultivated and nurtured, and we seek to identify a strategic triangle of critical resources for union success in a global economy.

The chapter is divided in two parts. We first examine the relevance of the two contending approaches to globalization and unions, i.e., an inevitable decline in union power, and a necessary renewal adapted to this new context. Drawing on the second of these two approaches and evidence gathered from Quebec unions, we then look at some of the avenues and conditions for union renewal. The purpose of this chapter is not to explain the structure and practices of the Quebec labour movement. Instead, we draw on our knowledge of Quebec unions to explore key ideas about the impact of globalization on union action. This exploration offers us the opportunity to highlight some aspects of the renewal process in different Quebec unions and, in so doing, also to shed some light on the relative success of the Quebec labour movement within the Canadian context. The underlying message, however, is not one of Quebec exceptionalism, but rather that the lessons learned from the experience of the Quebec labour movement are more widely applicable to unions both inside and outside of Canada.[2]

Global and local: the consequences of globalization for local union action

There are basically two competing approaches to understanding the impact of globalization on union action. According to a more pessimistic view, globalization leads inexorably to the weakening of union capacity, while a less pessimistic view sees globalization as a real but uncertain process where actors of all types are compelled to renew their practices and their resources in order to orient the results of what is an open-ended and uncertain process. Let us look in a little more detail at each set of arguments, because they have profound consequences for our understanding of the challenges and dynamics of union renewal.

The global incapacitation thesis draws on at least three types of change that illustrate how traditional sources of union power are being destabilized and undermined.

First, the phenomenal growth of multi- and trans-national firms underscores an ever greater disparity between increasingly global employers and, whatever their geographical label (regional, industrial, national or international), essentially local unions. There can be little doubt that these international firms account for an increasingly important part of global trade and employment, and that the velocity of change makes it quite difficult to estimate the full extent of their development. A 1999 United Nations estimate points to the existence of 63,000 international firms with 690,000 foreign subsidiaries, employing in total more than 75 million people, of which more than 50% are located outside of the country of origin. Probably more important again in terms of global reach is the rise of global production or value chains in which firms, be they national or transnational but increasingly the latter, organize their production of goods and services across borders through dense networks of sub-contracts and commercial partnerships (Dicken 2003). Thus, workers within such networks often have little recourse to an ultimate employer. Indeed, it can be difficult to locate the dominant firm or firms within the network. This is sometimes the dominant assembler, as in the case of world auto manufacturing firms. But it is sometimes the protector of the brand, as in the case of fashion and clothing firms (for example, NIKE), who have few direct employees engaged in anything other than the creation of product designs and marketing. Or, again, the dominant firm can sometimes be the retailer, as in the case of Wal-Mart, organizing global production networks of firms, none of which are owned by the lead firm, to produce goods to order for their retail stores across the world.

Wherever the locus of power in such firms and networks, they can transfer production from one site to another, and from one country to another with impunity. Moreover, their investment strategies are often designed to punish non-compliant sites and firms: for example, direct employees who do not meet benchmarked standards across their global operations or sub-contractors unable to implement required price cuts or quality improvements in order to secure contract renewals. In this new global universe, local unions appear terribly vulnerable—all the more so when faced with coercive comparisons between production sites in different parts of the world and the ever-constant threat of jobs moving from one location to another if workers prove unwilling or unenthusiastic about contract concessions, work reorganization, and fidelity to the firm.

While there is perhaps a tendency to exaggerate this new coercive universe, it is important to appreciate its real sway in the Canadian context. In a recent survey of industrial relations trends in the main industries in which national and international union organizations in Canada are present, Kumar and Murray (2001) found a combination of significant levels of workplace change and employer demands for concessions with enhanced employer bargaining power. For example, while more than half of respondents reported increases in the intensity of competition in their main industry, approximately four out of five industries had experienced increases in technological change, the extent of industry and organizational restructuring and employee workload. Employer bargaining power has either increased (42%) or stayed stable (51.3%), whereas union bargaining power is more likely to have decreased (32.2%) than increased (25.4%). In other words, despite the mixed trends in some industries, it would seem that unions are compelled to accommodate employer demands for competitive adaptations in order to protect employee jobs. Indeed, two recent observers of trends in France and Quebec have suggested that the common denominator of labour relations used to be wages, but it is now jobs, since the essence of most bargaining concerns the protection of jobs (Bélanger and Thuderoz 1998).

Secondly, the internationalization of competition between firms has prompted a search for and experimentation with new ways of organizing production and work, thereby accelerating the pace of change within workplaces and often challenging traditional union conceptions of job control. Our own research in the Quebec manufacturing sector shows how the extent and pace of change have been accentuated over recent years (Lapointe et al. 2000, 2001). For example, in the key metalworking industries, including primary transformation such as aluminium smelting, and a wide range of secondary metal manufacturing, managers and union representatives reported an average of seven major types of change in their workplace over the preceding three years (1999-2001). These changes covered new technologies and production management, quality systems, and work organization. Employee surveys confirm the same trends. For example, in a survey that we conducted with the FTQ (Fédération des travailleurs et travailleuses du Québec) and the Fonds de solidarité de la FTQ for the FTQ's 1998 congress, more than half of unionized employees (55.1%) indicated that significant changes had affected the way that they did their jobs in the three years preceding the survey.[3]

Some analysts suggest that these changes in the organization of production and work open up new possibilities for unions to negotiate, even to arrive at more participative forms of management. While not excluding such outcomes, which are the exception rather than the rule, most recent studies do not lend support to this analysis. In fact, changes in the workplace are most often introduced on a unilateral basis by management, and this tendency has been reinforced over recent years (Lapointe et al. 2000, 2001). Moreover, these continuing changes have tended to translate into increased workload and decreased job security. For example, in our FTQ-CROP study, roughly 60% of unionized workers reported an increase in workload, and more than 40% a decrease in job security over the preceding three years. This increase in workload and stress at work is thoroughly pervasive, as can be seen in two recent studies that we did with the Fédération des syndicats de l'enseignement (FSE) and with the Fédération du Comerce of the Confédération des syndicats nationaux or CSN (Lévesque, Murray, and LeCapitaine 2004, 2005). In the 2004 study of teachers, 89.9% of the 1,105 respondents indicated that their workload had increased over the previous three years. And in the 2005 study of 603 unionized employees in the financial sector, 62.8% of respondents had experienced an increased workload over the preceding three years, and 67.3% reported increased stress at work. In other words, if these comparable trends from quite different sectors (manufacturing, public services, and private service) are accurate (and they are certainly corroborated by a wide variety of research results), then unions seem less able to influence the terms and conditions of the work of their members in this new global context for work and employment.

A third type of change affecting unions concerns the link between the union member and his or her union organization. It seems that the many changes associated with globalization are weakening the link between unions and their members or potential members. One telling trend, of course, is the decline of the level of unionization in the private sector. Recent Canadian data identify a continuing change in the level of unionization: that the rate of unionization has declined from 35.9% in 1989 to 30.6% in 2004 (Morissette, Schellenberg, and Johnson 2005). Even if the threshold is much higher in Quebec (40.8% to 37.4%) than Ontario (32.8% to 27.3%), the trend is very similar. Another recent study of trends in the level of unionization between 1997 and 2004 identifies a decline of 0.8 percentage points in Quebec (to 40.2%) and 1.5 percentage points in Ontario (to 27.9%) and the other provinces of Canada (to 31.0%) (Labrosse 2005). Moreover, it is difficult to meet local unionists and discuss the state of their union without reports of individualism, generational change, and associated complaints that point to a shift in value frames or, at least, that "things are just not the way that they used to be."

Given the weight of the evidence put forward above, it would be foolish to deny that globalization has not exerted some impact on unions. Our second approach to the interpretation of the impact of globalization on union power suggests, however, that globalization is an indeterminate process. Not only does the precise impact on union power remain an open question, but it is up to unions to "renew" or "revitalize" their practices and resources in order to orient the process in favour of their members. We advance three arguments to support this interpretation.

First, even if the influence of multinational firms has been accentuated over the past decade, they by no means control their environment. Multinational firms, perhaps more than other organizations, are ridden with uncertainty of all kinds. The prolific self-help literature giving advice to managers is but symptomatic of a deeper malaise. Sklair's (2001) study of global managers elegantly illustrates how managers (perhaps even more than workers) are caught in the metaphorical "rat race" of competitive benchmarking. Their existential angst also reflects a deeper vulnerability within firms about the right strategic direction. That same uncertainty informs multiple changes in course and a profusion of sometimes ridiculous decisions, many generated from higher levels of the firm, in a desperate effort to stay ahead. Sometimes it works, but the more likely result is the daily reality of so many workplaces: arbitrary decisions.

The emergence of more sophisticated and highly integrated networks for ensuring the production of goods and services certainly offers the possibility of tremendous productivity and value gains, but these systems are also highly vulnerable. The interdependence between units means that a problem in one location can quickly reverberate throughout the production chain. A classic example was that of a Flint, Michigan strike in 1996, whose just-in-time production architecture quickly resulted in factory closures in Mexico, Canada, and the United States. Similarly, how else to explain Wal-Mart's 2005 decision to close a seemingly profitable but newly unionized outlet in Jonquière, Québec? Over and beyond the widely acknowledged anti-unionism of this employer, it highlights to what degree a part of the competitive advantage of the firm's business model seems to be predicated on low wages at both ends of its supply chain.

Another example is the vulnerability of firms to consumer and citizen pressures on the brand. This can be seen with regard to anti-sweatshop campaigns involving direct action with consumers, student organizations, ethical investors, pension funds, and the like. One of the more eloquent recent examples was the 2004 decision by Montreal T-shirt manufacturer Gildan Activewear to modify its labour relations and human resources policies in its Central American and Caribbean production facilities. This was the result of a prolonged civil society campaign coordinated by the Maquila Solidarity Network (www.maquilasolidarity.org). One of several key elements of this campaign was the decision by the FTQ Solidarity Fund to liquidate its substantial investment (approximately $100 million) in Gildan Activewear, a firm that it had helped to secure its financial stability only a few years earlier. In other words, the paradox of global firms is both their huge market power and their strategic vulnerability to organized and unorganized uncertainty, hence the preference to make rules, norms, and arrangements with other social actors to reduce the level of uncertainty.

Secondly, in addition to the fragility of organizing business across borders, the new ways of organizing the production of goods and services within worksites also appear vulnerable. This is because it is difficult to make the new forms of work organization, such as teamwork, just-in-time supply systems, and continuous improvement, work without the active collaboration of workers and their unions (Belanger, Giles, and Murray 2002). Indeed, they seem to require a more intensive labour-management collaboration because the employer often depends on union support in order to mobilize the good-will and knowledge of workers in making these systems work. Levesque's work at the former GM factory in Boisbriand highlighted how teamwork can take on a variety of forms, according to the under-lying social dynamics of a particular part of a workplace (Lévesque and Côté 1999). Similarly, our studies in the metalworking and transport equipment manufacturing industries in Quebec demonstrated that success in the implementation of these new systems is closely tied to the role played by the union. Indeed, on the basis of evidence gathered from local factory managers, it is clear that union involvement in work organization changes and processes contributes to improvements in both the productive performance, such as quality and productivity measures, and the social performance, such as skill enhancement, motivation, and guarantees about future prospects for work (Lapointe et al. 2000, 2001).

In other words, employers seeking to improve both productive and social performance are seemingly "condemned" to facilitate a role for the union in the change process. Moreover, contrary to popular belief, it is not in the subsidiaries of multinational firms that the union role is least developed. On the contrary, our study of the metalworking industry suggests that the union role in Quebec is likely to be more developed in worksites owned by multinationals and in establishments that are highly integrated into the global economy (Lapointe et al. 2001). Of course, it is important to consider other elements in this equation, but it is clear that unions in so-called globalized workplaces are more likely, rather than less likely, to play a role in changes affecting their members.

Finally, the notion that union members are less inclined to support their union does not withstand empirical scrutiny. The results of the FTQ-CROP survey point to an opposite conclusion: 87.9% of unionized workers believe that unions are necessary, 86.9% are favourable to unions, 75.2% express confidence in their union representatives to defend their interests, and 73.2% are proud to be union members. This same study reveals a reservoir of militancy, inasmuch as 40.8% of union members would be willing to give more time to their union. This kind of strong support for unions has been replicated in other studies. In a 2004 study of teacher delegates, 88.5% of the 1,104 respondents reported that their salary and working conditions would not be as good without a union, and 78.7% felt proud to be a union member (Lévesque, Murray, and LeCapitaine 2004). Similarly, in our study of union renewal in the financial sector in Quebec, 84.9% of the 603 unionized tellers and financial advisors indicated that unions are fairly or very necessary, and 71.7% felt proud to be a union member. In other words, despite a small decline in the overall level of unionization and the many challenges inherent to the unionization of less organized sectors, particularly in private services, support for unions remains quite vibrant.

The strength of these countervailing factors leads to the conclusion that the impact of globalization on union power is indeed an open question. Once one accepts the idea that globalization is not a steamroller flattening all in its path, the challenge of identifying the conditions for union renewal in this new context becomes vital.

Power resources and their renewal

The approach that we adopt here looks at the construction of power in terms of the resources that unions can access and mobilize in order to influence the processes of change in which they are involved in the workplace. The core hypothesis is that union renewal in this new context requires a reconfiguration of union power resources. The basic notion—and it is certainly not new—is that the employer, like any other social actor, must contend with the power of other social actors in particular contexts. As was illustrated above, the production of goods and services is typically characterized by strategic uncertainty. To take the case of any workplace, if the employer can mobilize his or her power and the union does not or cannot, then change is likely to take place on the employer's terms rather than on a negotiated basis. On the other hand, if the union is able to mobilize its power resources, then, subject to the specificities of that particular context, the prospects for the union's role in workplace change will be entirely different. We have sought to illustrate above that globalization further accentuates the need to think about the mobilization of actor power in particular contexts. This is likely to entail a wider range of resources, suggesting a need to develop new resources and a more systematic use of these resources.

We use the Quebec case and examples drawn from Quebec unions to illustrate this avenue of analysis. It is an approach that we have developed in working closely with Quebec unions over the last decade (see, for example, Lévesque and Murray 2002, 2003). In different partnerships with the major union confederations (FTQ, CSN, CSQ) and, using a range of quantitative and qualitative techniques, we have sought to develop an analysis of the union power resources that appear to be important in a global context.

On the basis of our work in several thousand different Quebec workplaces, three resources appear particularly relevant for the development of union power. These are 1) the strategic capacity to develop a vision or an agenda, 2) internal solidarity or democracy, and 3) external solidarity or the capacity to embed the local union in networks through alliances with the larger union movement, other unions and the community. These three resources are mutually reinforcing and constitute, according to our research findings, the conditions for union involvement in the processes of change at the level of the workplace. We have observed that unions able to mobilize these resources are more likely to play a role in the modes of implantation of change and in influencing the results of these changes for the benefit of their members. This does not mean that success is guaranteed, irrespective of context. However, it does mean that unions able to draw on these resources are more likely to influence outcomes in their particular context. Figure 1 illustrates this strategic triangle for developing local union power in the context of globalization.

Figure 1: Local Union Power Resources

STRATEGIC CAPACITY
Values, Vision, Agenda, and Discourse

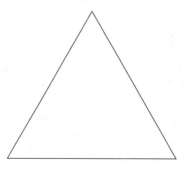

Internal Solidarity:
Democracy in the
Local Union

External Solidarity:
Alliances and Networks
with the Larger Union,
between Unions and with
the Community

These three resources, which we will develop in more detail and seek to illustrate below, could easily be packaged in other ways by subdividing, for example, the key resources to be mobilized into a greater number of categories. We have used the idea of a strategic triangle as a pedagogical device that is accessible to local unionists. It is meant to help trade unionists think in terms of a toolbox available for validating their own power resources and seeking to develop or reinforce resources likely to be relevant to the particular context in which they act.

The first union power resource relates to the union's capacity to develop a vision of its action (and the values underlying it) and to develop projects on this basis. At the heart of this resource is the union's strategic capacity, as well as the values, vision, agenda, and discourse that the local union can mobilize in support of its actions. Of course, projects have always been at the heart of union action. The hope, indeed the conviction, that things might be otherwise is at the very basis of the impulse to act. A union project is the rallying point for a community of interests among workers, and it is the promotion of this community of interests that becomes a tangible resource for union action. This first resource is both the narrative or value frame that informs worker action and the capacity to articulate it and mobilize it as an organization.

As argued above, globalization intensifies pressures on workers to subscribe to common projects with their employer. Such alliances are often seen as a way to preserve jobs, but such workplace and firm "patriotism" can suppress the formulation of alternative projects, inhibit the expression of other identities, and thereby weaken the union's capacity to mobilize its members. In particular, as has often been the case, the adversary becomes other workers and even, as is often the case in multinational firms, workers of other establishments within the same firm. The success of the union is then tied to firm and worksite performance rather than to the defence of workplace justice, working conditions, and local communities. That is why the capacity of the union to articulate its own strategic vision of change is a critical resource. It flows from a capacity to shape and articulate underlying values, and to translate this vision of purpose (or value frame) into an agenda for change.

Our research results on work reorganization in a wide variety of industries show that the reinforcement of union identity does not flow from either acceptance of or opposition to employer projects for changing the organization of work. Rather, it is the pro-active position on the part of the local union—its ability to formulate and communicate its own agenda for change—that reinforces the likelihood of strengthening membership identification with the union and negotiating the social performance of change initiatives on issues such as training, investment, and the protection of employment. Moreover, as is argued elsewhere in this volume, in the chapter by Kumar and Murray, the unions best able to articulate this kind of agenda for change are more likely to be informed by a broader set of values incorporating the importance of membership involvement, equity, and social justice.

Quebec unions have a long history of arguing for societal projects. This particular political culture was developed in the epic battles over the role of unions in Quebec society, first in the 1940s and 1950s vis-à-vis successive governments of Maurice Duplessis, and then in the 1970s relative to language rights, the national question, and the role of the public sector in the development of the Quebec economy and society. Over the past decades, Quebec unions have been characterized by an ebb-and-flow in their relations within the state and a relative war of positioning over strategic engagement with and within the state. Their engagement in a multiplicity of state bodies and the strength of their position within Quebec society translates into a vision with which any Quebec government must contend in the elaboration of economic and social policies. Moreover, it is no coincidence that the strong support of many Quebec trade unionists for sovereignty is informed by a social project which, it is believed, can be more easily promoted within a Quebec state that exercises greater control over its own economic and social destiny.

The existence of an autonomous project is, however, insufficient. To be legitimate, projects must be constructed from below. A second and fundamental union power resource is internal solidarity, or the strength of democracy in the local union. Internal solidarity is, of course, at the very heart of union action. It is not a given; it must be nurtured continuously. This resource concerns the participation of members in the life of the union, and their internal cohesion or strength of identification with the union and its actions. Such attributes not easily achieved, but we have consistently found that they are the result of the fairly basic mechanics of democracy, a structure of workplace delegates or stewards, the existence of internal networks to ensure communication within the union, paid time-off for union activities, educational support for workplace delegate training, and efforts to develop mechanisms to ensure the participation of different groups and types of worker in the life of the union and its governance. These basic tools are invariably associated with a more robust internal democracy and, in turn, stronger membership identification with the union.

In addition to reinforcing the union's capacity to intervene in the workplace, in-ternal democracy fulfills a dual role: first, it favours the emergence of union projects that are closely tied to membership concerns; and second, following logically from the first role, it strengthens the legitimacy of union actions and positions vis-à-vis the employer, who invariably makes a strategic assessment of union representativeness. In other words, internal democracy is a crucial power resource that must constantly be rekindled and strengthened.

Is this dynamic any different in Quebec? The answer is a qualified yes, and the explication can be linked to a more vigorous inter-union competition between contending union organizations operating in the same industries and sectors. A Quebec worker could plausibly be represented by at least three or four different union organizations in any sector, and that does not include the competition between FTQ-CLC-affiliated organizations to recruit new groups of workers. Quebec workers therefore have a wide choice of union organizations to which they can affiliate. Indeed, the Quebec Labour Code affirms the liberty of choice. The certification typically belongs to the association of workers concerned rather than to the larger union to which they are affiliated. For example, the CSN constitution gives any group of workers the right to change affiliation if the several steps of the fairly simple procedure to do so are respected. This means that there are both the possibility and the reality of movement between union organizations, mainly bi-directional between the FTQ and the CSN, but with other union federations and other non-affiliated union groupings also playing a significant role in both public and private sectors.

While this kind of competition could be perceived as harmful to inter-union solidarity (and sometimes it is), its effect is probably most beneficial in terms of union democracy. The ever-present threat that workers might exercise choice in terms of union affiliation means that there is a constant pressure on union organizations to ensure the respect of local groups of workers. This can be contrasted with the rest of Canada, where the hurdles to changing affiliation are significant and the sentiment of influence on union decisions, especially in industries where huge composite locals are the norm, can often be weak in a context where administrative efficiency takes precedence over certification unit autonomy.

Our own research in Quebec unions links stronger levels of internal union solidarity to very simple democratic mechanisms: the existence of delegate structures, participation at local union meetings, programs for delegate education, etc. The FTQ pioneered many of the worker-to-worker education techniques now used to train delegates elsewhere in Canada. The worker investment funds of the FTQ and the CSN (Fonds de solidarité de la FTQ and Fondaction of the CSN) both engage in economic education around the investments that they make. The FTQ has recently begun a program of training pension fund trustees on economic and social responsibility issues. The CSN, the CSQ, and the FTQ, moreover, all organize a wide variety of activities to train their local delegates, including many specialist conferences on subjects of interest to their members. They also have a tradition of working closely with outside experts, notably from the university sector, on studies and initiatives that feed back into membership training.

There has also been a concern to tackle the issues related to the renewal of union life at the local level. One of the more interesting initiatives in this respect was the decision of the CSN at its 2002 congress to adopt a "union life" program.

This prompted each of its industry federations to develop policies that would seek to improve the quality of union life at the local level. Its federation of workers in the paper and forestry industries, for example, used a technique of "estates general," in which local unions convened a conference of interested parties from inside and outside the union, mobilizing activists and non-activists, to reflect on the quality of democracy and the ability to involve new groups of members in the life of the union. The purpose was to make both a diagnosis and proposals for improving the quality of life in the local union.

Our research partnerships with unions in Quebec have often concerned the internal life of the union. In a 2004 study of teacher delegates in all primary and secondary school workplaces in the public education system, we focused on how to develop delegate capacity in the context of the decentralization of decision-making to the establishment level. Similarly, in a 2005 study of workers in the financial sector, the concern was how to renew union life for groups of workers whose link with the union was challenged by new forms of human resource management and work reorganization. The theme running through most of these initiatives is that internal solidarity or the democratic life of the union are resources that must be subject to continuing initiatives to rekindle or strengthen the ability of the union to act, and that local unions must make an effort to involve a new generation of members and new labour market identities in the life of the union. Moreover, we have consistently found that union democracy is a key tool in the ability of unions to develop membership identification with the union and its projects (Lévesque, Murray, and LeQueux 2005).

If internal solidarity is crucial to ensuring a union role in the workplace, it is arguably no longer sufficient in a global context. It must be complemented by external solidarity, a third essential resource for developing union power. External solidarity concerns the capacity of the local union to develop external alliances and networks within the larger union, relative to other unions and with the community, in the form of a variety of community groups. One of the paradoxes of globalization is that it simultaneously provides the means of communication and travel to multiple networks around the world while the competitive ethos "individuates" local unions into a sense of often desperate inter-site competition to avoid the loss of jobs. In the same way, outsourcing frequently places different groups of workers into competitive situations, underwritten by the survival of the "most compliant." It is evident, however, that turning inwards in this way is a source of weakness rather than strength for local unions. That is why we believe that it is important for the local union to become embedded in networks at multiple levels: regional, company, industry, national, and international. In this sense, participation in a wide variety of forums cannot be seen as a simple obligation or an interest of a few activists, but rather a crucial resource to be developed and mobilized. Local unions must be able to draw on these resources, notably because the multiple sites of external union action give access to kinds of expertise that would not otherwise be available and help to develop projects that might not otherwise see the light of day.

Our research with local unions has consistently demonstrated that local unions that are embedded in different types of external networks are more likely to play a stronger role within their workplace. This is especially true of links with community organizations around the protection of employment (FTQ 1999). It is also true of access to new forms of expertise. Drawing on the lessons of the recession of the early 1980s and its lack of capacity to intervene in the case of closures and attempts to revive firms, the CSN, for example, developed a consultancy agency to provide expertise and counter-expertise to local unions faced with work reorganization and financial solvency issues. The strength of the two major worker investment funds in Quebec (Fonds de solidarité de la FTQ and Fondaction de la CSN) also gives workers access to much greater financial expertise and potential sources of investment, not least because these worker funds offer tremendous multiplier effects in terms of their ability to leverage other interventions coming from state agencies. By the same token, Quebec trade unionists have been involved with the management of the state pension fund and sit on the board of the key public sector investment agencies. They are also involved in a wide range of bipartite or multipartite initiatives on vocational and workplace training and regional economic development (see, for example, Charest 2004). From the point of view of local unions, this is embedded and networked expertise that they can access at certain key moments.

External solidarity also entails more classic forms of inter-union solidarity. The history of the labour movement is, of course, related to efforts to find common cause among groups of workers that might otherwise be divided. The CSN has pioneered several significant bargaining breakthroughs in recent years in the ability to bring together groups of workers and achieve forms of broader-based or coordinated bargaining. In particular, not-for-profit child care educators developed coalitions and mobilized over many years, including strong support from parent and community bodies, in order to secure broader-based bargaining in this sector. This was particularly unique because, ceding to public pressure, the state provided a pension fund for workers who are not formally state employees. Similarly, Montreal hotel workers have developed a significant coalition in order to enforce pattern bargaining among the workers in this sector. Successive rounds of negotiations have seen substantial improvements in the terms and conditions of workers, notably in a sector where the reverse has often been the case.

The importance of external links between unions is just as important, if not more so, across borders. Indeed, we are just beginning to see some of the results of international solidarity for the way that local unions are able to negotiate with employers. For example, a recent FTQ document describes just some of the actions developed by different FTQ affiliated unions, notably through international worker solidarity centres (CISO), cooperation funds, and the like (FTQ 2001). Popular belief suggests that such alliances between unions in other countries or between unions and community groups are likely to be ephemeral, marginal at best. Moreover, it is often held that workers do not see their importance, but this point of view does not withstand empirical scrutiny. Our recent studies of local unions in the manufacturing sector indicate that 40% of these unions have participated in exchanges with community groups in their region over the last three years, and that 25% of these unions also participated in international exchanges with unions in other countries. Moreover, our FTQ-CROP survey of unionized workers revealed that union members now have a greater interest in international collaboration, and that 40% of respondents felt that it is important that unions in Quebec engage in joint actions with unions in the United States and Mexico. In other words, while globalization certainly exerts pressure on local unions to look inwards in an effort to save jobs, it also creates new opportunities to access expertise and develop alliances. Our research reveals that the capacity to utilize these opportunities systematically reinforces union power.

Conclusion

Our core argument is that globalization is fundamentally about the power of social actors. None of the social actors can really exert significant control over the context, but they can greatly influence the results of the renegotiation of rules about work through their ability to mobilize power resources that translate into social power in given contexts. Even if at first glance the context does not seem that favourable to workers and their organizations, we have argued that the process is much more open-ended. In particular, local unions able to enlarge their relative margin of manoeuvre through the mobilization of three kinds of power resources are better able to influence the processes of change in the workplace. On the other hand, those unions unable to draw on new power resources are more likely to experience the kind of unilateral employer actions that typify the stereotypical view of globalization that we presented at the outset of this chapter. The challenge for trade unionists is to think more systematically about the kinds of resources likely to enhance worker voice in globalized workplaces.

This argument is not merely theoretical, as our research results from Quebec systematically point to the importance of internal solidarity, external solidarity, and strategic capacity as sources of power likely to reinforce the role of the union in workplace change. In this respect, our research partnerships with different unions in Quebec merely highlight and seek to systematize what innovative unions are already doing in many regions of Canada. These results lay down the gauntlet for trade unionists to identify paths to renewal through the development of their power resources. They also suggest that unions should be developing education programs and services designed to nurture and develop these power resources. Our studies in Quebec consistently point to the importance of these paths to renewal. There is little doubt that many of these same observations can be generalized to other union movements also faced with the challenge of globalized workplaces.

Notes

1. We want to thank the many trade unionists in Quebec and elsewhere who, in the context of multiple studies and research partnerships with their union organizations, have generously shared their insights, experiences and time in order to help us better understand some of the dynamics of union renewal in a global economy. The research presented in this chapter has been supported by grants from both the Fonds de recherche sur la société et la culture (FQRSC) and the Social Sciences and Humanities Research Council of Canada (SSHRC). Particular thanks to Claude Rioux for his comments.

2. We have also conducted a comparative analysis of local unions in Mexico and Quebec and found strong support for this argument in two quite different institutional contexts (Lévesque and Murray 2005).

3. This study was conducted by the polling firm CROP in June 1998. In all, 1,196 persons participated in the survey, of which 442 were unionized. Some of the data presented in this chapter come from this FTQ-CROP study.

References

Bélanger, Jacques, Anthony Giles, and Gregor Murray. 2002. Towards a New Production Model: Potentialities, Tensions and Contradictions. In *Work and Employment Relations in the High Performance Workplace*, ed. Gregor Murray, Jacques Bélanger, Anthony Giles, and Paul-André Lapointe, 15-71. London, U.K. and New York, NY: Continuum.

Bélanger, Jacques, and Christian Thueroz. 1998. La recodification de la relation d'emploi. *Revue française de sociologie* 39 (3): 469-494.

Charest, Jean. 2004. Workforce Sectoral Partnerships in Quebec: A Positive Assessment. *Workplace Gazette* 7 (3): 61-70.

Dicken, Peter. 2003. *Global Shift: Reshaping the Global Economic Map of the 21st Century.* 4th edition. London: Sage Publications.

Fédération des travailleurs et travailleuses du Québec (FTQ). 1999. *Pour rétablir un rapport de forces: les alliances locales.* Montréal: Fédération des travailleurs et travailleuses du Québec.

———. 2001. *La mondialisation: la comprendre et agir syndicalement.* Montréal: Fédération des travailleurs et travailleuses du Québec.

Kumar, Pradeep, and Gregor Murray. 2001. Union Bargaining Priorities in the New Economy: Results from the 2000 HRDC Survey on Innovation and Change in Labour Organizations in Canada. *Workplace Gazette* 4 (4): 43-55.

Labrosse, Alexis. 2005. *La présence syndicale au Québec en 2004.* Quebec: Ministère du Travail, Direction de la recherche et de l'évaluation. Available at www.travail.gouv.qc.ca/actualite/index.html.

Lapointe, Paul-André, Christian Lévesque, Gregor Murray, and Francine Jacques. 2000. *Les innovations en milieu de travail dans l'industrie des équipements de transport terrestre au Québec: Rapport synthèse.* Québec: Comité sur l'organisation du travail de la Table de concertation de l'industrie.

Lapointe, Paul-André, Christian Lévesque, Gregor Murray, and Catherine Le Capitaine. 2001. *Les innovations en milieu de travail dans le secteur des industries métallurgiques au Québec.* Québec: Groupe de travail sur les ressources humaines de la Table de concertation de l'industrie.

Lévesque, Christian, and Pascale Coté. 1999. Le travail en équipe dans un univers de production allégée: contrainte ou opportunité? *Relations industrielles/Industrial Relations* 54 (1): 71-101.

Lévesque, Christian, and Gregor Murray. 1998. La régulation paritaire à l'épreuve de la mondialisation. *Relations industrielles/Industrial Relations* 53 (1): 90-122.

———. 2002. Local Versus Global: Activating Local Union Power in the Global Economy. *Labor Studies Journal* 27 (3): 39-65.

———. 2003. Le pouvoir syndical dans l'économie mondiale: clés de lecture pour un renouveau. *La Revue de l'IRES* 41:149-176.

———. 2005. Union Involvement in Workplace Change: A Comparative Study of Local Unions in Canada and Mexico. *British Journal of Industrial Relations* 43 (3): 489-514.

Lévesque, Christian, Gregor Murray, and Catherine Lecapitaine. 2004. *Enquête sur le renouveau syndical auprès des personnes déléguées d'établissement des syndicats membres de la Fédération des syndicats de l'enseignement (FSE): Résultats descriptifs.* Centre de recherche interuniversitaire sur la mondialisation et le travail (CRIMT).

———. 2005. *Transformations du vécu syndical des membres CSN du Mouvement Desjardins.* Montreal: Fédération du Commerce de la CSN.

Lévesque, Christian, Gregor Murray, and Stéphane Lequeux. Forthcoming. Union Disaffection and Social Identity: Democracy as a Source of Union Revitalization. *Work and Occupations* 32.

Morissette, René, Grant Schellenberg, and Anick Johnson. 2005. Unionization: Divergent Trends. *Perspectives.* Statistics Canada, Cat. 75-001-XIF. 5-12.

Murray, Gregor, Christian Lévesque, and Guylaine Vallée. 2000. The Re-Regulation of Labour in a Global Context: Conceptual Vignettes from Canada. *The Journal of Industrial Relations* 42 (2): 234-257.

Sklair, Leslie. 2001. *The Transnational Capitalist Class.* Oxford, U.K.: Blackwell.

PART II
Case Studies on Union Renewal

Chapter 6
The BCGEU: The Road to Renewal

GARY STEEVES

The B.C. Government and Service Employees Union (BCGEU) celebrated its 63rd birthday on February 19, 2005. The union has struggled with renewal in recent years and this case study outlines and analyzes the elements of that struggle.

Structure

The BCGEU began as a "union among government employees." It organized employees of the B.C. government service into geographic "branches." All provincial government employees in Victoria, for example, belonged to the Victoria branch, regardless of their occupation, the government ministry in which they worked, or the particular job they performed. Branches carried out the same role as geographic locals or lodges in other union structures.

The branch structure was replaced with a new "component" structure in the early 1970s. Created primarily to prepare for collective bargaining with the B.C. government, the new structure followed occupational or 'industrial' lines. All clerical workers were in the same component to facilitate discussion of clerical issues without interference from other occupational groups. The number of components varied over the years, but typically groups such as corrections workers, hospital workers, and liquor store workers had their own components.

To create a locally-based democratic structure, the union divided British Columbia into twelve "areas." Any component with 50 or more members in a particular area had a local in that area. The notion of province-wide locals with members in Prince George travelling to Vancouver to attend a local membership meeting was not acceptable. Local representatives from all locals in a component met to elect a component executive. The chairperson of the component executive represented the component on the provincial executive of the BCGEU. In the early 1990s, larger locals and components were permitted additional representatives on the component executive and the provincial executive, in keeping with a "rep-by-pop" system.

This hierarchical "industrial" component structure remains today.

History

The history of the BCGEU from its formation in the early 1940s until the mid-1980s was very much a top-down command-driven organization. In the 1940s, this was necessary to stabilize a fragile organization working to organize all government employees. A federated structure with autonomous locals was initially established, but quickly abandoned due to the weakness and isolation of many smaller branches.

In the 1950s, the fierce battle to acquire recognition and bargaining rights from W.A.C. Bennett's Social Credit government required a strong central leadership. By the 1960s, a deflated and under-resourced organization had little energy to defend itself against a vicious Bennett government counterattack intended to punish the union for its 1959 illegal strike. The loss of dues check-off, the termination of many activists and leaders, and the absence of any legislative support for public sector unionization presented formidable obstacles for the union. Nevertheless, even with a shop-steward-led voluntary dues collection system in place, the union maintained a rate of over 90% paid-up members in the government service.

The 1970s saw new leadership and energy in the union. The head-to-head battle for recognition with Bennett's weakened administration resumed. The test of wills with the Socred cabinet required a strong centralized union for strategic as well as tactical reasons. The union grew from 16,000 members in 1970 to 45,000 in 1979 as the strong central command leadership achieved results.

The election of Dave Barrett's NDP government in 1974 brought the modernization of labour relations and full collective bargaining rights for government employees, but the 1980s brought the maturation of the BCGEU. Bill Bennett's Social Credit government attempted to de-index public sector pension plans in 1981, and the BCGEU led a series of illegal walk-outs that forced the government to back down. The following year, the BCGEU engaged in its first full-scale province-wide legal strike. In many ways, the 1982 strike signalled the completion of the evolution of the organization from a small association to a large modern union.

Having reached organizational maturity, the philosophical shaping of the union was solidified the following year with Operation Solidarity. The BCGEU was cast into a prominent role as a political force within the highly polarized world of B.C. politics. The union saw itself clearly as a social union, rejecting the more traditional role of "business unionism" which it had assumed in the 1940s with its membership in the Trades and Labour Congress of Canada.

With the 1984 adoption of a policy paper entitled "Building for the Future," the union opened its doors to workers in both the public and private sectors. It launched major organizing campaigns in key service sectors, and the resulting successes brought a further restructuring of the union. By the close of the 1990s, membership in the BCGEU approached 60,000, with six components in the direct government service and five non-government components. Non-government components, some of which were in the broader public sector, represented about half of the total union membership.

For nearly 50 years, a high degree of membership involvement had been maintained through organizing campaigns, legal and illegal strikes, and political struggles. Renewal, as we understand it today, was not an issue. The strong central command model had maintained a very active and involved membership through its struggle to survive. Restructuring had played a role in facilitating activism, but the political, bargaining and organizing necessities had fuelled membership activism.

The union responded by developing programs to support membership activism. Programs such as the Temporary Staff Rep program and the Train the Trainers program, engaged hundreds of members in active roles within the union. The Temp Staff Rep program gave members the opportunity to serve for short periods as full-time Representatives in the union's area offices, while the Health and Safety Train the Trainers program broadened the base of membership involvement in occupational health and safety (OH&S) education and regulatory enforcement.

As the 1990s unfolded, the future looked much like the recent past. The union continued its aggressive organizing as its reputation in the community as a powerful social ally precluded any serious worry about "renewal." The union's organizing efforts in the first half of the decade averaged over 2,000 new members a year, but by the end of the decade that had tapered off to about 1,500.

Present profile

The BCGEU of the 21st century is a large, diverse service sector union with nearly 60,000 members. Its membership is almost evenly divided between direct government employees and non-government workers. Within the non-government membership, the union represents non-profit service workers in health, education, and social services; employees of for-profit corporations; financial institution workers; and employees in the hospitality sector. The union has 11 components, six representing direct government employees, and five representing non-government workers.

There are currently 112 locals and nearly 600 bargaining units in the BCGEU.

The union employs over 200 staff, more than half of whom are Staff Representatives engaged in research, education, advocacy, and bargaining roles. It has a full-time President and Secretary-Treasurer, with a governing provincial executive of 19 people, including four provincial Vice-Presidents. The President, Secretary-Treasurer, and the four provincial Vice-Presidents are elected at the union's triennial constitutional convention.

The annual operating budget of the union is approximately $38 million. It supports 13 union offices, including 12 "area offices" which are located in major regional centres throughout B.C.

The need for union renewal

In 1996 the union's Executive Committee examined a number of issues which indicated a much different future. It was felt that status quo may not meet the emerging needs in the context of economic pressures on union resources, an aging membership, the loss of local and workplace leaders, demands for deeper involvement in community and political affairs, and the necessity to mobilize against tight-fisted government policies.

Aging activists were retiring, and government funding cuts meant both government membership and non-government members, particularly in the non-government organization (NGO) sector, were being laid off. The recruitment and training of new activists had significant costs associated with it. Membership loss meant dues revenue was levelling off and could decrease. Components wanted a larger share of dues revenue, while organizing was becoming more difficult and costly. To heighten the Executive's concern, the defeat of the NDP government could reasonably be predicted, and the pending political campaign would increase financial pressures on the union.

The BCGEU Executive Committee took its deliberations on the need for change to the 1997 Strategic Planning Session of senior staff and Provincial Executive (PE) members. It was talking about "renewal," although that terminology was not used. The session concluded that the union must review its "servicing methods," suggesting that a new "servicing model" may be in order.

The union moved slowly into its future renewal strategy. An examination of its current servicing methods was carried out and, in a report to the 1998 Strategic Planning Session, senior officers and staff accepted the need for change. The report recommended that "pilot projects be undertaken to test assumptions and new approaches to servicing." In September, 1998, the Provincial Executive formally approved the recommendations to engage in a series of pilot projects.

Designing the program objectives

On November 27, 1998, the BCGEU Provincial Executive approved a list of 11 locals, one provincial government ministry, two government health institutions, and five other bargaining units to take part in the project as pilots.

Five objectives were established for these pilot projects. They were : 1) to increase the sense ownership of local activists in their union; 2) to increase the sense of ownership by local activists for the administration of their own collective agreements; 3) to improve and broaden the skill level of local union activists; 4) to maximize the utilization of union staff skills and expertise; and 5) to increase the authority and accountability of locals in the union.

The establishment of the five objectives was an important transition point to shift the mindset of "membership services" to that of "membership involvement" and "union renewal." Serious deliberation went into determining appropriate objectives. To a large extent, these deliberations moulded the growing body of thought that saw renewal as a more important objective than merely altering the union's servicing methodologies.

Objective #1: Reinforcing members' ownership of their union

The debate around the first objective of increasing the sense of ownership of members in their union was indicative of the movement away from "operational methodologies" to "movement renewal." The discussions centred on the organizational culture of reliance on union staff to do everything. The question was: "What kind of union did participants want?" Was the union like a machine into which you paid your money, pulled the handle and out popped services? Or was it a living organism made up of thousands of people active in the pursuit of social and economic change? Those at the centre of the debate were unanimous in supporting the latter proposition. The first objective enjoyed broad support.

Objective #2: Expanding local activists' sense of
responsibility for their own collective agreements

The second objective was closely related to the first, and enjoyed equally broad support. Virtually everyone understood it was impossible to hire enough staff to do everything. For locals too unmotivated to elect a shop steward, the organizational culture, financial reality, and dominant philosophy of the union provided little comfort. The notion that the union pay staff representatives to be shop stewards was firmly rejected, and the educational support required to achieve this objective was consistent with the BCGEU's generous and unwavering commitment to membership education.

Almost everyone participating in the leadership debate over the direction to be pursued was united in the belief that tangible benefits would be derived from this objective. Even those uncomfortable with the road to renewal believed in the second objective.

Objective #3: Expanding the experience and skills of stewards and local officers

The third objective was also consistent with the union's commitment to membership education. The turnover of shop stewards and local officers and the need to use education as a fundamental part of any renewal process made this an obvious objective. Even if the pilot projects failed, no one would argue that a more highly skilled and experienced body of stewards, committee members or local officers was a bad thing. The third objective was included, however, to recognize the clear connection to the first two objectives. After all, why increase skill levels and leadership capabilities if there was no role for them to exercise those skills and responsibilities in their workplaces, their locals, or their communities? The third objective also enjoyed unanimous support.

Objective #4: More effective utilization of union staff's time and expertise

The fourth objective was more contentious and had a very specific rationale. If renewal was to succeed, it needed the active support of the union's staff. The staff of the union had to know that renewal did not mean the elimination of their traditional leadership role within the BCGEU.

A large number of BCGEU staff had come through the ranks of the BCGEU while others had been recruited from outside the union due to their skills and accomplishments in the labour or social movements. The average age of staff was increasing, and many had been through the numerous struggles of the Social Credit years. Collectively, they were highly skilled, knowledgeable, and experienced. They were an important dynamic in the success or failure of any initiative within the union.

Equally as important, the staff was overworked and had endless demands on their time and attention. Performing shop steward and local officer duties detracted from their work. Clarifying roles and focusing expertise needed to be addressed.

Staff support for the renewal initiative was crucial. The fourth objective was a clear signal to staff that they were important to a renewed union and that their contribution was important.

Objective #5: Increasing the authority and accountability of BCGEU locals

The fifth objective was the most daunting and problematic. It created the most angst for senior leaders as it challenged the history and structure of the organization. It was, however, important to local members as it represented a commitment that there were no predetermined outcomes for the pilot projects. The road to renewal was to be a course set by them. Activists were free collectively to test their wings howsoever they deemed necessary.

Designing the pilot projects

The approach taken to the pilot projects was very important. Participants were to determine specific tasks to be carried out in pursuit of one or more of the objectives. The tasks chosen were completely up to the participants.

Considerable effort went into choosing these tasks. Meetings were held in each pilot project for all stewards, committee people, and local executive members. These meetings were a minimum of one day in duration, but in some cases they lasted three days. It was essential that all tasks chosen come from the members and leaders in the particular locals, bargaining units, and workplaces. There were no top-down edicts, and only tasks which enjoyed local activists' support were included in the project.

A tracking and evaluation sheet was designed to monitor pilot project progress. The aim was to report on the specific objectives, goals set, the tasks chosen to pursue an objective, the evaluation criteria used to determine whether or not the task moved the union closer to its objective, target date for completion, who bore responsibility for carrying out the task, and the current status of the task. Although the union staff assigned to "service" the particular local or group was responsible for submitting the tracking and evaluation sheets, the staff was encouraged to make the completion of these periodic reports a part of the locals' review of pilot project progress. This was the closest the project came to a bureaucratic structure—a fact that later analysis would identify as both a blessing and a curse.

Initial general findings

Many pilots demonstrated very good results, while others failed completely. Specific reasons were identified for the successes and failures. None of the failures was attributed to a lack of desire by members and activists.

At Riverview Hospital, for example, a plan was announced to downsize the institution and transfer it out of the provincial government service. Understandably, this caused great concern among members. The complete attention of local activists was concentrated on the work of the local reorganization committee which was negotiating options for affected members, including alternate employment and severance options. The pilot project was simply not a priority for local activists or the membership at Riverview Hospital.

At the Saanich Indian School Board, the focus was on gaining a first collective agreement. The formal pilot project took a back seat.

Although these pilots 'failed' in terms of formal evaluations, the principles of broadening the base of activism and having workplace activists taking on more authority to design their own strategies and solutions were still applied to the reorganization and bargaining processes, with some success.

It should be noted that, in choosing locals, bargaining units or other workplaces for pilot project status, the union deliberately chose groups where serious concerns existed as to the appropriateness of the project. It was believed that, unless a broad spectrum of situations was captured by the pilot projects, the successes and failures could not be properly assessed.

In general terms, the findings of the pilot projects were positive and provocative. They challenged members as to the type of union they wanted and the organizational culture they wanted to encourage. Changing the mechanics of union operation was relatively straightforward; changing organizational culture and dynamics was quite another matter.

General observations

Pilot project experiences were instructive. Some activists and members said, "We pay dues, hire staff, pay them well, and expect them to look after us. Why should we do their job?" Some staff thought the union was trying to make Staff Representatives out of every steward. Such suspicions and misunderstandings had to be dealt with quickly and directly. The BCGEU did so, and such views proved not to be a problem in the overall renewal initiative.

It was also obvious that many local leaders relied totally on Staff Representatives for direction. In local discussions among pilot project participants to determine what tasks would be used to pursue the objectives, local leaders frequently deferred to the union staff as to what tasks should be chosen. Union staff generally refused to do so, and reinforced the notion that the local activists were free to make decisions about their priorities.

Another issue centred on the difference between seeking direction and consulting with others in the union before making your own decision. Some fear existed that local leaders would do something which would compromise other locals or the union-at-large. Getting permission was the safe thing to do. The pilot projects, however, wanted to take members out of their comfort zone and provide greater opportunity for activists to assume responsibility and make their own decisions. Consultation was encouraged, while mistakes were expected and tolerated.

Although the pilot projects reinforced the BCGEU's belief that union education and training was fundamentally important, the pilots demonstrated a need to rethink and restructure its education program. Curriculum content, the range of courses, and the method of delivery were all called into question. Many local activists were eager to break out of the old mould but feared their lack of training would simply cause them to fail. Consequently, most pilot projects placed a huge emphasis on improving both hard and soft skills for stewards and local executive members. These findings eventually prompted a revision and expansion of the union's education and training program.

The general conclusion was that the renewal initiative was the right thing for the union to pursue. Of more significance, however, was the conclusion that "servicing methods" was no longer the issue. Union renewal had become the real issue.

Specific results

The specific findings on each of the five objectives were very informative. In terms of increasing the sense of ownership of local activists for their local and their collective agreements, activists were doing more and doing it well. The fears of failure simply did not overcome the energy and interest in increasing their union activity and recruiting others to join the activist ranks. Attendance at membership meetings increased as local executives canvassed members for meeting agenda topics. The number of vacant executive and steward positions declined. Local executive and committee meetings became "more interesting," were better attended, and included educational activities on their local meeting agendas.

Communications and organizational links within multi-bargaining-unit locals improved, and activists recognized these new arrangements as their own.

Activists in most pilot projects felt more willing and able to solve workplace "beefs," and phone calls to union offices for the assistance of a Staff Representative declined. In one project, where the workplace had a history of dozens of grievances a month, the bargaining unit committee arranged regular stewards/managers meetings to solve issues coming forward before they became formal grievances. This replaced a Staff Representative conducting case-by-case meetings with management. Stewards felt a sense of power, and an analysis revealed a high "win rate" with very high quality outcomes on grievance settlements.

Increasing the skill levels of activists was a huge success. Each pilot project had conducted a "needs assessment" of the education and training needs of union activists. Courses, seminars, and discussion groups on topics identified by local activists were quickly organized. The union established a budget to pay for the additional educational activities, and the union's education curriculum was amended to include new courses and seminars on such matters as time management, political action, and communications strategies. Union staff took on support roles as workplace leaders tested their new skills. The results showed a stunning change in some pilots.

Union staff stopped doing stewards work and local officer duties. Some pilot projects reported reduced demands on staff time as far as grievance advice was concerned. The nature of the Staff Reps' work changed in all the successful pilot projects. Staff had more time for training and supporting activists, providing education, and handling more complex matters. Stewards did more of the routine contract interpretation and dispute resolution work in the workplace.

It should be noted that union staff workloads initially increased at the start of the pilot projects. The increased load of facilitating the start-up of the projects was a harsh reality of staff life, but seemed to diminish dramatically as the local and its leaders assumed an increase in their authority and range of responsibilities. It was clear, however, that the union needed to plan more effectively for these start-up periods and provide more support for overworked staff.

The union made no effort to limit what increase in authority locals might assume. This did create some discomfort between some locals and their component executive. Most of these, however, involved the normal political jealousies and rivalries found in any union structure. Taking ownership of your issues and being accountable for the outcomes does not always come easily, especially in highly political organizations. The union must, however, recognize this dynamic and support the champions of change.

The pilot projects demonstrated that, as local unions assumed more responsibility for their own affairs, they soon came to consider these responsibilities as their regular business. As one local executive member said in a debriefing session. "It doesn't matter what the union decides as a result of the pilot projects, we're not going back to the old way of doing things."

The union found instances where local structures were dysfunctional. In two particular components, the need for structural change was evident. This issue was diverted to a separate process which had been set up to examine a variety of constitutional and structural issues for the union's next constitutional convention.

In evaluating how well locals and bargaining units accepted greater responsibility and accountability, the question of how one defines local accountability kept reoccurring. Implications for union structure, financial arrangements, and constitutional change proved to be major distractions for those pushing renewal. The old debate of local autonomy versus "one union with one voice" further plagued discussions concerning the fifth objective.

Recommendations

In May, 2000, the Provincial Executive adopted the 22 recommendations contained in the report on the pilot projects, and decided to implement them immediately. The recommendations called for the continuation and expansion of the pilot projects, and contained nine recommendations on the functions and responsibilities of locals, executive bodies, and shop stewards. Many of these were building blocks to support the renewal process and its five objectives.

Eight recommendations were made on the union's education program, calling for more resources, increased opportunities to participate, and an expanded curriculum of courses and programs. Three recommendations pertained to the operation of the union's network of area offices, and were support measures to promote the vision of union renewal.

The recommendations were extensive and far-reaching in terms of the BCGEU experience. They generated debate, particularly among locals which had not been previously involved in a pilot project and thus had no benefit of the valuable experience the pilot projects had generated. At the component executive level of the union, there was nervousness about the possibility of change outside their control. The debate was legitimate and intense.

One local, which had been designated as a pilot project, retained their view that "union staff were paid to do these things," while numerous other locals asked to be included in the expansion of the pilot projects. It was clear, however, that solid support existed for the renewal initiative.

Implementation of the 22 recommendations began immediately on a union-wide basis. The expanded pilot projects were given a mandate to push the initiative even further than the boundaries of the 22 recommendations. The idea was to have pilot projects on the leading edge of renewal, while the rest of the union worked at implementing the proven achievements of the pilot projects.

The BCGEU Executive, for the first time, gave the renewal initiative a name. It was called the Workplace Leadership Program (WLP).

Implementation challenges

The process of implementing the 22 recommendations was very slow work. Many locals and bargaining units, not involved in the initial pilot projects, had paid little attention to the pilot projects. A great deal of orientation was necessary in these locals, and the burden of the start-up efforts again fell on union staff and a handful of elected officers. There was, however, a genuine excitement for the Workplace Leadership Program, especially among the locals and bargaining units mandated to try new initiatives to broaden participation and activism in the union.

A committee was appointed to receive progress reports, clear impediments to progress, and make sure adequate resources were available for the WLP. Further, the committee was to be the clearing house for examining key questions raised in the renewal program in general, and the expanded pilot projects in particular.

The Campbell government attack

On May 21, 2001, the election of Gordon Campbell's B.C. Liberal government turned the province's social and political scene upside down. The threat to the BCGEU membership was unprecedented. An across-the-board tax cut plunged the province into a record deficit, providing the rationale for massive program, service, and employment cuts.

Within a year and a half, the government closed 12 hospitals, dozens of emergency and operating rooms; eliminated 3,300 acute and long-term-care beds; closed 113 public schools; eliminated 2,500 full-time teaching positions; increased Medicare premiums by 50%; cut corporate taxes by $790 million; and began the layoff of 8,700 provincial government employees. The BCGEU was staggered by the sheer volume of the cuts.

Collective agreement provisions were eliminated by legislative order, including wage and benefit cuts of up to 15% for health and social service workers, and the elimination of class size restrictions for teachers in K-to-12 schools. Privatized health care workers saw their wages cut on average from $19 an hour to as low as $9.50 an hour.

Privatization, contracting-out, and de-unionization initiatives in various forms were undertaken in every corner of the public sector. B.C. Ferries, B.C. Rail, and one-third of B.C. Hydro were privatized. Some $700 million in public health services were privatized, while legal aid and child care funding were each slashed by

40%. Government revenue collection services, as well as Medicare and Pharmacare administration, were contracted out to U.S. companies. In total, $1.3 billion worth of government services were contracted to American firms.

For government employees, the funding cuts and 8,700 layoffs meant the closure of numerous courthouses and correctional facilities; the loss of 70% of fish, wildlife and habitat protection staff, and the elimination of Victims' Services and the B.C. Human Rights Commission. It meant the closure of 46 provincial parks and the elimination of the Child, Youth and Family Advocate. Funding cuts reduced the operations of the offices of the Ombudsman, the Information and Privacy Commissioner, and Elections B.C. On average, provincial Ministries had their staff and budgets cut by 35%.

The union launched a full-scale fightback campaign. It involved, among other tactics, the organization of mass rallies, demonstrations, and illegal job action, and became the vehicle for membership mobilization and involvement. Formal evaluation, training, and support for WLP, however, fell by the wayside as mobilization and action replaced carefully planned and supported steps aimed at changing the culture of the union.

Although the campaign to stop Campbell provided real opportunities to mobilize the membership (a key goal of WLP), the government cuts, layoffs, and terminations decimated the local leaders who were driving the Workplace Leadership Program. By 2003, the devastating effects on local leadership were comprehensive and debilitating. In some cases, entire local executives were wiped out and whole new activist teams had to be organized. The union concentrated its efforts on fighting the Campbell Liberals, and the Workplace Leadership Program drifted.

Reflections

A 2003 report to the union's Provincial Executive took stock of the Workplace Leadership Program and what had occurred to date. Although local executives, stewards, Staff Representatives, and other activists made extensive efforts to implement the original 22 recommendations of the WLP, the Campbell attack was a huge setback. The loss of large numbers of stewards, committee people, and local executives meant recruitment and training for organizational survival trumped all other activities. The union sought feedback from WLP leaders on how to revitalize the renewal agenda.

In late July of 2003, union staff from all over the province met to discuss the situation and concluded the obvious: that the WLP was valuable and necessary to the future of the union. Much of the momentum created around the initial recommendations had been lost. The Campbell government's attack had decimated the ranks of local leaders who had the skill, enthusiasm, and spirit for the transformation of their union. Some fundamental decisions had to be made on how to re-invigorate the WLP, and the staff recommended that a formal audit of pilot project locals be conducted.

By September of that year, the audit was complete and it called for the identification of obstacles to moving forward with the WLP so that resources could be focused accordingly. It advocated the development of a revised plan of action. The report of the September review went to the Provincial Executive and outlined the situation in stark terms.

The report reiterated the importance of the Workplace Leadership Program to the future of the union and outlined the devastation that the Campbell attack had caused to the program and the union. It said that rebuilding renewal capacity was more than simply a function of time, money, and resource, that it was also a matter of leadership commitment. It observed: "With large numbers of new activists, stewards, and local officers, a renewed leadership commitment is seen in many quarters as critical to re-energizing the program."

The boiling issues

The call for a reconstituted political commitment was really a call for dealing with the deeper, more specific issues which had developed before and subsequent to the government's attack. Issues such as constitutional change, the appropriateness of union structures, the need for political support at the component executive level, as well as the Provincial Executive and staff relations, were all rolled into the call for a renewed commitment from the elected leadership.

What are the limits of local responsibility? Are fully autonomous locals the goal? If not, what is the real objective? Such questions were important because they called for consideration of numerous related matters. It would be difficult, some argued, to motivate local activists if the role and responsibility they are being asked to assume is unclear.

Structural and organizational questions persisted. How would a redistribution of power to the local level affect bargaining units, components, the structure of executives, financial policies, and other arrangements? The list seemed endless, but some refused to become mired in detail. Senior leaders saw the "bigger picture" and recognized the attempt to put building blocks in place to make the union truly membership driven need not ignite a constitutional debate. Constitutional, structural, and financial questions could be sorted out later. Some outside of the senior leadership ranks privately remarked that, if the WLP meant changing the union structure, constitution, and financial arrangements, they were opposed. Getting locals to be more active was one thing, but turning the union inside out was quite another.

The senior leadership of the union understood fundamentally that building support for local initiative and action depended in no small measure on the locals being confident that union headquarters and the Provincial Executive would support them.

The question of a political commitment was also meant to address the actions of a couple of Provincial Executive members. Although PE members had expressed support for WLP around the Executive table, some were somewhat less than supportive when visiting and addressing their locals. A practical political reality in any union, but one that had resulted in conflicting messages to local activists.

A significant disconnection between component executives and the WLP was associated with the question of political power. Component executives are the political power centres of the BCGEU. Thirteen of the 19 members of the union's

Provincial Executive are representatives of components. Moving any Provincial Executive initiative through to success requires the active participation, if not the passive acquiescence, of the component executives. In the case of the WLP, the PE had adopted a program which was centred on the locals and which devoted resources, time and attention directly to local activists. Some component executive members felt that encouraging locals to take more control meant ignoring components. The perception that the Workplace Leadership Program had bypassed component executive bodies was a real problem.

In hindsight, the lack of attention to component executives was a mistake, one that hindered the progress of the renewal movement.

Another reality percolating under the surface of the call for a political commitment dealt with staff relations. Historically, the staff of the BCGEU has been a central part of the union's leadership team. Although growth and routine over the years had prompted some staff to see their role in more narrow technical terms, many wanted the staff collective to remain a key element in the leadership core. Some staff feared a loss of influence in union affairs, and thus the dynamic of the WLP was coated with uncertainty.

The boiling issues of local authority, constitutional and structural change, component and Provincial Executive support, and staff relations were not all that stood between renewal and the status quo.

Re-charging the program

The Executive Committee decided to place the September 2003 report before the Provincial Executive in December of that year. A very significant portion of time was allotted for discussion and debate of the report. Some progress was made on the key underlying issues, but much of the enthusiasm for Workplace Leadership was unquestionably a victim of the Campbell attack. Many executive members saw WLP as another program to be discussed while their real concern was for the thousands of members they represented who were taking pay cuts or losing their jobs. The anti-Campbell campaign was foremost in the Executive's mind, and issues pertaining to the survival of the union took precedence.

Attempting to reconcile the important questions associated with the Workplace Leadership Program would be challenging enough in normal times. Asking the senior executive body to do so while their components struggled with massive job losses and pay cuts was unrealistic.

The Provincial Executive did make a re-commitment to the Workplace Leadership Program. With little time remaining in Campbell's mandate and a May 17 election date, the WLP continued to simmer rather than boil. There is no question that the leadership of the BCGEU remains deeply committed to the objectives of renewal. The practical realities and demands faced by the union's membership, however, remain a powerful force militating against progress on the road to renewal.

Observations and lessons

Any proposal for change must be carefully managed because most people react suspiciously to such proposals. Providing comfort levels for some is often enough, but messaging is critical. It must cater to members' understanding of their union reality, give them a reason to support change, and recruit their active cooperation and participation.

Champions of change must be developed in every corner of a union's structure. Like any organizing campaign, leadership for renewal must ideally be found throughout the organization and be relied upon to foster support for renewal. Simply broadening the base of support within the union for a renewal proposition without champions, advocates, or leaders in every corner will lessen the prospect of success. In the BCGEU case, efforts were concentrated on the pilot projects. Although general information and updates were made available to other locals and components of the union, the lack of developing "champions" at the component level exposed the Workplace Leadership Program to all manner of distractions.

Political realities in any organization cannot be ignored. Although the BCGEU experience generally dealt with these realities in an effective and up-front fashion, greater political attention needed to be paid to the sensitive relationship between the senior decision-making body and other levels of authority. This will maximize the potential for broadening participation and developing more active political support and "champions."

Pilot projects are a very good way of starting slowly and maximizing chances of success. It allows assumptions to be tested, support to be built, and provides an excellent basis for analysis and future decision-making. It also permits development of building blocks for expansion of renewal initiatives throughout the organization. Most importantly, however, it increases the opportunity for the road to renewal to be membership-driven. The BCGEU experience with pilot projects was extremely positive.

If there was only one conclusion to be drawn from the BCGEU experience with the road to renewal, it would be that any such initiative, regardless of its scope or design, must be membership-driven. It is fundamental to everything renewal stands for. The BCGEU placed complete and unfettered ability with pilot project participants to structure their projects. The mantra of "it must enjoy membership support" was more than a hollow saying.

Regardless of design of any initiative chosen to pursue renewal, the union must adequately resource its renewal initiatives. Not only does this demonstrate organizational commitment, but it also offsets the real dangers of "champions of change" getting burned out or browned off. Giving people the tools to inspire change is critical. Budget development, however, will be a key battleground for both advocates and opponents of renewal.

It became very clear in the BCGEU experience that changing union structure is a very difficult and contentious notion without first establishing a culture of renewal in the organization. Debates over future structure will divert attention from the more immediate demands of accommodating renewal. If unchecked, the side-bar debates will undermine the practical aspects of any renewal initiative.

The last point to be made on lessons to be learned from the BCGEU experience pertains to the unique culture of union organizations. Unions are high-energy, small "p" political organizations. They have within them an element that will seize on any potential to destabilize the leadership structure for reasons unrelated to anything other than a personal grudge. Attacks on individual leaders or activists for personal reasons are, unfortunately, an all-too-common an occurrence. The work of renewal must be insulated as much as possible from the regular cut-and-thrust of union politics. Fortunately, the BCGEU did not, with one minor exception, experience such ill-founded activity in the early stages. Dealing with the one incident, however, sensitized the BCGEU leadership to the potential and made those involved turn their mind to effective strategies to support the champions of change.

Conclusion

Renewal is a democratic, membership-driven belief in the possibility of engaging more effectively in the world around us. Its failure is a failure of people to take advantage of an opportunity to shape their own future.

Chapter 7
Union Renewal and CUPE

JANE STINSON AND MORNA BALLANTYNE

The Canadian Union of Public Employees (CUPE) has a long, rich, and varied history of engaging in practices that contribute to union renewal. How long, and what examples, depends on how union renewal is defined.

Some define union renewal as programs to renew (i.e., increase) union membership by organizing unorganized workers into the union. For some American unions, concerned about drastically falling levels of unionization, union renewal programs mean devoting much of the union's resources to organizing new members.

Increasing union density through organizing more members is one important element of union renewal. But union renewal should also include programs and policies to increase the internal strength of the union by building stronger union connections with members and increasing their engagement in union activities.

We find it useful to look at union renewal as being comprised of three fundamental cornerstones that are mutually reinforcing in building union power. There needs to be a vision, goal, or common project that the union is working together to achieve. The ability to achieve it requires internal solidarity—which means both working together and having active member engagement. External solidarity is the other important cornerstone. This includes alliances with other organizations and unions in the community and around the globe.[1]

In this paper, we use this theoretical conception of union renewal as a lens through which to view the national priorities of CUPE over the past 25 years, as articulated mainly through national policy papers and a series of union programs.

Background on CUPE, Canada's largest union

CUPE is Canada's largest trade union, with about 540,000 members (CUPE 2004a). It represents mainly blue- and white-collar workers who provide local government services, education support services, health and social services. As well, CUPE represents provincial hydro workers in Ontario, Manitoba, and Quebec, flight attendants, and workers with non-governmental organizations. Women make up more than half the union's membership.

As the Table 1 below shows the membership of the union has grown many fold since its inception in 1963. In particular the number of workers of colour has increased significantly over the last decade, especially in Canada's largest urban centres.

CUPE's membership is large, diverse, and spread across the country from St. John's, Newfoundland/Labrador, to Victoria, British Columbia. There is at least one CUPE local in most communities in Canada, except in the far north where federal public sector workers dominate. Approximately one in 25 working Canadian is a CUPE member.

Table 1: CUPE Membership, 1963-2004

Year	Number of Members
1963	80,000
1969	130,000
1975	210,000
1980	267,407
1985	306,835
1990	397,785
1995	452,711
2000	497,068
2004	538,850

Source: CUPE Membership Reports

CUPE members provide services to people from cradle to grave. You will find CUPE members working in maternity wards and digging graves in city cemeteries. CUPE members could look after your child in day care, in school as the education assistant or school secretary, and at university as a teaching assistant or sessional lecturer. CUPE members probably staff your community arena, fix your town's water and power lines and potholes, process your municipal taxes, and uphold public health regulations. They look after children and adults with developmental disabilities; provide foster care services, and staff battered women's shelters. They clean, prepare food, do the laundry, and provide other health care services in hospitals and long-term care facilities.

CUPE's size and diversity is both the union's strength and potential weakness. The potential power of 540,000 union members mobilized to fight for a common goal is tremendous. Reaching this potential is difficult despite continued efforts to encourage more grass-roots activism in the workplace and in the community. CUPE also faces the challenge of being a national union of workers in an increasingly decentralized country. Provincial laws and decisions govern most of CUPE's members. Regional interests and differences make it difficult to get all parts of the union to take common actions and move in the same direction at the same time.

CUPE members are organized into more than 2,000 local unions found in almost every community across Canada. Many of these—60%—are small local unions with 100 members or less (CUPE 2004b).

The origins of CUPE can be traced back to municipal workers who organized in their own local unions in the late 1800s. Over time, the number of public sector local unions grew and two Canadian (and often competing) public sector federations had emerged by the late 1950s: the National Association of Public Employees (NAPE) and the National Union of Public Service Employees (NUPSE). In 1963, these two unions merged (largely because of pressure from the Canadian Labour Congress) to form the Canadian Union of Public Employees (Crean 1995). The new union rode the wave of public sector growth, nationalism, democracy, and union organizing drives to become the largest union in Canada

Respect for the autonomy of local unions to set their level of union dues, to control their collective bargaining agenda, to decide which grievances go forward, and to decide their own governance structures and policies has been an underlying principle enshrined in the CUPE national constitution since its founding. On one hand, local autonomy represents an important democratic principle that supports grassroots decision-making. At times, however, local unions use this principle to justify their independent stance when they do not want to adopt or implement national policy or a set of common bargaining positions. It can hinder the union's pursuit of common goals. Ultimately, it means that the support of local unions and the members of local unions for common goals must be won over, one by one. This is difficult to achieve, but leads to powerful results when successful.

Bargaining structures, based on employment relations, also fragment the CUPE membership. Some small local unions and many large ones are made up of members divided into several bargaining units and therefore covered by separate and distinct collective agreements. In total, CUPE negotiates 4,000 collective agreements (CUPE 2004c).

In contrast to unions such as the Canadian Union of Postal Workers (CUPW) with one major employer (Canada Post) and most members covered by one major national collective agreement, CUPE has a multitude of agreements with a diverse group of employers. It devotes considerable national resources to negotiating, analyzing, and tracking collective bargaining outcomes in order to coordinate efforts to achieve bargaining priorities.

New Brunswick and Quebec are the only provinces where CUPE members tend to be covered by provincial collective agreements for the major sectors, including hospitals, long-term care facilities, school boards, and social services. These common terms and conditions of employment and centralized collective bargaining structures pull CUPE locals together, allowing major breakthroughs in collective bargaining. In Quebec, it was common front bargaining (by CUPE alongside other public sector unions) that won the first paid maternity leave provisions in the country. In New Brunswick, CUPE was able to beat back legislated provincial wage rollbacks through a province-wide general strike of 20,000 CUPE members in the 1992 (CUPE 2004d).

Given where CUPE members work, a common, over-arching goal for the union is to fight for the expansion and improvement of quality public services and to prevent them from being cut and privatized. This theme is central to the union's policies and practices of union renewal.

1989 Policy Paper and the Commission on structure and services

The ongoing process of union renewal in CUPE is rooted in the work of a Commission on Structure and Services, established at the 1989 national convention with the adoption of a policy paper called "CUPE into the 1990s."[2] The paper set out a number of specific questions for the Commission to review to improve the union's effectiveness. Central were questions about what structural changes were needed to develop the internal strength of the union to be able to deal better with the external challenges facing CUPE members as the union approached the start of a new century and millennium. Should the union be organized more on a jurisdictional or occupational basis? How could stronger links be forged between national policies, bargaining, organizing, and general union operations? How could mergers of local unions be increased? How could CUPE position itself to continue to grow and withstand the competition for members in the public sector from other unions, including private sector unions?

While the focus of the Commission was to be on how to improve existing union structures and services, the policy paper called for consideration of new approaches in wall-to-wall organizing, with a focus on organizing unorganized workers in CUPE's traditional jurisdictions. It suggested that new full-time organizing positions might be needed, and that consideration be given to reorganizing staff assignments so that first contracts could be negotiated as part of the organizing drive. This would relieve staff representatives of a task considered too time-consuming to do as part of their regular assignment.

Given the complex and controversial nature of these questions, the 1989 policy paper called for extensive consultation with CUPE locals, divisions, councils, staff, and staff unions. In the summer of 1990, the CUPE National Executive Board (NEB) appointed a commission composed of a member from each of CUPE's five regions and two staff to conduct this investigation. The NEB instructed the commission to conduct an independent and extensive consultation on—but not limited to—the questions raised in the policy paper, and to report back its findings before the 1991 national convention

One of the first steps of the commission was to produce a discussion guide with three main subject areas: 1) CUPE's organization, 2) its policies, and 3) its services and dues. It contained background information on each area so that locals could better understand the significance of the issues being considered. A copy of the discussion guide was mailed to all CUPE locals.[3] Provincial and regional hearings were organized, and members and local unions were encouraged to make written submissions as well. Over 2,000 local union representatives and staff participated in these discussion forums. Many questions beyond those specifically put to the commission were discussed and debated there.

After a year of consultation, the commission met and grouped its findings into three categories:

1. Issues where there was a great deal of agreement and could therefore be acted on relatively easily and quickly.
2. Issues that required more detailed work before being able to make specific recommendations.
3. Issues referred to the commission that should not be pursued because of insufficient membership concern.

Despite the specific mandate of the commission and the particular matters referred to it for consultation and consideration, what emerged from the consultations was a more fundamental discussion about what the union is, what it does, what it should be, and what it should do.

Building a stronger union to fight for public services

What emerged was a shared vision of what kind of union members, leaders, and staff wanted CUPE to be: a progressive, forward-looking, active union, responsive to the needs of both members and working people generally. They wanted a union that defended members' interests in the workplace, but they also wanted the union to advance members' concerns within the labour movement and society more generally. As public employees, they wanted CUPE to have an impact on both their workplace and broader public policy.

There was wide recognition of the need to act collectively to accomplish these goals. The vast majority of locals supported coordinated bargaining and coordinated political action on issues of common concern. They did not see local autonomy as a barrier to a strong cohesive union, as long as CUPE gave all locals, regions, and sectors meaningful input into collective decisions. They wanted CUPE to act democratically and with sensitivity.

Local unions wanted services from the union and its staff, but they were also concerned about excessive staff workload and wanted to be able to more effectively take action on their own to address their local issues. In this area, the commission recommended that:

1. CUPE's education program be reviewed with membership input so it could be re-oriented to give locals the training they needed to defend and promote the interests of their members at a local level;
2. the member-instructor program also be reviewed and expanded to help develop the capacity of members;
3. more priority be given to providing local union officers with more paid time off work to be able to effectively carry out their duties; and
4. the service and information needs of locals be regularly evaluated to ensure they are being met.

There was also a strong call for more staff to provide assistance to local unions, especially through staff specialists located across the country, not just in Ottawa.

Measures to improve co-ordination and effectiveness

Given the fragmented and decentralized nature of CUPE's local union structure, with separate collective agreements for different public sector employers, the commission focused on measures to improve coordination within the union.

It recommended strengthening CUPE's provincial structures (known as CUPE Provincial Divisions) to deal effectively with provincial legislation and budget decisions that directly impact CUPE members. The report of the Commission called for coordinated bargaining to be made a priority for CUPE, and suggested that staff and financial assistance be provided to achieve this. It also recommended that structural changes be made to encourage locals to merge. It was proposed that the national constitution be amended to allow a simple majority approval for mergers rather than a two-thirds majority vote, and that newly organized bargaining units be integrated into existing locals, where possible and appropriate.

The commission heard concerns that the union's convention process dealt with too many issues and did not set clear priorities for decisive, common action. Problems with not implementing policies adopted at convention were partly attributed to the National Executive Board's failure to allocate money and staff resources to implement policies. As well, concerns were raised that many small local unions where most of CUPE members are located often could not afford to send members to the convention, given the high cost of lost wages, accommodations, and expenses.

It recommended that:

1. a convention assistance fund be established to subsidize up to half of the cost for small locals to send a representative to the convention;
2. convention policy statements have an action plan and budget; and
3. the NEB, following national conventions, establish priorities for the implementation of policies and resolutions, that a detailed program of action be developed and communicated throughout the union, that regular progress evaluations occur, and that financial assistance be provided to locals engaged in the implementation of this action plan.

Equality

Promoting equality has been an important goal for CUPE, particularly since the mid-1970s when Grace Hartman was the National President and also the national president of NAC—the National Action Committee on the Status of Women. CUPE was the first union in Canada to have a full-time national equality officer. By the time of the Commission on Services and Structure, there was a national Equal Opportunities Department, and a national Rainbow Committee to address the problems and needs of workers of colour and Aboriginal workers. The commission's report included a number of recommendations to combat discrimination and the under-representation of women and equality-seeking groups in the union. It recommended that:

1. all CUPE staff undergo education on human rights issues and how to handle human rights problems;
2. each provincial division establish and fund a human rights committee and locals be encouraged to do the same,
3. human rights education be provided to CUPE leaders at all levels and to union activists;
4. women continue to account for half of those trained to become staff reps, and that the need for a special training program for workers of colour be considered;
5. CUPE develop its own affirmative action hiring program so that its staff are representative of the diversity of Canadian society;

6. CUPE develop a new educational program to develop the leadership skills of women members, particularly those also discriminated against because of race, disability, or sexual orientation; and
7. as part of skills development, to temporarily hire women members to help organize into CUPE the many unorganized workers in predominantly female sectors of child care and social services.

The report of the commission established a vision of change and renewal for the union to improve its effectiveness in representing its members and defending public services.

Over time, many of the recommendations of the commission have been implemented, such as more national and provincial priority and planning sessions to improve coordination; the expansion of the member facilitator program to conduct more union education and strengthen membership capacity; the establishment of a national convention assistance fund to support greater participation by many small local unions; NEB follow-up from convention to implement action plans; and the establishment of provincial human rights committees.

Some of the new programs that were recommended were implemented, but have lapsed over time, such as the requirement that half of those trained to be staff representatives be female. Others were never implemented, such as mandatory human rights training for CUPE leaders at all levels. Many of the recommendations that were not implemented continue to be issues the union is still grappling with. This includes some of the structural challenges examined by the commission, like how to reorganize servicing assignments and approaches to address the growing workload of staff representatives, and how to better centralize and coordinate bargaining. The later issue became a major focus at the 2003 national convention.

Organizing the organized—building union strength through activism

The adoption of the Organizing the Organized policy statement at the 1995 national convention was another important milestone in CUPE's process of union renewal. The policy started from the premise that the union must change to address a widening gap between the union and its members who do not feel connected to the union and don't want to be involved. More emphasis was placed on developing new activists and involving more members, especially to counter the growing trend for members to treat the union like an insurance agency where they pay their dues to get the service of a professional organization without having to get directly involved.

This national policy called on the union to change the way it did things, from filing grievances to communicating with members. The policy argued that all union activities should become opportunities to create union activists in the workplace and community. It called for more national union resources to be devoted to activism and leadership development, especially at the local level. And it called for special measures to be taken to reach out and involve in the union sections of the membership who were under-represented until then: workers of colour, Aboriginal members, young workers, workers with disabilities, gays, lesbians, bisexual and transgendered members. Outreach and involvement of these equity-seeking groups could only be achieved if a special effort was made to address and speak to their concerns, and if changes were made to the way the union carried out its business. The old way of carrying out union activities—from general meetings to conventions—would have to be revamped with a view to opening up the union to everyone.

The policy also addressed the need to change the union's way of communicating with members, replacing one-way communication from union to member with two-way communication. For example, ways would have to be found to make union discussions more present in the workplace and to engage members more in union decisions.

This policy direction took hold in the union to varying degrees. CUPE's education program was revamped, with more emphasis put on building broader understanding of the political and social factors at play in the workplace and community. Union courses were turned into opportunities to build leadership and organizing skills, not just narrow technical skills (such as how to interpret collective agreement language or legal rights). As well, CUPE's new Organizing the Organized policy allowed significant financial resources to be allocated to campaigns aimed at mobilizing members at the grassroots of the organization, and at connecting CUPE members to community coalitions with citizens' groups. Measures were taken to reach out to equity-seeking groups within the CUPE membership and in the community. Committees were established to advance the interests of these groups, and special human rights training was developed. Special measures were taken to ensure gender parity on national committees and to increase the attention paid to women's issues, particularly the problem of low women's wages. Thousands of CUPE members across the country received special training in how to reach out and involve members in the union, and the initiative sparked a new flame of militancy throughout the union.

At the same time, there were pockets of resistance to the new direction. Some were concerned that too much attention was being paid to broader political struggles against government policies at the expense of workplace struggles against the boss. There was a sense among some that the policy was being imposed on the grassroots from higher levels: a sense that many members don't want to get involved in their union and would prefer resources to be used to hire more professionals to carry out the work. In some cases, the initiative became a divisive issue between member activists and full-time paid staff representatives. In large part, this was due to the lack of understanding by both opponents and advocates about what the initiative was really about. Some took the call to transform the union into a place where members are the key organizers too literally and believed it to mean there was no place in the union for paid staff. Some were concerned that too much time and effort was being spent on the development of member activists without sufficient payback, and that the resources would be better directed to strengthening CUPE's staff structure.

Fighting privatization through internal and external solidarity

In any event, the Organizing the Organized policy paper was reaffirmed at the next national convention. By then, the attack on the public sector anticipated by CUPE at the previous two conventions was in full swing. It was time to put the principles and practices of organizing the organized in full gear to defend CUPE members' jobs and the services CUPE members provide to communities. With that in mind, the 1997 national convention adopted a major national policy paper called Stand Up: CUPE's Action Plan for Jobs and Services. It called attention to newly emerging forms of privatization, such as public private partnerships and competitive bidding, and new targets for privatization: power and water. The policy shed light on the problems, established the union's opposition to these schemes, and committed union resources to providing tools to mobilize members and their communities against these privatization initiatives. It also raised the global nature of privatization, explaining the connection between workplace privatization and international trade agreements.

CUPE's focus on fighting privatization through the mobilization of members and alliances with other unions and community groups intensified over the next few years, and continues into the present. CUPE became known as forcefully opposing all forms of privatization. A national campaign against water privatization was launched and continues to this day, giving rise to community water watch committees every time one of the big private water consortia moves in on a municipal water system. Several major public private partnership initiatives have been undone because CUPE was able to expose them as bad deals for everyone except the corporations. CUPE has also been able to broaden the base of opposition to privatization, having reached out to other unions and community organizations. CUPE has drawn attention to the detrimental impact of privatization on women's equality, on workers of colour, and on Aboriginal communities, thereby broadening the diversity of opposition to privatization. The privatization of Ontario Hydro, the largest privatization in history, was stopped when CUPE joined forces with the Communications, Energy and Paperworkers Union (CEP) and took the matter to the courts.

The union's campaign strategy to fight water privatization and public private partnerships are examples of how CUPE has gone about building both internal and external solidarity to achieve a desired goal or vision. CUPE's approach is first to bring these issues to the attention of local unions and members at a national convention where a common strategy of resistance can be discussed and adopted. As set out in the Organizing the Organized policy of CUPE, all the union's strategies are designed to involve members in their union and build union strength through grassroots education and action. As well, all of CUPE's campaign strategies include a component of community outreach and the building of alliances with community groups and other unions. This approach to union building and defending members has been fully accepted by all parts of the union. There is broad consensus that, to move forward, CUPE has to engage members to the greatest extent possible. There is also broad agreement that, to win, it is often necessary to mobilize the support of members for actions—including work stoppages.

External solidarity—from local to global

The union's struggles against privatization have also stretched the boundaries of external solidarity from local to global, taking many different forms. The union's privatization campaign has emphasized the global nature of this struggle:

1. that a few powerful, global corporations are actively seeking to privatize public services around the world;
2. that global corporations use international trade agreements like the GATS to open up public sector markets to private business takeovers, or NAFTA to make it costly to stop or reverse privatization; and
3. that there is much to learn from public sector union members around the world who are also engaged in fighting privatization.

The union commissioned legal opinions to warn local governments of the trade implications of privatizing their water systems. CUPE sought standing in the Metalclad case to support a Mexican town fined millions under NAFTA for trying to stop a U.S. corporation from operating a toxic waste dump in the community. It funded research on the impact of international trade agreements on health care, education, water, and municipal services. And the union mobilized its members to join protests against international trade agreements.

As the 2001 international solidarity national policy statement called "On the front line locally and globally" put it:

> We must think globally and act locally … we must build massive resistance to free trade and globalization on the ground and start by making the connections between local battles and the global struggles against corporate domination. Every fight a CUPE local takes on against job cuts, concessions, privatization, or the weakening of workers' rights must be seen as a fight against globalization. And every victory must be seen as a blow against globalization. (CUPE 2001)

The global dimension of privatization was once again emphasized. CUPE locals were encouraged to deepen their commitment to international solidarity by negotiating financial contributions to the union's Global Justice Fund in order to sponsor more international projects opposing the privatization of public services.

The privatization struggles of public sector workers in other parts of the world help to inspire and sustain CUPE members in their local struggles. CUPE delegates to the 2003 national privatization conference had the opportunity to hear an amazing account of how municipal workers in Cali, Columbia, stopped the privatization of services by occupying their local government offices. This was the result of years of community-based organizing to expose the problems with poorly funded public services and build support for community action to improve public services. It was an example of the type of organizing CUPE had promoted among its staff and members through the Organizing the Organized policy statement years before.

In its fight against public private partnerships, CUPE has closely monitored the experience in the U.K. with the equivalent Private Finance Initiative (PFI) hospitals. CUPE has used this information to explain to CUPE members and the public what is in store for Canada if we privatize our services through such partnership arrangements. CUPE's work is obviously having an impact. Two years ago, the Canadian Council for Public Private Partnerships declared CUPE to be the major obstacle standing in the way of its privatization plans.

Developing stronger alliances with sister unions engaged in similar privatization struggles in other countries has been another important dimension of growing global solidarity. CUPE has supported the South African Municipal Workers Union (SAMWU) with a project geared to analyzing restructuring and fighting the privatization of municipal services in South Africa. As well, CUPE has been a partner in the Municipal Services Project which brings together community-based groups and academics in South Africa to study the changes in public service delivery underway in that country.[4] This collaboration has resulted in sharing information and analysis about new forms of privatizing water and power, ways to respond through union and community organizing, and the development of alternatives such as public-public partnerships.

Organizing new members

CUPE's approach to organizing new members has largely been driven by the goal of increasing the union's bargaining strength by increasing density in workplaces and sectors where the union already exists. For CUPE, organizing is not just about increasing the numbers of CUPE members. It's about building solidarity among workers and building workers' power to take on the employers and those in power.

As the 1999 national policy statement "On the front line" put it:

> If we allow the unionization rate to drop in our traditional sectors, the bargaining power of all CUPE members will be eroded. If we sit back and allow a whole lot of other unions to move in and organize the un-organized in our workplaces and sectors, we lose the potential to build one strong and united front to confront our employers. We also risk having our collective agreements undercut by weaker unions—like a few who have organized workers in some privatized services at lower wage rates. (CUPE 1999)

Consistent with the union's goals of strengthening members' capacity, those who do the organizing in CUPE are largely members who are booked off work to undertake an organizing campaign. Over the last five years, CUPE has increased the number of full-time staff organizers, but member organizers who have received special training to carry out the majority of active sign-up campaigns. The theory of this approach is that workers are more likely to respond to an organizer who is from the workplace or sector and is familiar with the problems the workers are facing. As well, involving CUPE members as organizers contributes to their skills and leadership development. With this in mind, CUPE has made special efforts in the last year to provide training and engage members of colour and youth as organizers—after all, the fastest growing sector of unorganized workers in CUPE's jurisdiction are workers of colour and young, casual workers working in Canada's largest cities.

CUPE's organizing strategy contrasts sharply to that of most other unions. Unlike other unions, CUPE will not organize unorganized workers in jobs or sectors outside of its jurisdiction. The whole point of organizing is to reduce competition among workers and build solidarity to win better working conditions and wages for all. In CUPE's view, it makes sense for workers who provide similar public services to be located in the same union because it facilitates the development of common demands and bargaining strategies, and leads to better collective agreements.

With the increase in privatization, CUPE's organizing goals outlined in the 1999 policy paper also called for a strategy of "following the work" to organize private contract workers when CUPE members' work is contracted out. CUPE has taken the position that, even when public sector work is privatized, it should be considered part of the public sector and in CUPE's jurisdiction. CUPE should continue to represent and fight for the same working conditions and wages of public sector workers, especially because almost all privatized public services continue to by funded by the public sector. Further, CUPE should always fight to bring this privatized work back in-house where it belongs. If CUPE is able to reduce the wage differential between those working in the privatized services and those working directly for the public institution, the job of getting the work back is made easier. To take a different approach is to allow a different and lower standard of wages and working conditions in CUPE's jurisdiction, and all CUPE members suffer.

Not all unions take this position. The Service Employees International Union (SEIU) has faced the challenge of privatization by deploying a strategy of "corporate organizing." This strategy (which is also being advanced in Canada by the newly merged garment, textile, hotel and restaurant union UNITE–HERE) is aimed at sweeping the privatized workforce into corporation-wide bargaining units that include workers employed by the same corporation regardless of whether they provide service to public or private institutions. For example, the SEIU has launched campaigns to organize public sector food, laundry, and housekeeping workers whose jobs have been privatized by Sodexho. Part of the strategy is to force the corporation to voluntarily recognize SEIU as the bargaining agent for all those employed by Sodexho in a geographic area, regardless of where they work. This type of organizing strategy doesn't differentiate between workers employed at public institutions (like hospitals or universities), whose jobs have been privatized, and those who work in a private environment (such as food service outlets at office complexes). Under such an organizing strategy, the higher wages that the former public sector service workers made when they were employed directly by the public institution cease to be relevant when it comes to negotiating a collective agreement, making it impossible to maintain the higher standard.

Strategic directions and solidarity pacts

CUPE's push for union renewal continues today, guided once again by a national convention policy approved at the national convention in October 2003. Echoing previous policy directions, the convention adopted a strategic direction focused on three specific and ongoing challenges for the union:

1. strengthening bargaining power,
2. increasing the union's day-to-day effectiveness, particularly at the local level, and
3. intensifying the fight against contracting-out and privatization by moving from a defensive to offensive strategy.

The strategic direction was in response to the difficulties CUPE and other public sector unions were having in collective bargaining, particularly given the assault by governments at all levels. The actions of the B.C. government against public sector workers in that province, including the stripping away of hard-won collective agreement provisions through legislation, were the most vicious example of what CUPE members were up against in 2003. But the hostility of employers and governments was a problem across the country. Something had to be done.

The policy paper called on the union's leaders in every province to develop a strategic plan aimed at regaining worker and union power by consolidating bargaining efforts. Central to this was the notion of a CUPE solidarity pact where CUPE local unions would commit to take action in direct support of other CUPE local unions under attack. It was modeled on solidarity pacts adopted by CUPE locals in New Brunswick earlier that year as they prepared for collective bargaining. They had vowed that every local union would mobilize member support for strike action if any other local union in the province had its bargaining rights legislated away and a collective agreement imposed by law (CUPE 2003).

The strategic directions paper also addressed the need to increase CUPE's day-to-day effectiveness in protecting the rights of members in the workplace. The policy paper (as recommended by the Commission on Structure and Services 13 years earlier) pledged to carry out an extensive examination of the difficulties facing local unions in carrying out effective day-to-day representation of union members. The National Executive Board was charged with reviewing the findings so that it could allocate budget resources accordingly to address the problems over the next five years. As well, the paper stressed the need for CUPE to negotiate more paid time off for union leaders at the local level.

The third strategic objective set out at the convention was to intensify the union's campaign to stop contracting-out and privatization. The policy committed to providing national funding for strategic anti-privatization campaigns, better coordination of anti-privatization campaigns, more focused efforts to stop pension fund investment in public sector privatization schemes like investing in infrastructure and negotiating stronger job security protection. It also committed CUPE to organizing support for a broader labour movement strategy to stop privatization and calling on the Canadian Labour Congress to actively campaign against public private partnerships.

Conclusion

CUPE embarked on a major initiative of renewal 16 years ago, and the union has been working to make changes ever since. Many new programs and initiatives have been undertaken, all aimed at increasing the power of the union through increased membership involvement and greater solidarity among members. The challenge of change and renewal is made both more difficult and more important by CUPE's size and diversity.

CUPE's renewal program has been profoundly influenced by progressive thinkers and activists in the labour movement who believe that a union is only as strong as it is democratic; only as strong as it is active; and only as strong as it is ready and able to exercise collective action in defence of workers' rights in the workplace and citizens' rights in the community.

There is little doubt that CUPE is a different union today than it was in the early 1990s when the Commission on Structure and Services undertook its work. CUPE has grown significantly since then, at a much faster rate than any other union, and despite significant cuts in public sector funding and jobs, especially in the early 1990s. CUPE has also been able to hold the line against the push by employers and governments for collective agreement concessions and take-aways. CUPE has been able to make real wage gains for members, and CUPE members have been spared major layoffs. In large part, this is because protecting job security remains CUPE's top collective bargaining priority, and because CUPE members have been prepared to take action to defend employment. It is also because CUPE has taken a firm stand against contracting-out and privatization and has stopped major erosion of the public sector, along with other allied unions and community groups.

CUPE is also a more visible union now than it was a decade ago. A more active and militant union gets more media attention, and more attention in the community.

None of these changes occurred by accident. They came about because CUPE adopted policies and programs at national conventions and then allocated funds and resources to act on them. CUPE invested in member education and member mobilization because the convention decided it should. CUPE took on the fight against privatization because it adopted a deliberate program and strategy to do so.

Of course, there have been both advances and setbacks along the way. Many of the original recommendations for change made by the Commission on Structure and Services were not acted upon, despite repeated calls for the same change at subsequent conventions. For example, outside of Quebec, the union has not yet engaged in a thorough review of how union staff services are provided to members or how they could be reorganized to address the workload problems of staff or the growing needs of local unions. In Quebec, such a review was undertaken over a multi-year period, culminating in a full report to the provincial convention in 2005. The results are instructive, although not surprising. Some of the conclusions are similar to those of the national commission all those years ago: local activists need the tools and resources to better address the increasingly complex problems facing members, as do the paid staff.

Of course, there is a new challenge facing the servicing side of CUPE's operations. Like many other organizations, CUPE will be experiencing a large number of retirements in the next five years. The departing staff representatives will be taking years of experience and knowledge with them. The situation puts the issue of staff renewal on the front burner and may provide the impetus to carry out a serious evaluation of how staff servicing might have to change.

Another test of CUPE's capacity to continue the process of renewal is the changing demographics of Canada's largest cities, which inevitably impact on CUPE's membership. CUPE represents one in 60 Canadians. As the proportion of Canadians of colour and Aboriginal people increases, so too should the proportion of CUPE members of colour and Aboriginal members. Although CUPE has made significant headway in responding to the needs of these groups of members and involving them in the union, they continue to be under-represented on the union's leadership bodies at all levels. This must change.

Another area of concern is the question of women's participation. There are many barriers to women's participation in union life: women members continue to be economically disadvantaged, and many have to work multiple jobs to make ends meet, leaving little time for other activities. They continue to be the primary care-givers in their families, and they continue to do most of the domestic work. But even women who are active in the union encounter obstacles when it comes to getting elected to leadership bodies, especially at the provincial and national levels. There are currently no women on CUPE's National Executive Committee—a first in CUPE history. This issue will also have to be addressed.

One thing is certain: whatever direction the union takes with respect to renewal will be very important to the future of public services in Canada, and therefore to the future of all Canadians. Given CUPE's size and presence in almost every community across the southern part of the country, the union, with others, can play a central role in resisting the corporate takeover of public services. The union has done a good job of stopping the sell-off of vital services, but more needs to be done to advance a strategy to renew the public sector, and to revitalize communities through a reinvestment in public social and physical infrastructure. The union has launched a campaign to build communities, but sustaining such an initiative and broadening it to include rank-and-file members, community allies, and other unions will take a concerted effort.

The point is not just to protect the jobs and wages of CUPE members. The point is to work with others to win good full-time employment for all workers in the community, to promote environmentally sustainable policies of urban growth and development, and to fight for new services like child care, and to defend and expand public programs like social assistance, Medicare, employment insurance, and the Canada Pension Plan, making them truly universal and inclusive. Seen in this light, CUPE's union renewal has only just begun.

Notes

1. This is informed by the framework for analyzing local union power in Lévesque and Murray (2001).

2. Information on the Commission on Structure and Services comes from CUPE, *Shaping Our Future: Report of the Commission on Structure and Services.*

3. The guide was not mailed to locals in Quebec since a distinct consultative process was used in the province of Quebec.

4. More information on the Municipal Services Project can be obtained at http://www.queensu.ca/msp/.

References

Canadian Union of Public Employees (CUPE). 1999. *Action Plan. On the Front Line.* Adopted at the CUPE National Convention, Montreal, October 18-22.

————. 2001. *Policy Statement on International Solidarity. On the Front Line Locally and Globally.* As adopted at the 2001 CUPE National Convention, Vancouver, November 19-23.

————. 2003. Strategic *Directions Document. Priorities for the Next Two Years.* As approved by the CUPE National Convention, October.

————. 2004a. *Membership Report.*

————. 2004b. *Local Unions by Number of Members as of February 2004.* National Executive Board Meeting, September 14-16.

————. 2004c. Local Union Information System (LUIS) and Collective Agreement Information System (CAIS) data calculation, December 17.

————. 2004d. Honouring Other Picket Lines: Solidarity in New Brunswick and Beyond. *Table Talk,* Spring. Available at MACROBUTTON HtmlResAnchor http://cupe.ca/updir/TABLETALK_spring_2004.pdf.

————. *Shaping Our Future: Report of the Commission on Structure and Services.* n.d.

Crean, Susan. 1995. *Grace Hartman, A Woman For Her Time.* Vancouver: New Star Books.

Lévesque, Christian, and Gregor Murray. 2001. Mondialisation, transformation du travail et renouveau syndical. In *La FTQ, ses syndicats et la société québécoise,* ed. Y. Bélanger, R. Comeau, and C. Métivier, 189-202. Québec: Comeau and Nadeau.

Chapter 8
Union Resistance and
Union Renewal in the CAW

DAVID ROBERTSON AND BILL MURNINGHAN

The context for union renewal

It is fitting to be addressing the question of union renewal on the 20th anniversary
of the founding of the Canadian Auto Workers (CAW). By breaking away from the
U.S.-based United Auto Workers in 1985 to form an independent Canadian union,
we started an exciting, risky, visionary, collective project. At a time when many
unions and many progressive groups were struggling to stand still, we were building a union and shaping the future. The theme of our first collective bargaining
convention reflected the mood: "We're Building a Future Together." Twenty years
later, we are still building that future together. In many respects, the very formation
of the CAW represents a large-scale union renewal project, and our experience
since then highlights how renewal has been ongoing and central to the success of
that project.

Anniversaries are important in our union, giving us a chance to reflect upon our
past. And the CAW has a proud past whose measure is not just the last 20 years. In
sectors such as the auto industry, our history stretches back to the militant struggles
to establish industrial unions in the 1930s. In sectors such as rail, our roots are even
deeper, reaching back to the late 1880s, the first unions in the country, and historic
struggles like the 1919 Winnipeg General Strike. Ours is a young union, but we
have a long history.

Over the last 20 years, the CAW has grown considerably. In a period when
many unions were losing members, we were gaining new members, growing from
120,000 members in 1984 to 265,000 members today. The CAW is now the largest
union in the private sector in Canada. At the time of our formation, less than 10%
of our members were from outside the province of Ontario. Now we are a national
union with a major presence across the country.

Our union has grown through mergers and organizing, and the results have
altered its composition in important ways [see Figure 1]. Mergers with airline
groups and retail workers, and the recent organizing in the hospitality and health
care sectors, has raised the total number of women in the union to about 70,000.
In addition to more women, we have more workers of colour. And we have more
part-time workers.

As the CAW has grown, our structures have evolved. In our first constitution,
our National Executive Board (NEB), which governs the union, was established as
a group tied to our local unions and workplaces rather than a structure populated
by full-time officers. The CAW Council, often called our union's parliament and

Figure 1. Composition of CAW Membership

First CAW Bargaining Convention, 1987

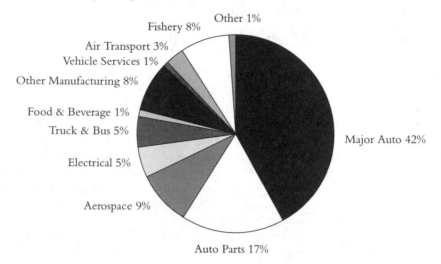

Seventh CAW Bargaining Convention, 2005

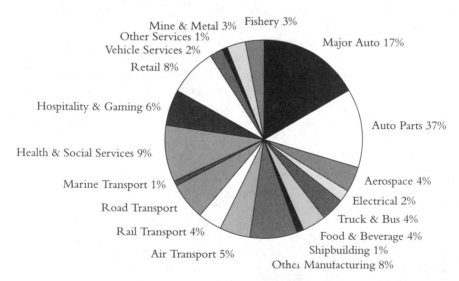

one of the most unique and democratic of union formations, was enshrined not just as a legal structure, but also as a forum for union building. Its role in building a strong and progressive union culture is widely recognized.

As the union has merged with other unions and workers from other sectors of the economy, we have created new forums for discussion and debate in sectors such as hospitality, health care, transportation, shipbuilding, retail, wholesale, rail, mining, and others. And, as different groups of workers have sought recognition, we have seen recognized caucuses develop within the union so that workers of colour, women, Aboriginal, and lesbian-gay-bisexual-transgender members have greater opportunities for union involvement and participation, as well as influence and leadership.

Over the last 20 years, we have stepped back from our day-to-day activities to examine particular issues and different aspects of our union. In 1993, we established a national task-force on the union chaired by NEB members. Through a series of extensive consultations, local leadership and activists all across the country raised concerns, submitted briefs, and offered ideas for union reform.

More recently, in responding to the crisis in social democracy, the union established a task-force on working class politics. In 2000/2001, union facilitators organized small group discussions with randomly selected volunteers from our membership. The goal was to canvass our members' views on important social issues, topics of broader politics, and the union's political work with our members. The follow-up work to the task-force involved discussions and debates at CAW Council, policy papers at conventions, and has now resulted in the launch of the Union in Politics Committees (UPCs)—a new locally-based, non-partisan, political structure, and a new political strategy across the union. A founding convention of the UPCs was held in the fall of 2004, and a first national campaign was launched in the spring of 2005 aimed at strengthening and securing public and employer pension plans.

Our ongoing renewal involves more than our structures. It is about what we do. For example, when we formed the CAW we already had one of the most innovative union education programs. Now it has expanded considerably to be one of the world's largest and most comprehensive union education programs. Our commitment to social unionism, already strong, was bolstered in 1990 by the creation of the Social Justice Fund, which provides ongoing solidarity assistance to humanitarian and development projects around the world. Over the years, our bargaining agenda has been developed and debated in Collective Bargaining Conventions. We have articulated a progressive bargaining agenda and, despite the wrenching fallout of the current wave of corporate restructuring, we remain determined to hang onto past gains and make progress for our members, their families and communities.

Our first priority is to make gains for our members at the bargaining table. It is, after all, why workers join unions. Over the years we have experienced both the ups and downs of bargaining—the breakthroughs and the struggles to preserve and secure what we have. The CAW's formula for progress is the combination of clearly identified bargaining priorities, a determination to make gains, and a commitment to generalize improvements from one workplace to other workplaces and other sectors. Equally important, in tough times we have resisted long-term agreements, gimmicky compensation schemes, and multi-tier wage systems. Where there have been setbacks, we have fought to limit them and prevent their spread to other workplaces.

In the last 20 years, the combination of fighting back and building a new union has led us to recognize the determinants of union strength (see Figure 2). These four determinants—membership level, bargaining power, the capacity to mobilize, and political influence—are the critical elements in our union's growth. Upon reflection, union renewal has been a defining feature of the CAW since its formation. Increasingly, our future is being framed in these terms. A major step toward formalizing a

Figure 2: Strategic Determinants of Union Strength

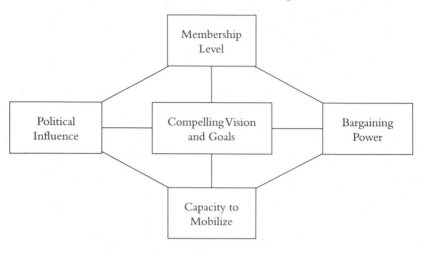

view of union renewal occurred at our most recent constitutional convention, held in August 2003. Gathering under the theme Unions: Resistance and Renewal, 1,100 delegates debated and adopted the policy paper Union Resistance and Union Renewal. The concluding chapters of that paper follow in Section II. Interviews with key union leaders and staff on the subject of union renewal are presented in Section III.

CAW constitutional convention paper: Union Resistance and Union Renewal

When working people are organized, we are one of the most powerful forces on Earth. Through our unions we have changed the course of human society. Our struggle for higher wages, pensions, job security, improved working conditions, and limits on employer authority has fundamentally altered the lives of workers.

Because we have unions, we have paid vacations, minimum wage laws, Medicare, public education, child care, health and safety regulations, and much more. When unions are strong we have achieved not only improvements in our own lives and those of our families, but also greater equality in the distribution of income, stronger regulations for all workers, and improved social programs for all citizens. Through our unions we have helped build a more vibrant democracy at home and we guard against the rise of tyranny around the world. When unions are strong, all workers make progress.

But what exactly defines a strong union movement? The rate of unionization among the workforce—union density—is a starting point. A high rate of unionization suggests a more powerful union movement. There is strength in numbers, for sure. But there are other critical measurements. "Do unions have real bargaining power with employers?" "Do unions have the capacity to mobilize their members to achieve their goals?" "Do unions have the ability to influence the politics of their country? "Are unions committed to compelling goals and principles?"

These then are the strategic determinants of union strength—membership levels, bargaining power, mobilizing capacity, political influence—all guided and shaped by a compelling vision. These things usually go hand in hand, though not always. We all know of situations where a relatively small group has had influence beyond what their numbers would suggest. Having said that, the goal is to achieve and maintain our strength in all strategic areas.

This is the challenge that is always in front of us: to build our numbers as well as the other strengths and capacities. It would be a mistake to view this challenge mechanically, like one more task at hand. It is so much more than that. This constant of union renewal is what gives the union movement its life's blood.

Union renewal is always deliberately constructed, though it is more obvious in hindsight. Think about the momentous decision in the mid-1980s to create a new, independent Canadian Auto Workers by breaking away from the American-based UAW. No one sat down and laid it all out as a union renewal project. In fact, there was tremendous uncertainty. Some argued that this decision would actually diminish our numbers and therefore our strength. But, without a doubt, that decision became one of the most important union renewal projects in the history of the Canadian labour movement. It changed forever not only our own union, but the shape of the country's labour movement as a whole.

Today, the CAW is the largest private sector union in Canada, stretching from sea to sea to sea, with more women and workers of colour among our members, and in sectors we never dreamed of representing in 1985. By focusing on the strategic elements of union strength, our numbers grew. The growth has been based on a combination of mergers and organizing. And the results have altered the composition of our union in important ways.

What also followed were new structures. In our first constitution, our National Executive Board was established as a body that was tied to our local unions and workplaces rather than a structure populated by full-time officers. The CAW Council, one of the most unique and democratic of union formations, was enshrined not just as a legal structure, but also as a forum for union building. Its role in building a strong and progressive union culture is widely recognized.

As the union has brought in other unions and workers from other sectors of the economy, we have created new forums for discussion and debate in sectors such as hospitality, health care, transportation, and others.

As different groups of workers have sought recognition, we have seen caucuses develop within the union so that Aboriginal and workers of colour, women, lesbian-gay-bisexual-transgender, and other members have greater opportunities for union involvement and participation, as well as influence and leadership.

Our evolution is ongoing. At times what is needed next can't be predicted in advance, but what is clear is our commitment to structures that recognize the touchstones of internal democracy: participatory, accountable, effective.

There have been other changes in our organization and other efforts to review and renew our capacities and goals. Along the way we have taken the time to examine different aspects of our union. For example, in 1993 we established a national task-force on the union chaired by rank-and-file NEB members. Through a series of extensive consultations, local leaders and activists all across the country raised concerns, submitted briefs, and offered ideas for union reform. Today, most of the task-force recommendations have been adopted and have found their way into union policies, structures, and programs.

More recently, in responding to the crisis in social democracy, we established a Task-force on Working Class Politics. In 2000 and 2001, union facilitators organized small group discussions with randomly selected volunteers from our membership. The goal was to canvass our members' views on important social issues, topics of broader politics, and the union's role in political work with our members. The follow-up work to the task-force was brought before the 2003 constitutional convention.

Our ongoing renewal involves more than our structures. It is about what we do. When we formed the CAW, we already had one of the most innovative union education programs. Now it has expanded considerably to be one of the largest and most comprehensive union education programs. Our commitment to social unionism, already strong, was bolstered by the creation of the Social Justice Fund. Over the years we have articulated a progressive bargaining agenda and, despite the wrenching fallout of the current wave of corporate restructurings, we remain determined to hang onto past gains and make new gains for our members, their families and communities.

Now, almost two decades after we formed our union, there are some very different circumstances confronting us. The challenge remains the same, but the context is different. There is a lot of very difficult news around us. And individual unions, as well as national labour movements, can become overwhelmed by these new circumstances. We need to continue our renewal—with deliberate, purposeful foresight.

As a leader in the labour movement, the CAW has been committed to the essentials of union renewal for many years—organizing, education, workplace strength, social unionism, and political action. The truth of these seem self-evident to us, and so part of union renewal is a further shaping of our efforts in each of these areas. And yet we also know that we need to respond to some new challenges and to inject fresh energy into our efforts to address the world of today and beyond.

Ten challenges to union resistance and union renewal:

1. Making gains in bargaining
2. Expanding democracy
3. Organizing
4. Deepening membership involvement and participation
5. Generational renewal
6. Strengthening social activism
7. Building alliances with social movements
8. International solidarity
9. Strengthening our capacity to mobilize
10. Defining ourselves by what we do

Making gains in bargaining

Our first priority is to make gains for our members at the bargaining table. It is, after all, why workers join unions. Our aspirations—to improve our conditions of work, our standard of living, and to increase our say in the workplace—have led to the development of an impressive bargaining system. It is a system that is both effective and accountable: elected bargaining committees, members involved in setting demands and ratifying agreements, a secure strike fund, staff and local and national leadership committed to successful negotiations.

Over the years, we have experienced both phases of the bargaining cycle: the breakthroughs as well as the struggles to hang on to what we have. Our formula for progress is the combination of clearly identified bargaining priorities, a determination to make gains, and a commitment to generalize improvements from one workplace to other workplaces and other sectors. Equally important: when we have bargained in tough times, we have seen the need to fight concessions, resist long-term agreements and gimmicky compensation schemes, and, where there are setbacks, to limit them and prevent their spread to other workplaces.

There are times when bargaining is extremely difficult. There are situations where our backs are against the wall, where even hanging on to past gains is a major achievement. Recently, we've had our share of those: Air Canada, Navistar, Bombardier. In those locations our bargaining committees have had to wrestle with overwhelming issues and have been forced to deal with problems that can't be resolved at the bargaining table. They can only be addressed through government policy.

At our 2002 Collective Bargaining Convention, delegates adopted an ambitious bargaining agenda which reviewed our bargaining philosophy, identified bargaining priorities, and outlined our strategy to achieve them. Even when bargaining in tough times, we remain committed to those goals and we are determined to achieve them. The impressive gains we achieved in the fall of 2002 in bargaining with the Big Three auto-makers established the pattern for others to aim for.

Expanding democracy

The attack on democracy has proceeded in step with the extension of neo-liberal policies. When investors are given stronger rights, freer access to more spheres of life, and protection against any interference, the corresponding rights and protections shrink for workers. When the free market guarantees freedom for investors, it undermines democracy for the rest of us.

In this period when the gap between the rich and the poor has become wider, when national governments abandon the job of protecting their citizens, the contradiction between capitalism and democracy is becoming more pronounced.

In some areas, the very idea of democracy is being challenged. It is being limited, in scope, to voting. It is limited, in substance, to the compromised "choices" in electoral terms. And it is limited, in extent, to the latest news events while important issues are drowned out by the given "spin."

The goal of the union is to counter those developments. It is to expand the notion of democracy—to have it mean more than elections. And it is to extend democracy in all areas of life: in the workplace, our communities, our union, in the broader labour movement, and in politics more generally.

Workers have built unions to be among the most democratic of institutions. As the CAW Statement of Principles explains:

> Unions are central to our society being democratic because:
> Unions bring a measure of democracy to the place of work, which is so central to people's lives.
> Unions act as a partial counterweight to corporate power and the corporate agenda in society more generally.

Democracy is built into our structures. It is defined in our struggles. It gets advanced in the way we challenge employers and governments.

We continue to build our own union in ways that are democratic, participatory, and accountable. Our internal democracy is the base upon which we have argued for more democratic choices in the labour movement. Our efforts can be seen in our decision to stand behind workers whose desire to join a union of their choice led to Canadian Labour Congress (CLC) sanctions against our union. Although the price was high and the process painful, the results were worth it. Not only were those particular workers given a choice of unions, but we were also successful in changing CLC procedures in a way which hopefully makes our labour movement more democratic.

In a broader context, our democracy project is about social transformation. It is about expanding democracy in all areas and at all levels of public policy—from how our kids' schools are funded to how trade deals are negotiated. Our democracy project is about workers gaining more economic and political influence. It is about winning stronger political rights, establishing more economic rights, and securing better social rights.

Such an ambitious agenda means overcoming a growing political cynicism among our members and Canadians in general. And it means continuing to challenge those forces and institutions that limit democracy. Our 2003 constitutional convention paper The CAW and Politics: Taking the Next Steps moves us forward in that direction.

Organizing

As a union, as part of a larger labour movement, we face a number of organizing challenges. We need to organize more members to strengthen our movement. We need to organize more members in the so-called "mature sectors" such as manufacturing where union coverage is falling. We need to find effective ways to organize and bargain gains in new sectors such as private services where the economy is shifting. In the process, we need to attract a broad range of the new workforce—workers of colour and recent immigrants, women workers in low-wage private services jobs, younger workers in their first jobs.

The challenge in organizing would be easier if the issue was just about a shift in resources from declining sectors to growing sectors, or a shift from one generation of workers to another. But it isn't. It is about organizing in both the traditional and the emerging sectors, and it is about organizing a broad range of workers in every sector.

We've had some notable successes. In manufacturing, we have used our leverage in bargaining such as in the Big Three auto-makers to gain a foothold in organizing non-union auto parts employers such as Magna. We've developed innovative approaches such as supplier neutrality agreements which have assisted workers at Sterling Truck and Johnson Controls to organize. And we continue to make breakthroughs in the service sector such as the recent success of workers at the Blue Heron Casino and the continuing successes of workers in our health care sector and in retail, wholesale, and department stores.

There is growing interest among unions in the current discussions on different approaches, models, and strategies of organizing. These are important discussions that will help strengthen union vitality. But just as important is our recognition that organizing can never be limited to the Organizing Department—no matter how effective it is. Organizing needs to be something we all do.

Recent research has shown a relation between support for unions and knowing what unions do. And that puts a responsibility on all of us. Our everyday discussions with friends and relatives, neighbours and acquaintances can make a difference in workers knowing what unions do. It is with that in mind that our hope is for every leadership person, activist—and, yes, every member—to become an organizer.

Deepening membership involvement and participation

A common feature of unions in decline is the lack of connection members have with their union. There can be different reasons to explain it. It could point to some particular shortcomings of the union itself or to increased managerial success in battling for the hearts and minds of workers. It could have something to do with contemporary social values where individualism is valued over the collective, or to the over-saturation of right-wing ideology. But, for whatever reason, when the membership doesn't identify with their union, the union is in trouble.

Our union has recognized that unions can't take their members for granted. Our campaign, captured in phrases such as "organize the organized" or "unionize the organized," recognizes the forces which pull us apart and has countered with deliberate strategies of involvement and participation.

These can be seen in local union efforts to make membership meetings more interesting and accessible. They can be seen in efforts to involve more members in the activities of the union by developing new local union committees (such as youth committees) and an expanded committee membership. They can be seen in new bargained programs such as the union awareness and the new member orientation courses at the Big Three auto-makers. They can be seen in our efforts to translate the enthusiasm generated by our educational programs into ongoing activism. They can be seen in our ongoing recreational programs where members get a chance to play together. They can be seen in forums addressed to particular groups of members, such as the youth conference or the annual conference of retired workers. And they can be seen in our union's efforts to build on the diversity of our membership as the accompanying convention papers do.

More than anything else, unions are vehicles. Their role is to get us somewhere. When members see the union as their own, the destination is more easily reached.

As the CAW Statement of Principles reminds us:

> Unions can only be effective if the membership know the union belongs to them. This means a union which reflects the goals of its membership, allows the members full participation, and encourages workers to develop their own skills and understanding.

A measure of our success continues to be the efforts we make in strengthening the links among our members and being open to the opportunities that arise to "organize the organized."

Generational renewal

In the labour movement, each new generation stands on the shoulders of those before it. What we leave and what others do with it puts an obligation on all of us. Part of understanding generational change in the union is in recognizing the context and the forces which shape different generations of workers.

Our union's first generation built the labour movement in the 1930s and '40s. The lives and attitudes of this generation were shaped by the Depression, the Second World War, and by their role in the growth of the social movements of the time. The second generation in our union was part of the rebellious 1960s. Workers in the '60s grew up in a context of expanding unions, workplace militancy, expanding social programs, and were influenced by new social movements against the Vietnam war and in support of racial equality and women's rights. Another generation is now with us. Young workers today are shaped by different forces and have grown up in a more contradictory time. Young workers have much to offer the union, and much to gain from being part of it.

For us, the test of generational change remains:

1. How we pass on what's best about our union while being open to the challenges younger workers bring.
2. How we attract more youth to our union and to more activities within the union.
3. How we strengthen the bonds between older and newer members.

Strengthening social unionism

From the early days of our movement, workers have inspired each other—to organize, to demand, to fight, and to win. Over the years, the sacrifices workers have made in their selfless acts of solidarity have done more than ensure that workers elsewhere have their support. They have established a basic principle of social unionism: the gains we want for ourselves we want for all workers. This is the ground on which our commitment to social unionism is built. Our Statement of Principles which introduces our constitution makes the point:

> Our collective bargaining strength is based on our internal organization and mobilization, but it is also influenced by the more general climate around us: laws, policies, the economy, social attitudes. Furthermore, our lives extend beyond collective bargaining and the workplace, and we must concern ourselves with issues like housing, taxation, education, medical services, the environment, the international economy. Social unionism means unionism which is rooted in the workplace but understands the importance of participating in, and influencing, the general direction of society.

Researchers have noted that in Canada the traditions of social unionism are strong. We know the breadth and depth of social unionism in our own union:

1. from flood relief to solidarity pickets;
2. from de-mining projects to Women's Day marches;
3. from funding of women's shelters to bargaining women advocates;
4. from child care campaigns to health care coalitions;
5. from "no sweatshop" clothing campaigns in city councils to the fight against child labour;
6. from the campaign for affordable housing and a living wage across the country to organizing Earth Days in our local schools.

We know that in these times, when the social fabric is being ripped and slashed, those commitments are more important than ever.

Building alliances with social movements

There is a relationship between the growth of unions and broader movements for social change. This was the case in the 1930s and '40s when industrial unionism thrived and where the membership of individual unions grew dramatically. It was again the case in the 1960s and '70s when public sector workers organized unions and swelled the ranks of the labour movement. Indeed, one of the reasons offered to explain some of the differences between the U.S. and the Canadian labour movement was the failure of U.S. unions generally to be part of the social movements of the '60s and '70s.

Building alliances with social movements is never easy. There is an ongoing tension between unions and social movements. It is a tension which can either threaten unity or lead to a renewed dynamism. In the mid-1990s, our union, through the Days of Action, helped build a coalition of unions, community groups, and social activists in Ontario. While the specific coalitions didn't last, the lessons and the networks did. Later, when our union joined the protests against meetings of the Asia-Pacific Economic Cooperation (APEC) in Vancouver in 1997, when we organized the teach-in and rally when the Organization of American States

(OAS) met in Windsor in 2000, and when we were part of the Peoples' Summit in Quebec City in 2001, we were part of a common struggle with movement activists whose tactics were quite different from our own. More recently, the anti-war demonstrations have given us the experience of marching in union contingents which were small compared to the size of the demonstrations. In each of these situations, the powerful and lasting experience of struggling together in common cause outweighed the at times difficult lessons each had to learn about working with the others.

The new social movements need unions. We have the financial resources, the organizational discipline, the leadership and activists, and the perspective on corporate power that can help build a broader movement for social change. And unions need to be part of the new social movements. This was the case in the 1930s and the '60s, and it is the case now.

When we organize around specific issues such as the campaign of the Coalition For A Living Wage, for example, our social justice work is more straightforward. At other times, it is more complicated, such as in the current period when the anti-globalization movement is recovering from the deep chill which set in as part of the aftermath of the atrocities of 9/11. But, either way, our efforts are fuelled by the hopes that our world can be changed, and that makes us part of the new social movements.

International solidarity and union internationalism

Our commitment to international solidarity gets expressed in a number of ways: through words of support, acts of solidarity, financial assistance, international cooperation, and, at times, common struggles.

1. It can be seen in simple letters of support which acknowledge other workers' struggles, which let workers elsewhere know that their struggle is witnessed, that the world is indeed watching.
2. It gets expressed in concrete acts of solidarity such as when the Norwegian union of Falconbridge went on strike in support of our members and in our own refusal to handle replacement parts from U.S. plants when General Motors plants were struck in the U.S.
3. It can be seen in our bargaining priorities when we first bargained the Social Justice Fund in 1990, first at Ford and then across the Big Three, and since that time in collective agreements across the union.
4. It can be seen in our affiliation to various unions, International Trade Secretariats, and through our support for common campaigns such as the Fatigue Kills trucking campaign, the letters of support to imprisoned Korean union leaders, or our recent hosting of the International Transport Workers' Federation Women's Conference.
5. It can be seen in the union exchanges as union delegations visit one another to learn more about each other, the struggles we are engaged in, and the ways we can provide ongoing support.

Our international solidarity is built on the recognition that capitalism is international and labour movements are national: that corporations are global, but unions are bound by national systems of labour legislation and industrial relations. Corporations become global quite easily, through acquisition or expansion, whereas unions have to build a union internationalism through cooperation and common struggle—a long and inevitably slow process.

We are in a period where international solidarity takes on additional emphasis. International trade deals have shrunk geography as the North American Free Trade Agreement (NAFTA), for example, inevitably brings us into either cooperation or competition with workers in Mexico, or where a move to a Free Trade Agreement of the Americas (FTAA) will mean that union positions, for example, in Argentina take on a closer and more immediate relevance.

In this period, there is growing union cooperation across national borders. It can be seen particularly in Europe, where, as a result of European Union directives, national labour movements work together around common employers. But there are also some beginnings in North America, where unions have engaged in common projects such as the campaign to end sweatshop practices, or in NAFTA-related campaigns.

It has also led to greater recognition that what a union does in one country affects unions in other countries. Our international solidarity will continue to be influenced by the realization that what we do at home has an effect elsewhere. If we strive to make gains here, then it influences what other workers can think about doing and actually achieve. If we fail to make gains, that too affects workers elsewhere.

From the early days of our union when Canadian workers were inspired by their American counterparts to organize industrial unions, when workers looked to Europe and adopted its unions' tactic of sitdown strikes, we have recognized the power of workers drawing inspiration from their sisters and brothers elsewhere. And we have recognized that international solidarity is in part about the struggle to make gains at home. As we go forward, we will continue to act in ways that might inspire others to act, to help create the room for them to do so, and, in turn, to struggle to match their gains.

Strengthening our capacity to mobilize

In the months preceding our 2003 constitutional convention, workers virtually shut down France in a nation-wide protest against the government's plans to reform the pension system. The photos of jammed streets and colourful banners in Canadian newspapers reinforce the point that, when workers are marching, the world takes notice.

Our success in organizing mass actions has been central to building the labour movement. Strikes and rallies, marches and workplace occupations have historically helped put the "movement" in the labour movement. They not only demonstrate a show of existing force, but they also strengthen our capacity to fight in the future.

Whether it is the community protests in Newfoundland against plant closings, the local demos against cuts to Employment Insurance, the political rallies against the government in British Columbia, the anti-war marches in Quebec, or on the picket line, we learn when we are on the street. The power of standing arm-in-arm with our sisters and brothers is an experience which shapes us in profound ways and stays with us forever. It is in common struggles with other workers where words like "solidarity" and phrases such as "the union makes us strong" take on their meaning. The preparation, education, organization, and leadership that is necessary to make those actions happen at all, and to make them successful, helps build unions.

Our capacity to mobilize our members is not just evident as a show of force. It is in the day-to-day building of our union. It is in our commitment to the education of our members, activists, and leadership. It is in our forums, our union structures, and in the issues we take on. It is what sets us apart from a model of business union-ism where the task of servicing members ends up a transaction much like those of the marketplace.

Our goal is to be even more effective in representing our members, to help build our union as a vehicle for social change, and to work for a more active labour movement.

Defining ourselves by what we do

One of our greatest strengths is our union's culture. Culture unifies and motivates. It binds together different sectors, different generations. It is the story we tell about ourselves that identifies who we are, what we are doing, the challenges we face, and the ways in which we respond to those challenges. The story we continue to tell describes a broad vision for social change and a continuing passion for social justice. It commits us to turn the tide in union decline, to build union strength, and to develop the labour movement's role as a powerful and progressive force in society.

Talking about union renewal

Two years after adopting the constitutional convention policy paper Union Resist-ance and Union Renewal, interviews were conducted by Bill Murnighan in the spring of 2005 with "Buzz" Hargrove, National President; Peggy Nash, Assistant to the President; Ken Lewenza, President of CAW Council and Local 444, and David Robertson, Director of Work Organization and Training and lead author of the 2003 convention paper on union renewal.

Q: Does the Canadian labour movement need to be talking about union renewal?

BUZZ HARGROVE: Constantly. We need to constantly be challenging ourselves with new ideas, new ways of doing things, and sometimes going back and looking to our history at the old ways of doing things. Sometimes the old ways are the best "new things" that we can be doing.

On the whole question of union renewal, you have to consider what gives unions strength. For real renewal to take place, unions have to constantly reject the agenda of the corporations and right-wing governments. We need to reject the idea that the wealthy, powerful élites can always take more while everybody else takes less. And we must reject an agenda that says we have to go out and sell concessions to our members, and tell our members that the times are "too tough" and that we can't make progress. We have to constantly fight for progress, regardless of how tough the circumstances.

Of course, there will always be limits on that progress, depending on what is going on in the economy, in a particular sector, or in a round of bargaining. But we need to be constantly ready to challenge ourselves, and be ready to defend our members and their families.

I look to the recent example in the East Coast crab fishery where our members had a dispute over new regulations. After several blockades of the harbour and the Newfoundland legislature, and hundreds of injunctions, the government found a way to back down gracefully. But the positive outcome only came about through fighting back. Our members never backed away and kept fighting.

At times, struggles like that seem commonplace in our union. They go by quickly without a lot of attention or discussion. But that is an example of how renewal is about always fighting for progress.

PEGGY NASH: Many unions, like the CAW, were born out of the CIO organizing in the 1930s. The world has changed dramatically since then in terms of the nature of the economy, the nature of the workforce, the growth of the private service sector, the loss of manufacturing jobs, the growing number of women in the workforce, the nature of Canada, huge numbers of newcomers to the country, and the rapid growth of new technologies. Add to this the attack on workers' rights from governments of all stripes. The world is changing constantly, and we need to be constantly challenging ourselves to respond to it. So, absolutely, we need to talk about renewal.

First off, however, we have to give ourselves credit for already doing a lot of things right. People join unions because they want the union to make progress for them, and in our union we're among the best at doing that in terms of the basics like wages, benefits, taking on the employer, and gaining respect in the workplace. We already do a lot of things right. When thinking about renewal, you have to remember that, if you don't look after the basics, nothing else matters.

But we operate in the broader society, and a broader labour movement, where one of the big problems we face is the growing gap not only between rich and poor, but also the growing gap between the declining numbers of good-paying industrial jobs and the growing numbers of jobs with poverty-line wages. Even many of those who are in a union in some of these sectors are not really seeing strong benefits. Unless these low-wage service sector workers, and the young people who often work these jobs, feel that they've got a hope of improving their lives though a union, then we're seriously undermining the labour movement's future.

The reality is that a lot of the today's union leadership came out of the struggles of the 1960s and '70s, and a lot of the baby-boomer leadership will be retiring soon. Young activists in the union will do some things the same, and some differently, but the challenge for us in terms of renewal is to keep the best of our culture and skills, while ensuring that the next generation of leadership brings new energy, but also reflects the new realties of today.

KEN LEWENZA: The term "union renewal" is often overblown. In our union I believe that we have constantly challenged ourselves to change with the times, while drawing on our history for strength. Look at collective bargaining, for example, and the issues we've taken on. You don't have to talk about renewal to fight against long-term agreements which unnecessarily exclude the members from the democratic process. Every workplace, small or large, is engaged during collective bargaining, which in our union is at least every three years. The longer a contract, the less engagement, and less reason members have to get involved.

Our position on long-term agreements is not really about renewal; rather, it is really about sticking to our traditional roots which have engaged our members, given the union strength, and shown the members about the need for their union. Our fights, and the issues that we've taken on, are not always about renewal as such. What we've said is that we take the strengths of our history and make sure that we continue on that same path, and, where there are weaknesses, we try to correct them.

For us, I don't know if we even talk about renewal in those terms. Our focus is about going back to our traditional strengths in the labour movement and reinforcing that strength against the odds. That is really what we're doing. We're challenging the status quo. People say that is renewal, but it not really renewal—in our union it's really maintaining the culture that we established 20 years ago when we formed the CAW, and working to keep it fresh.

DAVID ROBERTSON: Union renewal needs to be, and can be, an ongoing strategy. It is not a case of just moving from a position of decline to a position of growth. Renewal can be a frame of reference for a union, which I would argue is critical. If a union is not in constant renewal, then it becomes bureaucratized, and the structures and practices become outdated. Unions are fragile. They always have to be renewed. If they're not renewed, they fail. History shows that you can be strong today and gone tomorrow.

This means that renewal is not something you do when you hit a crisis. Renewal has to be something that is constant. You always have to be talking about your structures, your education, how you reach out to diverse groups in the union, how you build leadership. You have talk about all those things, all the time. If you stop doing that, then you are in a crisis.

Looking back at our 2003 convention paper on renewal, and the ten challenges that we highlighted, I see it less as a recipe for renewal and more as a set of ingredients. Any union that is engaging in a renewal project will need to address that list of issues. For us, it is a set of ingredients that shape a "union culture." Union culture becomes the central point. Today we have slogans like "fighting back makes a difference," or "you don't need a union to go backwards," which ultimately shape generations of leadership and get passed on.

The debate today about renewal is useful in order to have unions look internally to see what they are doing, and to look externally at their links with other unions, labour centrals, political parties, community groups, and social movements. The debate about union renewal becomes a vehicle that allows you to approach all these issues. And frankly, we wouldn't be talking about renewal so much today in the labour movement if in fact unions as a whole were constantly renewing themselves.

The fact that we haven't been talking about it enough as a whole labour movement underscores a certain potential crisis we face, not only in terms of declining membership, but also in terms of the ability of unions to deliver at the bargaining table, or to influence politics. On all these fronts, the right has been effective over the last two or three decades in terms of shifting the terrain, at winning ground. There is that old line that says that there is a class war going on, but only one side is fighting. That is the case: capital has been fighting the war and, for the most part, workers haven't been. Now, it is at a point for some national labour movements, particularly in the U.S., but also in other parts of world, that the labour movement and its member unions have reached a time to re-think where they are going.

The debates that emerge elsewhere may, or may not, be useful. For example, there is a debate now in the U.S. around general versus sector-based unions. It's an interesting debate, but resolving the debate doesn't resolve the crisis. The big questions remain about what are unions doing, how do unions see themselves, what is their role? And critically, what is their role in transforming the world, which might sound high-minded, but if unions don't have an agenda to transform the world, then what is it that we're doing?

Because we're talking about union renewal, it means that we can ask questions about whether new structures are needed for organizing different groups of workers. When the predominant unions were craft unions, it worked well for a time for those workers. But to organize the mass of industrial workers, the craft structure didn't make sense. Likewise, the industrial model that evolved didn't make sense for the public sector, which created new forms of organization. Today we need to see who isn't part of the labour movement, and the discussion of union renewal opens the door to ask question about whether we need to do things differently.

But in the end, all these challenges can't be dealt with by any one union. That is why we all talk about a labour movement. What a single union can do, in terms of renewal, is position itself. It can be ready for these challenges, and can be building internal structures and increasing membership involvement and commitment, taking on employers, and getting ready to confront governments. It can do all these things as a union, but it can't transform society as a single union.

Q: The Canadian labour movement has arguably had more success than movements in many other countries, and particularly when compared to the United States. What accounts for the difference?

BUZZ HARGROVE: The big difference in Canada, and particularly in our union, is our ability and willingness to fight back. A union can't have a discussion of renewal at the same time that they are out selling the corporation's agenda. For example, unions can't accept the logic of the auto companies that are saying today, particularly in the U.S., that health care and pension costs for retirees are the main problems that they face. As long as you don't challenge yourselves to identify the real problems and force governments and corporations to deal with them, then you're constantly going to go backwards, and the labour movement weakens itself. That is what is happening in the U.S.

I've watched the debates and read the materials about what is taking place in the AFL-CIO and not yet seen one idea that is going to stem the backward trend. Forced mergers among unions is not going to do it. Moving away from the Democratic Party is not going to do it. Endorsing the Democratic Party is not going to do it.

If the labour movement is not seen by its own members, their families and communities as working on their behalf, and fighting on their behalf, then the movement will be in constant decline. With few exceptions, the unions in the U.S. don't work with the social movements, provide no money to the social movements, except for token donations, and have little involvement. They end up isolating themselves.

Then, every once in a while, they will have a big debate that at the end of the day centres around who is going to be the president of the AFL-CIO or one of the major unions, then everyone relaxes for a few more years, then they decline a few more percent in density.

PEGGY NASH: We have been very good at adapting ourselves in the CAW, but there is a danger in patting yourself on the back too hard and sitting back and saying that we're doing fine, and all is okay. We have done better, for a variety of reasons, than many unions south of the border. There has been a willingness in our union to learn, grow, and adapt to changes in the workplace and in society.

I also look at our union's principles, which come out in our collective bargaining. It doesn't matter where you go, I run into workers who find out where I'm from and they say that our union fights for workers. The fact that people know about our union comes largely from sticking to our principles, and doing the work in collective bargaining. Of course, it is not about being perfect, but, critically, it is about never leading them backwards.

Another factor behind our success is being skillful with the media, and finding ways to get our story out. At times this is about taking actions that are controversial, that generate debate and attract attention. That's important, not because people like to see their picture on the television, but because you become part of the public debate. I look at our recent fight for an auto industry policy, or struggle against concessions in pensions in the airlines, or the harbour blockades in the crab fishery in Newfoundland. Our way of working with the media in these fights is about being part of the public debate.

At times it is easier for leaders, whether at the local or national level, to sit in their office all day, to not connect with the members, to not be front and centre when things happen. But our experience tells us that having that sense of responsibility for being out there, of having that public role to play, is really important.

There is also the whole notion of social unionism in Canada, about not getting isolated from the community, whether we are fighting for wages and benefits, or whether we are fighting with the community for child care, health care, or against the war in Iraq.

We are in a very different place today, different than the cyclical downturns in an industry, or in the economy, that we've seen in the past. Corporations have been incredibly radical. They decided that they needed to seize control of the agenda.

They put a lot of time, thought, and money into regaining domination of the public agenda and the political process. They also went after the hearts and minds of the people, especially working people.

They have been successful in some ways and unsuccessful in others. Here in Canada, they still haven't got people to back off from their support for public Medicare, and they still have not got into the kind of values-based right-wing movement that we've seen in the U.S. But they have been incredibly radical, no doubt. Around the world, this has put labour on the defensive.

Our success in Canada is in part because labour and progressive movements still work together here. In some ways, around the notions of women's equality, of social cohesion, of social programs, we still do dominate the public debate. People are very proud of the Charter of Rights and Freedoms, and they see immigration as an incredible strength for our country. But I also think that many people have also internalized the tax cut agenda. There are conflicting trends.

In spite of their absolute best efforts, the right-wingers have not succeeded in changing peoples' minds on many important issues here in Canada. On the other hand, has labour lost ground? Absolutely. Look at the rollbacks in labour laws, the erosion of Medicare, cuts to social assistance, and all the myriad cutbacks that we've seen. We have been on the defensive, but yet the progressive agenda has done surprisingly well.

KEN LEWENZA: The debate in Canada may be different because the Americans are losing union membership at an alarming rate. But we absolutely need to think about renewal. Although we haven't been nearly as affected as in the U.S., the labour movement in Canada needs to recall that having a union, and having membership, is not automatic. If you're not doing things to change with the times and to engage with the members, then you're in trouble.

Despite doing better than in some other countries, the labour movement in Canada should never be satisfied. Our strength is not about being satisfied and maintaining the status quo. Our strength is about building off our successes, and building a movement. We can take pride that we haven't lost as many members as in other countries around the world, but that doesn't mean we're satisfied. The reality is that we still have 70% of working class Canadians unorganized. As long as 70% are unorganized, that will continue to put pressure on the 30% who are organized. Nobody should be satisfied with 30%. Our ultimate goal is to give all working Canadians an opportunity to belong to a union.

In terms of what lies behind our relative success, I think our political and social activity in Canada is recognized by all political parties. Consider the period under the right-wing Harris government in Ontario. We took him on with the Days of Action community-wide strikes, and he didn't go as far as he wanted. He wanted to strip away the Rand formula that guarantees union security, and he didn't have the audacity to move ahead because of the recognition that the labour movement has gained, and the work that we do. And, critically, he didn't move ahead because of the recognition that we'll fight back in Canada. Those kinds of initiatives have been crucial.

I also look at the mean-spirited approach to privatization that we saw a few years back. I think organized labour played a huge role in getting government to reconsider that direction in education, in health care, and in other areas. The majority of the efforts to stop privatization came from the labour movement. We've had these kinds of successes because we've stayed connected to the needs of the general public. In the U.S., it is a different story. There seems to be a desperate approach to retreat.

Look at the last election in the U.S., where the unions spent more money than they ever did in their history in an effort to defeat Bush. But the reality is that it is not about money. It is not about how much you can spend. It is about reaching out to your constituency base on what's important to them between elections. What we've done in Canada is that we've stayed politically active. We're considered a respected force, even by our adversaries. And we're respected in Canada because of what we do, day in and day out, not just because of what happens during elections.

The labour movement can't act in isolation. We've come a long way over the years in expanding our support for coalitions, anti-poverty movements, supporting the unemployed, and we've got to continue to do that.

In the labour movement, you cannot be satisfied. It is not an automatic right to have a union. You've got to work hard at it. You've got to gain the respect of those who should join your union. It takes a hell of a lot of work to continue to advocate for the rights of unions, and for the right to join a union free from harassment. That work has to be ongoing. To be satisfied would be ridiculous.

DAVID ROBERTSON: In comparison to many other countries, Canada has done quite well. But we should recognize that some of the trends we've seen take their toll in other countries are at a turning point here. For example, we now have labour laws that make it tougher to organize; and we've got demographic changes and shifts in industries which mean that we represent a relatively small proportion of the working class, particularly in terms of youth, new Canadians, and in the private services sector.

We're also at a point when we should look at what unions deliver in terms of wages. As a labour movement as a whole, we haven't done that well in recent times. Some unions have done better, we have done better, but as a whole we've lost ground in terms of the share of national income going to workers' wages compared to the share going to profits. Some also argue that we've reached a possible turning point in terms of union density, particularly in the private sector. And, critically, unions are constantly under attack.

Considering our relative success here, I'm reminded that unions have tremendous influence on each other, despite relationships that are at times difficult. If all unions are making gains, it is easier for any one union to make gains. We are so interconnected that, if all unions give up, or the majority of unions do, then it is increasingly difficult for any one union to make gains. This is something we need to think about when we talk about renewal for the labour movement.

The debate on renewal is relevant here, but whether unions in Canada are in similar difficulties as the unions in the U.S. may not be the question. Rather, the questions are more about the changes taking place here. More unions today are Canadian unions, and increasingly there are more general workers' unions. Add to this the moves to increase democratic choice among unions in the Canadian Labour Congress, and increasingly workers could belong to any number of unions. So a key question for us in Canada is: What should those unions look like?

The point is that many of the conditions and challenges are similar in Canada as elsewhere around the world, but the terrain of the debate will necessarily be different.

Q: For unions that want to embrace the idea of renewal, what are the keys steps to take?

BUZZ HARGROVE: Unions need to be much more open, much more democratic. We are organizations of human beings, and at times, even in good unions, there are going to be disagreements. If a group of members feel that the union no longer serves their needs, or the interests of their families and community, and they want out, unions need to respect that. This forces everyone to work harder on all issues.

Unions also need to get rid of the gimmicks in bargaining where they sell workers on two-tier wages, lump sums, profit-sharing, bonuses, and all sorts of things that undermine the solidarity of the union. Unions have to reverse that trend. Most importantly, unions need to get away from the idea that they are responsible for the problems that the companies are in, and they have to fight like hell. And when they do, the whole labour movement has to join in.

I go back to the PATCO example, when striking U.S. air traffic controllers were summarily fired by newly elected President Ronald Reagan and the labour movement didn't respond; but that is a while back. More recently, I looked at the fight that the UFCW had with major U.S. grocery chains a few years ago. The labour movement should have shut the country down.

There are still 15 million union members in the United States. They should have taken a couple of days production out to send the message that we aren't buying this backward trend of attacking our health care system. Fighting back is critical. Agreeing to give it up is no way to build a movement, or an individual union.

PEGGY NASH: To embrace renewal, a union needs to find out where the members are at, to understand their views, and hear what their ideas are. Members will have a lot of ideas about what the union should be doing, what the union does well, what it could do better, and where it should be going. I would also get sharp minds to look at the economy, see what is happening politically, and look at other examples around the world.

And I would go out and talk to people who should be in the union, but aren't. I'd want to talk to young people just going into the workforce, talk to newcomers to Canada in non-union jobs, and ask them how they see unions.

While leading our unions' recent Task Force on Working Class Politics, I was struck by a change in today's culture that reflects a growing trend to what I would call "me-ism," where everything is about individuality and less about an association in solidarity with a large number of people. What the task force revealed was that a lot of people, including our members, get really isolated. And when that happens, they stop seeing the union as an important part of their lives. They may think about the union at bargaining time, but not as central to their lives.

What was reinforced while meeting with groups of randomly-selected members during the task force was that, when you create an opportunity for working people to get together and talk about issues that are important to them, the best comes out. They convince themselves of the importance of having the union on their side, not just for collective bargaining, but in terms of the union in the community, fighting for them on social issues and on political issues. And, ultimately, most end up viewing the union as a wonderful vehicle that they can access, and help build, to make change.

If we tap more into our members, the best of our members' aspirations in terms of what they want for themselves, their families and their communities, it is the best resource for union renewal. In order for renewal to take place, union leaders need to ensure that we are not just talking at our members, but creating opportunities for members to talk to each other. This means creating ways for them to be engaged throughout the union on a whole variety of issues.

In the CAW, our education programs are part of this: for example, bringing together the skilled trades for their own education program, and doing the same with women, people of colour, LGBT members, youth, and so on. It's about creating space for people to come together to talk about important issues in the union. And, in the process, we all listen and learn. If you want to keep renewing your union, you have to have good ears.

Ultimately, we will be judged as a union not by what we say, but by what we do. If we continue our tradition of action, of defending workers' rights throughout society, we will continue to grow.

KEN LEWENZA: From my perspective, you need to go back to the roots of your organization for renewal. You need to re-establish your roots and to look at what was the culture of the union when it was formed. I look at the UAW in the U.S., for example, and think that, if they go back to their roots, that you don't have to go too far beyond that for renewal.

In terms of concrete steps, education is key. Take a look in the auto sector, where we built programs to talk with our members about issues that are important to them, paid for by the employer. This is more important, in my view, than bargaining a paid holiday. We're talking to our members on an ongoing basis in terms of what's changing socially, what's changing politically, what's changing internationally, and what the union is doing to be pro-active in defending their interests.

Broadly speaking, what's different about today's generation is that members want more communication, and to talk more about what's important to them. They want to see the union working for them. It's pretty simple to me. All unions have to be looking in the mirror and asking: Are we doing what our members are asking us to do? Are we leading? Are we being advocates on their behalf, not just in collective bargaining, but nationally and internationally? In the CAW, we're doing reasonably well, but we've got to do more. That's what drives us.

I emphasize that having a labour movement is not automatic. It can't be taken for granted. You've got to continually work collectively to give those who are unorganized a good reason to join a union, and the only way we can do that is by reaching out to them before they pay dues.

DAVID ROBERTSON: One of our strengths is the number of forums we have for discussion and debate. Some unions don't get together often enough. One of our unique features is that we meet with such a large group of leadership three times a year, though the CAW and Quebec Councils and conventions. We basically have a convention every four months similar to the kind of meeting that some unions have every three years. We have structures that regularly bring people together, and that builds the culture of the union.

When our members and local leadership hear a fishery worker talk about blockading the harbour in St. John's, or an autoworker fighting on the picket line at a small auto parts plant in Windsor, or a hospitality worker from B.C. trying to make gains in bargaining, hearing that from each other and connecting with each other makes an incredible difference.

Unions need to have forums for engagement and debate. At times, those structures aren't always used, but the fact that the structures are there means that they are constantly connecting with each other, constantly debating issues. Essentially, it's about building class consciousness. To build democracy, you have to practise democracy. If unions don't meet, if national leadership doesn't meet with local leadership, if the members don't have channels and access, then I'm not sure how you move forward.

Another point to highlight is that, for renewal to happen, unions have to be willing to take risks and to challenge employers, governments, and themselves. We see that time and again, whether though plant occupations or in the Days of Action protests, that you always have to challenge and put yourself on the line. There is nothing like struggle to engage people. We see it at our council meetings when workers talk to the delegates about the fight they're in, their determination to resist and to fight back. You see what happens to the mood in the room. People are engaged and charged by that.

If you don't have the determination to struggle, and the mechanism to share it and engage in it, then I don't know how you talk union renewal. You could talk about union renewal as being about structures and specific projects, which may be useful and important, but without that central culture-building process then I don't think it will amount to enough.

We can look around at other unions, see who is doing what the most effectively. We can do that with education programs, organizing, the use of new media, and so on. But without the central piece being about a determination to struggle, a determination to engage in it, and having a way to share it across the union, then it's not clear where those other pieces go. That is the dilemma that the union renewal debate is in today.

Chapter 9
Rank-and-File Involvement in Policy-Making at the CEP

KEITH R. NEWMAN

At its formation in 1992, the Communications, Energy and Paperworkers Union of Canada (CEP) made a commitment to increase the role of rank-and-file members in decision-making. The merger agreement that brought the three founding unions together established the goal of having more rank-and-file members than officers on the National Executive Board. By 1998, this objective had been reached. One consequence has been an increase in the participation of members in establishing major union policy.

The purpose of this paper is to outline the process of decision-making the union has developed with regards to major policies, with a focus on development of the union's energy policy.

Major policies in the CEP are developed with the broad involvement of the union membership. A committee of union officers, local union leadership, and rank-and-file union members meets for several months to discuss issues. They seek expert testimony from outside specialists and input from other union members. They then draft a new policy.

The draft document is mailed to all local unions, posted on our union website, and presented at union conferences. Comments and proposals for amendment are solicited and, after due consideration, the committee incorporates the changes it deems appropriate. The final draft is brought before the convention, where it is open for debate, amendment, and adoption.

The CEP Energy Policy was written in a climate of strident public debate and strong industry pressure to reject the Kyoto Protocol. Nevertheless, the union unanimously adopted a policy strongly supporting the implementation of Kyoto. This policy now serves to guide the union in our support of Kyoto and our opposition to natural gas exports to the United States—exports that deprive Canadian industry and consumers of gas.

What is CEP?

CEP is a very diverse union. It was formed in 1992 when several unions whose members worked primarily in communications, media, energy, the manufacture of chemicals, pulp and paper, and other forest products merged. CEP has a total membership of about 150,000 workers who live all across Canada.

The significance of the diversity of the workers the union represents is that members from all sectors and regions determine together the course of the organization. This diversity set the stage for the union to initiate a new process of inclusion and consultation in developing major new policies.

The union is largely rooted in male-dominated industrial workplaces, but, as employment in those industries has declined, newly-organized members have increasingly been female. The union has a long history of pattern bargaining for much of its membership, and is currently working to expand the system of group and pattern bargaining to as many other workers as possible.

CEP is the Canadian leader for the reduction of weekly hours of work to save jobs and increase leisure time. It has carried out much research and education on the issue and provided strong support to workers seeking to negotiate shorter hours of work. CEP has been central in the ongoing struggle for pay equity for telephone operators working at Bell Canada, the largest pay equity dispute in the private sector. CEP has also played a key role in advancing environmental issues in Canada, notably on climate change. Union publications such as *Just the Beginning, Walking the Union Walk*, and major studies on hours of work provide further information on the union's history and priorities.

At merger, it was agreed that the sector-specific policy of each founding or-ganization would apply initially for the organization as a whole. The forest policy of the old Canadian Paperworkers Union and the energy policy of the Energy and Chemical Workers Union became the initial policies of the new CEP.

A few years into the merger, it became evident the new union needed to update these core policies. In 1998, a resolution to the convention from the Executive Board provided the mandate to develop the union's new forest policy and expand the policy of Just Transition.

Just Transition is the principle that workers and their communities should be treated fairly when society makes changes to production and consumption patterns to improve environmental sustainability.

It immediately became clear that there was no formal process to update major policies. In the past, each organization had relied on staff or a consultant to research the issues and provide a draft policy paper. The draft policy was discussed by the Executive Board and amended if necessary, then sent to the next convention for approval.

At convention, discussion of long policy documents is frequently difficult: time is in short supply, and delegates may have their minds on hotly contested elec-tions or on issues of lesser significance that are highly controversial at the time. While there are exceptions, this limited process resulted in policies that were often largely unknown within the organization, or not always fully taken into account by spokespeople when they took positions on behalf of the union

This old process was judged to be inadequate for the new organization. The founding unions did not know each other's issues. They wanted to understand them and to have a say in their development, and they wanted the policies to be as connected as possible with the new union.

A method to develop new policy was determined through discussion between the office of the President, National Union staff, and the Executive Board. A key proposal came from a colleague who had formerly worked in the environmental movement. The recommendation was to name a committee that would meet to discuss, research, and draft policy over a six-month period: Its members would include regional and administrative vice-presidents representing workers from the industry in question, and several local union representatives drawn from across the country and working in various parts of the industrial sector under study. The policy was then to be presented across the union at all major events in order to include comments and suggestions from as many members as possible.

This formal process was adopted, with the addition of an Executive Board member from another industrial sector entirely. The involvement of a member from an unrelated part of the union was intended to offer a different perspective on issues to the committee and also introduce a board member to the concerns of workers from another part of the organization.

This process proved highly successful in the development of the union's new forest policy and has been used for subsequent major policy development initiatives, with only very small modifications.

Energy policy

In 2001, the Executive Board mandated a committee to establish an energy policy. The committee was comprised of four officers and five rank-and-file union members. The committee was chaired by the Administrative Vice-President from Quebec, the Regional Vice-President for Western Canada, and the Administrative Vice-Presidents from Western Canada and Ontario elected to represent energy workers. The rank-and-file union members were from the Alberta tar sands, a rubber plant in Southern Ontario, a gas distribution company in Manitoba, a chemical factory in Montreal, and a forest company in Newfoundland.

The Policy Committee met over a period of four months. It consulted with a leading Canadian climatologist regarding the reality and effect of climate change, and with two trade specialists. It also commissioned studies on Canadian trade in oil and gas and the impact of the implementation of the Kyoto Protocol on jobs. Their purpose was to put before the members of the committee as much relevant information as possible. Full discussion of all issues was believed to be the best way to adopt principled positions and provide a good defence against the misuse of information by industry spokespeople.

At the time, the issue of the Kyoto Protocol was prominent in the news. While an exceptional employer or two in the energy sector did support action on climate change, most were opposed. Some stated that climate change was not yet proven. Others admitted climate change, but said the Kyoto Protocol was the wrong approach and would disrupt industry and result in job losses. Many within CEP were surprised at the sudden industry concern for lost jobs, as almost all companies in the industry, with the notable exception of those in the tar sands, had been reducing employment levels for many years.

CEP employers in the energy industry subjected workers to a barrage of industry positions questioning both climate change and the need for action to remedy it. This intense industry opposition to the Kyoto Protocol prompted concerns regarding the reaction of CEP members to the work and conclusions of the policy committee.

One staff member feared the work on the energy policy would end disastrously, "a train wreck waiting to happen," because the issues were too controversial and could tear the union apart over environmental issues. However, the process had already worked successfully for the forest policy, where very difficult environmental issues also had to be resolved. Issues that could not be resolved through consensus were set aside for future discussion, information gathering, and debate. If ultimately they could not be resolved through consensus, it was accepted they might have to be set aside and no policy position taken on them. While this would not be the best outcome, at least it would avoid a destructive confrontation over issues the union was not yet ready to face. As it turned out, there was no need to set difficult issues aside. The process of consultation over many months ensured that the "train wreck" did not occur.

Committee members were also aware of the potential significance of the union position on environmental issues. Ten years earlier, CEP had supported an environmental campaign for the elimination of chlorine in the bleaching of kraft wood-pulp. The campaign resulted in stricter federal and provincial regulations that the Ontario Minister of the Environment said would have been politically impossible to achieve without the support of CEP, the dominant union in the industry.

As part of the formal process, rank-and-file members of the committee were charged with discussing the policy as it developed with the membership of their local unions. This was an essential element, as it provided a way to communicate the research and discussions to the membership of the union. It also ensured that the committee was not getting out of touch with the members.

As the committee worked out its positions, it became clear that it was going in three main directions: support for the Kyoto Protocol, concern about Canada's rapidly depleting conventional oil and gas reserves, and Just Transition.

The geographical region that provided the most debate around the policy was northern Alberta. CEP represents nearly 2,000 workers in Fort McMurray, a major centre of tar sands development. Processing tar into usable oil creates large quantities of greenhouse gas, and some within CEP believed our draft policy, with its strong support for the implementation of the Kyoto Protocol, would be strongly opposed by these workers.

In fact, the opposite was true. While Kyoto was indeed the major area of discussion and concern in Fort McMurray, tar sand workers supported the policy for the same reasons most other Canadians did: the desire to slow climate change and breathe clean air.

The rank-and-file members of the policy committee from Fort McMurray and members of the local union executive board had been keeping workers informed regularly of the Energy Policy Committee's progress. As the committee positions evolved out of research and debate, the members of the local union were able to discuss them. The local union representative on the committee and other members of the local union executive felt confident in fielding questions and explaining the positions taken as a result of the extensive research and discussion.

The union's position in favour of Just Transition and the belief that changes in the industry would take place over a number of years also played a part in members' support for the committee's pro-environmental stand.

After four months, the draft policy was submitted to the Executive Board for review. Comments were included in the draft, and the draft policy was posted on the CEP website and also mailed to each local union.

Finally, the draft policy was presented to conferences of workers from specific industries, and at regional meetings for input over a period of several months. At these meetings, the issues and policy conclusions were explained and input solicited. Anyone wishing to contribute was encouraged to do so. All suggestions were dealt with seriously, and many were incorporated into the final policy document.

Not surprisingly, energy workers expressed the most interest at meetings. They wanted to discuss the effects of the Kyoto Protocol on jobs and energy prices, as well as the implications of NAFTA.

The final draft was submitted to the Executive Board for approval and sent to convention for debate.

A potential disadvantage of the wide exposure and debate of the draft policy prior to convention was that the desire to further discuss the policy could suffer. Indeed, this is what occurred with the draft forest policy at the previous convention. The policy had been so widely exposed that little discussion occurred and the convention proved anti-climatic.

To avoid a recurrence of that disappointment, two prominent speakers were invited to underline the importance of the main issues dealt with in the policy: the Kyoto Protocol, Just Transition, and job destruction in Canada resulting from excessively large exports of and oil and gas to the United States.

In the run-up to the convention, the debate over the Kyoto Protocol was raging in Canada. The United States government had indicated it would not ratify the agreement. The energy industry violently opposed Kyoto, claiming it would impose constraints that would make the industry uncompetitive. The Canadian Manufacturers Association claimed hundreds of thousand of jobs would be lost.

At the convention, the invited speakers dealt with the main points: Kyoto, energy security for Canada, jobs, and Just Transition. They underlined how important politically it was that the union representing workers in the energy industry was siding with Kyoto despite industry pressure, and that the significance of this would be well understood by the federal government. Indeed, there was an atmosphere of creating something significant at the convention. Many speakers rose in support of the policy, and, when the vote was held, it was adopted unanimously.

Conclusion

The new process was a success. It gave all members of the committee the confidence to debate issues with members, industry spokespeople, and others. It ensured that policy was well grounded in the union and reflected our membership. Finally, it ensured that all the issues were discussed and hammered out before convention, thereby facilitating the policy's adoption at convention.

Later, the President of CEP and the federal Minister of the Environment met to discuss the policy. The Minister subsequently noted CEP's support for Kyoto, and he committed to support Just Transition in the House of Commons.

CEP has continued to apply the policy in a variety of ways. In late 2002, the union opposed the export of offshore natural gas from Nova Scotia to the U.S. CEP ran local advertisements and made a submission to the National Energy Board (NEB) supporting the positions of New Brunswick and Quebec, demanding that the NEB apply its own rules to ensure Canadian supply first. Later, CEP conducted a public campaign to oppose the privatization of Petro-Canada, based on our energy policy. CEP continues to publicly support implementation of the Kyoto Protocol, most recently before the House of Commons Environment Committee in May, 2005.

Chapter 10
Mobilizing Young People:
A Case Study of UFCW Canada
Youth Programs and Initiatives

ANNA LIU AND CHRISTOPHER O'HALLORAN

Introduction

This case study examines how the United Food and Commercial Workers (UFCW) Canada developed youth programs and initiatives and successfully raised the participation and involvement of its young membership. An ambitious and long-term plan was devised to inspire new energy and commitment within UFCW Canada leadership and rank-and-file membership. The central points of discussion will examine what the union did, how it was done, and what has been gained.

UFCW Canada's experience is instructive for several reasons. Its young demographic membership, combined with an aging labour movement and harsh social climate, has triggered an urgency to mobilize and organize young workers at an unprecedented rate. The implementation of a dynamic strategy mobilized young members to really become organized within their union. What is remarkable about UFCW Canada is the way its leadership embraced building youth involvement, understood its value, and envisioned what it could be. Through an educationally-based strategy and the formation of a national youth internship program, local union youth committees and youth conferences emerged. UFCW Canada's ability to conceptualize a broader set of union interests away from service unionism redefined how young people perceive their union and has increased their participation through these programs and initiatives.

Background on UFCW Canada

The UFCW was formed in 1979 by the merger of the Retail Clerks International Union and the Amalgamated Meat Cutter and Butcher Workmen of North America (known in Canada as the Canadian Food and Allied Workers). UFCW represents 230,000 Canadian and 1.4-million U.S. workers in more than 20 sectors in the economy, including retailing, processing, manufacturing, health care, security, and other service sectors (Hinton, Moruz, and Mumford 1999). The majority of the membership is concentrated in retail food stores and services, and in food processing and production. In Canada, membership by gender is relatively equal, sitting at approximately 50% female and 50% male. Forty-four percent of the members work full-time, while 56% are in part-time positions. Of the female members, 37% work in full-time positions and 63% in part-time. Full-time and part-time work for the male membership is split in half, with 50% working full-time and the other 50% working part-time. Over 40% of the entire membership is under the age of 30, with the average age of a member at 35.[1]

While this case study is being written, UFCW Canada is celebrating the certification of 2,000 workers at Lakeside Packers, a division of Tyson Foods, in Brooks, Alberta. The Lakeside beef-kill operation, located about two hours east of Calgary, was at one point represented by the union in 1976, but lost support following a strike in 1984. Renewed commitment took place in 1994 by UFCW Canada Local 401 when Lakeside workers contacted the local office. With the support of the National Office and other locals, a permanent residence was established in Brooks. In the period leading up to and after this decision, the Canadian beef industry was undergoing restructuring and government-supported growth. At the same time, changes in ownership and expansion occurred at Lakeside. In the years leading up to the success at Brooks, the union provided workers with assistance in areas such as workers' compensation and arbitrary dismissals at the Brooks house (UFCW 2005). In August 2004, the majority of the Lakeside workers voted in favour of union representation.

The success in Brooks was due to a combination of factors. First, the leadership of the union was committed to organizing Lakeside workers, knowing very well that it would not be an overnight campaign, that it might very well take years. Second, long-term commitments tend to be costly, but this did not deter the union from devoting financial resources and assigning staff to the campaign. Lastly, in a town with a population of 5,000, approximately 40% of the residents worked at Lakeside Packers. The community itself is ethnically and culturally diverse. Working closely with leaders from these communities, the campaign became intertwined with local community life. All these efforts combined to shape the outcome of the success in Brooks.

With the same dedication, UFCW Canada has also taken on Wal-Mart in much the same manner. With sales of up to $2.8-billion a year and over 1.6-million employees worldwide, it is the largest retail company in the world. Wal-Mart's domination in retail sales and its growing share in grocery sales poses a tremendous challenge to the union's membership. With a membership base in retail food, the meagre pay and substandard benefits offered to Wal-Mart employees has a direct impact on the union's ability to negotiate improvements to collective agreements with companies in direct competition with the corporate giant.

Outside of the retail sector, Wal-Mart has also had a significant influence in the manufacturing industry. Suppliers are lining up to get their products onto Wal-Mart's shelves, and any contract is considered irresistible and lucrative. However, once they are tied into its web, Wal-Mart manipulates its suppliers into cutting costs from every angle so that Wal-Mart can purchase the product at an even lower price. As a result, many manufacturing companies, from garment to electronics, have closed their doors in western North America and moved their operations overseas to countries such as China. A prime example of this is the closing of the Levi Strauss plant in Edmonton, Alberta, with 200 employees, once represented by UFCW Canada Local 120G, and the closing of the Hamilton, Ontario plant with approximately 200 employees, once represented by UNITE.[2] In 2003, Levi

Strauss announced that it could not afford to produce a signatory series of jeans for Wal-Mart in Canada due to demands from Wal-Mart to lower the order price. As a result, good-paying union jobs were lost and now Levi Strauss jeans are made in China.[3]

Wal-Mart's formula is to keep labour costs extremely low, and it expects no less from its suppliers, even if it means moving across oceans to get the right price without any regard to the consequences for workers and communities affected. Wal-Mart is bringing down the standard not just for retail employees, but its business model affects workers in all sectors. In order to counteract this trend, UFCW has taken on the task of organizing Wal-Mart workers in Canada and the U.S. Taking on the world's largest retailer is critical to preserving the integrity of the union's membership. To date, a total of 12 applications for certification have been made before labour boards across Canada. As momentum grows, so does Wal-Mart's anti-union tactics, from intimidation to creating delays at the labour board to challenging provincial labour laws for automatic certification. Under the guise of worker democracy, Wal-Mart uses any means to remain union-free.

In its latest manoeuvre, Wal-Mart announced the closing of the first unionized Wal-Mart store in North America, citing low profits at the Jonquière, Québec location, after UFCW Canada Local 503 applied to the Québec Minister of Labour for binding arbitration leading to a first contract.[4] The effect of the announcement definitely sends an intimidating message to all Wal-Mart workers considering joining a union. Despite this setback, the union continues to conduct Wal-Mart organizing drives across the country. The latest victory for Wal-Mart workers occurred just before the Jonquière announcement, in mid-January 2005, when the Québec Labour Relations Commission granted UFCW Canada Local 501 certification at the Saint Hyacinthe, Québec location, making it the second unionized Wal-Mart in North America.[5]

Interestingly, in both the Lakeside Packers campaign and the Wal-Mart campaign, UFCW Canada youth played key roles in all stages of organizing two of the union's largest and most challenging endeavours.

Overview of youth programs and initiatives

To describe the development of youth initiatives within the union, it is important to start at Local 175 when Michael Fraser at that time was the president of the local union.[6] Locals 175 & 633 represent workers predominately in the retail food and wholesale industry in Ontario. In 1999, the membership of these local reached approximately 40,000, with approximately 25% of these members under the age of 25 (*Our Times* 2000).

In 1999, a vacancy became open on the Local 175 executive board. Michael Fraser decided it would be beneficial to the executive board to encourage a young person to fill the vacancy. However, the task proved difficult and the names put forward were all over the age of 30.[7] This brought to the surface a set of concerns over the current and future participation of a growing youth membership. This led to the formation of a task force, made up of young members from the local, to put together a comprehensive report on recommendations and strategies on how to improve participation among youth within the local.

To prepare for the report, the task force conducted telephone surveys and focus group discussions all over Ontario with young members in the local. In addition, the report also included proposals on youth-only education, training, and communication tools, as well as establishing a local youth committee.[8]

Later that year, Michael Fraser became the national director of UFCW Canada. In his new capacity, he saw an opportunity to develop a youth agenda at the national level. In consultation with UFCW Canada locals across Canada, the development of youth programs and initiatives began to take shape. At the same time, a staff position was designated, at the national level, to further develop and coordinate youth activities for the union.[9] One of the first programs implemented was the national youth internship program.

National youth internship program

The national youth internship program is an education and training program designed specifically for young members. Local presidents across Canada nominate candidates from their local and submit the names to the National Office. The National Office reviews the nominations and makes the selection based on geographical location, gender, and ethnicity, in an effort to ensure some form of demographic representation in the program. Lost wages, meals, travel, and accommodation are covered by the union. The program is four weeks long, divided into three intervals.[10] Week one is spent entirely on examining and discussing various topics in labour education. Topics include shop steward training, health and safety, labour history, labour economics, politics, anti-oppression analysis, and globalization. The second and third weeks are combined to focus on skills development and field training. Time is spent on public speaking, communications, and leadership training. Program participants are then placed into a local union and receive hands-on training.

Week four is devoted to visiting and interacting with affiliates and political parties. Tours are set up at the *Assemblée législavtive du Québec* and at the Canadian Parliament in Ottawa, where meetings are arranged with MPs from the *Bloc Québécois* and the NDP. In addition, participants also visit UFCW Canada local unions in Québec, the *Féderation des travailleurs et travailleuses, du Québec (FTQ)*, and the Canadian Labour Congress.

The national youth internship program laid the foundation for UFCW Canada youth to begin building a youth agenda within their local union. By the end of 2005, 78 members will have participated in the program. The internship is designed to build a core group of young active members for the union. Geographically dispersed, participants return to their respective regions equipped with the knowledge, skills, and drive to begin addressing youth issues at the local union level. As a result, UFCW Canada local unions across the country have taken on the task of getting more young people involved and listening to what they have to say.

After the pilot of the first youth internship program in 2000, local unions began strategically promoting the input of a youth perspective into the operations of the local union. What transpired for each local union was unique, as the directions each local took were all quite different. For example, Local 1518 in British Columbia elected a young member to sit on the Executive Board. In Alberta, Local 401 sent a survey out to all members under 26 and held a youth conference for 106 youth. Local 1400 in Saskatchewan began by taking the time to run workshops on global income disparity for a few young members. In addition, Local 1400 also began to work closely with the Saskatoon and District Labour Council and Saskatchewan Federation of Labour youth committees.

In Manitoba, Local 832 combined efforts with the Manitoba Federation of Labour to send youth into high schools and training schools to talk to students about health and safety in the workplace. Meanwhile, Local 1000A in Ontario focused on rallying youth in the local to participate in national and provincial youth initiatives. Locals 175 & 633 hired a young person to go into units to talk to youth about their issues. As well, the locals also began to explore how the arts and the experiences of young workers collide to produce music and popular theatre pieces.

In the short years following the pilot, there have been countless youth meetings, workshops organized, youth-oriented literature produced, youth alliances formed with affiliates, and other initiatives and programs focusing on outreach and making connections with young members. All of these efforts concentrated on providing education and training for the youth membership. While these components remain an important aspect of encouraging youth to learn more about their union and to participate politically within their union, the youth internship program has evolved to become a training ground for participants so that local unions and the National Office can utilize their skills for special projects. In the case of the 2004 youth internship program, program participants ventured into a successful organizing drive at a Winners department store in Saskatoon with the assistance of Local 1400. The positive results of the Winners campaign demonstrated not only the abilities of the youth, but it also made it clear what an asset the youth activism has become.

By providing basic labour education and training, UFCW Canada has created a pool of young union activists. The national youth internship could be credited as the catalyst for the spread of local union youth initiatives across Canada. However, it is the hard work of local union offices that facilitates the strength of youth involvement within the union. Much of the groundwork depends on the participation of young members who are involved with each local's youth committee. It is in this capacity that young members meet to discuss their issues and make recommendations to the local president on steps to take to increase youth involvement.

Local union youth committees

For the most part, interest for local union youth committees came out of the national youth internship program. The purpose of a local union youth committee is to provide a forum for young members to voice their concerns as members and to ensure an agenda is set to address these concerns. They are an essential component in the vitality of UFCW Canada's youth agenda, and comprise the base that upholds the success of the initiatives and programs created at the national and local union level.

Local 1518 in British Columbia was one of the first locals to establish a youth committee. The local was very active in recruiting young members to through the use of "*Super Servicing*." It took rank-and-file young members out of their workplaces and had them travel around with local union staff and talk directly to young members about their concerns. This helped Local 1518 to establish one of the first youth committees.

Local 401 in Alberta held the first UFCW Canada youth conference in August 2001. There were 106 young members from across the province of Alberta in attendance. The local used the youth conference to arrange provincial meeting with young members in the hope of establishing a provincial and regional youth committees. Since the establishment of the local youth committee, young members have played an active role in many union functions. One of the most notable was the G-8 protest in Calgary, where the youth committee played an active role in the planning and demonstrations.

One of UFCW Canada's largest and most active local youth committees is in Local 1400 in Saskatchewan. This youth committee has taken a leading role in organizing, servicing, and education, and has been instrumental in organizing 11 units in the youth internship program. Local 1400 has had a member graduate from the program in every year. These members have gone back to their local and taken up leadership roles on the shop floor, in the federation of labour, and on the local executive.

Local 832 in Manitoba has used social activity as a way to engage and involve new young members. It has held pub nights, and bowling and curling tournaments, all of which have had good turnouts from the membership. These events helped to get membership involved in their youth committee and other union activities. Local 832 held the second local youth conference in UFCW Canada in May 2005, when more than 50 participants attended a weekend of training and education.

Under the direction of then Local President Michael Fraser, Local 175 established the first UFCW local youth committee. This committee has been active since 1999, and most recently its members were travelling around the province of Ontario attending the local's steward conferences and working with the local to educate shop stewards about the issues and concerns of young members.

Local 1000A has taken on the *Talking Union* program in the Toronto area. *Talking Union* has young members go out and talk to high school students about unions and their rights at work.

In Quebec, Local 501 has taken an active role in the youth internship program and involving those graduates within the local. The local has members sitting on the national youth committee.

Local union youth committees' framework is set up for young people to actively participate in their local union. UFCW Canada has the most local youth committees set up across Canada.

Youth conferences

To date, the National Office has organized two youth conferences. The first youth conference UFCW Canada organized in 2001 had 60 participants and guests. It was one of the first of its kind: a national youth conference with workshops designed specifically to relate to young people's experiences and with young people facilitating the workshops for young people. Two years later, a second youth conference was organized, this time with 98 participants and guests. What was different about the second conference was that it was held for the Western and Prairie provinces only. The rationale behind organizing the regional conference arose from the political and social climate prevailing in these provinces at the time. Three out of the four provinces (Alberta, Saskatchewan, and Manitoba) anticipated provincial elections to be called shortly after the conference. In addition, the Western and Prairie provinces had the strongest leadership support for youth initiatives in the union. Not coincidentally, youth committees were heavily concentrated in this geographical region. In order to inform and mobilize young members around politics and how it affects the union and young workers, the conference served as the initial connection to the challenges facing the union.

The 2001 National Youth Conference and the 2003 regional youth conference were both a tremendous success. Overall, the two conferences turned out to be a huge investment for the union, particularly the regional conference. How the conferences were set up and coordinated determined the outcome of its success. The location, dates, agenda, outreach, facilitation, selection of guests, coordination during the conference, and other logistics were placed in the very capable hands of youth activists. In other words, the conferences were run entirely by youth for youth. What fuelled the conferences was the support of the union's leadership. The youth had real decision-making power over the conferences, and there was commitment to providing the necessary resources to make the conferences the best they could be.

In many ways, the 2001 National Youth Conference was one of the principal building blocks leading up to the crescendo of events at the 2003 regional youth conference. By incorporating the recommendations from the national conference and taking advantage of the existing youth framework already set in place by the national youth internship program and local youth committees, the union moved into an elevated level of organizing with young people. From a workshop aimed at creating further youth initiatives and programs at the local union level, conference participants made presentations to one another and local union executive officers. The following day, local union executive officers—individually, on behalf of their respective locals—responded to their youth delegation and to the rest of the conference participants. The response was tremendous, especially from Locals 401, 1400, and 832. In fact, members of Local 832 were delighted to discover that, in addition to the local youth conference they proposed, a $10,000 budget was allocated to them to pursue the other ideas drafted.

Meanwhile, under the direction of National Director Michael Fraser, an organizing meeting was called during the conference. The meeting dealt strictly with the union's efforts in organizing Wal-Mart. At the meeting, approximately 30 young members talked about strategies the union could explore, possible leads that could be followed, and who would be interested in working on the campaign. This was a real meeting, beyond brainstorming and note-taking, that produced real results. After the conference, a team of young people were taken out of their workplaces and placed on a Wal-Mart organizing drive in North Battleford, Saskatchewan. Not surprisingly, the organizing lead came directly from the meeting held at the conference. Local 1400, with the assistance of the National Office and other locals across Canada, successfully made an application for certification to the Saskatchewan Labour Relations Board in March of 2004.[11]

Education conferences in general are often good energizers for union members. UFCW Canada youth conferences have been extraordinary. They have been meeting places for young members and the union's leadership to get together and discuss how existing and new challenges can be tackled. Bringing it one step further, the regional youth conference has set the pace to demonstrate concrete commitment and innovative organizing strategy with young people. Without the groundwork already laid out by the national youth internship program and the strength of local youth committees, the youth conferences would have been drastically different. By incorporating past experience and work into the conferences, it has pushed the union to the next level. Plans were made to hold the next regional youth conference in Atlantic Canada in August 2005.

Challenges ahead

UFCW Canada has been able to mould a heightened level of interest and commitment from a segment of the union's membership virtually untouched and gone unnoticed in the past. While the accomplishments are immense, there is still a lot of work ahead. In the process of increasing youth participation and incorporating their role into the operations of the union, a set of challenges has evolved alongside the process.

First of all, not all local unions within UFCW Canada are actively and consistently participating in youth initiatives and programs. The National Office can set up national youth programs and initiatives, but it is up to the local unions to send the members. Second, if a local youth committee does not exist, there is no set structure in place for further involvement when youth return home from participating in any youth action or education program. Youth who come out of smaller local unions often do not have the resources or staff readily available to facilitate the development of any youth initiative or program. Thirdly, youth tokenism is easy to fall into. Designating a youth spokesperson or calling on the same group of young people again and again is an issue that needs careful and consistent monitoring. The participation of young Aboriginals, immigrants, and workers of colour has fluctuated since the inception of the union's youth agenda. The issue of youth representation within the union should be reflected in a balance of participation from all youth across the spectrum, including more marginalized youth.

While measures to address these challenges have been implemented at the National Office—such as special youth project funding for locals and rotating youth facilitators for the national youth internship program—there is a need to coordinate further measures with local union offices to ensure these challenges are minimized, with particular emphasis on diversifying and enhancing the strategies already set in place.

Conclusion

Young people are one of the most vulnerable groups of workers in the workforce. Regressions in public policy, coupled with declining union density and an aging labour movement, have forced the labour movement to re-invent itself and move away from more conventional methods of organizing, servicing, and membership participation. As one of the demographically youngest unions in Canada and the U.S., the UFCW has focused its resources on mobilizing its youth membership. UFCW Canada's leadership most fundamentally understands power: how to build it and how to share it, by nourishing and encouraging youth to get involved in their union and by giving them a voice within their union. By setting out a long-term youth agenda, it has been successful in transforming itself into a union of which young people want to be a part. The development of the national youth internship program, local union youth committees, and holding youth conferences have created a space for young members to become both empowered and active. While some challenges have been identified in the process, they are certainly not considered setbacks. Instead, these challenges are viewed as opportunities to make the union even stronger.

UFCW Canada has seen the benefits of involving young members with increased participation in committees, servicing, and organizing. It has been the training and education of young members, along with a bottom-up approach, that has allowed young members within UFCW Canada to become: shop stewards, service representatives, organizers, Executive Board members, and local union and national full-time staff. UFCW Canada and its local unions have established a practical and feasible system of integrating young members into every level of the union. The direction UFCW Canada has taken to be a more representative and inclusive union is an exemplary definition of union renewal.

Notes

1. UFCW Canada, research department, 2004.
2. Both Levi Strauss plants closed at approximately the same time in March 2004.
3. Interview with Andrew Mackenzie, 2004.
4. The Québec Labour Relations Commission certified a bargaining unit at the Jonquière, Québec Wal-Mart store on August 2, 2004. On February 1, 2005, Local 503 applied to the Québec Minister of Labour for binding arbitration leading to a first contract. On February 9, 2005, Wal-Mart announced it would close the store in May 2005. On April 29, 2005, Wal-Mart shut the store a week earlier than scheduled.
5. The Québec Labour Relations Commission certified a bargaining unit at the Saint-Hyacinthe, Québec Wal-Mart store on January 18, 2005.
6. Michael Fraser was the president of Local 175. Local 633 is a craft union local, which represents retail meat departments and meat processing workers. The two locals are separate, but Local 175 performs administrative processing and services for the members of Local 633.
7. Interview with Michael Fraser, 2002.
8. From internal documents of the UFCW Canada Locals 175 and 633. Data collected in 1999.
9. Interview with Debora De Angelis, 2002.
10. In 2000, the youth internship program was piloted and ran for six weeks.
11. Certification has not yet been issued; an application is pending at the Saskatchewan Labour Relations Board.

References

Hinton, Louisette, Josefina Moruz, and Cheryl Mumford. 1999. A Union Perspective on Emerging Trends in the Workplace. In *Changing Work Relationships in Industrialized Economics*, ed. Isik Urla Zeytinoghi. Amsterdam: John Benjamins.

United Food and Commercial Workers (UFCW) Canada. 2005. Organizing the Unorganized. *Our Union: Membership Magazine for UFCW Canada Members* 22 (Winter 2004/5): 4-5.

Youth Need Unions. *Our Times* 18 (December/January 2000): 30-35.

Chapter 11
Renewal from Different Directions: The Case of UNITE-HERE Local 75

STEVEN TUFTS

Introduction

The stagnation of union growth in Canada is usually attributed to the relative decline of highly unionized manufacturing employment and the continued low rates of unionization in expanding private sector services. As a result, we often overlook the historic and significant presence of unions in those few organized service industries such as accommodation. In Canada, hotel and tavern workers have been organized since the 1890s, but the history of hospitality unionism is uneven at best. During much of the post-war period, there were occasional bargaining and organizing victories, but these were often overshadowed by incidents of union corruption and a failure to organize large numbers of hospitality workers, even as accommodation and food services experienced rapid growth. By the late 1980s, however, some unions representing hospitality workers in Canada began using new strategies to organize workers and strengthen bargaining. The result has been a period of union renewal in selected hospitality labour markets.

UNITE-HERE Local 75, representing 7,500 hotel workers in the Greater Toronto Area, is a significant case of a re-invented local that emerged from a period of questionable leadership, followed by international trusteeship in the mid-1990s, to become one of the more innovative unions in the city.[1] It is difficult to discuss Local 75's renewal in terms of a single organizational change, ideological shift, or strategy. Instead, the re-invention of Local 75 involves *multiple strategies* emerging from different organizational levels of the union. Some of these strategies are developed, implemented, and refined by the local itself, while others are orchestrated by the international office in Washington, D.C. These strategies come at employers from different directions. They are *integrated*, reinforcing one another as a systemic approach to renewing the union's strength. The use of multiple and integrated strategies is necessary, given the context of a global hospitality sector that employs large numbers of marginalized workers.

Union renewal in a global sector with global workers

Toronto's accommodation sector, employing the majority of Local 75's members, is an increasingly global industry. The unique ownership-management structure of the industry forces unions to deal frequently with two employers: the owner of the property and the management company or "brand" that runs the hotel. In recent years, there has been significant consolidation in the sector as large international

Table 1: Selected Toronto CMA Labour Force Characteristics, all Occupations, all Industries and Hotels, Motels and Tourist Courts Industry (Standard Industrial Classification 911), 2001

2001 Census	Total population 15 years and over in labour force	% immigrant population	% entered country within the last 5 years	% neither English or French as mother tongue	% visible minority population	Average employment income (C$)
All Industries, All Occupations						
Total	2,522,025	47.9	7.8	38.7	34.2	39,006
Male	1,326,115	48.5	8.2	39.9	33.8	47,033
Female	1,195,905	47.3	7.4	37.5	34.6	30,263
SIC 911, All Occupations						
Total	13,855	68.1	10.8	48.6	54.2	28,749
Male	5,985	66.8	11.2	51.0	55.8	32,819
Female	7,870	69.2	10.5	46.9	53.0	25,543

Source: Ottawa: Statistics Canada, March 16, 2004. 2001 Census of Canada. Catalogue number 97F0012XCB2001047.

hotel management companies such as Fairmont and Marriott have expanded their brands across the globe. Multi-national hotel companies are able to invest large amounts of resources to resist unionization and to suppress the demands of workers. Hotel companies have become increasingly sophisticated in resisting attempts to organize hotel workers in Toronto, employing union-busting consultants and in some cases responding to the "union threat" by offering wage rates above those prevailing in unionized hotels.

Perhaps the largest challenge to organizing hotel workers, however, is the diversity of the "global" hotel workforce. In large metropolitan centres, hotel workers are drawn from the most vulnerable segments of the labour market as hotels employ recent immigrants, women, and people of colour with limited employment opportunities (Ghosh 2003). These workers speak different languages (with English as a second, third, or fourth language), are often unfamiliar with Canadian labour regulations, and in some cases may be undocumented, working in fear of state authorities. The challenges to organizing a largely Latino hotel workforce in Southern California and the strategies used by UNITE-HERE to reach these workers have been documented (Wells 2000). While some of the challenges and strategies identified are applicable to Toronto, it must be realized that the hotel labour force in the city is even more heterogeneous and fragmented.

First, the accommodation sector employs a higher number of women, immigrants, and visible minorities, who earn significantly less than the average worker (Table 1). Within the sector there is a pronounced racial and gender division of labour among occupational categories. The divisions are often between "front-of-the-house" and "back-of-the-house" occupations. For example, room attendants or "light-duty cleaners," the largest occupational category in Greater Toronto Area (GTA) hotels, are mostly women of colour born outside of Canada. Such "back-

Table 2: Selected Greater Toronto Area Labour Force Characteristics, all Occupations, all Industries and all Selected Occupations in Hotels, Motels and Tourist Courts Industry (Standard Industrial Classification 911), 1996

Occupational Category	Total non-institutional population	% Female	% "Visible Minority"	% Born in Canada	Income as % of all industry average
All occupations, all industries	1,275,995	47.8	33.6	48.3	100 ($32,635)
All occupations, SIC 911	12,485	47.9	52.8	30.5	72.9
Accommodation Service Managers	750	32.0	25.3	56.0	136.1
Accounting and Related Clerks	145	37.9	62.1	37.9	76.3
Bartenders	290	5.2	37.9	39.7	82.9
Chefs	310	17.7	43.5	30.6	94.3
Cooks	610	26.2	66.4	29.5	70.3
Dry Cleaning and Laundry	200	65.0	67.5	10.0	57.0
Executive Housekeepers	135	74.1	63.0	11.1	73.5
Food and Beverage Servers	1,770	42.4	44.1	22.9	54.1
Food Service Supervisors	105	28.6	52.4	38.1	67.2
Hotel Front Desk Clerks	1,350	58.5	42.6	45.1	60.8
Janitors	555	17.1	51.4	33.3	90.2
Kitchen and FS Helpers	575	15.7	70.4	10.0	51.5
Light Duty Cleaners	2,360	80.3	82.0	6.4	53.2
Hosts/Hostesses	110	63.6	36.4	45.5	47.1
Restaurant and FS Managers	210	23.8	31.0	42.9	116.9
Senior Managers	30	50.0	33.3	33.3	272.8
Other Occupations	2,965	48.4	43.1	41.8	85.2

Source: Custom tabulation ordered by the author from Statistics Canada, 1996 Census.

of-the-house" work pays significantly less than other "front-of-the-house" occupations (e.g., bartenders) staffed by more male (and white) workers (Table 2).

The gender, ethnic, and income segmentation of the hotel labour market creates challenges for solidarity and new organizing. Challenges range from the ability to communicate with workers in their own language to racism among workers. Nevertheless, in 2003, 37.9% of the 27,550 accommodation workers in the Toronto Census Metropolitan Area were unionized, well above the 20.1% all-industry city average (City of Toronto, 2003 Industry Profiles). The unionized hotel sector is among the few sectors that serve as a strong base for increasing the incomes for large numbers of immigrant workers. Recent research, however, indicates that, while unions in Canada have become more diverse in the 1980s and 1990s, there is still work to be done in organizing and collective bargaining to realize a significant union differential between unionized and non-unionized immigrant workers (Hunt and Rayside 2000; Reitz and Verma 2004).

Figure 1: Downtown Toronto Hotels by Size and Bargaining Agent

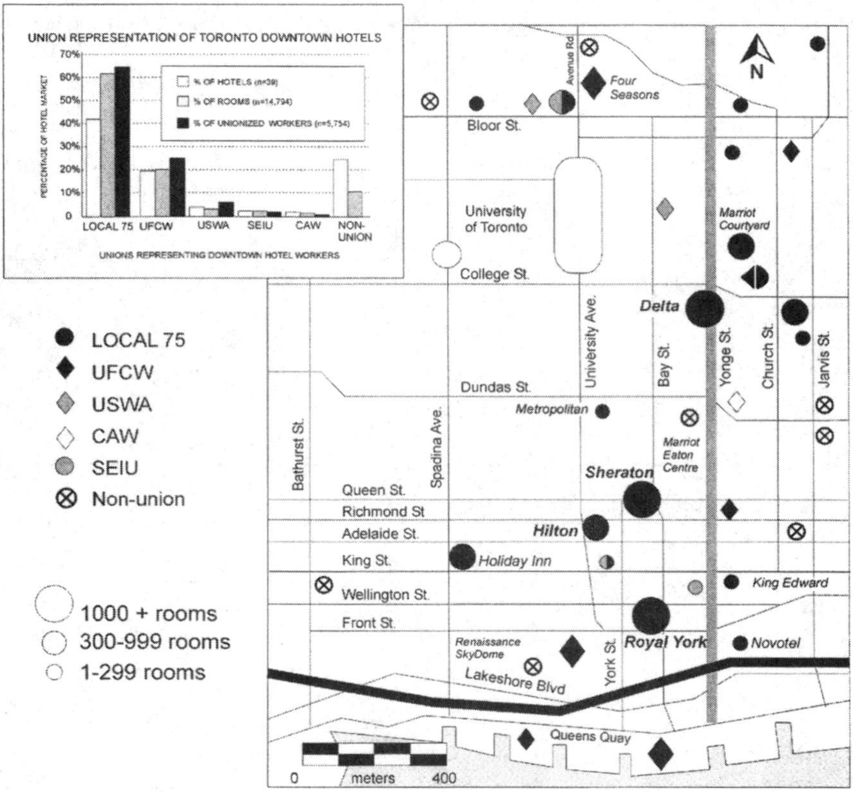

There are several challenges to organizing workers from diverse communities (Milkman 2000), but the relatively high union density in accommodation services indicates that immigrant workers and workers of colour are organized and are capable of organizing themselves despite a sometimes ambivalent and often fragmented labour movement. In the case of Toronto's hotel sector, there are several unions representing hotel workers. While Local 75 is the largest hotel workers' union in the city, representing approximately two-thirds of organized accommodation workers, the UFCW, USWA, SEIU, and other unions also represent hotel workers (Figure 1). For the most part, all these unions continue to organize in the sector. Jurisdictional conflict and competition to represent hotel workers in Toronto can, however, undermine union renewal efforts and are barriers to implementing multiple and integrated strategies. Besides draining each other's resources as unions defend themselves against raids, representation of hotel workers by multiple unions also limits collective bargaining and organizing. Competition among unions can sabotage organizing efforts and render sophisticated strategies useless.

For example, even though the USWA successfully organized workers at the Intercontinental Hotel in the late 1990s, its attempt to organize the non-union Marriott Eaton Centre hotel in 2001 failed. For some unionists in the sector, the failure stemmed from the "blitz" approach adopted by the USWA, which involved signing the required number of workers for a certification vote over a short period and then immediately applying to the Ontario Labour Relations Board for an election. While the union gathered a significant number of signed cards, it failed to counter an aggressive anti-union campaign launched by the company prior to the vote, and lost the certification election. Under Ontario labour law, workers must wait another year before re-applying. At the same time, Local 75 was running a concurrent campaign in the hotel (e.g., internal committee building, house visits) that was aimed to build worker involvement over a longer period. The Local 75 approach was designed to manage the anti-union backlash from the employer. The failed campaign by the USWA, however, also delayed Local 75's campaign.

Conflicts between unions with different organizational structures—the USWA's general industrial model compared to UNITE-HERE's international sectoral unionism—continue to challenge organizing efforts. Hotel workers are seen as integral to the renewal efforts of many industrial unions seeking to diversify their declining sectoral (i.e., manufacturing) and geographical (e.g., suburban, rural) bases. The case is just one example of how jurisdictional conflict among unions can limit potentially successful organizing efforts. Successful bargaining and organizing in a segmented labour market, however, requires that unions overcome the conflicts associated with jurisdictional conflicts.

At the same time, it is important to recognize that the presence of multiple unions in Toronto's hotel sector played an important role in the re-invention of Local 75 as an active organizing union. After an extended period of suspected corruption in the 1980s and early 1990s, Local 75 was put under trusteeship only after questionable leadership threatened to facilitate a "raid" by another union and secession from the International. The trusteeship allowed the union to build a more participatory and innovative leadership and change the overall culture of the union (Aguiar, Kainer, and Pupo 1998). The contradictions of multiple unions representing workers in the same industry continue to typify hotel labour in Toronto.

Multiple strategies: Attacking from different directions

In 1997, Local 75 faced a difficult period of bargaining with the Novotel airport hotel and its union-busting HRM consultant, John Platz. Management was pursuing an aggressive negotiating position that was leading to a strike and threatened decertification if an agreement could not be reached. Fortunately, Local 75's international union had been active with the trade secretariat International Union of Food, Agricultural, Hotel, Restaurant, Catering, Tobacco and Allied Workers' Associations (IUF) that had established a trade union rights agreement with ACCOR, the French multinational hospitality firm that owns Novotel. The IUF coordinated international pressure on ACCOR to respect the agreement and deal fairly with Local 75. In her detailed study of the ACCOR-IUF agreement, Jane Wills (2002) argues that pressure to apply the trade union rights agreement to organizing hotels in places where workers "fear" organizing is crucial to trade union growth, but it is not an absolute substitute for local union action:

In organizing workers in the hotel sector, for example, there is no substitute for local organizing and, if possible, for defending such activity
with national agreements. However, should those workers be part of
a [transnational corporation], there is also scope for using an international framework agreement as an extra lever in support such activity
and even ensuring the activity is a success. (Wills 2002, 695)[2]

It is the *extra lever* that is so important in organizing fragmented and marginalized
workers. But this does not mean that "local organizing" is displaced, but rather
that it is assisted. Further, it is the integration of local strategies with international
support, and vice-versa, that is the key to organizing successfully in the sector.
Multiple integrated strategies are central to Local 75's master bargaining and new
hotel organizing campaigns.

Master bargaining in the North American hotel sector

Removing geographically diverse wages and working conditions from competition is among the primary goals of trade unionism. The most effective way to
reduce capital's ability to relocate from high-wage regions to low-wage regions
is to bargain a common "pattern" covering large areas. For hotel capital, however,
international relocation is not an immediate threat to workers, as the service produced (i.e., accommodation services consumed at the place of "production") is
not mobile in the short to medium term. International companies can divest and
develop hotels in more compliant hospitality markets around the globe, but this is
a long-term strategy. Downward pressure on wages is most likely when hotels with
similar amenities, and similar vacancy and daily room rates in *the same market*, have
different cost structures. For example, if a four-star hotel is forced to raise its room
rate to cover the cost of a wage increase, and other four-star competitors are not
pressured by a similar wage increase, the first hotel is at a competitive disadvantage.
If all four-star hotels face across-the-board wage increases, room rates are more
likely to increase in order to compensate. Across-the-board room rate increases
can occur up to the point where visitors start staying away from the city's four-star
hotels or avoid the destination altogether—a point that global cities such as New
York and London never seem to reach.

Local 75 managed to negotiate a master agreement with the employers of several Toronto hotels, but the agreement was broken during the period of trusteeship
in the early 1990s as large hotels—such as many hotels outside the downtown
core (e.g., Inn on the Park, Westin Prince)—abandoned the agreements. Remnants
of the master agreement between Local 75 and the Hotel Employers Group of
Toronto (now the Central Hotel Group comprised of the Delta Chelsea, the Toronto Hilton, and the Sheraton Centre) survived, but the scope of the agreement
and number of hotels covered was limited. Although there may be some benefits
gained from bargaining together and stabilizing labour costs, many hotels prefer
individual contracts. An individual contract gives the hotel some flexibility to bring
wages into competition and adjust to property or chain-specific conditions. For
example, head office pressure to increase levels of service may require a hotel to

become temporarily more labour-intensive and reduce labour cost per worker to compensate. In this case, hotels may be less willing to enter into a master agreement with higher wages. At the same time, a high-performance hotel may wish to settle an agreement other hotels cannot afford in order to escape labour unrest in the competing hotels as unions attempt to "bargain-up" to the higher wage level.

Removing wages from competition by rebuilding and maintaining a master agreement has been a priority of Local 75. Local 75's collective agreements with the "Big 3+1" (the Central Hotel Group hotels and the Royal York) generally set the pattern for negotiations with the smaller hotels throughout the GTA. While base wages and benefits are relatively lower in the smaller properties, the same percentage increases to wages and improvements in benefits are often adopted. A master agreement with several big city hotels also gives the union greater leverage over the sector. While some argue that striking single properties exerts pressure on hotels, given that guests can be diverted to non-striking hotels, the argument assumes hotels always have some vacancies. Vacant rooms are rare during peak seasons in large urban markets, so guests who do not have the option to transfer to another hotel must suffer picket lines and decreased levels of service. At the same time, there is the possibility of collusion among hotels who may agree not to accept each others' guests during a work-stoppage. The ability to strike hotels city-wide gives hotel workers the power to affect the entire tourism market, especially during major events, as was the case in Toronto when strike action threatened to disrupt the Pope's visit to World Youth Day events and the International Carnival (Caribana) during the summer 2002 negotiations.

Rebuilding a strong master agreement and improving wages and working conditions through strike action are challenging tasks. The tactics used to pressure employers in mature industrial relations systems in manufacturing or public services do not easily apply to the hotel sector. While hotels risk significant financial losses and damage to their customer base during a work-stoppage, management can often operate striking hotels with reduced staffing levels (Siemieruk 2001; Leong 2002). The structure of hotel work and Toronto's hotel workers' unions make strikes a less feasible alternative to unions and hotel workers than they are for other sectors. Much hotel work requires limited training, and employers can quickly replace striking workers with management or replacement workers. The use of casual and seasonal labour (easily secured through employment agencies) by the industry creates a reserve army of hotel workers anxious to access more hours of work. The low wages paid to the majority of union members and a low dues base limit the funds available to support workers and their families during a strike. Weekly strike pay for Local 75 members is approximately $100 per week, less than half of the strike pay from larger unions.

For these reasons, a host of actions and different strategies are needed to pressure employers during collective bargaining. Tactics that do not involve the complete withdrawal of Local 75's member's labour proved to be effective in terms of mobilizing member participation, exerting pressure on employers, and attracting media attention without formal strike action.[3]

These multiple and integrated tactics were all evident in the 2002 round of bargaining.

The summer of 2002 in Toronto was unusually hot, especially for many of the city's hotel workers. Local 75's contracts with the city's largest hotels had expired in the late spring, launching a period of intense bargaining. After months of negotiations and a series of job-related actions and rallies held throughout the city, Local 75 had contracts with its "Big 3+1" properties that significantly narrowed the gap between other leading hotel sector collective agreements in the city and across Canada.

The campaign reflected the new model initiated by Local 75 President-Administrator Paul Clifford, encouraging greater participation of rank-and-file members and increased visibility of hotel workers in the community (Clifford and Kainer 1998). Generating this participation involves staff representatives engaging in intensive "internal" organizing with all departments inside the hotel. Through contact with departmental shop stewards and other workers (often during break periods), members are informed about actions occurring at the hotel or at other sites. These actions often involve establishing a presence in the community with a series of visible rallies before any strike or lockout with formal picket lines. The numerous events organized by Local 75 involve the selection of an accessible site, such as Fairmont's downtown Toronto head office or outside a large hotel (e.g., Delta Chelsea). The rallies often involve a picket march with colourful banners and signs (the recent trademark being yellow circles with purple stencilled lettering of various hotel positions), loud music and chanting, with speeches by rank-and-file activists, leaders, and supporters from other unions. The demonstrations are usually short in duration (one or two hours) and are scheduled during shift changes to allow workers beginning and ending shifts to participate. The scheduling and duration are important, as they allow members living throughout the GTA to attend without sacrificing other commitments (e.g., child care).

The numerous public events held by Local 75 during the summer of 2002 began to intensify in June as negotiations progressed slowly with the Big 3+1. On Monday, June 10, Reverend Jesse Jackson attended a large downtown rally. Addressing the hotel workers, who were now in a legal strike position, Reverend Jackson told the crowd, "When you trust in God, He will get you a hotel contract." Reverend Jackson has been a supporter of hotel workers in North America for a number of years. In 1998, President-Administrator Paul Clifford read a letter of support written by Jackson to Toronto hotel workers at an International Hotel Workers' Day. When asked about his reasons for coming to Toronto, Reverend Jackson replied, "I don't accept the artificial barriers of state, mountains, oceans, or lakes" (CP 2002). The decision to expend effort and resources to secure Jesse Jackson, an American clergyman, may be questioned by some Canadian nationalists and secular unionists. But it is important to realize that Reverend Jackson represents something different to many hotel workers, especially those from black diasporic communities, than he may to others on the left who have different relationships and affinities with the religious community.

In July, the union's bargaining committee at the Royal York agreed to allow members to vote on a management offer without endorsing the contract. According to the official spokesperson, the company was "saddened" when 70% of the workers rejected the offer and set a 72-hour strike deadline (Leong 2002). With

World Youth Day approaching, the Royal York and the other large hotels were under pressure. Following the rejection of their offer, the Royal York countered with a proposal endorsed by the bargaining committee and ratified by 80% of the members. The major settlement reached with Fairmont Royal York was a three-year deal that included a 13.5% increase for non-gratuity workers and a 9% increase for gratuity earners over the life of the agreement. Other gains included increased employer contributions to health benefits, paid personal days, and an agreement for employer-subsidized transit passes.

The union tried to duplicate the agreement with the Central Hotel Group, but the agreement at the Royal York set a high pattern for the other three large hotels to follow. These employers were not only resisting the wage settlement, but they were also determined to obtain a five-year agreement. These conditions challenged the union's attempt to rebuild the master agreement including the Royal York, since, before wages can be removed from competition through pattern bargaining, collective agreements have to expire at the same time so simultaneous negotiations can begin. The conflict between labour and management was intensifying. By the end of July, the provincially-appointed mediator ruled there was no chance of a settlement.

By August, Local 75 rallies and demonstrations became more aggressive. During the days before "Carnival" weekend, the union held "study sessions" outside the hotels. These sessions involved four-hour walkouts by the workers and information pickets outside the properties. The goal was to inform members, guests, and the public about hotel workers' demands, and "educate" hotel management about the difficulties of running a full hotel during a strike. The media (print and television), covered the walkouts. The line-ups of discontented International Carnival visitors waiting to check into rooms not yet cleaned were of particular interest. When the union threatened to engage in a full-scale strike, management claimed they were prepared to service guests with replacement workers (Keung 2002). Local 75 threatened to begin rotating strikes for the month of August, but the Central Hotel Group countered that, if one of the hotels struck, workers at all three hotels would be locked out. Talks broke-off in early August, and the posturing continued, but an end game was finally reached on August 26 in New York City. HERE Local 75 recommended a four-year agreement for ratification.

The four-year agreement between the union and the Central Hotel Group, signed and witnessed by head office representatives of the multinational corporations and union officials in New York, did not match the pattern set by the Royal York. The settlement did, however, include a 16% wage increase for room attendants, dishwashers, and laundry workers, a 14% increase for other non-gratuity workers, and a 9% increase for gratuity earning positions. The agreement was ratified by 83% of the workers (80% at the Hilton, 75% at the Sheraton, and 90% at the Delta Chelsea). Taken together, the agreements made significant gains for workers, including a 30% increase in general health and welfare benefits, as well as increases to pension plans. The gains were also achieved despite the impacts that the events of September 11, 2001 had on the industry. Furthermore, the agreement was reached without a full-scale work stoppage. The negotiations marked a significant milestone in the history of Local 75. In a period of "union renewal" since the mid-1990s, it

Figure 2: Room Attendant Hourly Wage Rates, Selected Toronto Hotels, 1994–2005

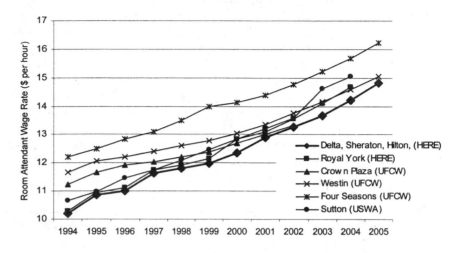

Source: Data gathered from collective agreements. Wage rates have been annualized to allow for comparison.

signified the union's commitment to (re)building a strong master agreement and pattern bargaining. The agreements also significantly reduced the gap between wage rates negotiated by Local 75 and other unions representing hotel workers in Toronto that were significantly higher throughout the 1990s (see Figure 2).

While the agreement did achieve important gains for the hotel workers, the attempt to (re)establish the local master agreement was less successful. The wage increases were slightly below that of the agreement reached with the Royal York. More importantly, the four-year deal makes collective bargaining with the "Big 3+1" more difficult, as the Royal York agreement expires half a year earlier. The failure to re-establish a local master agreement with the "Big 3+1" may, however, *benefit* Local 75 in the future as it takes part in more global bargaining strategies

The symbolism attached to signing the agreement in New York with upper-level union and company officials signalled a shift in the scale of future bargaining from the local to the national and international level. The international office is in the process of building agreements with multinational hotel companies that establish, among other things, protocols for organizing campaigns, guidelines for bargaining, as well as chain-wide agreements as explained by a member of Local 75's staff:

> We are looking at these new transnational corporations where we have the density on an international basis. If we look, for example at Fairmont [and its subsidiary Delta Hotels], that used to be Cana-dian Pacific, we have in excess of 50% of Fairmont's hotels unionized throughout North America. Of that, the vast majority are represented by HERE. The collective strength we can have is by lining up our

bargaining dates. So we are looking at having a North American-wide expiry date. In 2006, you would have Chicago, New York, LA, Boston, Toronto, and Honolulu having all lined up their expiration dates. If we were representing the majority of Fairmont workers, the amount of power we would have to secure decent agreements and get these companies to accept, for example, card-check neutrality agreements on their new developments, or to be able to bring in their residual units that are non-union, such as front desk, I think we'd have an incredible amount of strength and power by utilizing this international approach. (Scott, Local 75 staff member)

Although Local 75's master agreement with the three large hotels expires a year later than the Royal York's, it is now in-line with other master agreements in large metropolitan centres that all expire in 2006. It is here where we may be seeing the beginning of hotel labour's rescaling of bargaining from the local to (inter)national multi-employer agreements. Recent developments in the U.S. and abroad point to the increasing importance of 2006 as an opportunity to "scale-up" bargaining. In October 2004, San Francisco employers locked out 4,000 hotel workers of HERE Local 2 in response to a strike of a small number of city hotels. A major issue in the negotiation is the duration of the agreement as hotel employers do not want a two-year deal expiring in 2006.[4] There is even potential to bargain chain-wide agreements that extend outside of North America, since key agreements with the Liquor, Miscellaneous and Hospitality Workers Union in Australia also expire in 2006.

"Jumping-scales" (Smith 1990, 1993) from local to international pattern bargaining may be a viable alternative for Local 75, as an agreement with all of the large Toronto hotels remains elusive. Although Local 75 represents the most hotels workers and the largest hotels, premier properties such as the Westin Harbour Castle, the Sutton Place, and the Four Seasons (arguably Toronto's only luxury hotel) are represented by the USWA and UFCW. In bargaining a local master hotel agreement, the ideal process is to set the top-performing property as a target and push similar hotels into the same wage structure. Even if Local 75 establishes a collective agreement with all its larger hotels, master bargaining on the scale of New York, Chicago, or Vancouver is a challenge for Toronto's hotel workers.

Furthermore, the fortunes of Local 75 workers will inevitably be influenced by the outcomes of negotiations between hotels and other unions. This situation may have benefited Local 75 in the recent past as its agreements, negotiated in organizationally weak periods, lagged behind those of other unions. During its present rebuilding period, there was great incentive to match these agreements. But, now that Local 75 has built a stronger organizational structure, it will have to ensure that bargaining is not influenced by substandard agreements negotiated by weaker unions. Hotel workers would likely hold a much stronger bargaining position if they negotiated *together*, but the deeply embedded competitive relationships among unions with different organizational models makes any cooperative bargaining seem impossible. In simple terms, jurisdictional conflict and the lack of local sectoral bargaining strategy among different unions limits labour's ability to bargain a local pattern.

Mobilizing support for bargaining is an intensive task in the hotel sector. Although the diverse membership and the limited resources of unions make full-blown strikes difficult to sustain, low-wage hotel workers are militant and capable of solidarity. The exercise of union power does, however, have to take different forms. Organized actions outside striking and sanctions inside the workplace, such as informally "working-to-the-rule" of collective agreements, are legitimate forms of labour action for marginalized workers. At the same time, organizing and making members visible on the street and in hotel lobbies is how workers launch effective struggle against employers. A similar multifaceted approach is integral to the local's ongoing renewal efforts that also include innovative tactics and campaigns to organize new members.

New hotel development campaigns

By the mid-1990s, it became clear that the booming U.S. economy was leading to a new round of hotel development in many U.S. cities—often funded with public money. For hotel unions, a window of opportunity was opening to increase the membership by developing new strategies to organize workers in these newly built and renovated properties.

Campaigns would have to begin *before* workers were even hired. In a hostile regulatory environment, labour organizers realize that it is important to limit anti-labour responses to union drives and in some cases force employers to agree to terms that differ from legislative frameworks favouring firms. In the U.S., unions have attempted to establish their own regulatory framework by entering "card check" and "neutrality" agreements with employers (Bronfenbrenner 2000). In simplest terms, employers agree to recognize the union voluntarily (i.e., without a labour board supervised vote) when the union demonstrates that a specified percentage of union cards have been signed. Often a respected community member (e.g., a local official or cleric) is assigned the responsibility of checking the cards. Similarly, employers may also sign agreements with unions to remain neutral during an organizing campaign, meaning there will be no interference or intimidation of workers.[5] In exchange for entering the agreement, unions agree that they will not disrupt normal business operations during the drive.

These strategies have particular relevance for the hotel industry. First, the sector employs many immigrants and undocumented workers who are vulnerable to employer intimidation and require as much "neutrality" and freedom as possible from employer threats during union drives. In a consumer service that is based on providing guests with a secure, peaceful, comfortable space away from their homes, actions and picket lines in hotel lobbies are unwelcome. For new hotel developments to be profitable, they must be completed in a timely fashion. Delays are costly. This is precisely why UNITE-HERE has actively tracked new developments in North America, planning campaigns well before official groundbreaking ceremonies. The new hotel development project was largely coordinated by Lee Strieb, a senior research analyst with the union. Besides tracking new developments, the major tasks were to develop and share campaign strategies with all locals. To this effect, the union held a conference on new hotel development in Providence, RI, in the fall of 1998.

Disruption of hotel developments involves diverse tactics, ranging from using political influence with members of local councils to organizing community groups around zoning issues. The entire hotel development process must be analyzed from the leasing of property through financing and zoning bylaws. When a point of leverage is identified, the developer can be approached. For example, in San Leandro the developer of a marina conference centre agreed to a card check agreement in exchange for Local 2850 halting a push for a local referendum on the project's zoning and ceasing its campaign for a withdrawal of public investment (Wakeland 1998).

Interested in these tactics, Local 75 sent several staff to the 1998 conference, even though there was little new hotel construction in the city at the time. Ontario Labour Board certification practices are not as harsh as those in U.S. "right to work" states, but changes to the *Employment Standards Act* by a Conservative provincial government in the 1990s led Local 75 to consider campaign strategies developed in the United States for future organizing drives. Although there was little new hotel development in Toronto throughout the 1990s, there was evidence that Ontario was poised for some new development activity. Some 1,766 rooms were added to the provincial hotel supply in 2001, and another 3,028 were expected to open in 2002, accounting for over 60% of all estimated new rooms in Canada (Colliers 2002). In Toronto, while there has been some new construction activity, these have largely been smaller "boutique" hotels or smaller executive suites properties (hotels for extended stays, usually smaller with two-room [living + bedroom] accommodations) built around the airport and northern limits of the city.[6] Local 75 has tracked these developments since the program (succinctly defined below) was conceived:

> In terms of the union's immediate interests, if the hotels aren't going to be union hotels, then it's better for us that they not be built ... Our position is: sure, build new hotels, but once they're built they are going to have to have HERE members running them. And our strategy, part of our research strategy, is to track new developments and try to think of ways, frankly, to screw them up if developers are non-union." (Dan, Local 75 staff)

A current project of significant size in downtown Toronto is the 305-room luxury "five-diamond" Ritz Carlton project, supposedly led by Donald Trump, with others in early stages of development (Wong 2000). The Ritz Carlton project, originally slated to open in late 2002, has been delayed (McNish 2001). In part, some of these delays were due to actions of Local 75. The union secured the services of a well-known urban planner to assist in identifying weaknesses in projects such as the Ritz Carlton that can be exploited for leverage. Hiring a planning professional indicates how "knowledge-intensive" these campaigns have become. The planner prepared a document outlining ways a project of this size could be delayed (e.g., application for building permits, zoning processes). The union worked with its political allies on Toronto's city council to question the project, and it was delayed for approximately 18 months.

Table 3: Major Provisions of Neutrality Agreement for a New Hotel

1. Language defining Employer and Employees (i.e., union coverage).
2. Labour peace agreements limiting union action against employer during campaign (e.g., picketing).
3. Employee rights establishing employer neutrality during organizing drive and guarantees against union coercion of workers.
4. Union involvement in hiring processes (e.g., furnishing employer with applicants).
5. Rules outlining union access to workers including guarantees of access to lists of employees.
6. Card count recognition language requiring only a majority to sign union cards for certification, negating the need for a vote supervised by the Ontario Labour Relations Board.
7. Arbitration language (final and binding) for the first agreement if negotiations fail along with no strike/no lockout provisions.
8. Successor rights language if the hotel is sold during the campaign.
9. Duration language (e.g., agreement is in place for four years from the hotel's opening).

Source: *Neutrality Agreement for a New Hotel-Memorandum of Agreement*, signed with developers of 311 Bay Street (Ritz Carlton) HERE Local 75, 2003.

In interviews with Local 75 research staff, Toronto City Councillors Olivia Chow, Jack Layton, Kyle Rae, and Pam McConnell were particularly valuable in delaying the project. A complex hotel development of this size provided many opportunities for experienced politicians to question aspects of the project, given the numerous application and approval processes. Furthermore, the actions of other parties also attempting to delay the project helped Local 75. Owners and tenants of the Scotia-McLeod building, a neighbouring office tower, were concerned about the impact the new building would have on views from its offices, as well as the effects of shadows and wind tunnelling (communication with informant). In the spring of 2003, the project's developers signed a neutrality agreement with the union in exchange for support at City Hall. The agreement outlines a number of provisions the union and employer will adhere to during the organizing campaign (Table 3). An evaluation of the new-hotels campaign's success in downtown Toronto is premature, but a few points about the promise and challenges of the strategy can be made.

First, there is a tension in the strategy between the new-hotels campaign's "top-down" orchestration and other "bottom-up" strategies often associated with grass-roots union-renewal (e.g., house visits, internal committee building). Neutrality agreements are most successful when used in concert with other organizing tech niques. Establishing an agreement with a future employer to allow organizing of new employees (in some cases the union sets up an information table outside the offices where hiring occurs) is not a substitute for interaction and building strong participation with new rank-and file members. Strategies such as house-calls and committee building among workers are effective, however, if an employer is forced to adhere to fair play during the organizing campaign. For example, neutrality agreements can prevent employers holding anti-union "captive audience" meetings in the workplace or demanding that employees divulge who has signed union cards.

Reduced employer intimidation increases the chance a worker will allow an organizer into his or her home without fear of reprisal. Strategies developed to pressure employers into neutrality agreements are necessary to facilitate grass-roots organizing campaigns that involve techniques such as sending rank-and-file members to the homes of unorganized workers. Similarly, pressuring employers can involve a significant amount of rank-and-file participation. For example, the union can mobilize workers from unionized hotels to picket a hotel construction site, or implement work-to-rule strategies in a hotel operated by the same firm. These strategies build rank-and-file activism that includes members in the organizing process.

At the same time, campaigns to establish neutrality agreements can be very knowledge-driven. Knowledge-intensive strategies that manipulate urban development processes by challenging zoning regulations, building regulations, and/or hotel finance arrangements require specialized knowledge outside of the membership. Over-dependence on lawyers challenging municipal by-laws at city council meetings, or back-room negotiations between local staff and developers rather than rank-and-file activism, can counter efforts to build more participatory unionism. It takes an extra effort on the part of the union to educate rank-and-file activists about the processes involved, the importance of the strategies, and how members can be directly involved in the corridors of power. Campaigns that include protests in the street or in a hotel developer's existing unionized property are the more direct forms of worker mobilization that can leverage labour peace in hotels and provide a chance to organize future hotel workers.

Combining specialized tactics developed at the international and local levels with grassroots organizing techniques is necessary in sectors such as accommodation. In a recent study of the campaign to organize the Dorchester Hotel in London's West End, Wills (2005) argues that grassroots organizing strategies on their own are less effective because they overburden a small group of activists who are less inclined to organize and represent other workers unless they see evidence of real union power (in other words, that they are not alone). Using existing union density and expertise is not a substitute for worker involvement in organizing, but it may very well be necessary to facilitate unionization in the accommodation sector. A balance must be maintained between the "top-down" orchestration of organizing campaigns and grass-roots involvement.

A second point of discussion is the ability to transfer a campaign largely built in the American context to Canada. For example, in the United States, municipal subsidies play an important role in new hotel development and unions have more leverage over hotel developers because public funds are part of the project. Unions encourage local politicians to support investment in hotels open to unionization in exchange for membership votes at the polls. As a consequence, there is significant negotiation between the union and City Hall. In Canada, municipalities are forbidden to subsidize private development by various provincial municipal acts. The question is whether or not this American strategy can be applied to Canada. The response from Dan, a Local 75 staff researcher, was that "we have to use other tricks." These "other tricks" include having the researcher send a copy of a new hotel's building permit to the city when he knew the property was being built in a residential zone. In this case the developer attempting to build the small hotel without prior proper zoning had failed to respond to the union's request for a meeting about a neutrality agreement. After being contacted by the city, the developer contacted the union.

Third, multiple unions representing hotel workers in Toronto are less likely to develop sector-specific organizing campaigns such as those used by UNITE-HERE. They will continue to organize in the sector and potentially interfere with strategies adopted by Local 75. The new-hotels development campaign, for example, is premised on the assumption that a single union is organizing workers in the sector. Even if the international office is able to transfer the necessary knowledge for a successful campaign to Local 75, with three or more unions seeking to represent the sector, how many neutrality agreements would an employer be willing to sign? Or how would an employer react after signing an agreement with one union, only to have another disrupt operations? As unions compete, the potential effectiveness of these intensive strategies will be tested.

These considerations are not meant to downplay the potential of the new-hotels development campaign. It is by far the most ambitious and comprehensive project to organize the hotel sector's workers. It is also far more imaginative and productive than "blitzing" non-union hotels. Being part of an international union specializing in the hotel sector, Local 75 will be able to refine the process developed by its international and U.S. locals as it embarks on campaigns to organize a spate of new properties currently being developed in Toronto. Furthermore, the local can share its refined techniques with other North American locals through the international office.

Conclusion: Recent developments and the future of integrated strategies

In February 2004, it was announced by the international leaders of HERE and UNITE that they would formally merge the unions over the summer months into UNITE-HERE, with an inaugural convention to take place in July. The merger was consistent with the long-term plans of the New Unity Partnership (NUP), a coalition formed in 2003 among the SEIU, UNITE, HERE, Carpenters, and Laborers unions. The NUP is committed to forming larger unions capable of sustaining organizing campaigns in specified private sector industries and pressuring the AFL-CIO to adopt a more aggressive organizing agenda (Johnson 2004).

The merger has generated a range of critical commentaries on its motives and efficacy. HERE and UNITE officials claim that the merger will be helpful in their organizing campaigns that often involve immigrant workers in a select number of private sector industries (e.g., hotels, commercial laundries, gaming, and retail). Sceptics attack what Chaison (1996) has termed a "survivalist" motivation as organizations in crisis look to solidify declining memberships. In the case of UNITE, merging in order to address the structural problems associated with a declining membership in a global sector (i.e., garments and textiles) seems a continuation of a strategy that gave birth to the union when the ILGWU merged with the textile workers in 1995. The newly-merged union, UNITE-HERE, creates a labour organization with 440,000 workers with a base in a growing sector of the economy. As for HERE, following September 11, 2001, the union (with a limited dues base in any case) was facing financial challenges as well. UNITE's significant assets (such as its majority stake in the US$3.2 billion Amalgamated Bank of Chicago) will obviously reduce HERE's financial burden.

The UNITE-HERE merger may, however, be viewed as part of the complex multi-scaler strategies used by labour. For example, there was speculation in the American labour community that, following the merger, HERE President John Wilhelm would run with the support of the NUP for President of the AFL-CIO against John Sweeney in order to implement a national organizing agenda and secure support for the NUP unions. In the case of "bargaining-up" in 2006, with the added resources of UNITE, strike benefits may be secured for perhaps tens of thousands of hotel workers engaged in prolonged battles with international hotel chains. As both HERE and UNITE organize in marginalized communities, shared expertise (such as that developed in the new-hotels campaigns) can be diffused to a greater number of workplaces. The merger is also part of UNITE's geographical strategy to expand its rural manufacturing base into new urban sectors. While it is difficult to ignore the more obvious instrumentalist motives behind the merger, it is possible to situate the newly-formed UNITE-HERE in a broader union renewal context.

Local 75 is clearly engaged in a union renewal program that takes place at local and international levels, but these diverse organizing and bargaining initiatives will continue to be challenged by the sector's specific labour geography. First, local union rivalry will continue to limit the success of local master bargaining and intensive organizing. Currently, multi-union cooperation to establish city-wide master agreements in Toronto is unlikely. For the time being, Local 75 will have to "jump scales" and enter master agreements negotiated with transnational hotel corporations. Organizing campaigns, such as the effort to organize new hotels in Toronto, are also designed for an environment in which one union has jurisdiction over hotels. Even if Local 75 has sophisticated strategies, it can be thwarted by other unions running concurrent campaigns. In other large cities, broad sectoral and occupational based union structures are viewed important to organizing in accommodation services (Wills 2005), but there is limited evidence of any local coordinated bargaining and organizing strategies between Local 75 and other unions such as the UFCW at this time in Toronto.

Second, the hotel sector shows very few signs of abandoning its practice of hiring workers from marginal segments of the labour market. It will continue to be a difficult sector to organize, even with the advanced campaign techniques developed by UNITE-HERE. While organizing immigrants, women, and people of colour does require an understanding of the different circumstances and capacities of workers to resist, "traditional" tactics involving picket lines and public protests making hotel workers visible in the landscape are still important. Knowledge-intensive campaign strategies do, however, provide support for workers engaged in these struggles.

Lastly, employer resistance to hotel unionism is firmly embedded in the sector even when the majority of large properties are unionized. Even though labour markets limit the economic gains of hotel workers in several North American cities, the union differential in wages and benefits still affects the bottom-line of firms. Furthermore, the potential disruption to hotels during each round of collective bargaining will be resisted by managers maintaining discipline in the hotels. Increased policing of labour unrest and the privatization of public space threaten many of the strategies used by hotel workers to coerce employers. The neo-liberal state is capable of regulating union strategy, adding another layer of complexity and frustration. Boyer (1995, 554) states that the "innovativeness of unions is not a perfect substitute for changes in trade union legislation," warning us that there are limits to even the most successful organizing strategies. The test for Local 75, and hotel worker unionism in general, will be their ability to respond when hotel companies and the state react to the gains that workers have made in recent years through renewal efforts.

Notes

1. Over the summer of 2004, HERE formally merged with UNITE to form UNITE-HERE, a new international union with 440,000 members. For the most part, the research is drawn from a larger dissertation project (Tufts 2003, 2004) involving interviews with rank-and-file union members, staff, and union leaders in the hotel sector (the names of the participants have been changed). As this research and the strategies discussed are in the context of HERE prior to the merger, I will refer to the union as Local 75.

2. Although I share Wills' (2002) enthusiasm for international framework agreements as a way for labour to regulate global capital, it must be noted that, shortly after Local 75 reached a collective agreement with Novotel, the hotel was closed due to airport expansion.

3. Frustration was expressed in interviews by two union staff over the lack of media attention given to their numerous rallies. One staff member was told by a Toronto reporter that labour-related protests were not usually newsworthy unless they were part of a strike/lockout. The inability to attract media coverage (especially local television) is one disadvantage of protests without strikes. In the summer of 2002, when Local 75 escalated the tactics and the threat of a work stoppage at three large hotels loomed during a peak tourist season, media coverage was plentiful.

4. According to a report in the *San Francisco Chronicle*, tension emerged between the international office and some Local 2 negotiators with different commitments to the demand for a two-year agreement (Raine 2004). While it can be speculated that the companies may have been supportive of these different voices, conflicts between national offices and locals bargaining national agendas are common.

5. By the mid-1990s, the ability of labour to do an "end run" around NLRB votes was proving to be a useful tool (Greenhouse 1997). The technique overcomes the insanity of the NLRB election process that occurs months after application for certification. In this period, support for the union usually drops off (and union supporters are often fired).

6. Working from a list of new properties compiled by HERE staff in 2002, the author estimated that there are over 1,000 potential new members for the union. The crude estimate is based on an average number of employees per room for the type of hotel (excluding management) calculated from existing properties.

References

Aguiar, L., J. Kainer, and N Pupo. 1998. H.E.R.E. to Stay: Re-inventing a Union as a Social Movement. Paper presented at the Canadian Sociology and Anthropology Association Meetings, University of Ottawa, Ottawa, Ontario.

Boyer, R. 1995. The Future of Unions: Is the Anglo-Saxon Model a Fatality, or Will Contrasting Trajectories Persist. *British Journal of Industrial Relations* 33 (4): 545-556.

Bronfenbrenner, K. 2000. Uneasy Terrain: The Impact of Capital Mobility on Workers, Wages, and Union Organizing. Submission to the U.S. Trade Deficit Review Commission, Washington DC.

Canadian Press (CP). 2002. Jesse Jackson Rallies Toronto Hotel Workers. Wire story, June 10. Available at www.thestar.com.

Chaison, G. 1996. *Union Mergers in Hard Times*. Ithaca, NY: ILR Press.

City of Toronto. 2003. *2003 Industry Profiles*. Available at www.toronto.ca/economic_profile/.

Clifford, P., and J. Kainer. 1998. Building a Union: Reflection on Organizing in the Hospitality Industry. *Briarpatch*, October, 27-30.

Colliers International Real Estate. 2002. *2002 Canadian Hotel Investment Report*. Available at www.colliers.ca.

Ghosh, S. 2003. Left Out. *THIS Magazine* 36 (4): 16-20.

Greenhouse, S. 1997. Bruised Unions Trying an End Run. *New York Times*, March 10, A10.

Hunt, G., and D. Rayside. 2000. Labour Union Response to Diversity in Canada and the United States. *Industrial Relations* 39 (3): 401-444.

Johnson, W. 2004. The UNITE-HERE Merger: Is It a Step Forward…or Business as Usual? *Labour Notes* 4.

Keung, N. 2002. Hotel Staff Stage Walkout. *Toronto Star*, August 2, B4.

Leong, M. 2002. Hotel Workers on Verge of Strike. *Toronto Star*, July 13, B3.

McNish, J. 2001. Trumpeting Sky-High Luxury. *The Globe and Mail*, November 30, A3.

Milkman, R. (ed.). 2000. *Organizing Immigrants: The Challenge for Unions in Contemporary California*. Ithaca, NY: Cornell University Press.

Raine, G. 2004. Hotel Talks Run Into a Snag: Negotiations Will Resume Next Week After Stalemate. *San Francisco Chronicle*, November 13. Available at www.sfgate.com/chronicle/.

Reitz, J., and A. Verma. 2004. Immigration, Race, and Labour: Unionization and Wages in the Canadian Labour Market. *Industrial Relations* 43 (4): 835-854.

Siemiernik, C. 2001. Analysts Unanimous: Hotel Strikes Always Hurt. *Toronto Business Journal*, August 13, 3.

Smith, N. 1990. *Uneven Development: Nature, Capital and the Production of Space*. Oxford, U.K.: Blackwell.

———. 1993. Homeless/Global: Scaling Places. In *Mapping the futures. local cultures, global change*, ed. J. Bird, B. Curtis, T. Putnam, G. Robertson, and T. Tickner, 87-119. New York, NY: Routledge.

Tufts, S. 2003. A Contemporary Labour Geography of Hotel Workers in Toronto, Ontario, Canada. PhD dissertation, Department of Geography, York University, Toronto.

———. 2004. Building A Competitive City: Labour and Toronto's Bid to Host the Olympic Games. Special themed section on A New Geographies of Trade Unionism, *Geoforum* (35):47-58.

Wakeland, J. 1998. Union Steps Aside For Marina Deal. *Oakland Tribune*, June 24.

Wells, M. 2000. Immigration and Unionization in the San Francisco Hotel Industry. In *Organizing Immigrants: The Challenge for Unions in Contemporary California*, ed. R. Milkman, 109-129. Ithaca: Cornell University Press.

Wills, J. 2002. Bargaining For the Space to Organize in the Global Economy: A Review of the Accor-IUF Trade Union Rights Agreement. *Review of International Political Economy* 9 (4): 675-700.

———. 2005. The Geography on Union Organizing in Low-Paid Service Industries in the UK. Lessons From the T&G's Campaign to Unionize the Dorchester Hotel, London. *Antipode*, 139-159.

Wong, T. 2000. Hotel Project Aims to Bring Ritzy Luxury to Toronto. *Toronto Star*, August, E1, E6.

Chapter 12
Building Capacity for Global Action: Steelworkers' Humanity Fund

JUDITH MARSHALL AND JORGE GARCIA-ORGALES

The power of one question

During the 1990s, Steelworkers members working for mining companies in British Columbia found themselves dismantling equipment in Canada to ship to Chile while their managers used their lunch hours to learn Spanish. Mining sector activists felt a strong need to understand the lure of Chile. They asked themselves: what is happening in Chile? Is there somebody we can talk to?

The Humanity Fund was the tool the Steelworkers used to find an answer to their question. That quest for an answer started a path the Steelworkers and their union partners in Chile and Peru are still walking.

Steelworkers' Humanity Fund

1. Founded at the Steelworkers National Policy Conference in 1982.
2. Bargained in 33 new units in 2004; about 600 bargaining units now contribute.
3. Based on member contribution of penny/hour worked.
4. $1.2 million contributed by members through collective agreements in 2004.
5. Co-financed with Canadian International Development Agency, (CIDA).
6. Long-term projects in 10 countries, plus education, worker exchanges and policy action.

The United Steelworkers, like every other union in the world, is confronted with an economic system that works the planet as a single chessboard. This game is commonly known as "globalization." In the developed world, "corporate" globalization has meant the closing of large number of well-established facilities due to the open competition with imported products produced in countries with less or no protection for workers and the environment, and the transfer of jobs to those countries. For Steelworkers in Ontario, this process was accelerated through NAFTA. Management threats to close up operations in Canada and supply the now borderless North American economy through low-wage jobs in Mexico became a weekly occurrence. Our mining sector in B.C. watched in consternation as Canadian mining companies scrambled to position themselves in a mining boom in Chile where rich mineral resources and newly open-to-private-investment economies beckoned.

The union realized very quickly the need for an effective response. For many, that response was the difference between the survival or the disappearance of the union. We could either let mining companies trigger a race to the bottom, unimpeded, or we could begin to build connections with mining unions in Chile and fight together for strong mining sectors and safe mines in both countries. In other words, work with other unions at the international level was fundamental as a response to globalization. The renewal of the union in this century was linked to that ability to work with others internationally and it was genuine solidarity, driven by needs on both sides.

This chapter is about how the Humanity Fund of the Steelworkers became one of the tools to build international connections. The main research methodologies on which this paper is based are participant observation and a conference event. The participant observation was carried out by the authors during a series of worker to workers exchange visits between 1994 and 2004 in which they participated both directly and indirectly. The activities during these exchanges included visits to mine sites and smelters, training courses, focused exchanges on topics of common interest, two international meetings, and conference and community events. The other major source of data comes from the written presentations to a Commission of Inquiry on Corporate Conduct in the Americas which was held in Quebec City on April 19, 2001, in the context of the People's Summit of the Americas. More than 400 people gathered to hear testimonies from workers and community activists in Brazil, Chile, Peru, Mexico, and Canada about their common transnational employers.

In the paper, we will first situate the context by a brief description of the United Steelworkers. We will then look at the way that working the global connections in our organizing and our bargaining in the mining sector through links with Chile and Peru has contributed to union renewal. What we have learned from a decade of intense work in this sector has provided useful lessons that we are applying today as we establish a broader practice of global exchanges and alliances.

USW—Everybody's union

United Steelworkers: A proud history

The roots of the Steelworkers go back more than 100 years. Founded in 1876, the Amalgamated Association of Iron, Steel and Tin Workers rose to organize large numbers of workers in steel-making towns across the United States and Canada in the post-Civil War period. At one point, the Pittsburgh-based Amalgamated was the largest affiliate of the American Federation of Labor (AFL).

The Steel Workers' Organizing Committee was formed with the assistance of the United Mine Workers in 1936. SWOC confronted the steel barons well known for their wealth, power and ruthlessness. In addition, significant differences in the cultures, nationalities, and even languages of the workforce in most steel towns posed what many considered insurmountable obstacles to organizing. By the end of 1937, U.S. Steel, the largest company, finally signed a nation-wide agreement with SWOC. Steelworkers paid a horrendous price to gain this recognition. One of the bloodiest days in modern labour history occurred on Memorial Day, 1937, in Chicago, where, at the entrance of Republic Steel, police fatally shot nine steelworkers and one bystander, and injured hundreds more. These workers were taking part in what is known as the Little Steel Strike in which workers struck 10 steel companies.

The Amalgamated joined the Steel Workers' Organizing Committee (SWOC) of the Confederation of Industrial Unions (CIO) on May 22, 1942, to form the United Steelworkers of America (USWA).

Many proud unions merged with USWA over the years. Here are some of those mergers:

Aluminum Workers of America—1944
International Union of Mine, Mill and Smelter Workers—1967
United Stone and Allied Products Workers of America—1971
District 50, Allied and Technical Workers of the U.S. and Canada—1972
Upholsterers International Union—1985
United Rubber, Cork, Linoleum and Plastic Workers of America—1995
Independent Workers of North America—1991
Aluminum, Brick and Glass Workers International Union—1997
Canadian Railroad Workers—1999
American Flint Glass Workers Union—2003
United Fish and Allied Workers Union (Canada)—2004
Industrial, Wood and Allied Workers of Canada—2004

In a historic convention in Las Vegas, April 2005, the USWA merged with the Paper, Allied-Industrial, Chemical and Energy Workers' International Union (PACE) to form the largest industrial union in North America, the United Steel, Paper and Forestry, Rubber, Manufacturing, Energy, Allied Industrial and Service Workers' International Union (USW). USW today has 850,000 active members, 256,000 of them in Canada.

PACE is a product of a merger between the United Paperworkers International Union and the Oil, Chemical, and Atomic Workers International Union in 1999.

USW workplaces are found in nearly every sector of the North American economy, from metals and mining and manufacturing to health care, utilities, and various private and public services. Here is a snapshot of the USW membership:

Forestry, Wood and Paper	21%
Stone, Clay, Glass and Concrete	5%
Equipment and Machinery	10%
Rubber and Plastic	8%
Fabricated Metals	10%
Primary Metals	14%
Petroleum and Chemicals	7%
Other Manufacturing	6%
Mining	4%
Transportation, Trade and Services	16%

The USWA at the beginning of the 21st century barely resembles the mostly-male industrial union of the 1930s, '40s and '50s. But the increasing diversity of the membership has only strengthened the basic principles on which the union was founded.

Figure 1: Total Membership over the Years

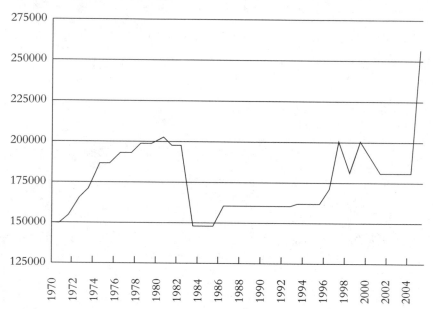

Workers employed in the steel industry and in mining—two of the union's traditional jurisdictions—total about 65,000, out of a total membership in Canada of 256,000. Steelworker members can be found in every sector of the economy—from factories to offices, to hospitals, university campuses, hotels, warehouses, bakeries, banks, transportation and communication workers, and many more. More than 20% of Steelworkers now are women,[1] and there is a growing membership among visible minority workers.

Over the years, the Steelworkers have learned how to re-invent themselves as a union (see Figure 1). Steelworkers know how to rebuild in tough economic times. The most serious challenge to union came in 1981-82 with the deepest and longest recession since the 1930s caused by policies of Regan administration in the United States.[2] The unemployment rate rose over 9% (Bedard and Grignan 2000). The union was hammered, in both Canada and the United States. In Canada, our membership dropped from 200,000 to less than 110,000.

The tens of thousands of jobs lost in that recession never came back, but new organized workers filled the ranks

The first big step was the decision to organize thousand of poorly paid, exploited security officers, and hotel and restaurant workers in Quebec. That move provided a sparkling example for the rest of the union to follow. Ever since that pioneering effort, which created the largest multi-location Steelworkers local union, we have not hesitated to target and embrace all kinds of service industries.

Steel did not abandon manufacturing. On the contrary, it targetted the growing problem of low-wage women in manufacturing ghettos. Several high-profile strikes, boycotts, and public campaigns—Radio Shack, Fotomat, Irwin Toy, among others—put the Steelworkers in the forefront of a remarkable surge in organizing working women in Ontario.

In the West, Steelworkers broke new ground when credit union clerks and University of Victoria Student Society employees joined the Steelworkers' ranks.

In 1985, the Upholsterers' International Union merged with Steelworkers. The Upholsterers International Union of North America was founded in 1883. It brought a 103-year history and 35,000 furniture workers into the USWA.

The 1989 National Policy Conference officially adopted the "Everybody's Union" theme in recognition of the growing linguistic, racial, occupational, and gender diversity of the Steelworkers in Canada. By the end of the 1980s, Steelworkers membership in Canada was back to over 160,000. It was an amazing recovery. Ten years later, in 1990-91, another recession, created by trade policies of Mulroney and Bush, hit us. Dozens of plants closed. The unemployment rate soared to 10.2% during the first half of the 1990s (Bedard and Grignan 2000). Employers took advantage of free trade to consolidate their production, and to run away from high dollar and high interest rates. Members of bargaining units that had been part of the Steelworkers for decades lost their jobs as companies closed or moved south of the border. Old industrial empires crumbled. Steelworkers took another hit. Its membership dropped as low as 135,000. Again, Steel fought back. We organized thousands of new members.

We brought in new Steelworkers through mergers with other unions: the Aluminum, Brick and Glass Workers Union; the Rubberworkers; and the Canadian section of the Transportation and Communications Union.

The Aluminum, Brick and Glass Workers Union (ABG) was formed in 1982. The Aluminum Workers International Union, the United Brick and Clay Workers of America, and the United Glass and Ceramics Workers of North America had merged over the years to strengthen their bargaining position against their employers and to provide quality service to their members. Approximately 40,000 members of the ABG merged with the USWA in 1996.

The United Rubber, Cork, Linoleum & Plastic Workers of America (URW) was founded in 1935 in Akron, Ohio—then the "Rubber Capital of the World" and home-base for most of the major tire and rubber companies. The 90,000 URW members voted to merge with the USWA in 1995.

In 1999, the Canadian Division of the Transportation Communications International Union merged with the USWA, bringing to the union a diverse membership of 5,000 working in all areas of the transportation and communications industries in Canada.

In fact, some of our best organizing years in the past two decades across the country were in the late 1990s as major units of employees in manufacturing industries, as well as employees in new sectors such as post-secondary education, chose to join the Steelworkers.

In 1998, the administrative staff of the University of Toronto voted to join the Steelworkers. More than 5,000 members formed Local 1998, the largest single local in Toronto, in Canada, and the second largest in the union.

In August 2004, the 55,000 members of the IWA (Industrial, Woodworkers and Allied Union) voted to merge with the Steelworkers. In their last convention, in

Figure 2: Membership by Sectors, 2005

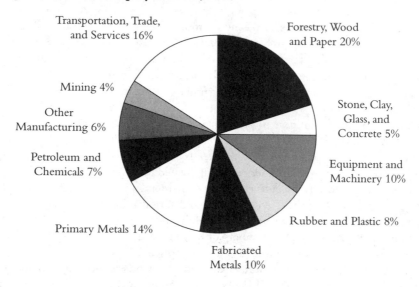

April 2005, PACE (Paper, Allied-Industrial, Chemical and Energy Workers International. Union), representing more than 275,000 workers, also voted to merge with the Steelworkers.

The new union is called the United Steel, Paper and Forestry, Rubber, Manufacturing, Energy, Allied Industrial and Service Workers International Union, or the USW for short.

The combined union will have over 850,000 active members in over 8,000 bargaining units in the United States and Canada. It will be the largest industrial union in North America, and will be the dominant union in paper, forestry products, steel, aluminum, tire and rubber, mining, glass, chemicals, petroleum, and other basic resource industries. The importance and presence of USW in the service sector will continue. After the merger, the new USW will have more than 16% of its members working in services. In Canada, there are 256,000 active members as of May 2005 (see Figure 2 for membership by sector).

The Steelworkers have discovered over the past 25 years that you can't fight corporate globalization only at home. One of their most effective tools for renewal has been to go global as a union, expanding the mandate of a tool created for global social solidarity into a tool for new global alliances of workers.

The Steelworkers' Humanity Fund

The capacity of the Canadian Steelworkers to respond to corporate-led globalization has been greatly strengthened by the creation of the Steelworkers' Humanity Fund. The Fund was created in 1985 in response to the famine in Ethiopia. As people throughout the world reacted to the images of suffering projected into their living rooms from Africa, Canadian Steelworkers came up with a uniquely union response. Several local unions decided to bargain an international development fund into their collective agreements—a penny for each hour worked. The Fund became national union policy within a year. Four other major Canadian unions— CEP, CAW, CUPE, and IWA—established similar Funds in the early 1990s. The Canadian Labour Congress and the five unions have together formed the Labour International Development Committee (LIDC). The LIDC has bargained a co-funding arrangement with the Canadian International Development Agency (CIDA) whereby CIDA provides $1.7 million annually, divided proportionally among the LIDC members.

The Fund raises about a million dollars a year from the penny-an-hour contributions of members. Adding the revenue from the co-funding arrangement with CIDA, this creates an annual budget of about $1.5 million.

The Fund has grown both organizationally and also in terms of its mandate. In the early 1990s, our union's members were flooded with management pressures for concessions, all couched in the language of global competitiveness. At the same time, our members were active players in the coalitions that formed to fight the free trade deal with the U.S. and later NAFTA, the MAI, and the WTO. There was recognition among Steelworkers leaders that, if the Humanity Fund was to remain relevant to our members, it would have to address the global issues facing workers on a daily basis—issues like NAFTA and company relocation to low-wage jurisdictions. As a result, the Fund has become an important space in the union for innovative new responses to globalization.

The Fund works in three main areas. The first is long-term development projects with both labour and community partners. True to our original mandate, we continue to respond to floods and famines at home and abroad, but the main work of the Fund is support for labour and community organizations in 14 countries, in long-term development projects. Each project is seen as a door through which we can create some traffic north and south, enabling working people to stand in each other's shoes and come to know the global economy from different perspectives.

The second main area of the Fund is education and worker exchanges. The international solidarity education program is delivered as part of the broader Steelworker education program. More than 500 Steelworkers have taken the week-long "Thinking North South" course, which uses popular education methodology to introduce workers to the functioning of the global economy. A shorter course called "Facing Global Management" is run regularly for large locals and area councils.

The education carried out through these courses is deepened through worker-to-worker exchanges. Steelworkers who do anti-racist education or labour housing work in Canada have connected with counterparts in Africa working in these areas. Women activists link up with the work of women's committees in partner unions or community groups in Mozambique or Bolivia. But the most innovative links have been those that bring together workers in different countries with a common transnational employer like Cominco-Teck or Placer Dome or Noranda:

> The objective of the visits are primarily education and solidarity. The hosting organization is requested to prepare an educational process for the Canadian Steelworkers. Members are asked to speak from their own strength and experience, as social activists in Canada, carrying out

their activism through their unions. Often during the visit, it becomes evident that the stereotyping of the South is no worse than the stereotyping of the North. Latin American activists are surprised that behind the glitter of consumer society [in Canada] there are strong labour and social movements, along with serious problems of unemployment, poverty, and racism. (Marshall 1997, 62)

The education and exchange programs play a vital role in the success of the Humanity Fund. International visitors have gradually become less exotic. They are now seen more as fellow-employees of the companies we work for, working families who happen to live in another point in the global economy.

The third major area of work is lobbying and policy work. As the Humanity Fund broadened its work in the early 1990s, its Board stated clearly a desire to have a labour signature on the work of the Fund. It was not enough to create another Oxfam, excellent as that organization may be. The challenge was to create an international development fund that reflected labour's issues and perspectives. This has meant not only a dramatic increase in the number of labour partners supported through the Fund, but also a choice of policy issues of particular interest to labour. We have led a policy initiative within the Canadian International Development Agency (CIDA) itself to begin to develop a labour screen for its work. In the same way that public funds spent by CIDA must be subjected to a gender and environmental screening process, we have made some inroads in establishing the need for a labour screen. With this in place, the impact of any given project on working people would become part of the criteria for eligibility to access Canadian development assistance funding.

Another major area of policy concern for the Humanity Fund has been international trade agreements. We have been active members of coalitions like Common Frontiers, a table that brings Canadian labour and social organizations together on trade issues.[3] From Seattle to Washington, Santiago to Quebec City and Miami, we have mobilized our members to carry out a mixture of lobbying, education, street demonstrations, and direct action. More than 300 Steelworkers attended the forums and teach-ins of the People's Summit in Quebec in April 2001 with more than 3,000 members participating in the demonstration on the final day.

Finding answers—The path to Chile

Once NAFTA came into effect in 1994, attention focused on Chile as the country most likely to sign on to an expanded NAFTA. Chile's relations with Canada had been undergoing a dramatic transformation, with a mining boom in Chile that had prompted some major Canadian mining companies to literally close up explorations in Canada and move operations to Chile. More than $4 billion of Canadian mining capital went to Chile between 1987 and 1993, and the pace has not abated in recent years.

Moises Labrana, President of the Chilean Confederation of Mining, had this assessment to offer of the role of the mining companies at the Inquiry on Corporate

Conduct held in April 2001 in Quebec City in the context of the Peoples' Summit of the Americas:

> In Chile, more than 53% of our economy is in the hands of big tran-
> snational corporations.... In the area of mining investment, 41% are
> Canadian, 18% are Australian, and 14% are from the United States.
> These investors determine the internal policies in the country....They
> have formed a Mining Council where they define the strategies they
> want to impose on Chile and how to destroy mining unions.
>
> Testimony of Moises Labraña,
> Inquiry on Corporate Conduct, April, 2001[4]

The Steelworkers were drawn to Chile not so much in response to Chile's needs, but to our own. Our members' job security and the future of our mining communities were at stake. We needed to understand what was luring Canadian mining companies to Chile. The Chileans needed to understand the logic of foreign private mining companies taking over the mining sector in their country, and how to relate to the Canadian mine managers flooding into Chile. These needs led us to a powerful global alliance with Chilean and Peruvian mining and smelter workers.

Building connections with labour and social movements in Chile began in the early 1990s. Chilean political exiles who had become active Steelworkers during their years in Canada played a critical role in helping the Humanity Fund establish contacts with major mining and metalworker unions in Chile. Through Common Frontiers, the trade network in Canada of which the Steelworkers are active members, we made contact with a newly formed Chilean network on trade. Over a three-year period, five Steelworkers from the mining sector and two staff representatives visited Chile to attend conferences and workshops and begin to learn about Canada's role in the mining boom in Chile.

Recognizing the importance of health and safety and environment in establishing global competitiveness, the National Health, Safety and Environment committee of our union took on a project of hosting worker exchanges from Chile. The Chilean Confederation of Mining identified a miner from the Quebrada Blanca mine owned at the time by Cominco, and one from the Placer Dome mine. The two came to Canada for a month-long exchange. The Chileans were billetted in the homes of Canadian local union activists, and they—and their full-time translators—basically shadowed local union officials through their day-to-day activities. They participated in bargaining, in lunchroom talks, in membership meetings, in social events, and finally in a national policy conference of the Steelworkers in Vancouver in 1995.

Our members had expected the Chileans to recount stories of dirty, unsafe mines back home. Instead, the Canadians learned that their company's new Quebrada Blanca mine was a state-of-the-art operation, with technology slightly more advanced than their own open pit operation in Canada. Our members implicitly assumed that the Chilean visitors would be less skilled than they were. The electrician and welder who came on the exchange visit from Chile, however, were trades-people with skills that would have allowed them to operate in the Canadian mines at a moment's notice.

Perhaps the biggest surprise for the Chileans was the active presence of the union in the workplace itself, and the civility, regularity, and depth of the interaction with management on a week-to-week basis. There is a dramatic difference between the detailed collective agreements bargained between workers and management in Canada and the modest collective agreements that prevail in Chile. In Canada, a multi-layered system of officers, shop stewards, and health and safety committee members monitor the implementation of these agreements and have activate mechanisms for compliance when necessary. Implementation of the typical 200-page agreement that a big mining company is likely to sign in Canada is also backed up by the union's national legal and research staff. Yet that same company is likely to sign a 20-page agreement in Chile with a union that has little capacity to monitor its implementation, crippled as it is by a labour code still largely intact from the Pinochet era.

The exchange visits were followed up by periodic conference calls in which a translator was included on the line to facilitate communications. Meanwhile, the Canadian Steelworkers made sure that company management knew that they were in regular contact with its operations in Chile. Return visits were organized. Interestingly, the arrival of the Canadian unionists in Iquique on the return exchange resulted in the first meeting of the Chilean union executive with the Canadian owner-manager. Up until that point, the Chilean Human Resources Director had been the only point of contact with the Canadian transnational.

The two Canadians who made a return exchange visit to Chile were not able to spend much time shadowing the Chilean unionists in the workplace. The mine site is four hours from Iquique at 4,500 meters of altitude. A one-day visit brought two major shocks to the Canadians. The first was the meager union presence in the workplace, where, by law, only the five members of the executive can carry out union business in any way. The other shock was altitude sickness and what it means to take a four hours' trip to work, starting at sea level and climbing 4,500 meters. The nausea, headaches, and faintness that the Canadian trade unionists experienced on their one-day visit to the mine site are the reality with every shift change for the Chilean workers. Every seven days, their physiological systems have to adjust to the changing oxygen content in the air between their sea-level homes in Iquique and their workplace high in the Atacama Desert.

Although the exchange included only one day at the mine site, the activities at the union office in town were lively. The Canadian miners were asked to do impromptu training sessions on bargaining and local union financial management, as well as give some hands-on assistance with computers and modem.

A full exchange on bargaining strategies was set up for the following year, one which brought together miners from seven different mining companies in Iquique and Copiapo. The bargaining exchange with the Chilean miners marked a new high in the relationship. The atmosphere was electric. The course took place on the eve of Quebrada Blanca's first negotiations with Cominco, so the Chilean bargaining committee members were anxious. From the Canadian side, we did our utmost to make our knowledge of the company and our experiences in bargaining available to the Chileans without presuming to dictate to them how they should bargain. We were all too aware of the vast difference between the bargaining contexts in Chile and in Canada. We were also tremendously conscious of the fact that, if bargaining went badly, the role of the Canadian unions on the eve of the negotiations could easily be perceived as having been the cause.

In one role-play exercise during the workshop, a Canadian miner took on the role of Cominco management. During the debriefing, the Chileans commented on how shocked they had been that he seemed to know exactly what management had been saying to them in Chile, even though he'd just arrived. The Canadian replied that "management-speak" in bargaining is the same in every country, and not to be taken seriously. Steelworker irreverence about management may well have been one of the most important ingredients in the exchange. One of the Chileans remarked that, when the Canadian managers first came, the Chileans had placed them on a pedestal. After hanging out with the Canadian miners and hearing tales of these same Canadian managers on their home turf, the Chileans were left with a very different impression. They approached the bargaining table with a great deal more confidence and achieved what was, at the time, the best collective agreement in Chile.

Along with direct links between local unions, the Humanity Fund has also given continued program support to the Chilean Mining Confederation. The Confederation has utilized the funding strategically, organizing a series of training seminars for union leaders from mines owned by transnationals from Canada, the U.S., Australia, and South Africa that have arrived since the mining boom. Working the links both at national and local union levels, we have continued to build a network, with information exchanges, participation in each other's events, and joint strategies.

In recent years, the connections have also expanded to Peru. Workers from the Cominco smelter in Peru have forged strong links with zinc smelter counterparts here in Canada, following much the same pattern as the early connections with the Chilean workers. The Chileans themselves have played a strong leadership role in connecting with the Peruvian union, inviting Peruvians to their events in northern Chile.

A very significant step forward was taken by the Chilean Confederation of Mining in February 2000, when it convened the first international meeting of Cominco workers, bringing together workers from five Cominco operations in Canada, Chile, and Peru. The delegations met for seven days in Iquique, Chile. The meeting ended with a declaration committing each union to continue the collaboration. A second international meeting took place in Peru in October, 2002.

Over the years, there have been periods of both intense activity and lulls. Changes of leadership in the local unions have had an impact on the overall momentum of communications. There have been times in each country when members have questioned the value of the international connections, voicing a preference for their union leaders to devote more attention and resources to members' needs at home. The new possibilities created by these connections keep reasserting themselves, however, and today active working links are firmly established, going several layers deep in our respective organizations.

We have chosen to present a case study of the paths that have linked mining and smelter workers in Canada, Chile, and Peru into a strong network. The Steelworkers have also promoted many other exchanges that bring together workers with a common transnational employer, including meetings of workers employed by AL-CAN, DANA, Noranda, and, more recently, an expanding Brazilian transnational steel producer, Gerdau.

Purchase of major Canadian companies by foreign investors poses new challenges. During 2004 and 2005, we have been faced with the possibilities of a Russian company buying Stelco, and Brazilian and Chinese companies buying Noranda. Coordination with unions in other parts of the globe was a fundamental part of the strategy to ensure job security for our members and protection of our communities in front of these new possible owners. The previously developed networks made possible quick exchanges of information and coordination of actions.

Let us look at the Noranda situation as an example. In June 2004, rumours started that Companhia Vale do Rio Doce (CVRD) SA, a very powerful Brazilian transnational in the mining sector, was planning to purchase Noranda. Soon the news fizzled, and shortly thereafter Noranda signed an agreement to have exclusive negotiations with China Minmetals Corp, the largest government-owned importer of metals with subsidiaries in 17 countries. This meant that Noranda was not able to pursue sales negotiations with other possible buyers. Large numbers of officials from Minmetals visited Noranda and Falconbridge facilities around the world. The parade continued for more than two months but, once again, the sale fell apart.

Steelworkers were concerned about Noranda's intentions to sell the company. They needed to respond. In December 2004, the Canadian leadership held a meeting with the Noranda locals to discuss the implications of the sale of Noranda to Minmetals, or any other buyer. In the meeting, Steelworkers established a set of principles the union will use to evaluate any sale by Noranda. The principles included:

1. Workers and communities must not be collateral damage in the purchasing process.
2. The voice of the workers must be heard and respected during the purchasing process.
3. The potential owner must commit to keep operating/owning all of its facilities and to a substantial reinvestment into the business.
4. The federal government must ensure that the purchase of Noranda is used to protect and create processing and transforming facilities upstream from primary resources operations.

In the meeting, Steelworkers discussed how to proceed in the future. The need to connect with mining unions in Chile and Peru quickly came to the top of the agenda. First, the decision to translate the principles to Spanish and circulate them among partners in the network was easily approved.

Second, an international meeting of Noranda workers was discussed and approved. Steelworkers present at the meeting understood immediately that a national response was not sufficient, and they knew their union had the connections to act globally.

A few months later, in March 2005, Noranda announced that it was merging its operation with Falconbridge into a single operating company. Even though an imminent sale of the company is no longer on the agenda, the need for Noranda workers to share information and strategies remains.

The Humanity Fund's 20th Anniversary was the occasion to bring together union leaders from Brazil, Chile, Peru, Mexico, and South Africa to reflect on the first two decades of the Humanity Fund and to chart future collaboration. It was also the occasion to bring together Falconbridge-Noranda workers from Canada, Chile, and Peru and to work out plans for ongoing communications and joint action. During this same period, Canadian, Chilean, and Brazilian workers from the Brazilian steel transnational Gerdau met in Oshawa. Although the company refused permission for a site visit, once again reinforcing its position that meetings bringing together its workers throughout the Americas are not recognized by the company as valid, the workers themselves planned out an action plan for 2005 which will include a Gerdau gathering in Argentina on the occasion of the Third People's Summit of the Americas in Argentina in November 2005.

Conclusion

Today, the workers' exchanges and global alliances facilitated by the Humanities Fund have become a powerful force for revitalizing the union and equipping our members to better contend with corporate globalization. At the USW founding convention in Las Vegas in April 2005, the merger with PACE and the creation of the largest industrial union in North America were not the only cause for excitement. We also celebrated new global alliances with key union partners in Germany, Brazil, Australia, and Mexico. We are putting contract language on the bargaining table to pressure companies to allow worker monitoring of company codes of conduct. We are negotiating international framework agreements through the Global Union Federations to establish common standards in all of a company's global operations. We are setting up Company Councils and bargaining company financing to facilitate international gatherings of workers to hammer out common policy platforms. And we are continuing to consolidate the relationships at the local shop steward level.

The challenge is to operate at these multiple levels in our quest not only to invent new mechanisms of control over today's unregulated global corporations, but also to do so in a way that can revitalize our union and empower our local union activists.

As Nestor Munoz, one of the union leaders from Quebrada Blanca involved in the Cominco Teck work over the years, puts it:

> ... we have the right form of trade union globalization, not from the top down but at the level of workers employed in a particular company. We can feel this now. Every worker at Quebrada Blanca knows that we have brothers and sisters in Canada and Peru who are fighting alongside us. We have learned how to act in each of our countries. Now we have to develop more active forms of solidarity.

Testimony of Nestor Muñoz,
Inquiry on Corporate Conduct, April 2001

Notes

1. United Steelworkers of America, District 6. *A Guide to Everybody's Union*, 7.

2. The recession affected the Canadian economy far more seriously than that of the United States, creating high levels of unemployment and closing many manufacturing facilities. Real output fell 5.3% between 1981 and 1983 in the U.S. and 7.7% in Canada (Card and Riddell 1993). Pierre Trudeau was the Prime Minister of Canada at the time. He was unseated by Brian Mulroney, leader of the Progressive Conservative Party, in the next election. Mulroney ran under the slogan "Jobs, Jobs, and Jobs" and won the election.

3. Common Frontiers is a coalition of labour and social organizations that was founded in 1987 when Mexican participation in NAFTA first came onto the agenda. Common Frontiers has collaborated actively since that time with counterpart networks in Mexico (RMALC) and the U.S. (ART) on trade issues. In recent years it has played an active role in building a Hemispheric Social Alliance with membership from organizations throughout the Americas.

4. Moises Labraña's testimony and those that follow were presented at a Commission of Inquiry into Corporate Conduct in the Americas organized by the Canadian section of the United Steelworkers jointly with the Confederation of Mining and CONSTRAMET from Chile, the National Confederation of Metalworkers, Brazil, the Authentic Labour Front, Mexico, and the Federation of Mining, Metallurigcal and Smelter Workers of Peru, during the Second People's Summit of the Americas in Quebec City, April 19, 2001.

References

Bedard, Marcel, and Lois Grignan. 2000. *Overview of Evolution of the Canadian Labour Market from 1940 to the Present*. Research Paper R-00-9E. Ottawa: Human Resources and Skills Development Canada.

Card, David, and Craig Riddell. 2003. A comparative Analysis of Unemployment in Canada and the United States. In *Small Differences that Matter: Labor Markets and Income Maintenance in Canada and the United States*, ed. David Card, and Richard B. Freeman, 149-189. Chicago: University of Chicago Press.

Marshall, Judith. 1997. Globalization from Below: The Trade Connections. In *Adult Education and Training: Impacts and Issues*, ed. Shirley Walters. London: Zed Books.

PART III
Unions and Community:
Campaigns and Organizing

Chapter 13
Community Unionism and Labour Movement Renewal: Organizing for Fair Employment

CYNTHIA J. CRANFORD, MARY GELLATLY,
DEENA LADD, AND LEAH F. VOSKO[1]

Community unionism is essential to the renewal of the Canadian labour movement. Most commonly conceived of as alliances between trade unions and community groups to organize the unorganized, community unionism includes such alliances but entails much more. It also supports the work of autonomous workers' organizations. Increasingly, workers' centres and other organizations mobilize workers who fall outside of contemporary labour protections, target employers who engage in unfair labour practices and pressure government to reform labour law. These efforts are emerging to address the growing segment of workers who are precariously employed—workers who are hired through a temporary employment agency or work on short-term contracts or at the bottom of multiple sub-contracting chains. Some may be out of work all together. Others may be full-time and permanent but concentrated in low-wage sectors where employment standards are not enforced, or do not apply, and where it has been difficult for trade unions to organize. Precarious employment disproportionately affects recent immigrants, people of colour and women. Recently arrived immigrant workers are often required to gain "Canadian experience" and many engage in temp work and other precarious employment as a consequence. Only a broad conception of community unionism, and of labour movement renewal, is capable of tackling these profound inequalities of class, race-ethnicity and gender. What is needed is a deep commitment to and ongoing support of the self-organizing that would allow precariously employed workers to take ownership over their own struggles.

In this chapter, we demonstrate the potential of community unionism for labour movement renewal through a case study of one "community union"—Toronto Organizing for Fair Employment (TOFFE).[2] In the first section, we give a brief overview of the growth of precarious employment in Canada, which is prompting the need for community unionism and labour movement renewal. We give several contemporary examples of community unionism in the second section, ranging from organizing among community-based groups to trade union–community alliances. In the third section, we conceptualize community unionism as occupying the middle range along a continuum with community organizing at one end and trade union organizing at the other. Finally, we describe the practices of Toronto Organizing for Fair Employment in the fourth section. We conclude by arguing that community unionism, broadly defined, is central to achieving labour movement renewal in Canada.

The need for community unionism: precarious employment in Canada

A growing number of people in Canada have only temporary or contract work, although most people still have full-time permanent jobs. Full-time permanent wage and salary employment fell from 67 per cent in 1989 to 63 per cent in 2003, while temporary employment rose from 6 per cent to 10 per cent in the same period (Vosko 2005). Statistics Canada measures "temporary" jobs as all jobs with a pre-determined end date. This includes those employees working on term or contract, a casual or seasonal basis or those working through a temporary agency. Temporary agency workers are more precarious than other temporary workers in many ways. They earn less money and receive fewer benefits and are less likely to be covered by a union. These workers do not have one employer but are party to a triangular employment relationship that allows both the temporary agency and client company to evade employer responsibilities. The temporary help industry now provides a broad range of staffing services and places workers in light manufacturing, construction and de-skilled clerical work (Vosko 2000).

More companies are following the garment industry model of offloading the costs of doing business through multiple levels of sub-contracting. Those at the bottom of these organizational pyramids are often treated as "self-employed" contractors. In addition to garment homeworkers, those treated as "self-employed" include home care workers, mail and newspaper carriers as well as door-to-door salespeople. However, many of these workers do not have the capital and control akin to entrepreneurs (Cranford, Fudge, et al. 2005). These self-employed contractors are captured in Statistics Canada measures as the "own-account self employed," that is, the self-employed who do not have employees. Own account self-employment grew from 7 per cent to 10 per cent of total employment between 1989 and 2003 (Vosko, Zukewich, and Cranford 2003).

Recent immigrants of colour and women are disproportionately concentrated in the most precarious employment. Recent immigrants face discrimination in the Canadian labour market and are often pushed into temporary agency work upon arrival; temporary agencies justify paying low wages and providing few benefits by arguing that recent immigrants are receiving valuable "Canadian experience" and that women are gaining the "flexibility" to combine work and family (Vosko 2000, 186-195). West Asians and North Africans are more likely to be in part-time temporary work, among the most precarious type of wage work, and the proportions of South Asians and Filipinos are also high (Cranford, Vosko, and Zukewich 2003). Challenging these precarious employment relations, and the racialized and gendered inequalities that both shape and are shaped by them, requires a (re)turn to community unionism.

Community unionism in contemporary Canada

The term "community unionism" is used to refer to many different aspects of labour movement renewal. Most broadly, it has been used synonymously with social movement unionism to refer to the need to bring the movement aspect back into the labour movement by focusing on both internal and external organizing rather than just servicing (Clawson 2003; Gindon 1998; Robinson 2000; Wilton and Cranford 2002). There is a fairly substantial literature on efforts within trade unions to bring feminist and anti-racist organizing and structures into unions as well as other strategies of internal organizing or internal union renewal (Briskin and McDermott 1993; Brofenbrenner et al. 1998; Leah 1999). In our brief review here, we focus only on external organizing in alliance with community groups and more autonomous community-based organizing.

Community unionism includes the efforts of unions to connect with non-labour community groups in order to organize workers into existing trade union structures or into pre-union associations allied with trade unions. There has been much recent focus on this aspect of community unionism, which has been successful in organizing janitors, garment and hotel workers and other low-wage, largely immigrant and women workers, in both the Canadian and U.S. literatures (Cranford 2004; Banks 1991; Ladd 1998; Leah 1999; Lévesque and Murray 2002; Yates 2002; Milkman and Voss 2004; Robinson 1994; Russell 1992; Tufts 1998). One of the most remarked upon efforts is that of the ILGWU (now UNITE-HERE) to organize immigrant women garment homeworkers into pre-union associations in cities ranging from Toronto to Los Angeles in the 1990s (Bonacich 2000; Tufts 1998). In Toronto, the campaign began in 1991 and involved a Coalition for Fair Wages and Working Conditions for Homeworkers that lobbied for legislative reform to impose joint liability on employers up the corporate pyramid, a Clean Clothes Campaign that mobilized consumers to pressure garment retailers, outreach to the Chinese and South Asian communities where homeworkers were concentrated and chartering a Homeworkers Association as an associate member local (Borowy, Gordon, and Lebans 1993; Das Gupta 1996; Fudge 1994; Yalnizyan 1993). More recently, unions and community groups have sought to organize migrant farm workers from Mexico and Jamaica, despite this group of workers' lack of access to collective bargaining. The CLC, in partnership with the UFWA Canadian office and the UFCW, began the Global Justice CareVan Project in 2001 and opened the Migrant Agricultural Workers Support Centre in 2002 in Leamington, Ontario in order to document migrant workers' living and working conditions, provide them with information, especially on health and safety, and to support eventual organizing (UFCW Canada and CLC 2002; Zwarenstein 2002). Justicia for Migrant Workers, a group of volunteers from labour, student and faith groups is also engaged in outreach to migrant farm workers.

Community unionism is also about building the power of non-unionized workers and the broader working class community. There has been less written in Canada about community unionism as the practices of community-based groups focusing on labour issues. In contrast, there is a large literature on community-based labour organizing outside of recognized trade unions in the United States where

a weaker labour movement density-wise, combined with autonomous organizations of Black, Chicano/Latino and Asian Americans, has cultivated a large number
of workers' centres and associations of immigrant workers and workers of colour
who are employed in precarious service and factory work, including day labour
and paid domestic workers, temporary agency workers and garment workers (Fine
1998; Gordon 1995; Hondagneu-Sotelo and Riesgos 1997; Louie 2001; NAFFE
2002; O'Conner 1964). This type of community unionism includes organizations
that are hybrids between immigrant service organizations and immigrant workers'
organizations, and these are found in Canada although not recognized as a form of
unionism. One example is INTERCEDE, the Toronto domestic workers' organization. Like the campaigns mentioned above, INTERCEDE acts as an advocacy
group and has worked in coalition with others for broader-based bargaining as well
as changes in immigration policies that limit the citizenship and labour rights of
domestic workers (Fudge 1997; ILGWU and INTERCEDE 1993).

Workers' Centres are also sites of building non-union workers' power. They do
so through education, networking, legal advocacy and reform work and organizing.
One example is the Immigrant Workers Centre/Centre des Travailleurs et Traval-
leuses Immigrant (IWC/CTI) founded in October 2000 in Montreal to work with
immigrants from South and Southeast Asia, Eastern Europe, and the Caribbean
who labour below legal standards, including home workers and domestic workers.
The IWC/CTI has three main activities: 1) they give classes on education and
rights, including labour history, labour laws and organizing training; 2) they provide
individual services to immigrant workers and their families on issues of paid work;
3) they facilitate links between immigrant communities and unions seeking to
unionize new workers. They have also launched a campaign to amend the Labour Standards Act to better protect immigrant workers and to raise the minimum
wage.[3] The Workers' Organizing and Resource Centre in Winnipeg is also a site
for advocacy, community organizing and union organizing (Bickerton and Stearns
2002). The significance of these community union practices is more fully fleshed
out in a conceptual discussion of community unionism.

Conceptualizing community unionism

We conceptualize community unionism as occupying the centre range along a
continuum of union organizing and community organizing (see Cranford, Das
Gupta, et al. 2005 for an extensive conceptual discussion). In order to demonstrate this idea, we contrast the currently dominant model of trade union organizing—industrial unionism—to the community development mode of community
organizing. We contrast these two ideal types, the latter very process oriented and
the former a model of representation solidified in laws and policies, because, in our
view, a greater focus on processes of worker empowerment is needed to build a
stronger labour movement (Ladd 1998; Leah 1999).[4]

There is a large body of scholarship on the limits of the industrial trade union
model in Canada. The early struggles of industrial unions included elements of
community unionism, for example the Wobblies organizing of immigrant seasonal
workers through transferable membership cards (Avery 1979) and the bringing

together of skilled and unskilled workers in strategic geographic areas by the One Big Union (Palmer 1992). These radical unions were repressed by the state, which negotiated instead with the 'responsible' unions (Fudge and Tucker 2001). The industrial labour relations regime that emerged from these struggles in the Post WW II period narrowed the activities of unions and their scope has been further limited with recent employer opposition.

In exchange for union recognition from employers, the 'responsible' industrial unions consented to a collective bargaining regime that was largely taken out of their control and placed in the hands of labour boards (Ursel 1992, 199-201). Labour board policy emphasizes the single employer, single location bargaining units (O'Grady 1992; Fudge 1993). In addition, the industrial labour relations regime emerged from the struggles of predominately white, citizen, male workers during the late 1930s and early 1940s. Initially, the industrial unions, concentrated in the non-competitive manufacturing and resource-extraction industries characterized by large, bureaucratic workplaces had enough power to pressure employers to bargain at an industry wide level. But since broader based bargaining is not required by law, employers have chipped away at industry-wide agreements. The industrial model never worked for the predominantly female and immigrant workers concentrated in small workplaces in competitive sectors (Ursel 1992; Fudge 1993). Furthermore, the worksite-based model does not provide an incentive for unions to organize small workplaces in competitive industries (Fudge 1993; O'Grady 1992). Within this context, many trade unions have become organizations of collective bargaining between an employer and paid workers in a single workplace, rather than organizations to organize and mobilize those who need collective support the most.

There is a growing awareness of the need for legislative reform so that collective representation is not tied to a single employer at a single worksite (Fudge and Vosko 2001; ILGWU and INTERCEDE 1993). Temporary agency workers, for example, labour in multiple locations and switch from one occupation to another (Vosko 2000, 261). Contractors must first prove that they are an "employee" in order to have access to collective bargaining rights; but even if they are found to be employees they may not be found to be employees of the entity with the ultimate power over their wages and working conditions, for example, the garment retailer, the real estate developer or the government funder (Cranford, Fudge, et al. 2005). This important attention to legislative reform is usefully complemented by studies focusing on the processes of organizing.

A separate body of work on anti-racist, community development among immigrant women, and sometimes men, draws attention to the processes of organizing essential for building broader working class power. This work also elevates how racialized and gendered inequalities intersect with class relations to influence modes of working class resistance (Carty 1993; Das Gupta 1986; Stall and Stoecker 1998).

Community development refers to community work to enable people from oppressed groups to bring about change in their lives, as women, as immigrants, as people of colour and sometimes as members of the working class (Das Gupta 1986). The goal of this kind of community organizing is building community power rather than a specific demand or benefit. Community development reflects a particular philosophy of how to build, and sustain, community power. It begins with personal empowerment. Empowerment is the feeling that one has the capacity to affect change (Ladd 1998, 13). Personal empowerment pushes individuals to engage in collective reflection and action, particularly through popular forms of education (hooks 1994; Friere 1996). Community development is a process whereby individuals begin to see personal problems as broader political issues and to think about how to address those problems collectively. A broad base of empowered individuals, rather than leadership by a few charismatic individuals, is thought to be more enduring, bringing potential for widespread social change (Das Gupta 1986, 12, 37; Stall and Stoecker 1998). Methods of organizing focus on critical learning and popular education in order to formulate a critique of systematic racism, sexism and classism. Also used are collective problem solving and strategizing and some-times direct action. One group that has, perhaps most successfully, joined individual empowerment with collective organizing and a broad notion of unionism is the Self-Employed Women's Association in India (Rose 1992).

Organizations that adhere to a community development philosophy view the involvement of members at every level as a principal objective. They are also very effective with poor, working-class immigrant women and women of colour (Cranford, Das Gupta, et al. 2005; Das Gupta 1986; Rose 1992; Stall and Stoecker 1998). Networks of community-based self-help organizations serving immigrants in Canada have been sites of empowerment and anti-racist organizing (Das Gupta 1986; Leah 1991). However, the reliance of some of these groups on state funding may conflict with the goals of building community power (Cranford, Das Gupta, et al. 2005; Ng 1990). Furthermore, it is becoming more difficult for these organizations to focus on empowerment in the contemporary climate of cuts to funding agencies supporting recently arrived immigrants and constraints on certain types of action, often labeled as 'advocacy' amongst such groups. Insights from community development must be joined with a more explicit focus on labour organizing.

Neither the industrial union model nor the community development mode, are able to address the issues of precariously employed workers alone. Joining useful components of each tradition could lead to a powerful community unionism fostering labour movement renewal characterized by fundamental rather than incremental change. One version of how this community unionism can take shape is described in the next section on Toronto Organizing for Fair Employment.

Toronto Organizing for Fair Employment (TOFFE)

The case of Toronto Organizing for Fair Employment (TOFFE) illustrates the power of drawing together aspects of both union and community organizing. TOFFE is a community union working with workers in precarious employment who confront a range of different situations—including temporary agency workers, self-employed contractors, and increasingly workers with permanent jobs that lack decent wages and benefits and routinely have their employment rights violated. Many of the people that TOFFE works with are in and out of work and constantly looking for stable jobs. Thus, like early industrial unions, TOFFE also organizes with the unemployed. TOFFE consciously outreaches to recently arrived immigrant women and men of colour and sees their work as part of a broader resistance to racialized and gendered class inequalities, as is the case in much community organizing. In Spring of 2005, TOFFE merged with the Workers Information Centre[5] (W.I.C.) to become the Workers' Action Centre. This decision reflects both TOFFE's and the W.I.C.'s long-range concern to foster improvements in workers' conditions of work and health through a self-organizing model geared simultaneously to educating and mobilizing workers and their communities, confronting employers and targeting the government to improve laws and enforce existing ones. The merger signals both groups' growing realization that precarious employment is directly connected to the erosion of standards for workers in all types of employment. This article reflects some of TOFFE's past work as well as the more recent integrated work with the W.I.C.

A self-organizing model guides TOFFE's work. This model integrates leadership training and education in all the work in order to build extensive worker participation and a culture of organizing around precarious employment as well as a public response to it. The method of self-organizing involves workers in strategizing to improve working conditions in their own lives as well as in their sector. It highlights the links between critical learning, self-reflection and action, akin to the philosophy of community development. However, TOFFE targets not only workers and their communities but also government departments, especially the Ontario Ministry of Labour, and employers contravening basic employment standards.

TOFFE seeks to create a culture of organizing *vis-a-vis* employers and the government by developing worker committees. For example, one committee active in TOFFE practically since its inception is the Tamil Temp Workers' Committee. The group of workers has a range of overlapping solidarities of sector, geography, race-ethnicity and gender. It is made up of Sri Lankan Tamil women who live in Scarborough and are primarily assigned to light manufacturing work. In the early 2000s, the committee focused on several problems related to the lack of enforcement of employment standards, including entitlements for vacation and holiday pay and minimum three-hour pay. It also participated in the campaign to raise the minimum wage in Ontario in which many social action groups participated, and worked in solidarity with the Downtown Temp Workers' Committee, another longstanding committee of TOFFE, in a highly successful campaign for public holiday pay in 2003.

TOFFE engages in a three-pronged strategy. By this, TOFFE means first that it strives to build workers' involvement and leadership through specific campaigns and, more generally, build a workers organization. Second, TOFFE targets employers to both obtain direct gains for workers and increase workers confidence in asserting their rights while challenging employers' confidence in breaking the law. Third, TOFFE puts forward demands for change in labour legislation, policy and practice. One example of this strategy in action is the public holiday campaign of 2003, a large-scale initiative aimed at a key grey area in the *Employment Standards Act* as it applies to temporary agency workers. After several members were not paid for public holidays, TOFFE committee members and staff informed other temporary workers about their right to public holiday pay, and urged them to get involved in claiming this right through a segment on a Tamil radio station and by putting up posters in English and Tamil around temp agencies, community centres, popular shopping places and neighbourhoods. TOFFE faxed a public information bulletin on the statutory requirement of payment for public holidays to over three-hundred temp agencies before Victoria Day that year. Finally, TOFFE and its members engaged in discussions with the Ministry of Labour over this issue and ultimately ministry officials wrote to the temp industry group, ACSESS, regarding its incorrect recommendation to agencies that temporary agency workers are in the elect-to-work category and therefore ineligible for public holiday pay. In the process, TOFFE also supported two workers in filing claims with the Ministry of Labour through Toronto's Parkdale Community Legal Services (for a detailed case study of this campaign see Cranford, Das Gupta, et al. 2005).

The public holiday campaign is but one example of TOFFE's work in assisting temp workers in both asserting their rights to basic employment standards and helping to build a base of worker leadership. TOFFE's self-organizing activities, involving extensive training about basic workers' rights, helped workers demand holiday pay from the temporary agencies. Committee members gained confidence after securing their own rights and they told others in their community about their success. Consequently, the group grew in numbers as well as in its leadership abilities.

TOFFE's three-pronged strategy of organizing workers, targeting employers and holding government accountable, has been strengthened by its alliance with the Worker's Information Centre (W.I.C). In 2002 TOFFE began to work more closely with the W.I.C. Together, the W.I.C. and TOFFE have worked to turn individual advocacy into the collective mobilization of workers in a range of campaigns. One example is an initiative to support, primarily recently arrived immigrant, workers selling high speed internet or digital cable services door-to-door hired by different sub-contractors who contracted with a large telecommunications company. Treated as "self-employed" by the sub-contractor, in this particular case, workers were promised a commission for each sale they made. However, if the customer cancelled their subscription a month or two later or the cable could not be connected the commission was taken away. Many of the workers also did not get paid for any of the sales they made. When the subcontractor was contacted, it blamed the client company. When the client company was contacted, officials claimed that their company was not their responsibility and that they were not the employer. The workers affected felt that it was important for the client company to take responsibility. Consequently, the W.I.C., Kensington Bellwoods Legal Clinic in Toronto and TOFFE assisted them in launching a related employers complaint to the Ministry of Labour. The coalition also engaged in a public education campaign (Cranford and Ladd 2003).

Partly as a consequence of such successful campaigns, TOFFE and the W.I.C. worked together throughout 2004-2005 in building a broad constituency of workers in precarious employment, ranging from temp agency workers to independent contractors, including the telecommunications, garment and building cleaning industries, and focusing on workers facing problems such as unpaid wages and benefits. At the same time, TOFFE continued its work with community-specific committees, such as the Tamil Temp Workers and the Downtown Temp Workers.

Pooling their resources, TOFFE and W.I.C. were also able to devote greater attention to creating employer-specific committees in order to target employers that are not abiding by the *Employment Standards Act*. This was the beginnings of the soon to come merger of the two organizations. In 2004-2005, for example, TOFFE was approached by many groups of workers from different firms struggling with unpaid wages and against employer discrimination. At the same time, W.I.C. was also receiving phone calls from workers facing similar problems (i.e., unpaid wages and benefits). In response, W.I.C. and TOFFE decided that it was important to assist workers tied to particular employers or sectors to support each other in understanding their rights and collectively seeking solutions to their common problems. TOFFE and W.I.C.'s employer-specific committees consist predominantly of recently arrived immigrant workers and young workers. Staff provide training and support for workers to speak publicly about their experiences, conduct media interviews, and determine what improvements are needed in the *Employment Standards Act*. In response to these calls for assistance, the creation of a number of employer-specific committees were supported across a range of constituencies, including garment workers, information technology workers, young service sector workers, machine operators, and fast-food workers. The work of TOFFE and W.I.C.'s core committees, both the employer-specific committees established in 2004 and 2005 and longstanding committees of temp workers, led these organizations to launch joint policy campaigns on specific issues related to employment standards.

The "Bad Boss" campaign is the foremost contemporary example of how TOFFE and W.I.C. organized campaigns around unfair employment standards. In early Spring of 2004, on the basis of calls from workers the two organizations began documenting cases of employers that repeatedly violate the *Employment Standards Act* and ignore the Ministry of Labour's orders to pay lost wages in order to illustrate to the Ministry of Labour, the media and its allies the extent of violations of workers' rights. In so doing, TOFFE came upon many cases where workers were owed thousands of dollars with little hope of ever recovering their lost wages because, in some instances, employers file bankruptcy, only to reopen under a new name, while in others they continue to operate without any response to orders imposed by the Ministry of Labour. In its research, conducted with Parkdale Community and Legal Services, TOFFE found that half a billion dollars in workers' wages went unpaid between 1989/90-2002/2003, which is 71 per cent of the monies that the Ministry of Labour ordered employers to pay went unpaid.[6]

In addition to compiling comprehensive data on unpaid wages, case profiles were developed for use in public education and discussions with the Ministry of Labour. The case profiles are based on self-organizing with workers who documented their experiences as well as those of others. For example, they documented the case of a Toronto garment manufacturer with a history of bouncing checks and failure to pay overtime to workers who regularly work over sixty hours per week. In this case, one worker sewed clothes for 8 months only to be owed $6,000 in wages by December 2002. Even though the Ministry of Labour ordered the employer to pay the wages in July 2003, it never investigated whether the employer was failing to pay other workers. Nor did it enforce the order or penalize the employer for breaking the law. New workers were hired only to face the same situation. Now the employer owes 6 workers over $35,000—none have been paid and the employer is still operating. TOFFE used cases like this one to illustrate the serious gap in employment standards enforcement in the province and make demands for changes in ESA enforcement. These cases also provided concrete targets for workers' organizing in a way that involves workers, challenges employers and, hopefully, obtains workers' wages.

Several other elements of the 'Bad Boss' campaign brought increased public pressure on the Ministry of Labour and individual employers. One such effort was the 'Bad Boss Bus Tour', organized by TOFFE and W.I.C. in July 2004. This tour involved over 100 members, who drove around the Greater Metropolitan Toronto Area and involved targeting employers and subcontractors known to be in violation of employment standards. The tour brought together worker committees of all sorts, building solidarity across TOFFE and W.I.C.'s growing constituency, and it developed all three prongs of its strategy of targeting employers, community organizing with workers, and calling on the government for the effective enforcement of employment standards. One outcome of the tour was the investigation of two companies visited by workers on the 'Bad Boss Bus' by the Ministry of Labour. In one case, the employer was ordered to pay almost $1 million in severance (although the employer is now appealing) and, in another, a full investigation found the employer owed low wage workers close to $160,000 in unpaid wages. The Ministry promised to take all possible enforcement measures to recover wages owed in the cases that were profiled. Another outcome of the 'Bad Boss' campaign was the establishment of the Minister's Employment Standards Action Group, and the invitation of TOFFE to participate. Still another outcome was the creation of a video, for public education, documenting this campaign and linking it to the broader issue of gaps in protections for the precariously employed.

Together, these successful campaigns led TOFFE and the W.I.C. to create an Action Committee in the Fall of 2004. This committee aims to build solidarity within TOFFE and the W.I.C.'s base and thus involves workers across sectors and communities through representation from all of its committees. It is involved in organizing rallies to continue to 'protect workers, not bad bosses,' to paraphrase one leaflet, and to remind the Ministry of Labour to honour its Spring 2004 promise to "increase awareness of employment standards rights and obligations, and strengthen enforcement to make sure those rights are protected" (Ministry of Labour 2004).

The goal of the Workers' Action Centre, formed as a result of the merger of TOFFE and the W.I.C. in the spring of 2005, is not only to see the enforcement of labour standards, although individual victories are very important. Rather, through critical learning and teaching, fighting back against employers and pressuring the government, workers become empowered. The W.A.C. aims to cultivate a culture of organizing as workers support and mobilize one another and create new solidarities not tied to a single worksite. The ultimate goal is to build a base of workers able to demand fair employment.

Conclusion

Community-based labour organizing efforts, such as workers' centres and workers' associations, are essential to a renewal of the labour movement. Like union-community alliances and renewed efforts at internal organizing among trade unions, community-based labour organizing should be supported by the labour movement. Indeed, the importance of workers' centres as a key organizing strategy in immigrant communities was recognized at the 2002 CLC Women's Symposium.

Neither trade union organizing nor community organizing addresses sufficiently the issues of precariously employed workers. In the U.S. context, Dan Clawson (2003) has recently argued that a fusion of the labour movement and new social movements is essential for the resurgence of labour in this context and Janice Fine (1998) has called for uniting labour market unionism and a community unionism. In addition to the range of social justice issues brought by new social movements and the focus on reforms for particular groups emphasized by workers centres and other forms of community unionism, some of the principles of community development should be merged with union organizing tactics. These include attention to critical learning and teaching, self-organizing and the link between individual empowerment and community power. A combination of a deep, process-oriented self-organizing, with a targeting of employers and pressuring of governments, the type of fusion found in TOFFE's strategy, could bring about a powerful renewal of the labour movement in Canada.

Notes

1. This chapter emerged out of a Community-University Research Alliance on Contingent Work funded by the Social Sciences and Humanities Research Council of Canada. Authorship is alphabetical to reflect equal contribution.

2. TOFFE is now called the Workers' Action Centre. An explanation of the changes in the organization resulting in the new name is given in the text under the heading Toronto Organizing for Fair Employment (TOFFE).

3. This information is from a pamphlet describing their activities and supporters and their newsletter, *IWC Rumblings*, sent to us by the Immigrant Workers' Centre of Montreal.

4. Much of the union renewal literature instead contrasts various unionisms, such as business unionism, social unionism, or social movement unionism. For an example, see Robinson (2000). In practice, particular unions, as well as community groups, fall at different places along this continuum in different times in history. Community-based organizing falls along a continuum as well, from more radical groups, such as the Ontario Coalition Against Poverty, to community agencies funded by the government focusing largely on servicing.

5. The W.I.C. provided phone-based and drop-in information to workers on employment standards and other workers' rights. In addition, they provided workers' rights training and educational workshops to a broad range of community- and immigrant-based organizations.

6. These figures were compiled from the Fiscal Year Reports of the Employment Standards Branch, Ontario Ministry of Labour, 1989-90 to 2002-03.

References

Avery, Donald. 1979. *"Dangerous Foreigners": European Immigrant Workers and Labour Radicalism in Canada, 1896-1932.* Toronto: McClelland and Stewart.

Banks, Andy. 1991. The Power and Promise of Community Unionism. *Labor Research Review* 18:17-32.

Bickerton, Geoff, and Catherine Stearns. 2002. The Struggle Continues in Winnipeg: The Workers Organizing and Resource Centre. *Just Labour: A Canadian Journal of Work and Society* 1:50-57.

Bonacich, Edna. 2000. Intense Challenges, Tentative Possibilities: Organizing Immigrant Garment Workers in Los Angeles. In *Organizing Immigrants: The Challenge for Unions in Contemporary California*, ed. Ruth Milkman, 130-149. Ithaca and London: ILR Press.

Borowy, Jan, Shelly Gordon, and Gayle Lebans. 1993. Are these Clothes Clean? The Campaign for Fair Wages and Working Conditions for Homeworkers. In *And Still We Rise*, ed. Linda Carty, 299-330. Toronto: Women's Press.

Briskin, Linda, and Patricia McDermott, eds. 1993. *Women Challenging Unions: Feminism, Democracy, Militancy*. Toronto: University of Toronto Press.

Carty, Linda, ed. 1993. *And Still We Rise*. Toronto: Women's Press.

Clawson, Dan. 2003. *The Next Upsurge: Labor and the New Social Movements*. Ithaca: Cornell University Press.

Cranford, Cynthia. 2004. Gendered Resistance: Organizing Justice for Janitors in Los Angeles. In *Challenging the Market: The Struggle to Regulate Work and Income*, ed. Jim Stanford and Leah F. Vosko, 209-29. Montreal and Kingston: McGill-Queen's University Press.

Cranford, Cynthia, Tania Das Gupta, Deena Ladd, and Leah F. Vosko. 2005. Thinking Through Community Unionism. In *Precarious Employment: Understanding Labour Market Insecurity*, ed. Leah F. Vosko. Montreal and Kingston: McGill-Queen's University Press.

Cranford, Cynthia, Judy Fudge, Eric Tucker, and Leah F. Vosko. 2005. *Self Employed Workers Organize: Law, Policy and Unions*. Montreal and Kingston: McGill-Queen's University Press.

Cranford, Cynthia, and Deena Ladd. 2003. Community Unionism: Organising for Fair Employment in Toronto. *Just Labour: A Canadian Journal of Work and Society* 3:46-59.

Das Gupta, Tania. 1986. *Learning From Our History: Community Development by Immigrant Women in Ontario 1958-86*. Toronto: Cross Cultural Communication Centre.

———. 1996. *Racism and Paid Work*. Toronto: Garamond Press.

Fine, Janice. 1998. Moving Innovation from the Margins to Center. In *A New Labor Movement for a New Century*, ed. Gregory Mantsios. New York, NY: Monthly Review Press.

Friere, Paulo. [1970] 1996. *Pedagogy of the Oppressed*. Revised 20th Century Anniversary Edition. (Orig. pub. 1970.). New York: Continuum.

Fudge, Judy. 1993. The Gendered Dimension of Labour Law: Why Women Need Inclusive Unionism and Broader-based Bargaining. In *Women Challenging Unions*, ed. Linda Briskin and Patricia McDermott, 231-48. Toronto: University of Toronto Press.

———. 1994. Community Unionism: Coalition Fights to Clean Up the Garment Industry. *Canadian Dimension* 28 (2): 27-29.

———. 1997. Little Victories and Big Defeats: The Rise and Fall of Collective Bargaining Rights for Domestic Workers in Ontario. In *Not One of the Family: Foreign Domestic Workers in Canada*, ed. Abigail Bakan and Daiva Stasiulis, 117-45. Toronto: University of Toronto Press.

Fudge, Judy, and Eric Tucker. 2001. *Labour Before the Law*. Don Mills: Oxford University Press.

Fudge, Judy, and Leah Vosko. 2001. By Whose Standards? Re-Regulating the Canadian Labour Market. *Economic and Industrial Democracy* 22 (3): 327-356.

Gindon, Sam. 1998. Notes on Labor at the End of a Century: Starting Over? In *Rising from the Ashes? Labor in the Age of "Global" Capitalism*, ed. Ellen Meiksins Wood, Peter Meiksins and Michael Yates, 190-202. New York: Monthly Review Press.

Gordon, Jennifer. 1995. We Make the Road by Walking: Immigrant Workers and the Struggle for Social Change. *Harvard Civil Rights-Civil Liberties Law Review* 407.

Hondagneu-Sotelo, Pierrette, and Cristina Riegos. 1997. Sin organización, no hay solución: Latina Domestic Workers and Non-traditional Labor Organizing. *Latino Studies Journal* 8:54-81.

hooks, bell. 1994. *Teaching to Transgress: Education as the Practice of Freedom*. New York: Routledge.

ILGWU and INTERCEDE. 1993. *Meeting the Needs of Vulnerable Workers: Proposals for Improved Employment Legislation and Access to Collective Bargaining for Domestic Workers and Industrial Homeworkers*. Toronto: ILGWU and INTERCEDE.

Ladd, Deena. 1998. No Easy Recipe: Building the Diversity and Strength of the Labour Movement. Feminist Organizing Models, Canadian Labour Congress Women's Symposium.

Leah, Ronnie Joy. 1991. Linking the Struggles: Racism, Sexism and the Union Movement. In *Race, Class, Gender: Bonds and Barriers*, ed. Jesse Vorst. Toronto: Garamond Press.

————. 1999. Do You Call Me "Sister"? Women of Colour and the Canadian Labour Movement. In *Scratching the Surface: Canadian Anti-Racists Feminist Thought.* Enakshi Dua and Angela Robertson, 97-125. Toronto: Women's Press.

Lévesque, C., and G. Murray. 2002. Local Versus Global: Activating Local Union Power in the Global Economy. *Labor Studies Journal* 27 (3): 39-65.

Louie, Miriam Ching Yoon. 2001. *Sweatshop Warriors: Immigrant Women Workers Take on the Global Factory.* Boston: South End Press.

Milkman, Ruth, and Kim Voss, eds. 2004. *Rebuilding Labor: Organizing and Organizers in the New Union Movement.* Ithaca: Cornell University Press.

NAFFE. 2002. *Worker Center Strategies.* North American Alliance for Fair Employment Strategy Series. Working Paper One. Boston: NAFFE. Available at <www.fairjobs.org>.

Ng, Roxanna. 1990. State Funding To A Community Employment Center: Implications for Working With Immigrant Women. In *Community Organization and the Canadian State,* ed. Jacob Mueller. Toronto: Garamond Press.

O'Conner, James. 1964. Towards a Theory of Community Unions. *Studies on the Left* 4 (2): 143-148.

O'Grady, John. 1992. Beyond the Wagner Act: What Then? In *Getting on Track: Social Democratic Strategies for Ontario,* ed. Daniel Drache. Montreal and Kingston: McGill-Queen's University Press.

Palmer, Bryan D. 1992. *Working Class Experience: Rethinking the History of Canadian Labour, 1800-1991.* Second Edition. Toronto: McClelland & Stewart.

Robinson, Ian. 1994. NAFTA, Social Unionism, and Labour Movement Power in Canada and the United States. *Relations industrielles / Industrial Relations* 49 (4).

————. 2000. Neoliberal Restructuring and U.S. Unions: Toward Social Movement Unionism? *Critical Sociology* 1 (1/2): 109-138.

Rose, Kalima. 1992. *Where Women are Leaders: The SEWA Movement in India.* New Delhi: Vistaar Publications.

Russell, Bob. 1992. Reinventing a Labour Movement? In *Organizing Dissent: Contemporary Social Movements in Theory and Practice,* ed. William K. Carroll, 117-33. Toronto: Garamond Press.

Stall, Susan, and Randy Stoeker. 1998. Community Organizing or Organizing Community? Gender and the Crafts of Empowerment. *Gender and Society* 12:729-56.

Tufts, Stephen. 1998. Community Unionism in Canada and Labour's (Re)organization of Space. *Antipode* 30 (3): 227-250.

United Food and Commercial Workers Canada (UFCW) and Canadian Labour Congress (CLC). 2002. National Report: Status of Migrant Farm Workers in Canada. Brief presented to the Honourable Jane Stewart, Minister of Human Resources Development Canada.

Ursel, Jane. 1992. *Private Lives, Public Policy: 100 Years of State Intervention in the Family.* Toronto: Women's Press.

Vosko, Leah F. 2000. *Temporary Work: The Gendered Rise of a Precarious Employment Relationship.* Toronto: University of Toronto Press.

————. 2005. Precarious Employment: Towards an Improved Understanding of Labour Market Insecurity. In *Precarious Employment: Understanding Labour Market Insecurity in Canada,* ed. Leah F. Vosko. Montreal and Kingston: McGill-Queen's University Press.

Wilton, Robert, and Cynthia Cranford. 2002. Toward an Understanding of the Spatiality of Social Movements: Labor Organizing at a Private University in Los Angeles. *Social Problems* 49 (3): 374-394.

Yalnizyan, Armine. 1993. From the DEW Line: The Experience of Canadian Garment Workers. In *Women Challenging Unions: Feminism, Militancy and Democracy,* ed. Linda Briskin and Patricia McDermott, 284-303. Toronto: University of Toronto Press.

Yates, Charlotte. 2002. Expanding Labour's Horizons: Union Organizing and Strategic Change in Canada. *Just Labour: A Canadian Journal of Work and Society* 1:31-40.

Zwarenstein, Carlyn. 2002. Small Town, Big Issues: Migrant Workers Organize. *Our Times,* July, 14-21.

Chapter 14
The Workers' Organizing and Resource Centre in Winnipeg

GEOFF BICKERTON AND CATHERINE STEARNS

It is Thursday evening in Winnipeg. The two meeting rooms at the Workers' Organizing and Resource Centre (WORC) are full. Past and present collide as these activists plan future activities. Grass Roots Women are meeting in the Helen Armstrong room, named after a leader in the 1919 Winnipeg General Strike. Mayworks is meeting in the Lawrence Pickup room, named after a postal worker who lost his job as a result of participating in the Workers' General Strike Committee of the historic 1919 strike. Other folks drift in. They are trade unionists, peace activists, people of colour, women. There are pensioners and youth. They wait for 7:30 when the meeting rooms will free up and two other groups, the Workers of Colour Support Network and the No War Coalition, can begin their meetings.

You can feel the sense of friendship and solidarity in the hallways. As they wait, the discussions range from the upcoming Mayworks festival to the plans for staging an outdoor musical about the General Strike in a city park in the summer. These activists are the brains and the backbone of the left. It is definitely a good place to hang out.

The WORC began in 1998 as an initiative of the Canadian Union of Postal Workers and community activists drawn from several communities. The WORC mission statement reflects the commitment of the Winnipeg CUPW local and regional office to community unionism:

> The union movement must again become the moral, strategic and political center to build a movement dedicated to fighting for the rights of all workers, defending workers' democracy and improving the lives of the ever increasing numbers of people forced to live in poverty. (WORC 1998)

Originally, the Centre was housed in a storefront located in the shadows of the bank headquarters that tower over the intersection of Portage and Main. In March 2003, it was forced to relocate and found a new home on the mezzanine floor at 280 Smith St. What it lost in accessibility it gained in space. The Centre now boasts two meeting rooms and four separate offices.

The staff at the Centre consists of one paid part-time position and a network of volunteers drawn from the progressive community and the organizations that use the Centre. The Central Committee, which governs the operations of the Centre, meets monthly and is comprised of representatives of the groups using the Centre and CUPW. Where possible, decisions are reached through consensus, although a vote may be called to break a deadlock. Although CUPW holds a majority of seats on the Central Committee, it has never used its majority representation to impose a decision.

The mandate of WORC

During the initial discussions on the Centre, activists identified many areas to be addressed. These included outreach to youth, especially those unemployed, under-employed, non-unionized and students, and assistance to workers with problems associated with labour standards, employment insurance, workers' compensation, and human rights. The need was identified: to work with both community coalitions and social justice groups, as well as with organizations representing ethnic groups in their struggles to achieve equality, recognition, education and employment opportunities.

It was agreed that the Centre should foster an understanding that unions are an integral part of our communities, and that union members must actively participate in struggles to bring about changes that benefit workers, their communities, and society as a whole. There was also a consensus that the Centre should promote community campaigns to fight unemployment. Outreach to schools, for both labour and community groups, was also seen as another role for the Centre. Finally, promoting the organizing of the unorganized was identified as one of the Centre's chief objectives.

From this process emerged the Workers' Organizing Resource Centre mandate, which is:

1. to help establish, maintain and facilitate community organizations that represent and enforce people's rights within our community;
2. to advocate on behalf of unorganized workers for protection of their rights in the workplace and beyond; and
3. to organize the unorganized.

This paper will evaluate the experience of WORC in meeting each of these three dimensions of its mandate. The information used in this evaluation is drawn from personal experience at the WORC, interviews with leaders of groups which use the Centre for meetings and offices, examination of the briefs presented by WORC, examination of the meeting room log-book, a review of the intake statistics, and interviews with union and community activists in Winnipeg.

Strengthening coalitions

Does the Centre assist local coalitions and progressive community organizations? Has it helped foster greater cohesion between progressive organizations in Winnipeg? Does the Centre contribute to enhancing the awareness of union members that they and their unions are an integral part of their communities and that union success depends on the strength and vitality of local working class movements?

The answers to these questions can be found by examining how the Centre's facilities are used by progressive groups and asking activists.

The short answer to each of these questions is Yes.

The Centre provides free meeting space, use of office equipment, and some office supplies to numerous groups. The following are some of the observations of activists within these groups.

Grass Roots Women is an independent women's group in Winnipeg. It meets twice a month at WORC and uses the office equipment, telephones, and photocopiers. As a low-budget organization, the group appreciates the free meeting space, which is not available anywhere else in downtown Winnipeg. The location of WORC, at the intersection of several major bus lines, is also an important advantage for organizations with members relying on public transit. The group is very supportive of WORC for several reasons, which go beyond the facilities. Veteran activist Marion Yoe points out that she has learned much about the CUPW and the other groups that use WORC. She is clear that the value of bringing activists together goes way beyond monetary efficiency: "Today there is nothing more important than solidarity. We are in the struggle of our lives. The WORC is a gift to our community."[1]

The Winnipeg Chapter of the Council of Canadians has been meeting at WORC regularly, on the first Tuesday of every month, for the past three years. The availability of free space is important for the Council, as is the central location. The stability of having regular meetings at the same location has helped the Council grow. The proximity to other groups at WORC has also helped them to promote public events that they organize. Cinthya Vargas, chairperson of the Council, believes that it is important that the "political bandwidth" of WORC remains very wide. "It is really important," she says, "that WORC appeals to a wide range of issues. Meeting here helps us to break down the isolation which occurs when we rely on e-mail to publicize our activities. WORC is also one of the few places that you see unions working with community groups."[2]

The organizing for the annual Mayworks festival also occurs at WORC. Mayworks uses more than the meeting rooms. The WORC staff and volunteers also help organize and promote several of the Mayworks activities. WORC volunteers answer phones, provide information, and take reservations for Mayworks' activities such as the General Strike Bus Tour. Glen Michalchuk is a co-chair of the Mayworks Committee and also serves as First Vice-President of the Winnipeg Labour Council. He notes that the ability for groups who do not have their own office space to receive messages through WORC is extremely helpful when groups are organizing public events. "Organizing our activities at WORC helps us to share information, promote our activities, and learn about what other groups are doing."[3]

The Workers of Colour Support Network is comprised of unionized and non-union workers. It has been meeting at WORC for many years. While they meet and plan activities using the WORC facilities and office equipment, the actual events are usually organized in other venues, as the WORC meeting rooms are not big enough. For the Network Coordinator, Louis Ifill, WORC's role as a meeting place of working class organizations is essential: "WORC pulls together people who have a conscious identity as workers. This is crucial for us. Locating ourselves at WORC helps build our working class orientation."[4]

The Winnipeg local of the Canadian Union of Postal Workers frequently uses the WORC for meetings of its membership, local executive, and shop stewards. Located near Winnipeg's major sorting plant, the WORC provides easy access to the local and its membership. While the local contributes $175 a month to the WORC, it actually saves more than this amount by having many of its meetings there instead of at the Winnipeg Union Centre, which charges for its meeting rooms.

Bruce Tascona, CUPW Winnipeg Local First Vice-President, is a 29-year veteran of the union's many struggles with Canada Post and within the labour movement. Tascona helped develop and implement the union's literacy project, which uses a focus on workplace heath and safety to assist members in developing their literacy skills. Using the availability of free meeting space at WORC as "in-kind support," he was able to leverage funding for the project from the Workers' Compensation Board. Tascona has no shortage of ideas of how the WORC could be used as a location for a broader adult education program. His experience in developing programs at WORC has also led him to consider numerous ways by which the Centre could be used by the local union for social and family activities, in addition to union events and meetings: "The WORC is like our own community centre. It has tremendous potential for building solidarity between the members. It is also a sanctuary for the unorganized."[5]

Winnipeg is the only city in Canada where CUPW has three locals. This is due to the success of the Winnipeg Local and Prairie Region in organizing workers in the courier industry. The WORC plays a major role in providing cohesion between the three locals. The locals use it for meetings during organizing campaigns for couriers. The CUPW Red River and Muddy Waters locals also hold their meetings at the WORC. The National Union used it for meetings during its successful campaign to sign up the Rural and Suburban Mail Carriers, and has held many meetings at WORC for various union committee sessions that have been held in Winnipeg.

The Low Income Intermediary Project (LIIP) is a very active organization, with its office located at WORC. In Winnipeg, the LIIP is recognized as the foremost organization performing advocacy support for low-income people and people with welfare problems. Over 40 organizations in Winnipeg, including health clinics, churches, unions, and government services, now refer people to LIIP. Harold Dyck, the current coordinator for LIIP, began his association with WORC as a volunteer doing advocacy work on poverty issues. As WORC became better known and the caseload increased dramatically, Dyck helped to establish the LIIP as a separate organization located in the WORC. Together with volunteers from the community and trade union movement, Dyck uses the organizing and advocacy skills he developed as a union activist in the Canadian Auto Workers Union and the Manitoba Government Employees Union to help hundreds of low-income people access support from social service agencies and resolve welfare problems.

Having built a solid reputation LIIP, Dyck is now often able to resolve problems with telephone calls to appropriate agencies and case workers. The initial contact for almost two-thirds of LIIP's caseload comes from telephone contact, with the rest being referrals from the WORC or walk-in visits.

In addition to his involvement with LIIP, Dyck is an active member of the WORC Central Committee. He sees WORC as an important place to build cross-sectoral solidarity, in addition to providing a central meeting place for progressive groups and advocacy organizations: "WORC is an ideal tool to counter the culture of individualism and free trade. Any person who comes in with an anti-union attitude leaves with a positive view of what labour can do for the community."[6]

In addition to CUPW locals, CAW Local 4209 is the only other union to have located its offices at the WORC. Local 4209 represents 13 bargaining units in the transportation, hospitality, and service sectors. The location at WORC was a conscious decision by the local to locate itself within the centre of community activism represented at WORC. According to local President Don Lajoie, the decision to locate at WORC, as opposed to the Winnipeg Union Centre, was not difficult. "We have to get out of the mainstream cannibalism of the establishment labour movement," he says, "and get back to where we came from."[7] Lajoie would like to see WORC relocate to a larger storefront where more union locals could locate their offices and pool their resources to underwrite the cost of meeting space and equipment.

Other groups that hold regular meetings at WORC include the NO WAR coalition, which is the main peace group in Winnipeg, the Cuba-Canada Solidarity Network, the Youth and Landmines Project of the Mennonite Council for International Cooperation, the Industrial Workers of the World (IWW), Eco Mafia, a University of Manitoba youth group, the Structured Movement Against Capitalism (SMAC), the Red Boine Metis Local, and The Delivery Drivers Alliance of Manitoba (DDAM), which includes delivery drivers from various workplaces.

Is WORC fulfilling its mandate to help establish, maintain, and facilitate community organizations that represent and enforce people's rights within our community? Yes. In the words of CAW union representative and community activist Karen Naylor: "WORC is an extremely important initiative. It is a hub of progressive activity in the city, assisting labour and strengthening the social justice movements."[8]

Advocacy on behalf of unorganized workers

It is much easier to quantify the amount and quality of advocacy work at the Centre. Here again the mandate of WORC appears to have been fulfilled far above the initial expectations when WORC was created. The three major areas of advocacy work are in the areas of welfare (Low Income Intermediary Project), employment standards (WORC itself), and rights and working conditions of courier workers (Delivery Drivers Alliance of Manitoba). In addition, the WORC Coordinator and several volunteers provide information on other issues, such as tenants' rights, human rights violations, and immigration problems. However, advocacy work on these issues is usually referred to other organizations with specialized knowledge.

The Low Income Intermediary Project (LIIP) is the only organization in Winnipeg doing advocacy for welfare clients. Harold Dyck and his volunteers handle between 15 and 30 cases per week. About two-thirds of these are direct contacts through LIIP's dedicated phone line, and about one-third are referred from WORC. Currently, over 40 community organizations refer clients to LIIP.

The LIIP itself is actually a creation of WORC. It did not exist when WORC was created. However, the high number of welfare problems and the very high success rate of WORC in pursuing claims led to increased demand for its services. WORC's reputation of high-quality advocacy work on behalf of welfare claimants led several social service agencies to refer clients needing advocacy services to WORC. As a result of the increased demand for assistance, Harold Dyck, together with other caseworkers, initiated the creation of LIIP as a separate organization to deal exclusively with welfare issues.

It is highly unlikely that LIIP would exist if it were not for WORC. Currently, LIIP is seeking government funding, which, if successful, will contribute to WORC's efforts to become financially self-sufficient by renting the space.

WORC itself, through its part-time coordinator and volunteers, performs advocacy work for workers on a broad range of issues. Thanks to a study undertaken in 2003 by Jay Short, a WORC volunteer doing pre-master studies in Industrial relations, there exists a detailed analysis of WORC's activities between January 1999 and June 2003.

In his study, entitled *Fairness For Whom?*, Short found that WORC has assisted almost 2,400 people in its first four-and-a-half years of operation. Short reviewed all of these intakes and found that approximately 1,200 of them dealt with issues directly relating to Manitoba Employment Standards jurisdiction. It is important to note that this number included only instances where an official intake form was completed. The nature of the WORC environment is such that WORC volunteers and associates do not always fill out intake forms, as they are constantly answering telephones and fielding questions while attending to their own union and advocacy work.

The types of employment standards problems ranged from unjust dismissal, harassment, unauthorized pay deductions and other pay problems, rights of independent contractors, failure to pay for holidays and severance pay, and many other violations of the law.

Most of the contacts answering the question were workers experienced in the labour force. Contacts ranged in age, with 42% being workers between 25 and 40, 16% older than 40, and 17% younger workers between 16 and 24, who had less experience in the workforce.

Short found that the majority (64%) of all employment standards intakes came from WORC's use of a weekly advertisement in the *Winnipeg Free Press*. The ad is placed in the Saturday classified section and informs workers that WORC is willing to help with information and referral services dealing with all issues of workplace rights. The ad catches the attention of both unemployed workers and employed workers searching for new employment due to poor employment conditions in their current job. Many of these workers contact the WORC to inquire about their rights regarding the current or past actions of an employer.

The second most common way for workers to discover WORC was through referrals by the Manitoba Human Rights Commission. About 12% of intakes came by way of the Commission. Many workers who were being subjected to harassment in their workplace contacted the Commission to complain. Unfortunately, arbitrary discrimination and harassment of workers by their employers finds no protection under human rights statutes. Regardless of this, the people referred to WORC by the Human Rights Commission were assisted through an explanation on ways to collect EI if they had lost their jobs due to harassment, possible solutions through unionization and collective bargaining, as well as advice on how to deal with bad bosses by using safety and health legislation.

WORC's established record within the community also leads to intakes. Short found that WORC received 8% of contacts through word of mouth or past experience with the Centre. Another 7% of WORC's intakes came through its website.

In the majority of cases (56% of intakes) WORC provided information to individuals relating to their rights, or lack of rights, under the Employment Standards Code. In 41% of WORC's cases, a referral was made to another organization or avenue that workers could access for assistance. In some instances, WORC volunteers acted as advocates on behalf of the client, either with their employer or another government agency.

In 16% of cases, workers were referred to resources assisting in the organization of a union. WORC distributes the CUPW "Why Do Workers Join Unions?" booklet, as well as providing contacts of local union organizers. The percentage of referrals to unions is not as high as expected because many of WORC contacts had already left the employment relationship and therefore unionization was not of immediate concern. However, everyone accessing WORC's services is informed about their rights to join a union and the benefits from unionizing.

In addition to general advocacy work on labour standards, welfare, and poverty issues, WORC is a centre for courier workers to organize and resolve workplace issues. This is largely due to the combined efforts of the CUPW and the Delivery Drivers' Association of Manitoba (DDAM). DDAM was founded in 1997 and provides education and advocacy for all delivery drivers in Manitoba, including couriers.

Until recently, many couriers have been told by companies and the government that they are not entitled to protections. That restrictive interpretation of the law was overturned in the precedent-setting case in the courier industry found in *Dynamex v. Mamona* (2003). This decision, which has been affirmed by the Supreme Court of Canada, found that couriers are employees for purposes of labour legislation and therefore entitled to vacation and holiday pay. Since that time, DDAM, with the assistance of CUPW volunteer advocates, have been successful in winning more than a total of $50,000 in compensation for dozens of courier workers from 11 same-day courier operations who have been denied their rights under employment standards.[9]

DDAM has also been successful in improving the lives of delivery drivers on a number of fronts. It negotiated vehicle dashboard decals for delivery drivers which allow them greater flexibility when parking in loading zones, no-parking areas, and free meter parking when a laneway is not provided to serve the business. Additionally, DDAM and WORC worked together to lobby the Employment Standards Branch to ensure that couriers were recognized in having access to legal tests determining employee status and protections under the Employment Standards Code.

In addition to advocacy for individuals, WORC is also involved in public advocacy. In 2004, it made presentations on workers' rights to high schools and youth services centres, to learning centres on adult re-training programs, submitted briefs to the Manitoba Workers' Compensation Board, and made presentations to numerous groups and conferences.

Organizing

WORC has a mandate to assist in the unionization of workers. Indeed, part of CUPW's original motivation for funding the Centre was the hope that the advocacy work of the Centre would inspire workers to start organizing drives in their workplaces.

From the outset, the CUPW leadership was clear that it did not wish to use the Centre as a means of organizing outside of its traditional jurisdiction in the transportation and communications sector. Organizing leads in other industries were to be forwarded to unions associated with the appropriate sectors.

Unlike coalition support and advocacy work, it is more difficult to quantify the contribution WORC has made to unionizing workers in Winnipeg. During its seven years of existence, WORC volunteers have proposed to hundreds of workers that they consider the advantages of unionization. Specific organizing leads have been forwarded to the Canadian Union of Public Employees (CUPE), the United Food and Commercial Workers (UFCW), the Canadian Auto Workers, (CAW), and the Communications, Energy and Paperworkers Union (CEP).

While it is impossible to attribute any one single successful organizing drive to these initiatives, there is significant evidence of WORC's contribution to the success of CUPW's local organizing efforts.

Within CUPW, the Winnipeg local has been a trailblazer in the unionization of courier drivers. Winnipeg was the first location in Canada in which CUPW established a separate non-post-office local, The Red River Local, comprised totally of courier workers employed by Dynamex.

The organization of these workers was a long-drawn-out process in which the existence of WORC played a major role. Initially, the employer challenged the employee status of the owner-operators all the way to the Supreme Court. These legal manoeuvres were a transparent attempt to wear down the resistance of the drivers and generate significant employee turnover.

For its part, CUPW decided to apply the research of Brofenbrenner and Juravich (1996), and Cornish and Spink (1994), and implement a community organizing model involving a comprehensive grassroots approach relying on an already established organizing committee. During this period of more than seven months, WORC played an invaluable role providing a place for Dynamex workers to meet regularly, socialize, and plan their organizing strategy (Short 2004).

CUPW Regional Education and Organization Officer John Friesen is clear that WORC was central to the union's organizing drive at Dynamex: "Without WORC, I do not believe we would have been successful in unionizing Dynamex. The atmosphere and the location of WORC was totally compatible with the union-building model that we used in our organizing campaign."[10]

Following the successful certification effort, the newly-created Red River local located its office within WORC in order to work with the Delivery Drivers' Alliance of Manitoba, and build upon the recognition WORC had earned within the community of courier workers. WORC has provided a home for the Red River local, and the local frequently assists the CUPW Winnipeg local and the national union in other organizing drives.

Obstacles and potential

In its seven years of operation, WORC has provided assistance to thousands of workers, assisted in the development of new and existing working class institutions, and gained the respect of organized labour and the progressive community within Winnipeg.[11]

A number of factors contributed to facilitate its development. The solid support received from the Winnipeg CUPW local and regional office, and the progressive community of Winnipeg, has been essential. WORC could not exist without the dedication of the large number of volunteers. Likewise, the non-sectarian character of the left community in Winnipeg has provided the political framework that enabled WORC to develop. Finally, the sustained funding from the CUPW national union has provided WORC with the financial base to sustain its operations.

The importance of WORC extends beyond the city limits of Winnipeg. Within CUPW, WORC represents a tangible symbol of the union's belief in community unionism. Currently, it is unlikely that many other CUPW locals could match the commitment of the Winnipeg local and Prairie Region, which has been necessary to sustain WORC. However, the experience of the union in Winnipeg may yet inspire other locals, and perhaps other unions, to undertake similar initiatives in other cities. Much depends on the culture and character of the progressive communities and the relationships that have been built between labour and the political left.

Seven years after its creation, WORC continues to be a vibrant centre of progressive working class activity. With continued support, it will grow and serve as a model of union-community solidarity and cooperation.

Notes

1. Interview with Marion Yoe, March 30, 2005.
2. Interview with Cinthya Vargas, March 30, 2005.
3. Interview with Glen Michalchuk, March 30, 2005.
4. Interview with Louis Ifill, March 31, 2005.
5. Interview with Bruce Tascona, March 30, 2005.
6. Interview with Harold Dicks, March 30, 2005.
7. Interview with Don Lajoie, March 31, 2005.
8. Interview with Karen Naylor, March 31, 2005.
9. WORC Case Awards, April 5, 2005.
10. Interview with John Friesen, May 1, 2005.
11. Interview with John Doyle, Communications Officer, Manitoba Federation of Labour, November 2001.

References

Bickerton, Geoff, and Catherine Stearns. 2002. The Struggle Continues in Winnipeg: The Workers Organizing and Resource Centre. *Just Labour* 1:50-57.

Bronfenbrenner, Kate, and Tom Juravich. 1996. It Takes More Than House Calls: Organizing to Win with a Comprehensive Union-Building Strategy. In *Organizing to Win*, ed. Kate Bronfenner, Sheldon Friedman, Richard Hurd, Rudolph Oswald, and Ronald Seeber. Ithaca, NY: Cornell University Press.

Cornish, M., and L. Spink. 1994. *Organizing Unions*. Toronto: Second Story Press.

Dynamex Canada Inc. v. Mamona. 2003. Federal Court of Appeal 248 (A-241-02, June 4, 2003).

Short, Jay. 2003. *Fairness For Whom: A WORC Report On Manitoba Employment Standards Legislation*.

———. 2004. *Straddling the World of Traditional & Precarious Employment: A Case Study of the Courier Industry in Winnipeg*. Winnipeg, Manitoba: WORC.

Worker's Organizing and Resource Centre (WORC). 1998. Mission Statement of the Worker's Organizing and Resource Centre.

———. N.d. http://www.mts.net/~worc/.

Chapter 15
A Community Coalition in Defense of Public Medicare

NATALIE MEHRA

This is a case study of unions working in coalition with community groups to defend public Medicare. Although the campaign was nation-wide, this account focuses on the plans and actions that were undertaken in Ontario. In this case, unions took the lead in creating an education, organizing and mobilization campaign in response to an external catalyst. The campaign was conducted internally, in unions, but also externally, in coalitions with community groups and individual residents.

Although there were some elements of an offensive struggle, the campaign was overwhelmingly defensive. It was not a struggle for a new social benefit, but to defend the well-established public Medicare system from dismantling through cuts and privatization. It was developed in response to a government initiative and therefore did not create the initiative.

This campaign is important for those studying union renewal for several reasons:

- the campaign was forged in response to a public policy issue that would affect the social and economic equality of millions of workers and community members, but was not a direct collective bargaining issue
- it was a large campaign—reaching millions of workers and households
- it mobilized massive community response across Ontario, and ultimately across the country
- it was undertaken by unions across the public and private sectors working collectively, internally and externally
- it was conducted in true partnership between unions and community groups that are not part of the labour movement
- it was, ultimately, successful in forcing into retreat—at least temporarily—the forces working to privatize the public health insurance system.

The catalyst for the campaign was the establishment of a Royal Commission into the future sustainability of the public Medicare system in Canada. In April 2001, a Committee of the Privy Council, on advice of Prime Minister Jean Chretien, appointed former Saskatchewan Premier Roy Romanow to conduct the Commission. Amid an escalating lobby and public relations campaign by the business-funded think tanks and private health industry to privatize the public health system, this Commission was set up under the following mandate:

- To recommend policies and measures to ensure the long term sustainability of a universally accessible, publicly-funded health system; a system which offers quality services to Canadians.
- To recommend policies and measures which would strike a balance between investments in prevention and health maintenance and investments directed to care and treatment.

Romanow announced a two-stage process:

I. Fact-finding stage that would culminate in an interim report to be issued in January 2002.
II. A dialogue with the Canadian public and "interested stakeholders" based on the interim report.

The final report would be issued in November 2002.

The campaign was organized beginning in the fall of 2001, through the winter and spring of 2002 to have maximum impact on the Commission as it was researching and writing its report. Further combined efforts were planned to coincide with the release of the report.

Political context

Public Medicare in Canada has been under pressure from the very beginning. Doctors, private insurance companies, the health industry and right-wing politicians worked from before Medicare's inception to try to stop the program. Once it was created, these same forces continued to push for two-tier access and other modifications of the health system that would provide additional revenue streams and access to the "market" for private insurance corporations, and later, as the industry grew and consolidated, for the private for-profit health provider industry.

The anti-Medicare forces received a big boost from public spending policies through the 1980s and 1990s. The deficit-fighting mania of the 1980s, the recession of the early 1990s and poor government planning were beginning to erode confidence in the public health system. It is unlikely that the forces working against Medicare would have made such inroads, however, had it not been for the provincial tax cuts and the federal budget of 1995. In this budget, then federal finance minister Paul Martin planned for a cut of 40% to transfer payments over two years to provincial and territorial governments and restructured the transfer system (Barlow 2002, 80). At the same time, provincial political parties were running election campaigns on platforms of significant tax cuts. In Ontario, Mike Harris' Conservative government was elected on a mandate to cut taxes by 30%. Combined with the withdrawal of federal funding, the impact on the public health system was devastating.

In the mid-1990s across the country, provincial governments moved quickly to step up their cuts to hospitals. In Ontario, from 1995-1997 approximately $800 million[1] was abruptly axed from transfers to hospitals. A restructuring commission was set up, travelling across the province ordering the closure and amalgamation of dozens of hospitals with the justification that services would be shifted from hospitals to community care systems that were cheaper. Almost 9,000 critical, acute and chronic care hospital beds were slated for closure[2] and 26,000 hospital worker positions—including nurses—were axed (CCPA 2000, 14). Hospitals shrank to core services, "load-shedding" physiotherapy, speech pathology, chiropody and other rehabilitation services, and stepped up their cuts to and privatization of support services. Planned construction for cancer-treatment centres was axed, redevelopment and building of new hospitals were put on hold, and existing hospitals spent down their reserves and ran huge deficits as they scrambled to deal with the cuts. The community services that were to take the place of hospitals were slow to be funded and in some cases never materialized.

The capacity of the combined community care and facility services was not enough to meet demand. Patients were left waiting on stretchers in hospital corridors. Well-publicized "hallway medicine" and health care horror stories echoed in news media headlines month after month. Waiting times for surgeries and cancer treatment ballooned. Ambulances travelled from hospital to hospital searching over-capacity emergency rooms for those that were open to taking their patients. Patients were sent at exorbitant costs for cancer treatment and other procedures in the United States while capacity withered at home.

By 1997, Ontario's government was forced to re-fund hospitals. By 2001, funding was back up to 1994 levels, but the billions that were mis-spent cutting staff and closing hospital beds would not be recovered.[3] By the time the Conservative government lost the election in 2003, hospital bed cuts rested at about 5,000.[4] Acute homecare services saw increased funding as a cheap alternative to hospital care and 20,000 new long-term care beds were created to deal with wait lists that had grown to tens of thousands of elderly residents. Even so, with a growing and aging population, refunding was not sufficient to meet demand and clear backlogs. A festering problem that pre-dated the Conservative government of people unable to get family doctors continued to be a growing and well-publicized problem. As acute care patients took up homecare budgets, home support services for the frail elderly, disabled and those with chronic illnesses were drastically cut, forcing tens of thousands of clients to pay out of pocket or go without. Successive rounds of delisting of publicly-insured procedures were cutting access to physiotherapy, audiology and approx. $100 million in formerly covered services. The provincial government carried through with promised tax cuts, reducing their revenue base while demands for increased funding came from all parts of the health system and patients continued to have difficulty accessing timely care.

While the cuts to public financing were being undertaken and fought, a twin trend of health delivery privatization was deepening. Diagnostics in hospitals were being moved out to free-standing for-profit clinics housing lab, x-ray and ultrasound operations. The growing acute homecare sector was re-designed to open the door to for-profit corporations under a system of "market competition" in which non-profits that had delivered services for decades were forced to compete with for-profit corporations for service contracts. The market was deliberately set up with revolving contracts to destabilize the workforce in order to keep staff costs low resulting in chronic and severe staffing shortages. The majority of the new long-term care beds, developed to move patients out of hospitals into cheaper nursing home arrangements, were contracted to for-profit corporations. For the first time, these corporations were given long-term financing to build beds that they would then own and run for-profit. As the beds became operational, long term care corporations were reporting unprecedented profits from the increased funding and deregulation of care standards. As long waits for cancer treatment hit the head-lines, a new publicly-financed cancer treatment centre was set up at Sunnybrook Hospital in Toronto, but for the first time ownership and control of the facility was handed over to a for-profit corporation. As the contract was eventually exposed, it became clear that the treatment centre was being funded at a higher rate than the non-profit cancer treatment centres were paid for the same work (Provincial Auditor 2001). New MRI and CT clinics were announced, again contracted to for-profit corporations to own and operate.

The new capacity that was being created in the health system was being pri-vatized. The higher costs and profit-taking of the for-profit sector were placing a significant competing demands on scarce resources. The for-profit drug industry was contributing to this competition. Drug costs were escalating to become the fastest growing cost in hospitals and in health systems across the country. The for-profit lobby was growing in size and power and with their easy access to Ontario's government, was winning policies and funding to benefit themselves.

While defenders of the public health system were busy fighting funding cuts and privatized delivery systems, an aggressive campaign was being launched from another quarter. Private clinic owners and the private health insurance industry were clamouring for the dismantling of the public health insurance system. Busi-ness-funded think tanks and politicians geared up to push for changes that would privatize piece-by-piece the insurance system and allow clinics to charge for serv-ices. The insurance industry had an interest in diminishing the public insurance system so that it would have a new market for private health insurance. The for-profit clinics wanted the ability to charge patients for services in a two-tier health system so that they would have access to an additional revenue stream to enhance their profits.

These groups used the horror stories and long waits created by the cuts agenda to promote the false idea that the private sector could alleviate pressure on the public health system and build capacity. They created campaigns to instill fear that the public health system was unsustainable and inefficient. Business-friendly government officials and politicians assisted by creating provincial commissions and campaigns to support the claims about the unsustainability and inadequacy of the public health system. The solution, repeated over and over again, that two-tier health care, user fees, and privatization were the panacea to cure the ills created in large part by government cuts and poor planning.

The Romanow Commission was created by the federal government in response to these pressures. Although there is no public account of Prime Minister Jean Chretien's motivation in setting up the commission and in appointing Roy Ro-manow as the Commissioner, it is clear that pressures and counter-pressures were at a high ebb. Leadership had been taken by the right-wing in the Senate and provincial governments to force the hand of the federal government with respect to health reform. Prior to the establishment of the Romanow Commission, Senator Michael Kirby—a board member of private nursing home giant Extendicare—had won a mandate to review the public health system in Canada and planned to release a series of five reports culminating in a final report early in 2002 to generate public debate about its future.[5] In August 2000, Alberta Premier Ralph Klein established an advisory council on health reform to be headed by Mulroney cabinet minister Don Mazankowski and others with ties to the private health insurance industry.[6] The Clair Commission in Quebec and the Fyke Commission in Saskatchewan had been set up to forge plans for health reform in those provinces.

Non-governmental action on the issues was also at a high level. Polling showed that concerns about the health system were continually at the top of the public agenda. While the private health industry was aggressively pushing its agenda of cuts to public services, deregulation and privatization, the defenders of the public health system were pushing the federal government to do more to protect and promote the principles of the public insurance system. Across Canada, there were increasing reports of two-tier health services and charges for medically-necessary services, expressly banned in the *Canada Health Act*. The federal government was under pressure from groups and individuals across the country to use its powers to stop provinces from allowing these contraventions. All levels of government were under pressure to deal with the problems in accessing the health system and the perception of growing costs. It was clear that the federal government needed to be seen to be taking action to deal with the problems in the health care system, the demands of provincial premiers for restoration of federal transfers, and the pressures of citizens' groups and the private health industry.

In many ways, the establishment of the Romanow Commission was a testament to the power that the privatization lobby had amassed by the turn of the century. It was also a testament to the damage incurred by the deficit-fighting and tax-cutting agendas of all levels of government. Finally, it revealed the inability or unwillingness of the federal government to act on its own to develop a clear set of policies and practices to defend, enhance and modernize the public health system and to resource that system adequately.

The seeds of the campaign

Throughout the winter of 2001, the private health lobby was repeatedly garnering headlines with its campaign to make Canadians believe that public health care was inadequate, inefficient and unsustainable. Administrative committee members of the Ontario Health Coalition (OHC), community organization leaderships and heads of unions in Ontario were painfully aware that the control of the public debate was shifting into the hands of those who wanted the public system dismantled. By the time the Romanow Commission was announced in April, anxiety about the ability of the private sector and its contacts in governments to win the privatization of the health system was very high.

The idea to mount a massive community outreach campaign originated with the activists, staff and leadership of the Ontario Division of Canadian Union of Public Employees (CUPE). Union leader Sid Ryan spoke of the inspiration provided by a municipal strike in Thunder Bay in which union members went door-to-door throughout the community to successfully win public support for protection of their working conditions. Worn out by years of protests that had not provided the pivotal change in government policy direction that was needed, activists were looking for new ways to organize and broaden support. The time was ripe to talk about deep community outreach and organizing as a possible method of moving the population to support a progressive agenda for health reform. After some discussion, the leadership of CUPE pushed for a cross-province door-to-door campaign to win public support to protect and enhance the public health system.

They brought the idea to the Ontario Health Coalition (OHC) and the Ontario Federation of Labour (OFL). The health coalition had been busy building up an infrastructure of local coalitions across the province in order to increase its capacity. By the beginning of the campaign there were a dozen or more local chapters of the health coalition operating across the province. In the previous two years, the local coalitions had moved into a pattern of coordinated activity on identified issues and were proving successful in getting privatization onto the public agenda.

The Administrative Committee of the OHC discussed how across-province door-to-door campaign, bigger than anything that it had tried before, might be done. The union leaders, health professionals and community activists together developed a plan to attempt to build the coalition infrastructure to accomplish the goal of a province-wide door-to-door campaign. The Ontario Federation of Labour agreed to support the campaign. There was a consensus that such a campaign would require unprecedented financial and volunteer resources for the coalition. All groups worked to find additional resources to fund and people the campaign. All concurred that work on the campaign should happen through their individual organizations, but the public rallies and door-to-door elements should be done in coalition. It was also agreed by the key large union, health professional and community groups of the coalition to hold a large meeting of local coalitions and activists to try to win support for the idea and launch the campaign. The wheels were set in motion.

The campaign plan

The campaign consisted of a building and planning stage, a public lead-up campaign, and a finite-time period to conduct the door-to-door effort. In addition, the coalition planned rallies at the three hearings held by the Romanow Commission in Ontario. A series of following goals and methods to accomplish these were set out over a timeline that stretched from September 2001 to May 2002. It was agreed to evaluate the campaign and plan for the next phase at that point.

Goal 1: Establish a common set of policy objectives and ensure that these were communicated broadly across the province;

Method: The OHC produced its submission to the Romanow Commission, a summary and fact sheets and distributed them widely;

Key member groups created their own submissions echoing that of the OHC, and distributed their submissions and the OHC's widely.

Goal 2: Win mandate from local activists for an action plan; start planning; establish goals, campaign events and timelines.

Method: A large assembly of several hundred coalition activists was held in December 2001. The assembly debated and adopted the action plan including the door-to-door campaign and its lead-up publicity campaign, and planned participation in the Romanow Commission's consultations and rallies at the Romanow Hearings.

Goal 3: Organize community lead-up campaigns in as many communities as possible across the province to garner publicity for the campaign and the policies agreed upon.

Method: It was planned that each community would conduct a series of initiatives and events in an attempt to make the campaign and our goals "rise above the noise" in each community. Regional training sessions on the policy issues and campaign plans were held in every part of the province with reps from each local health coalition.

The local campaign plan that was developed in partnership with all of the central and local organizations was as follows:

January-February 2002: Hold local spin-off assemblies to win mandate and develop local action plan; hold a public media event/rally to launch the campaign.

February-March 2002: Find and open a local campaign office to establish a community presence; Put up lawn signs and hang street banners and other public messaging to raise awareness of the threat to public Medicare and the campaign to protect it.

Hold an office opening ceremony as a media event and to bring community members and activists into the campaign planning; distribute literature and visuals as widely as possible in the community; bring a resolution to municipal council in support of public Medicare and progressive reform of the health system; organize media conferences with local community agencies to raise awareness of how public Medicare helps community members; ask faith organization leaders to issue public policy statements supporting the public health system.

Hold vigils, candle-light ceremonies, church-bell ringing ceremonies and other events to build involvement of faith and social justice communities; hold community forums, rallies and other events to raise public awareness; hold mall displays, market tables and speaking events at community clubs and agencies to get petition signatures and support for the campaign.

April-May 2002: Conduct the door-to-door campaign; put up red ribbon and lawn signs saying "Yes! National Public Medicare" as widely as possible; get signatures on a petition that called for protection of the public health system and progressive reform.

May 2002: Hold a rally or event with the red ribbon to finish off the campaign at the same time across the province.

Goal 4: Ensure that Romanow heard from large numbers of people inside and outside his hearings in support of the public health system.

Method: Notification about the hearings was sent out by every organization as broadly as possible; large rallies were planned outside each hearing in Ontario to deliver a common message.

Goal 5: Evaluate the response to the campaign and plan next steps.

Method: OHC reps traveled across the province to each community to meet with local organizers and assess the campaign to date.

Feedback was compiled and reviewed by the Administrative Committee and next steps were planned.

What was accomplished

- Over 55 communities organized citizens' groups to conduct the door-to-door campaign.
- Over 215,000 households were visited by over 3,000 volunteer canvassers across the province.
- Over 170,000 signatures were received on petitions from across the province.
- Over 70 town hall meetings, forums and public meetings on the Yes! National Public Medicare Campaign were held across the province between February-May 2002. Over 3,500 people attended these gatherings.
- Over 1,000,000 feet of ribbon and approximately 20,000 lawn signs were put up at households across the province.
- 55 municipalities passed the Ontario Health Coalition resolution in support of National Public Medicare.
- Rallies were held at Romanow Hearings in Ottawa, Toronto and Sudbury. The Toronto rally, which was the largest, featured a gathering of approx 1,500 people in a blizzard outside the hearing. Commissioner Romanow joined the rally to hear the assembled group read en masse a common statement appealing for protection, and progressive reform of the public health system.

The national campaign

At the same time that ideas and planning were being undertaken in Ontario, unions at the national level were promoting the idea of a cross-country door-to-door campaign. A joint meeting was held by the Canadian Health Coalition and the Canadian Labour Congress in the autumn of 2001 to develop the national action plan. Provincial health coalitions agreed to take on the door-to-door campaign, as well as to organize community education initiatives and to mobilize community members to participate in the Romanow hearings and consultations.

The community campaign was organized by the Canadian and provincial health coalitions. As the Ontario campaign got underway, other provinces signed on and built their own initiatives. Lawn signs were put up across the country, community forums and events were held, and community members flocked to the Romanow hearings to appeal for protection of the public health system. Plans culminated in a set of cross-country events and rallies timed to coincide with the May wrap-up events planned in Ontario.

A parallel labour campaign was organized through the health committee of the Canadian Labour Congress (CLC). The unions planned and coordinated a mass outreach initiative through all major union affiliates. Materials about the threats to the public health system and the importance of public medicare were distributed to millions of union members. In addition, unions in the private sector—notably the Canadian Auto Workers Union (CAW) and Communications Energy and Paperworkers (CEP)—organized to get major private sector corporations to issue public and written statements supporting public health insurance. They were successful in obtaining support from the major auto manufacturers and several other large corporations. Public sector unions, notably the National Union of Public and General Employees (NUPGE) undertook press initiatives to show that public healthcare was important to the economy.

Union participation

Participation in the national and provincial campaign from unions affiliated to the umbrella labour organizations was very high.

Participants in the CLC organized worker outreach through mass distribution of literature and petitions in workplaces included.

Private sector unions
Canadian Auto Workers (CAW)
Communications Energy and Paperworkers Union of Canada (CEP)
Industrial Wood and Allied Workers (IWA)
International Association of Machinists (IAM)
United Food and Commercial Workers (UFCW)
United Steelworkers (USW)

Public sector unions
Canadian Union of Public Employees (CUPE)
National Union of Public and General Employees (NUPGE)
Service Employees International Union (SEIU)
Public Service Alliance of Canada (PSAC)
Union of National Defense Employees (UNDE)
Confederation of Nurses' Unions

In Ontario, several unions—notably CUPE, OPSEU and USW seconded members to help organize the canvassing and community campaigns. Several unions assisted with printing of materials and lawn signs. Other unions donated space and phones in union halls to provide free campaign offices. CAW retirees and SEIU members organized buses to Romanow hearing rallies. CAW, CUPE, Elementary Teachers Federation of Ontario (ETFO), Ontario Public Service Employees Union (OPSEU), Ontario Nurses' Association (ONA), Ontario Secondary School Teachers Federation (OSSTF), SEIU, USW, and the UFCW, provided extra support in the coalition and conducted their own internal campaigns to enhance community efforts. All of these unions actively supported joint decision-making between the community and organizations and the unions. Other unions participated through the Ontario Federation of Labour.

Community participation

Leadership of the local coalitions and action groups that organized the community campaigns was a mixture of seasoned community activists, union activists, faith community members and less experienced concerned citizens. Many of the community coalitions found it difficult to attract large numbers of union members to the door-to-door canvassing. Most canvass volunteers were non-union community members, supplemented by some participation by health care workers, auto workers, steel workers, nurses, teachers and members of several other unions.

Notably, large ethnic and cultural groups were deeply involved in the campaign in urban centres—especially in Toronto—and developed materials and petitions in six languages. These initiatives were exclusively done by non-union community members. Rallies of Portuguese and Spanish women were held to support the campaign. These communities organized in downtown neighbourhoods to conduct door-to-door canvassing in the appropriate languages. An extensive lawn sign campaign was conducted by Sikh groups. The Korean Canadian Association organized to get over 10,000 signatures on Korean petitions translated from the OHC petition.

Also noteworthy was the leadership and participation of many large seniors' organizations, community non-profits, and the Council of Canadians. Community social service agencies, including health centres and co-ops were deeply involved in distributing lawn signs, ribbons and petitions. The Council of Canadians organized a cross-country tour with several stops in Ontario to raise awareness and join in the campaign. The Council also provided leadership on the steering committees and central organizations at the federal and Ontario levels, and Council chapters at the local level led several of the community campaigns. Seniors' groups were instrumental in distributing policy positions and campaign plans through their large networks. Many United, Unitarian, Anglican and several Catholic churches organized petition-signing, vigils and other events, along with a few diverse faith communities.

Community/union relationship

At a central level in Ontario, the goals of the community coalitions, health professionals and unions were so similar and relationships *so* well-established that there were few difficulties in establishing common policy positions and campaign plans. Unions supported key community goals of extension of homecare to provide home support services that had been cut, to enhance community health centres, to support the determinants of health and prevention initiatives, and to promote primary care reform. Community groups supported union desires that the labour force be

treated with dignity, care standards be regulated and sound human resources planning be undertaken. All supported maintaining and extending public funding and
promoting public non-profit delivery.

At a local level, there were similarly few differences about policy goals and
campaign plans, but there were a few difficulties in building coalitions between
community, faith and union members. In a few towns, community members and
union activists had some difficulties in understanding and getting used to the each
others' cultures, etiquettes and organizing styles. There were class differences to be
overcome between the largely middle and upper-middle class community volunteers and the working-class union volunteers. Some community members objected
to the overwhelming use by unions of placards and flags emblazoned with union
names at events, as they overshadowed the smaller hand-made signs of the community groups and individuals. In several cases, community members expected unions
to "save the day" and could not understand why union members were not already
deeply and broadly mobilized like the general community. In other cases, community members were challenged to overcome biases and preconceptions about
unions. Similarly, the community groups and faith communities needed, in some
cases, to learn to see their similarities but also to respect their different organizing
cultures and needs. Most of these issues were resolved to some extent over time and
as volunteers worked together, and many resulted in a deeper understanding by the
non-union volunteers of the issues facing unions and workers.

Outcomes of the campaign

The primary goal of the campaign was to mount an effective opposition to the
empowered forces that were campaigning to dismantle the public health insurance
system. There were also secondary goals. The coalition wanted to promote ideas for
progressive reform within the public health system including an expansion of the
system to cover home and pharmacare, to win restoration of federal transfers and
to maintain a national health system, to push the national government to enforce
the principles of the *Canada Health Act*, and to stop the increasing privatization of
health delivery systems. Internal organizational goals included winning community
and union members to the idea of deep community outreach and organizing as
a method of fight-back, developing a large and strong infrastructure to deal with
ongoing threats to the public health system and the broadening of the coalition.

The primary goal of the campaign was met successfully. Ideas for privatization such as medical savings accounts, two-tiering and increased delisting gained
some initial ground with the work of the Kirby and Mazankowski committees. By
the end of the community/labour efforts, combined with the work of academics
whose research supported the public health system, there was no serious debate in
policy-making circles about any of the privatization initiatives for the health insurance system. In his report, Romanow (2002) clearly rejected the dismantling of the
public insurance system and called for significant restoration of federal transfers to
deal with the funding crisis in the health system. This was a significant victory that
effectively closed the door to health insurance privatization for several years.

The secondary goals of enhancing the national role and enforcement mechanisms and stopping the privatization of delivery systems were not successful. To the extent that the federal government restored transfer payments, it bought itself a slightly greater role in the health system. The federal government ultimately signed a health accord[7] with the provinces that significantly increased federal funding and directed monies to particular parts of the health system, including reduction of wait times and homecare funding, among others. However, none of the directed funds were enforceable through any mechanism. Moreover, the accord called for a disputes resolution mechanism that watered-down the federal role in enforcing the *Canada Health Act*.

Although Romanow rejected privatization of health delivery systems in general, he did not provide any recommendations that would create systems to stop such privatization, with the exception of calling for the end to two-tier access for workers' compensation cases which could dry up much of the funding that was supporting the private clinics across the country. In addition, Romanow's report contained a gratuitous reference to privatization of support services such as hospital cleaning and laundry, stating that privatization of these services was acceptable. This was an unexpected blow to public sector unions, and was based on no research by the Commission and was included with no prior warning or consultation with those groups that would be most affected. This made it difficult for many of the public sector unions to support Romanow's report and was used by provincial governments and the health industry to push further privatization of these services.

The campaign also failed to win enhancements to the public health system. Romanow supported some moves towards creating a national pharmacare program, but as of the time of this publication, nothing has come of these. He also recommended a homecare program, but he drew the line at acute homecare—excluding the home support services that are so important to seniors' and others' ability to live independently. He also chose not to mention long term care facilities entirely. Although the federal government created a funding transfer for homecare including those services identified by Romanow, there is no enforceable program and no standards attached to the money.

The internal organizational goals of winning support for deep community outreach and organizing, a broadening of the coalition, and enhancement of coalition infrastructure were partially reached. After the initial post-campaign fatigue, more activists than previously have been regularly willing to undertake deeper outreach and organizing. Coalitions have the *attention* of local politicians who know that these community groups are willing and able to go door-to-door in their ridings to win particular policy issues. Local groups have more extensive contact lists and better connections. Many new local groups were formed and continue to work on issues. The commitment and sophistication of local leadership has deepened.

This work is never done. More could have been accomplished, more groups could have been involved more intimately, and we have much more work to do on this. But this campaign proved to those involved that we could pull exceptional levels of work, involvement and commitment when we needed to. The level of activity of the coalition has increased dramatically ever since. Importantly, both centrally and locally, expectations of our own movement have heightened.

Analysis

This campaign revealed some significant strengths, but also some weaknesses that should be noted. This is by no means a rigorous analysis, and not everyone involved would agree with all of these ideas. However, a few possible conclusions about this type of organizing follow:

- There is consensus that the method of outreach used in this campaign—lead-in publicity campaigns, local organizing, and household-by-household outreach—works. Our experience in this campaign was that we were able to mobilize powerful public consensus around the public health system despite a well-coordinated and superiorly funded campaign by the private health industry with high-level ties to governments.
- The campaign successfully pushed back the attempt to privatize the health insurance system for several years. However, the Fraser Institute and Alberta premier Ralph Klein have attempted to create ways to re-open the question. The Institute has recently embarked on a media campaign touting a new report by Preston Manning and former Ontario Premier Mike Harris that includes devolution of powers to provinces and a re-opening of the privatization discussion. In Alberta, Ralph Klein has recently organized an international conference in an attempt to inject new life into the debate about privatization. The weakness of a "one-off" campaign in the face of a relentless global industry is evident. The need to develop strategies to deal with this remains.
- We failed to anticipate the potential for Romanow to hive off support services for privatization, though it was known that industry was working for the privatization of those services. This was a mistake that may have been avoidable.
- We failed to ensure that long term care issues were on the agenda. We will need to find a way to ensure that the systems set up to provide this care for the aging population are public and follow the egalitarian principles of the public health system. This will be difficult.
- We learned that the organization of a deep outreach campaign required finite timelines as community members could undertake such work in large numbers only for pre-determined amounts of time. This was done successfully in the campaign.
- Although more could always be done, significant outreach to union members was accomplished using flyers and petitions. However, we learned that the mobilization of workers required member-to-member phoning which we did not undertake as systematically as needed. The structures to do this on an ongoing basis do not exist in most unions and many local leaderships are organized solely around collective bargaining and direct workplace issues and do not have enough time, resources and/or plans to do community outreach.
- We needed to discuss and assess more fully what could have been done to ensure that more of Romanow's progressive recommendations were adopted

and that the federal government take a more active role in enforcing and/or extending the *Canada Health Act*. Perhaps if we had organized a major mobilization for the meetings of the federal-provincial-territorial first ministers at which the accords that followed the Romanow Commission were signed, we may have enhanced the profile of the anti-privatization fight and won more ground. Perhaps there are other strategies that would have been more effective. This has not been discussed within our organizations.

- The ongoing work of the coalitions and labour movement to protect the health system is important and is slowing down privatization. However, a larger strategy to deal with the power of the global privatization forces has not been developed and will be necessary if we are to be successful.
- This campaign did not move us from a defensive to an offensive position. More work needs to be done to develop policy options and strategies to enhance and extend the public system and public supply and delivery within it. Progressive options for planning, human resource issues, increased democracy within the system, reform of health institutions and delivery systems need to be developed and promoted more effectively.
- The effectiveness of a coordinated coherent strategy undertaken by groups across large geographic areas at the same time was shown in this campaign.
- The partnership between the labour movement and community groups strengthened the effectiveness and improved the policy positions of all involved. This campaign is evidence of the viability and importance of such initiatives.

Conclusion

It is now 2005, three years after the Romanow Commission did its work. The latest health insurance privatization initiative of the right wing think tanks, Ralph Klein, Mike Harris and Preston Manning has suffered a temporary blow as the national Conservative Party leader, Stephen Harper, has distanced himself from health privatization in anticipation of a federal election. The power of popular support for public health care is evident in the unwillingness of the right wing to openly propose privatization in election season.

But privatization continues to eat away at the public health system. In Ontario, British Columbia, Quebec and Alberta, privatized hospitals (known as P3s or public private partnerships) are being pushed by provincial governments, both Liberal and Conservative. Huge community fightbacks are underway to keep our hospitals public. New private clinics and day surgery hospitals are popping up across the country, finding ever new ways to can get around the *Canada Health Act*'s prohibition against selling two tier health services. In Quebec, two tier services for medically necessary procedures are being sold, in flagrant contravention of the *Canada Health Act*, in a bevy of private clinics and surgeries. In Ontario, private health insurance and two tiering have been stymied by the public health care campaigns of the coalition and allied groups, but privatization of health service delivery and delisting of services continue. So too, the community outreach campaigns, huge rallies and protests, lobbying and other activities of our side continue.

Situated, as we are, next to the United States which houses the largest private for-profit health industry in the world, Canadians will always have to fight to protect our health system from the encroachment of the private market. As the global private health industry grows and continues to consolidate into corporations larger than governments, our struggle will become more difficult. The survival of our universal, one-tier public health system, and the protection of public non-profit service delivery, will depend on our ability to learn the lessons of campaigns such as that we mounted during the time of the Romanow Commission. It will depend on our ability to forge a renewed public vision and clear policy options, to organize and mobilize effectively against a global industry that far surpasses us in wealth and resources but lacks popular human support, to protect and extend democratic processes and structures, and to build resistance to the commodification of our health care and social systems.

Notes

1. See Government of Ontario, Ministry of Finance, Annual Statements 1996/7, 1997/8.
2. OHA: Key Facts and Figures November 1998. Beds staffed and in operation as of March 31, 1998 from MOH 1990-92 Hospital Statistics and 1993-98 Daily Census Summary.
3. Calculated from Government of Ontario, Ministry of Finance, Annual Statements 1995-2001.
4. Calculated from Ontario Hospital Association reports on hospital beds staffed and in operation.
5. See Senate of Canada, Standing Committee on Social Affairs, Science and Technology, proceedings from 2001-2002.
6. For more on Mazankowski see Friends of Medicare-Alberta, *Analysis of Mazankowski Report*, 2002.
7. See *First Ministers' Accord on Health Renewal 2003*, and the statement issued September 16, 2004, by the Government of Canada from the First Ministers' meeting on Health Care, *A 10 Year Plan to Strengthen Health Care*.

References

Barlow, Maude. 2002. *Profit is Not the Cure: A Citizen's Guide to Saving Medicare*. Toronto: McLelland & Stewart.
Canadian Centre for Policy Alternatives (CCPA). 2000. *Public Pain Private Gain Summary: A Report to the Ontario Health Coalition*. Ottawa: CCPA.
Office of the Provincial Auditor. 2001. Special Audit. December 13.
Romanow, Roy. 2002. *Building on Values: The Future of Health Care in Canada*. Report of the Commission on the Future of Health Care in Canada.

Chapter 16
Organizing Call Centres:
The Steelworkers' Experience

JULIE GUARD, JORGE GARCIA-ORGALES,
MERCEDES STEEDMAN, AND D'ARCY MARTIN

The United Steelworkers' (USW) successful organizing in the call centre industry is a useful model for unionists seeking ways to respond to the challenges of the new economy. Working together, inside organizers and experienced professional organizers can develop winning strategies that enable unions to organize these hard-to-organize workplaces.

The organizing strategies that have overcome the obstacles in this industry demonstrate the importance of rank-and-file organizers, whose specialized knowledge of the workplace, capacity to respond quickly and creatively to management tactics and ability to communicate effectively with their co-workers are crucial to a successful campaign. Good strategy is important, but collaborative organizing practices that treat workers as equal partners are far more effective than those that rely primarily on the abilities of professional organizers. Workers with little or no union experience may lack the tactical skills and knowledge to organize their own workplaces, but without their specialized knowledge of the industry and the workplace, campaigns don't succeed. With a basic education in unionism and on-going mentoring, they can be full partners.

Method

The research was conducted in two phases. In the first phase a case study approach was used to interview union organizers and activists involved with the USW call centre unionization drive in Canada. We chose Omega Direct Response in Sudbury, Ontario because it had been recently organized. Omega Direct was the first call centre to enter the Sudbury region. The company, with head offices in Toronto, was a young Canadian-owned company offering both inbound and outbound financial services to a mainly American market. Management's attempts to ignore minimum legal standards, together with an unusually high union consciousness in the area, contributed to the USW's success. In recent years the city had undertaken an aggressive call centre marketing campaign, offering financial incentives to potential employers. Omega Direct Response was the first to arrive in Sudbury with a 1,300 employee operation. But when call centre workers at Omega began to complain about being required to work on Thanksgiving Monday, a statutory holiday, the situation began to unravel. Because most of the corporate contracts were with American companies, Omega planned to have employees take the American holidays instead of the Canadian ones. Employees' complaints quickly found voice in suggestions for unionization.[1] Sudbury is a heavily unionized community in which the USW has been a key player, so even non-unionized workers were familiar with unions or had a unionized family member.

The research team conducted interviews with rank-and-file organizers who participated in organizing their own and other call centres and with USW staff involved in organizing and servicing call centres. These interviews provided information about successful and unsuccessful organizing strategies, the particular problems of organizing in this sector and the nature of the call centre workforce. Using a purposive sampling strategy to identify key informants with knowledge and experience related to the union organizing campaigns, we interviewed union staff who were directly involved with the campaign, activists who were directly involved as volunteer organizers, and rank and file members who signed cards but who were not actively involved with the union organizing campaign. The interviews were conducted shortly after the union negotiated the first contract. Interviews were supplemented with documentation on Omega Direct corporate management released by the union and media coverage of the organizing campaigns and first contract negotiation.

The second phase of the research was gathered from a conference, "Organizing Call Centres from the Workers' Perspective," held in Toronto in September 2003. This invitation-only conference brought together rank-and-file organizers, union staff from Canada, the USA, and the UK, and academic researchers to share experiences and develop strategies for successful organizing in this sector. These unionists and researchers offered useful comparisons and provided an international perspective. The research team paid particular attention to encouraging effective communication among conference participants through the use of popular education techniques that valorized different kinds of knowledge and helped to overcome communication barriers among academics, unionists, and call centre workers. The presentations, discussions, and observations that emerged at this conference were taped, transcribed and analyzed by the researchers. They form a significant part of this study.

Call centres and the new economy

Call centres are so integral to the "new economy" of information and communication services that they are virtually ubiquitous. Both private and public sector employers now use call centres to provide a vast array of products and services as diverse as health care, including pharmaceutical and medical products; technical support; freight transportation; insurance, banking and financial services; customer complaints and inquiries; pre- and post-sales customer service; reservations; help lines; collections; message-taking; operator services; warranty and repair service. Nearly half offer services 24 hours a day. An estimated two to three percent of the workforce in the major industrialized countries now works in call centres, although because electronic communication is a nearly universal aspect of so many services, the real proportion is probably even larger (Holman 2003).

Indeed, Peter Bain contends that any workplace in which most of the work is performed in front of a computer and using a telephone is a call centre. Even within the "call centre industry," conditions are so different that, Bain suggests, it is more accurate to identify call centres as a technology-based work arrangement than a distinct industry (Bain 2003; Taylor and Bain 2001).

Today call centres are a major component of Canadian business support services. Employment in this sector jumped more than fivefold (447 percent) from 20,000 to 112,000 between 1987 and 2004. In 2000 there were an estimated 13,400 call centre operations in Canada employing 570,000 workers. The sector has grown rapidly, experiencing an annual growth rate of approximately 26 percent in most recent years, yet the vast majority of workers (75 percent of the industry) are located in call centres with fewer than 25 operators. Ontario, with more than 7,000 call centres, has nearly half of Canada's call centres and one of the highest concentrations of call centres in North America (Statistics Canada 2005).

Many communities, hoping to recover from the job losses caused by decades of de-industrialization or reverse long-standing patterns of regional underdevelopment, have adopted a "call centre ready" policy. Regional strategies include maintaining low telecommunication costs on local, long distance, 1-800 calling, data communication, and wireless services as well as offering direct subsidies to call centres that locate in the region. Training is frequently provided at no cost to the employer through public institutions such as community colleges and universities. Government subsidies, low overhead costs, and the promise of a job-ready workforce willing to work for low wages are key to call centres' location decisions (Ontario Call Centres Brochure 2005; Buchanan and Koch-Schulte 2000). But even with financial incentives and regional support, call centres are uncertain vehicles for local economic development. When it opened in 1998, Omega Direct promised 1,300 jobs. Today the number has dwindled to 250. At one time the company had two locations in Sudbury. Today it occupies two floors of the old police station and has recently given notice that it will contract further to one floor. In addition to Omega, nine other Sudbury call centres employ 4,000 full- and part-time workers but, like Omega, jobs in these centres are precarious.[2]

Working conditions and wages in call centres vary enormously. In the low wage sector of the industry, which includes telemarketing, fund raising, reservations, and credit collection, employers tend to require only a high school diploma and possibly some language skills in addition to a "neutral accent," clerical and interpersonal skills. The latter tend to be perceived as "feminine" abilities rather than real skills and are usually poorly remunerated. Better-paid jobs involving web-based computer technology (sometimes in web-based multi-media centres) are emerging as the industry evolves, suggesting that the skilled labour requirements in this sector may expand. At present, however, the industry remains "feminized" and poorly paid. According to Statistics Canada, in 2004, over 60 percent of jobs in the industry were held by women, while youth made up almost one-third of the job holders in business support services. Wages are low, averaging $12.45 an hour in contrast to the average service sector wage of $18.50 an hour (Statistics Canada 2005). In some cases, employers have adapted to the evolution of call centres by redesigning work arrangements to offer services in new ways. Others have seized the opportunity to reduce costs and streamline operations by out-sourcing work to private-sector for-hire call centre companies. Not all of these are the high stress, insecure jobs described in much of the literature. In many call centres, particularly where workers provide customer services in-house or as part of the public sector, wages and working conditions are not significantly different from those in more traditional work settings in the same industry. In the public sector, and occasionally in the private sector when they are part of a large business rather than a separate, stand-alone operation, call centres may even be unionized. In contrast are the "electronic sweatshops" of the private sector, for-hire call centre industry that sell telephone services, mostly out-bound telephone sales ("telemarketing") and in-bound customer service on a contract basis to other businesses. These call centres are the flagship new economy industry—notoriously footloose, aggressively anti-union, and able to tap a highly vulnerable and diverse workforce with little experience of unions.

These private-sector, for-hire call centres are exceptionally well-positioned to take full advantage of a wide range of union avoidance strategies. Research on call centres argues convincingly that the management strategy of virtually the entire private call centre industry is predicated on successful union avoidance (Fernie and Metcalf; Good and McFarland 2003; McFarland 2002). Out-bound, for-hire call centres are capable of moving to another region, or even another country—a strategy that those in the industry call "off-shoring"— to ensure a union-free environment. Aside from the telecommunications infrastructure and a literate workforce willing to work irregular hours for relatively low pay, the requirements of a call centre are minimal. Their technology is relatively simple and very portable: computers, telephones, headsets, desks, chairs, and cubicle dividers. Rental warehouse or office space in an industrial park or plaza is adequate. This extraordinary mobility enables private sector call centres to bargain favourable conditions from governments and helps keep workers insecure and compliant.

USW organizing in the new economy

Despite these obstacles, since 1999 organizers in District 6 (Ontario) and District 3 (Western Region) of USW have been successfully organizing and servicing the different segments of the industry.[3] At one end of the spectrum is CIBC-VISA, located in a large urban centre and part of a complex corporation. Most of the work is in-bound (receiving calls from clients), responding to questions, offering services, and recruiting new clients. Unionized with USW for several years, these workers have a mature relationship with the employer. While some issues can be easily resolved and others lead to confrontation, sometimes to the point of strike actions, both parties see merit in maintaining a working relationship that allows them to get the job done. On the other end of the call centre spectrum is Omega Direct, an out-bound (workers call out and do not receive calls) "telemarketing" centre in which workers sell an ever-changing array of products, primarily to customers in the United States. At Omega, Telephone Service Representatives (TSRs) make cold calls (to people who do not expect their call), most of which are automatically dialled by a computer, and read a script to potential customers. Omega epitomizes the hard-to-organize "electronic sweatshop." Yet in December 1999, USW Local 2020 at Omega was certified, with 65% of workers voting for the union. Members of the research team followed these events closely, either as members of the local Sudbury community or as research staff in the USW national office. Interviews conducted with key participants in the drive almost two years later, including two staff organizers, two members of the inside organizing committee, and a local shop steward, provide informed, first-hand accounts.

The story of USW's campaign to organize Omega offers a compelling demonstration of the Steelworkers' determination to make good on their promise to become "Everybody's Union." By integrating the key insights advanced by advocates of the new "organizing model" of unionism, and by targeting workers in the service sector, USW is responding to the needs of workers in the "new economy," long overlooked by the organized labour movement. The Steelworkers is shedding its industrial white-male image as organizing in new sectors changes the face of the union. Almost 10,000 post-secondary institution support staff, most of them women, are part of the new face of Steel. In Northern communities, Aboriginal forestry and mining workers are redefining the look of Steel. The Steelworkers' urban membership in Toronto and other urban areas is close to fifty percent workers of colour. The increasing diversity of its membership is enhanced by the organization of call centres, whose workforce typically includes young workers, some of them students, single parents, recent immigrants, retirees living on low incomes, homemakers seeking part-time jobs, and people with disabilities.

Progress in organizing this industry has been slow, in part because organizers deliberately target small to medium sized private sector call centres, the ones that are typically the most difficult to organize. Yet, as senior USW organizer George Casselman explains, without union protection, these workers are "open targets" for exploitive employers who ignore their legal rights, abuse and infantilise them.[4] Perhaps more than any other group of workers, they need unions. Despite a number of failed campaigns, Canada's Steelworkers now has over 2,000 call centre workers under contract in eleven workplaces, concentrated in Ontario (District 6) but also in Manitoba and British Columbia (District 3). The Steelworkers' success in this "new economy" industry, notorious for its employment of particularly hard to organize workers and its eagerness to avoid unions, points to a reversal of some District leaders' apparent reluctance to promote new organizing strategies and target service sector workers, previously identified by Gregor Murray (1998). Its success in organizing call centres is part of a larger trend toward service sector organizing in the USW. In 2005, USW completed its mergers with the Industrial, Wood and Allied Workers of Canada (IWA) and the Paper, Allied-Industrial, Chemical and Energy Workers International Union (PACE), to become the United Steel, Paper and Forestry, Rubber, Manufacturing, Energy, Allied Industrial and Service Workers International Union (USW). Service sector workers in call centres, banks, post-secondary institutions, hotels and restaurants, nursing and retirement homes are now sixteen percent of the union's membership.

Organizing Omega

The USW's 1999 campaign to organize Omega Direct, a for-hire call centre in Sudbury, incorporated elements that some advocates of the new "organizing model" have identified as the key components for success: the support of the union leadership and a skilled and determined organizer (Milkman and Wong 2001). Denis Dallaire, the lead organizer, is a clever, committed, and innovative strategist. Organizing Omega demanded exceptional energy and an ability to work extremely long hours. Over the seven months of the campaign, Dallaire often worked eighteen hour days. Although professional organizers expect long days during the crucial periods of a drive, the demands at Omega were almost too much for George Casselman, a senior USW organizer who joined Dallaire for the final six weeks. Dallaire recalled, "I had no mercy for him. ... We'd be there at 8, 8:30 in the morning ... [and] I'd keep him there 'til 2. I don't need much sleep. After two weeks he said, 'I gotta go home and rest.'... I tried everything in my power not to let him go. He would take off every couple of weeks for a couple of days to re-energize, and I'd come up and say, 'You know, every day you're gone we fall back a week.' I did everything I could [to keep him]."[5] USW District 6 Director Wayne Fraser, who was staff co-ordinator in the Sudbury area during the campaign, gave solid support to the campaign. He approved Dallaire's plan to devote himself to a months-long drive and requested and got two more staff organizers from the District office, five volunteer organizers and one support staff to assist in the final six weeks of the campaign. He approved financial support for both 'normal' expenses, such as leaflets, buttons, stickers, and postage, and less typical costs such as pizza dinners for the inside committee's weekly meetings.[6]

"If I needed the cash," Dallaire said later, "it was there." But he acknowledged that the unorthodox nature of his costs created problems for his director. "At one point [Wayne] pulled me in and said, 'You're going to get me fired. I don't know how much you're spending but I need to know how many cards have you got?' And I said, 'That's confidential.'"[7] Dallaire brought in guest speakers to educate the inside committee members, developing a program that addressed topics of direct relevance to call centre workers, including work-related stress and health and safety hazards. USW leaders and activists from the district office helped train the committee in organizing and inoculation strategies.

These resources were important, but the campaign's success turned on the collaboration between the staff organizer and the inside committee. This collaboration was possible because Dallaire, himself a former inside organizer, treated the inside committee as full partners in the campaign. Advocates of union renewal generally agree that organizing works best when workers take ownership of the campaign and identify themselves, rather than the organizer, as the union (Clawson 2003). Yet most accounts emphasize the role of professional organizers or officials, rather than the workers, as the lynch-pin of a successful campaign. Experienced organizers with dozens of hard-won organizing struggles to their credit are understandably reluctant to hand over control to inexperienced amateurs. But the hard truth is that workers are unlikely to take ownership of an organizing campaign or regard themselves as the union unless the organizer treats them as partners, acknowledges their expertise and knowledge, and demonstrates trust by giving them some control over the process. Dallaire recalled, "The people [in the inside committee] were just excellent. ...We had folks from all walks of life [working] in the organizing drive. ... Initially I had different 'cells', but then we realized we could trust them all."[8]

This diverges from research on union renewal that places primary importance on organizers' extensive repertoire of new organizing strategies. To be sure, the success at Omega points to the importance of clever strategy, a comprehensive, union-building approach and careful use of situation-appropriate tactics (Bronfenbrenner and Juravich 1998). But it also reveals the key role of the inside committee.

The winning strategies at Omega were developed and implemented collaboratively by the organizer and the inside committee. This is consistent with the path-breaking work of Kate Bronfenbrenner and Tom Juravich, who argue that "rank-and-file intensive strategies" are most likely to succeed. These tactics include "acting like a union from the beginning of the campaign," encouraging rank-and-file organizers to participate in and take responsibility for the campaign, emphasizing "person-to-person contact" including small group meetings and house calls, and focussing on dignity, justice, and fairness rather than "bread-and-butter issues" (Bronfenbrenner and Juravich 1998, 24-5). We argue that, in the call centre industry, organizing campaigns succeed when staff not only recruit and train rank-and-file organizers, but also acknowledge that these workers have knowledge and skills that differ from their own but are just as important in advancing the campaign. What worked at Omega was a combination of highly skilled professional organizers, supported by the union leadership, working together with enthusiastic inside organizers.

The USW victory at Omega challenges the view that union rejuvenation depends primarily on the efforts of decision-makers at the top of the union hierarchy and the skill and resolve of professional organizers. Rick Fantasia and Kim Voss, for instance, have recently argued that successful new organizing in sectors that unions have tended to see as too hard to organize depends largely on the enthusiasm of the union's top leadership. They identify the crucial components of a union's transition from a service to an organizing model as the willingness of the union's top leaders to foster an organizing culture among organizing staff, allocate union resources to new organizing, and replace senior organizers who resist new ideas with young activists who have social movement experience (Fantasia and Voss 2004). Taking a different but still institutional focus, Charlotte Yates argues that industrial unions can adapt to the changing demands of organizing in the "new economy" by transforming their internal structures to accommodate and integrate an increasingly diverse membership (Yates 2004, 221-3). Even those who regard strategy as crucial, regardless of whether it fosters increased union democracy, assume a leadership-driven organizing model. Ruth Milkman and Kent Wong, who examined both failed and successful campaigns involving largely immigrant workers, argue that success depends less on whether the campaign is top down or grassroots than on the organizer's skill and the adequacy of the resources available: "We argue that what really matters is not whether a union organizing campaign begins as a strategic effort to put pressure directly on the decision makers in an industry or as a bottom up, grassroots mobilization of workers on the ground. Rather, success seems to depend on effectively combining the two approaches into a comprehensive strategy (Milkman and Wong 2001, 103)." But Milkman and Wong's emphasis on tactics presupposes the support of the leadership to provide legal and financial resources not available to the grassroots (Bronfenbrenner and Juravich 1998).

Steve Early disagrees with these arguments, pointing out that an emphasis on the support of powerful gate-keepers within the organization to institutional change assumes a top-down approach that overlooks the role of rank-and-file participation and increased union democracy. He argues that real renewal in the labour movement demands wholesale structural change that will put workers in charge of their own unions (Early 2004). Dan Clawson, similarly, argues that genuine rank-and-file control of a labour movement that is truly a movement and not a constellation of bureaucratic institutions led by staff and executive with a vested interest in maintaining the status quo is the only solution to labour's current dilemma. Participatory democracy at all levels of the movement, he contends, is essential to the rebuilding of a labour movement capable of responding to the new political and economic realities facing working people (Clawson 2003). Chris Schenk contends that social unionism, that mobilizes workers around a "worker-centred way of seeing the world" and links collective bargaining with social justice is essential to labour's revitalization (Schenk 2003). USW experience suggests that, while strategic organizing and a supportive union leadership are important, so is the participation of inside rank-and-file workers at every step of the campaign. The key component of USW success is the partnership between full-time, seasoned organizers, who oversee strategy, wangle resources, and keep an eye on the long view, and inside organizers, who know the workplace, its culture, and the needs of their fellow workers and can keep abreast of the employer's moves.

When he began the drive at Omega, Denis Dallaire was a seasoned organizer, experienced with anti-union employers and adept at accessing the resources necessary to mount a successful organizing campaign. But what kept the Omega drive on track was Dallaire's willingness to listen to and learn from call centre workers. Management's vast array of union avoidance strategies together with their extraordinary capacity to intimidate job-hungry workers conditioned by harsh circumstance to tolerate dictatorial and coercive control pose particular challenges for organizers. Many of these workers have little expectation of respectful treatment, autonomy, or decent pay and regard the kind of working conditions unionized workers take for granted as unachievable. Sowing the seeds of a union culture that construed respectful treatment and decent working conditions as achievable took time. Denis began spending time at the work site, getting to know the job and the workers. With management hiring a lot of new workers, it was easy for him to walk in unnoticed. "I could walk in with a group when they were on their breaks, just check the place out. Wow! This is what a call centre looks like."[9]

Like other call centres, Omega targeted young workers, women, single mothers, recent immigrants, people from impoverished backgrounds and people on social assistance especially vulnerable workers whom they expect to accept irregular shifts, unscheduled overtime and fast-paced work without complaint. According to George Casselman, who had worked on a number of call centre organizing drives before joining the one at Omega, call centre workers are harder to organize in part because they are more vulnerable than industrial workers and have little experience of unions. Typically, these workers are more fearful of losing their jobs if they are caught trying to organize than industrial workers and may have a negative view of unions.[10] But by making himself available to them without attempting to push the union, Dallaire gradually won their trust. A member of the inside committee explained that workers appreciated his unaggressive style:

> The way he talks to people, he doesn't talk to them about the organ-
> izing drive, he talks to them about what they want and how they feel
> they should be treated. Then he tries to explain to them why having a
> union would benefit them. Basically, he's not an arm twister. He tells
> them the facts and lets people see the facts and that he's not there just
> to get a card. He's there actually to help. People were signing [union
> cards] on the backs of people when they were coming out [of the
> workplace].[11]

In time, the workers began to see him as an ally to whom they could bring their concerns about bad working conditions and problems. "People got so they'd expect you to be there. So they'd come out and they'd be looking, 'Where is he?' They had something to talk about. So that was the important thing ... There was a lot of venting. You gotta give them time for venting and then focus on the issues."[12]

Omega opened the first of its two call centres in Sudbury in April 1999, hiring approximately 1200 workers. Over the summer, Dallaire recruited an inside com-mittee from among the people he met outside the call centre. He also "dropped in" on barbeques and birthday parties organized by his son's girlfriend, who worked at Omega and was one of the first inside committee members. From the start, he used the strategies advocated by proponents of union renewal.[13] Even before the drive was officially underway, Dallaire began training workers at Omega to begin "acting like a union," educating them about their rights, encouraging them to insist on respect and fair treatment at work, and helping them find remedies for their workplace problems. His strategies emphasized "person-to-person contact" and small group meetings, usually at someone's house, where workers shared their ex-periences and began to forge a sense of common purpose. He used these meetings, as well, to start "inoculating" them about what to expect from the employer when they tried to organize, training them in union tactics and giving them ammunition to use in the workplace to recruit other workers. The campaign focused more on issues of dignity and respect than on wages or job security. Not only were these the issues of most pressing concern to the workers, but they were more "winnable" in a call centre than the bread-and-butter issues that have traditionally been the focus of unions. But most importantly, he encouraged rank-and-file participation and handed the primary responsibility for the campaign to the workers themselves. Dallaire earned a reputation for his ability to work collaboratively with the inside committee. According to one committee member, "Denis is probably the greatest organizer for the Steelworkers because he shares information with the inside com-mittee."[14]

Over the summer, Dallaire and a tiny core of volunteers developed an initial list of workers, and in September, the committee called everyone on the list and invited them to the Steelworkers Labour Day picnic, using the opportunity to mention the organizing drive. Attracting Omega workers to the Labour Day picnic not only gave the committee a way to distribute information and sign up new members; it also linked these workers to Sudbury's vibrant union culture. Representing mainly industrial workers, USW has been a powerful voice for workers at INCO, Sudbury's biggest employer, for over fifty years. But although they lived in a union town, many of the Omega workers had no personal experience of unions and regarded them with trepidation. One of the most energetic members of the inside committee recalled that, before she became active in the drive, she'd been frightened of the union. "At first, it was kind of scary, the thought of being involved with a union. Because all those fears come to you: 'I'm going to lose my job.'... it's unknown territory."[15] Others, however, were members of USW families and had worked in unionized workplaces before coming to Omega. They were able to use their experience to advantage when confronted with anti-union arguments from other workers. Gail, a member of the inside committee, recalled, "We explained to [workers who were critical of unions] that their union dues were like basic insurance, that there's going to be an avenue if you have a grievance, or there's going to be some kind of pay rate that's going to be obtainable. You're not going to have to go in and beg for a raise every six months."[16]

Members of the inside committee, some of them new to unionism themselves, were sometimes able to communicate more effectively than the professional organizer with other workers who were unfamiliar with the terms and concepts organizers take for granted. Despite her own union experience, Gail was initially reluctant to get involved in the drive. Her interest increased when, at her first meeting, she intervened to translate Dallaire's explanations into terms other workers could understand. She recalled:

> People ... kept asking the same question over and over again. That really frustrates me, because there are different ways that people learn and understand. Poor Denis was standing up at the front, and I could see, he was trying to think about how he could say it in a different way. ... It was about their job security and why they couldn't fire us. Why would we be visible? People were so worried that they were going to be targeted [if they signed a union card] and fired automatically. And Denis had explained to them that they can't do that and that one way of securing that is to sign a card, because that shows that you are actually involved with the union. People couldn't grasp the concept. ... I just stood up and said, "If you don't mind, I'd like to explain this one." And I looked at the person next to me, and I explained it, how she might understand it. Only because I knew her a little bit better. ... I just basically said, "Look, if you believe in this, you need to sign a card to show your support. Because, if you go back tomorrow and they fire you, you can say, 'Why did you fire me? I've got the good record here, here, here and here. Is it because you think I'm involved in this union organizing drive?' If all the evidence points to that, you actually have a card to back it up." But people didn't understand that. ... And she says, "Oh, okay." And I turned to this other lady who had asked the same question three times, and I said, "Do you understand now?" And she said, "Yeah, well that makes sense." And I said, "Okay," and I sat down.[17]

Inside organizers can translate unfamiliar concepts and terms for their co-workers far more easily than professional organizers, for whom these terms have become second nature. And their personal accounts of the advantages of a union have far more relevance to other workers than advice from a union organizer who has not shared their daily experience.

Omega workers, like others, were reluctant to demonize their employer, preferring to encourage management to treat them respectfully and fearful that an aggressive approach would aggravate, rather than improve, their relations with management. As Larry Cohen and Richard Hurd observe, fear of increased conflict at work is at least as serious an obstacle to organizing as fear of employer reprisals, and workers are often quick to blame union organizers, rather than the employer, with whom they have an on-going relationship (Cohen and Hurd 1998). One of the inside organizers explained that standing up for your rights "doesn't always have to be negative. I think the fact that there were a lot of women involved in the drive ... [meant that although we] never cowered back from management, we were never rude. ... We were there because we had legitimate concerns. The fact that they didn't want to answer and skirted these issues just basically showed us who they were."[18] When a local reporter with a pro-union perspective published an article exposing Omega as a bad employer in the local newspaper, Dallaire and the inside committee intervened. Six or seven members of the inside committee persuaded him that bad-news stories about Omega would hinder their campaign. Dallaire explained, "We didn't want to trash [Omega] because employees want to feel good about their workplace. ... That's what we based the campaign on, that we needed to improve things, that we wanted to work with management."[19]

Dallaire seized every opportunity to cultivate congenial relations with management to emphasize the union's desire to solve problems, not create them. Strategic mistakes by management, many of whom were inexperienced at union avoidance, made his job easier. "When we filed those unfair labour practices, we got to know the HR Director ... There would be incidents ... and I would call him up and say, 'We could be filing all kinds of charges, criminal charges, human rights issues, health and safety issues. I don't know if you want to go through this. Personally, it ties me up and I've got a job to do. I know your [job] is to keep [the union] out, but you've got a centre to run.' And he'd say, 'Can we talk?' And he'd let me come in. And I'd make sure I paraded through the whole place so people would know." Until the HR Director was terminated for being too friendly to the union, Dallaire made a point of being seen with him. "He would look for me. In the mornings, he'd be having a smoke between the buildings, and he'd wave at me. ... We developed a rapport."[20]

Despite the friendliness of the HR Director, Omega's managers expected that the precariousness of their jobs and the lack of comparable work in the area would allow them to intimidate the workers with impunity. Like other call centres, Omega counted on the ease with which it could pack up shop and move to a more accommodating region to discourage any attempt to unionize. But a core of union-savvy insiders, trained by the organizer and aided by management's over-confidence, helped turn a potential disaster into a union victory. The ability to respond quickly and effectively made the crucial difference.

Early in the campaign, when Dallaire was spending time "just hanging around" the workplace, when only a night-shift inside committee was formed, he was approached by one of the workers in the day shift who was eager to start organizing. The worker was so pushy that Dallaire was concerned. "This guy's a loose cannon," Dallaire recalled. "He scares me." The worker called Dallaire early one morning after the employer accused him of passing a petition in favour of a union. "I think they are going after me." Within a few hours, he was fired. Dallaire filed charges against the employer with the Ontario Labour Relations Board immediately. Not content with terminating this worker, the company called a meeting of approximately 380 people, threatening that if any of them started organizing, they'd be "terminated on the spot." Managers also warned the workers that, "if the Steelworkers were voted in, they would pack up and leave. They've done it before. ... It takes just two hours to clean this place out."[21]

While Steelworkers pushed for the case to be heard by the Labour Board, the company offered a substantial amount of money if the worker would resign. Dallaire recalled, "I went to his house and said, 'You have a kid, you can get a job in the call centre across the street and make a dollar more per hour ... this is a good settlement. Are you sure you don't want it?' His wife intervened and told me, 'You don't know him; he wants to do this. He would not be able to live with himself if he does not go back to Omega'." The union continued the fight at the Labour Board and won. The settlement was a clear victory for the USW. According to the terms of the settlement, the worker returned to his job and Omega sent a written apology to the other workers. In addition, the company paid for a mail-out to the entire workforce of an organizing leaflet promoting the union and a union card to be signed. Sixteen Steelworkers with flags and signs accompanied the returning worker triumphantly to Omega's front door while everybody looked on. "It was extraordinary," recalled Dallaire. "It was the turning point in the campaign."[22] The Labour Board-ordered mailing generated a spectacular response, higher than any other mailing during this or any other USW campaign. By acting like a union at the Labour Board while continuing to negotiate with the company, USW demonstrated to the Omega workers that it could defend their rights aggressively while maintaining a good working relation with the employer.

The inside organizers at Omega took ownership of the campaign, challenging the climate of fear and intimidation on a daily basis, something even a skilled organizer like Dallaire could not do. After the Labour Board-ordered mailing, the campaign heated up and the inside committee of a dozen workers began meeting with Dallaire every night. Inside the workplace, personal connections among workers became increasingly important, as the inside committee mobilized a large contingent of volunteers. Research on organizing strategies demonstrates that virtually all workers are more likely to join a union when the campaign relies on personal contact rather than on leaflets (Bronfenbrenner and Juravich 1998; Milkman and Wong 2001). Personal contact is even more important when the workers are highly vulnerable and unfamiliar with unions, but an organizer's ability to make contact with workers is limited, particularly when scarce union resources are already stretched by the lengthy campaigns that are required to organize call centres. The intensive personal contact that was essential to the success of this campaign was possible only because of the active participation of Omega's active and well-trained inside committee. With over 150 card collectors, card-signing became pervasive. Some collected only one card, but with so many people handing out union litera-ture and working to build the union, the mood in the workplace began to change. Gail recalled, "A lot of people were turning to their friends, and they would sign [a union card]. ... Which was kind of neat, because it made them feel like they were involved."[23] Some got bolder. Some of the inside committee started displaying their union sympathies openly, applying the USW sticker to their employee identifica-tion tags. "We all did that. We all put stickers, union stickers, on our swipe card."[24]

Wendy, one of the leading card collectors, reported, "We'd have our [hand]bags open, you'd sign your card and drop it in the bag and just keep going. Or I'd go to the swipe machine [where workers signed in] ... and I had union cards on me, and I'd spill them all over the floor. And I got people helping me pick them up. Just crazy stunts that we pulled, and it worked."[25] Building the union themselves, day by day and worker by worker, created a new workplace culture that is inherently democratic, in which the union is "us." Because the workers were treated as part-ners in the campaign and allowed to participate in important decisions, rather than merely being assigned specific tasks, they began to believe that they and not the organizer were the union. Gail explained that, during the drive, workers would ask members of the committee what to expect when the union "came in." "I'd say, 'No, we are the union, we're right here, we're the people. The people are the union. You could be a steward, you could be a staff rep, you could be on health and safety,' and I'd start telling people, 'You can do that ... When we get our first contract, you need to step forward and become a steward.' ... So we started grooming people around us, to show them that they were the ones that were going to make all this happen."[26] When the campaign was over and the day-to-day work of running the union began, workers who participated in organizing had some of the skills and experi-ence they need to maintain their local. The active participation of the members in the daily business of the union helped forge a "social union" culture. Workers who practice their unionism from the moment they start organizing are better placed to continue their activism, which helps the local stay organized. Rank-and-file organizers from Omega were also a valuable union resource for other campaigns, contributing in energy and enthusiasm what they lacked in experience.

Skilled organizers like Casselman and Dallaire understand that workers in call centres, like those elsewhere, often want respect, fair treatment, and reduced stress more than they want higher wages.[27] Insiders can apply this knowledge concretely in the workplace, fostering enlarged expectations among their fellow workers and designing organizing tactics to address particular instances of abuse. Working collaboratively, they turned some of the worst aspects of the work environment at Omega into organizing opportunities. Before they had the union, one inside organizer reported, management often abused workers. "We had management just yelling at people on the floor. ... One friend of mine was docked fifteen minutes [pay] because she went to the bathroom and took too long. ...Things like that were constantly happening."[28] When workers began to perceive the union as a real pos-sibility, management's unrelenting bad treatment of workers became an organizing opportunity. According to Wendy, management "helped us. They treated people like shit every day. We told them that repeatedly, 'If you wouldn't have done that, we wouldn't have won.'... Management treats people like dirt on a regular basis and then you wonder why people inside decide to organize?"[29] "It wasn't just about the organizing drive," says Gail. "It was about pumping up a set of people who went into a minimum-wage job with a minimum-wage mentality and came out of that job or maybe progressed from that job with a mentality that they could actually succeed because somebody had confidence in them."[30] Emphasizing dignity and respect helped build a union culture around compassion and solidarity. Many young workers in call centres aren't willing to organize because they regard their jobs as temporary. Gail explained that she would prompt younger workers to consider their co-workers who had fewer options. "Phyllis is the sixty-year-old lady who sits beside you, whose husband has died and she's here supporting herself. ... Do you realise Phyllis isn't going to get any dignity and respect here if her co-workers don't support her in this drive?"[31]

At Omega, USW had educated the inside committee about what to expect from management during the drive, and they were able to track the employer's anti-union activities and respond quickly, 'inoculating' their co-workers on a continual basis. When management announced a raise, Gail immediately gave credit to the union: "Oh, isn't that wonderful? Just the threat of having a union is getting us money. Imagine, when we get in here, because we're going to build on what we already have. So good, give us all the raises you want beforehand, because now we can build on that." Having the backing of the union gave people like Gail the confidence to talk back to management when they tried to bribe the workers with words and bonuses. "I'd say, 'It's very obvious that you guys realize that the attack didn't work, so now it's the nice guy approach. Let me see, what's the next one going to be? Can I predict this?' And we always had predictions because we were very well educated through the Steelworkers."[32] They also educated some of the USW leadership. Women on the inside committee sometimes had to confront sexism in the union as well as in the workplace. Gail explained that the men in the "male-dominated Steelworkers ... have this very male knuckle-dragging attitude sometimes towards women." Union leaders, accustomed to dealing with male in-dustrial workers, may also need education about the skills and abilities of service sector workers. "I remember [USW District 6 Director] Wayne Fraser saying at a meeting, '[working at a call centre] isn't brain surgery.' And I ... was very insulted. ... I told him, 'Don't ever, ever insult a group of people I represent again. ... I'd like to see you sit down and actually do a call, do the job.' ... and [Wayne] said, 'Yeah, you're right.'"[33]

Conclusion

The USW victory at Omega could not have been won without the combination of an able and committed organizer, generous allocation of union resources, and rank-and-file activists' energy and determination. By treating the inside committee as full partners, acknowledging their specialized knowledge of the workplace, and col-laborating with them to develop winning strategies, lead organizer Denis Dallaire forged a team capable of overcoming the obstacles to organizing this call centre.

The campaign illustrates the potential of workers mobilized to struggle collectively for dignity and respect and supported by a skilled organizer and an enlightened union leadership. Democratic, rank-and-file participation creates discomfort in unions, pushing them to allocate resources to support unfamiliar initiatives with unpredictable outcomes, threatening long-standing institutional arrangements, and forcing union leaders to re-evaluate their priorities and assumptions. But it also encourages union members to see themselves, rather than the organizer or the leaders, as the union. Omega workers who organized their workplace were transformed by the experience, becoming the core activists in their newly forged union. That transformation was articulated by the organizing committee member who self-confidently asserted, "we are the union."

Notes

1. *Sudbury Star*, October 3, October 7, 1999.

2. "Call Centre Employees Losing Dial Tone," *Northern Ontario Business*, June 3, 2005; "Pulling the Plug," Northern Ontario Business, August 2003; "Omega Axes Sudbury Call Centre," *Northern Ontario Business*, October 2002. Available at http://www.nob.on.ca/ (accessed June 3, 2005).

3. For similar evidence of successful organizing in call centres, see Peter Bain and Phil Taylor (2000, 2003), and Sarah Koch-Schulte (2002).

4. George Casselman, Interview #5. Interviewed by Jorge Garcia-Orgales, Vancouver, BC, June 2001.

5. Denis Dallaire, Interview #001. Interviewed by Mercedes Steedman and Jennifer Keck, Sudbury ON, February 3, 2002.

6. Denis Dallaire, Interview #001.

7. Denis Dallaire, Interview #001.

8. Denis Dallaire, Interview #001.

9. Denis Dallaire, Interview #1.

10. George Casselman, Interview #5.

11. Gail (pseudonym), Interview #2. Interviewed by Jennifer Keck and Mercedes Steedman, Sudbury ON, February 14, 2002.

12. Denis Dallaire, Interview #1.

13. These are the strategies advocated by Bronfenbrenner and Juravich (1998, 24-5).

14. Gail, Interview #2.

15. Wendy (pseudonym), Interview #3. Interviewed by Jennifer Keck and Mercedes Steedman, Sudbury ON, February 24, 2002.

16. Gail, Interview #2.

17. Gail, Interview #2.

18. Gail, Interview #2.

19. Denis Dallaire, Interview #1.

20. Denis Dallaire, Interview #1.

21. Denis Dallaire, Interview #1.

22. Denis Dallaire, in conversation with Jorge Garcia-Orgales, April 25, 2005.

23. Gail, Interview #2.

24. Wendy, Interview #3.

25. Wendy, Interview #3.

26. Gail, Interview #2.

27. George Cassleman, Interview #5.

28. Wendy, Interview #3.

29. Wendy, Interview #3.

30. Gail, Interview #2.

31. Gail, Interview #2.

32. Gail, Interview #2.

33. Gail, Interview #2.

References

Bain, Peter. 2003. Presentation to Organizing Call Centres conference, Toronto, Ontario, sponsored by United Steelworkers of America B Canadian National Office (USWA), Laurentian University and the University of Manitoba, September 11–13.

Bain, Peter, and Phil Taylor. 2000. Entrapped by the Electronic Panopticon? Worker Resistance in the Call Centre. *New Technology Work and Employment* 15 (1).

———. 2003. Call Center Organizing in Adversity: from Excell to Vertex. In *Union Organizing: Campaigning for Trade Union Recognition*, ed. Gregor Gall, 153–173. New York and London, Routledge.

Bronfenbrenner, Kate, and Tom Juravich. 1998. It Takes More than House Calls: Organizing to Win with a Comprehensive Union-Building Strategy. In *Organizing to Win*, ed. Bronfenbrenner, Sheldon Friedman, Richard Hurd, Rudoph Oswald, and Ronald Seeber, 19–36. Ithaca and London: ILR Press.

Buchanan, Ruth, and Sarah Koch-Schulte. 2000. *Gender on the Line: Technology, Restructuring and the Reorganization of Work in the Call Centre Industry.* Ottawa: Status of Women Canada.

Clawson, Dan. 2003. *The Next Upsurge: Labor and the New Social Movements.* Ithaca, NY: Cornell University Press.

Cohen, Larry, and Richard W. Hurd. 1998. Fear, Conflict, and Union Organizing. In *Organizing to Win*, ed. Bronfenbrenner, Sheldon Friedman, Richard Hurd, Rudoph Oswald, and Ronald Seeber, 181–196. Ithaca and London: ILR Press.

Early, Steve. 2004. Reutherism Redux: What Happens When Poor Workers' Unions Wear The Color Purple. *Labor Notes* (September). Available at http://www.labornotes.org/archives/2004/09/articles/j.html.

Fantasia, Rick, and Kim Voss. 2004. *Hard Work: Remaking the American Labor Movement.* Berkeley and Los Angeles: University of California Press.

Fernie, Sue, and David Metcalf. (Not) Hanging on the Telephone: Payment Systems in the New Sweatshops. In *Advances in Industrial and Labor Relations*, Volume 9, ed. D. Lewin, and B.E. Kaufman, 23–67. Stamford, CT: JAI Press.

Good, Tom, and Joan McFarland. 2003. Technology, Geography and Regulation: The Case of Call Centres in New Brunswick. In *Challenging the Market: The Struggle to Regulate Work and Income*, ed. Leah Vosko and Jim Stanford, 246–264. McGill-Queen's University Press.

Holman, David. 2003. Call Centres. In *The New Workplace: A Guide to the Human Impact of Modern Working Practices*, ed. Holman, Wall, and Clegg, 115–34. Chichester, U.K.: John Wiley and Sons.

Koch-Schulte, Sarah. 2002. Cheeky Operators: Resistance Tactics in Canada's Call Centers. In *Just Doing It: Popular Collective Action in the Americas*, ed. G. Desfor, D. Barndt, B. Rahder. Montreal: Black Rose Books.

McFarland, Joan. 2002. Call Centres in New Brunswick: Maquiladoras of the North? *Canadian Woman Studies*, special issue "Women, Globalization and International Trade" 21/22 (4/1).

Milkman, Ruth, and Kent Wong. 2001. Organizing Immigrant Workers: Case Studies from Southern California. In *Rekindling the Movement: Labor's Quest for Relevance in the Twenty-First Century*, ed. Lowell Turner, Harry C. Katz, and Richard W. Hurd, 99–128. Ithaca and London: ILR Press/Cornell University Press.

Murray, Gregor. 1998. Steeling for Change: Organization and Organizing in Two USWA Districts in Canada. In *Organizing to Win: New Research on Union Strategies*, ed. Bronfenbrenner, Sheldon Friedman, Richard Hurd, Rudoph Oswald, and Ronald Seeber, 320–338. Ithaca and London: ILR Press.

Ontario Call Centres Brochure. 2005. Available at http://www.2ontario.com/software/brochures/call_centre.asp. Accessed May 24, 2005.

Schenk, Chris. 2003. Social Movement Unionism: Beyond the Organizing Model. In *Trade Unions in Renewal: A Comparative Study*, ed. Peter Fairbrother and Charlotte A.B. Yates, 244–262. London and New York: Continuum.

Statistics Canada. 2005. *The Daily*, May 25.

Taylor, Phil, and Peter Bain. 2001. *Trade Unions, Workers' Rights and the Frontier of Control in UK Call Centres.* Economic and Industrial Democracy 22 (1): 39–66.

Yates, Charlotte A.B. 2004. The Revival of Industrial Unions in Canada: The Extension and Adaptation of Industrial Union Practices to the New Economy. In *Trade Unions in Renewal: A Comparative Study*, ed. Peter Fairbrother and Charlotte A.B. Yates, 221–23. London and New York: Continuum.

PART IV
Leadership Development and Education

Chapter 17
Increasing Inter-Union Co-operation and Co-ordination: The BC Federation of Labour Organizing Institute

JOHN WEIR

As unions renew their focus on organizing, the appropriate role of central labour bodies in these efforts continues to be the subject of much debate in Canada, and recently a very sharply divided debate in the United States.

In 1996, the British Columbia Federation of Labour decided to increase its activities in support of union recruitment by launching an Organizing Institute. The Institute is not a separate bricks-and-mortar institution, but rather an institutional initiative to increase co-operation and co-ordination in affiliate recruitment organizing activities. The Federation, a 380,000-member provincial labour central chartered by Canada's national trade union central, the Canadian Labour Congress, was the first Canadian central to formalize its efforts in this way.

The purpose of this chapter is to review the history of the Institute, give readers a sense of its work, and discuss the Institute's role as a central labour body project.

Origins

The Organizing Institute came to life in late 1996 with a mandate from the Federation's Convention. In many ways, the circumstances that preceded its creation were not significantly different from those in other jurisdictions. At 37% union density, B.C.'s workforce was comparatively higher in union density than other North American jurisdictions, but B.C. unions had experienced the same prolonged decline since the 1960s, notwithstanding a spurt of growth in public sector unionization in the 1970s.

Prior to 1996, the Federation's involvement in organizing was largely limited to advocating improvements to labour relations legislation. While the Federation had formed an organizing committee following the Federation's formation in 1956, the committee was dissolved in 1962 (the latter date coinciding with the culmination of union density growth and the beginning of decline). Inter-union cooperation in organizing was limited.

In the late 1980s, some limited internal discussion took place about the role of the Federation in regard to promoting renewed growth in the labour movement, but the issue was not at the forefront of concern at the time. Instead, the Federation's preoccupation was the political struggle over labour rights that unfolded in the polarized political environment of B.C.

Since the labour law reforms of the early 1970s, the B.C. Labour Relations Code had been the subject of a seesaw legislative battle over organizing and union security rights.

In 1973, the NDP government of Dave Barrett made significant amendments to the Labour Relations Code, introducing union certification based on membership card evidence. Government employees gained full collective bargaining rights. Union density and coverage grew significantly following these amendments, briefly breaking the pattern of decline—a pattern not unlike most Canadian jurisdictions.

On the heels of the economic recession of the early 1980s, the succeeding Social Credit governments of Bill Bennett and then Bill Vander Zalm introduced a series of amendments to the Code to limit union organizing success, and reduce union security against employer evasion of bargaining obligations. In 1987, a sweeping legislative bill designed to weaken organizing rights and union security prompted a one-day province-wide general strike.

Bennett and Vander Zalm also took direct aim at public sector unionization by pursuing an aggressive privatization strategy throughout the 1980s, both in the direct public service and contracted services. Open shop construction provisions were actively promoted in government projects such as construction for the British Columbia World Fair, known as Expo '86.

There were several important effects of this political struggle that made conditions ripe for the concept of the Organizing Institute to take hold in B.C.

First, privatization prompted the British Columbia Government Employees' Union (BCGEU) to develop organizing capacity in order to re-establish the union in work moved to the "private" sector.[1] As one of the largest unions in the province, the BCGEU's influence was significant in the affairs of the Federation, and its novel interest in organizing issues provided an impetus at the Federation.

Second, the broad attack on labour by government and employers had also unified the labour movement in British Columbia. Affiliation to the Federation increased to include virtually every union in the province, with the exception of the B.C. Nurses' Union and the B.C. Teachers' Federation, but even here, strong working relationships existed.

Third, the increase in union density that followed the 1973 Code changes, and the decline in union density coinciding with the Social Credit legislation in the 1980s, convinced many in labour that the legal environment was the prevailing factor in determining union density. And so, with the election of the New Democrats in 1991 and a reversal of direction in labour law policy, union activists hoped for a resurgence in organizing success.

But, by 1995, it was clear that the density decline was continuing at much the same rate as in the 1980s, and that union organizing was falling far short of maintaining density. Union security had been improved and liberal support for organizing restored—including limits on employer "union avoidance" strategies and the reintroduction of card-based certification—and the success rate for union campaigns had shown an improvement. Yet the volume of organizing drives was at a level that only half of the number of union members lost due to technological change, contracting-out, and closures were being replaced through recruitment.

Finally, organizing efforts of affiliates were increasingly being pre-empted by the growing presence of three unaffiliated unions typically given favourable treatment by employers. These unions were actively promoted as an "alternative" to the mainstream labour movement, and had gained ground by exploiting a legislative provision in B.C.'s employment standards legislation allowing a union to negotiate contract terms inferior to the minimum public standards. The growth of these rivals—commonly derided as "rat unions"—prompted an ad-hoc group of affiliate organizers to call on the Federation to co-ordinate a joint effort to address the problem.

As awareness of these difficulties in organizing increased among Federation activists and leaders, the Federation officers and staff considered what steps the Federation could take to respond to the situation.

The search for models

In examining the potential role for a labour central body beyond policy advocacy, the Federation first looked south to the AFL-CIO Organizing Institute as a primary model. First established in 1989, the U.S. Organizing Institute was seen as breaking important new ground in training organizers and promoting inter-union cooperation around organizing projects. Co-ordinated organizing models such as the Los Angeles Manufacturing Action Project were also part of the review.

Federation staff audited the Institute's training program, and U.S. speakers attended several Federation events during the fall and winter of 1995/96 to discuss their experiences.

The Australian Council of Trade Unions' "Organizing Works" program, begun in 1994, was another central labour body organizing project examined as part of the Federation's research.

In the spring of 1996, the Federation officers agreed to propose the creation of a Federation-sponsored Organizing Institute to serve B.C. unions. A report was prepared for the convention, and agreement was reached that a 3 cents per-month per capita increase would be proposed to fund 55% of the Institute's annual budget, with the rest of the budget funded from the existing per capita, and program cost recoveries.

First steps

Following the 1996 Convention, then-President Ken Georgetti moved quickly to implement the proposal and create the Institute. It was decided that the full Executive Officers' committee would be the governing body of the Institute. (One small but symbolic change at this level was that organizing would be made a standing agenda item at each Federation Officers' and Executive Council meeting, reflecting the intention that organizing work should receive greater attention by the leadership.)

An Organizing Advisory Committee (OAC) was created, comprised of a mix of senior staff and organizers from various affiliates. The Committee was tasked with developing the training program, and providing advice to the officers on possible initiatives for the Institute.

The initial plan for the Institute contemplated a full-time staff director, and long-time Canadian Auto Workers activist Len Ruel was appointed to the post by the Federation officers.

Together, the officers, Organizing Advisory Committee and staff director comprised the Institute, and for ease of reference in the material that follows, I have chosen to encompass all three by reference to the Institute.

Initially, the Institute focused on developing a training program modelled closely on the AFL–CIO example. This program would include an initial period of intensive training, followed by a short-term internship in an affiliate organizing project, and then a longer-term "apprenticeship" assignment for candidates who had shown promise during the internship. In order to develop a broader range of experience, the program envisioned an inter-union exchange of program participants for internships and apprenticeships.

Anxious to move ahead, the Institute scheduled its first training session in October of 1997. While well attended by 42 participants, the training program opened to mix reviews because of two main problems. The first related to the rawness of the curriculum, which the Organizing Advisory Committee had not had adequate time to fully develop. The second and more perplexing problem was the rivalry and competition between the organizer/instructors, which, in the absence of well-defined curriculum, played out in conflicts over teaching methods.

Ruel and the Committee worked diligently to develop the internship and apprenticeship elements of the program, but with only limited success. While many of the first session graduates went on to organizing projects within their own union, practical problems with the availability of formal on-the-job training opportunities meant there was limited uptake of course graduates by other affiliates.

Then, at the end of 1997, Ruel decided to accept a new posting as regional director for the Canadian Auto workers, and the Federation appointed this author as his successor in early 1998.

The Organizing Institute program lost some of its initial momentum in the transitional period between directors, so the OAC undertook to evaluate its efforts and refine its direction.

The Institute moved to formalize the training program. Regular spring and fall sessions were instituted in the hope that this would encourage affiliates to structure increased internship and apprenticeship opportunities around that schedule.

The Committee also formed an instructors' sub-committee to gain a consensus about the training curriculum and improve the material, with a focus on both the learning needs of union activists newly entering the organizing field, and providing materials that could be used as training tools for organizing campaign volunteers.

By the spring of 1999, the curriculum was well defined, and regular training sessions were in place.

The organizer training program

The cornerstone of the Organizing Institute is its training function. The training program has four main elements:

- providing centralized organizer training opportunities delivered by the Institute;
- developing course materials and training resources for affiliates to use in their internal training programs;
- training instructors to enhance our capacity to deliver the program, both through the Institute and through affiliates; and
- developing placement opportunities for newly trained organizers.

To date, nearly 600 union activists have attended the Institute's intensive three-day training program to prepare them for leadership roles in organizing campaigns. While the training curriculum is regularly re-evaluated and adjusted, the fundamental features have remained constant from the outset, with the main emphasis on developing an organizing skill set that equips activists to plan and execute campaigns in the field.

There is a low ratio of students to instructors (one instructor for every four participants), and special attention is given to the mix of instructors. Organizing Institute instructors bring current experience working on recruitment organizing campaigns, and convey that hands-on knowledge of current developments they encounter. They are also selected for their diversity, both in the sectors where they normally organize and in their personal characteristics.

Most importantly, to the greatest extent possible, the course tries to replicate the real-world experience of organizing, using a variety of techniques. Role-playing is used extensively, from reproducing the experience of a captive audience meeting, to working with individuals and groups in organizing campaigns. Hours are long and tightly scheduled, with little personal time available to participants. Group activities, and even meal seating assignments, are all planned so that participants are required to interact with all of the other participants, regardless of their individual background or characteristics. In this way, participants also learn about the personal experience of union organizing work, in addition to understanding campaign methodologies.

Surprisingly to some, there is limited labour law and legal advocacy content, reflecting our philosophy that organizing campaigns must be won on the shop floor. While participants are familiarized with the legal concepts and pitfalls they will encounter, most of our attention is paid to winning the campaign on the ground and at the ballot box.

To support affiliate training, the Organizing Institute curriculum and course materials were made available and widely distributed in electronic form to affiliates, as well as interested labour organizations in other jurisdictions.

In order to expand training capacity, the Institute also has a policy of recruiting and training one or two instructors at each session.

Building the organizer network

One of the strategic directions the Institute consciously took from the outset was to build a network of organizers. Unlike most important areas of union activity—such as equality rights, occupational health and safety, or political action—the Federation in 1996 had no established network of activists interested in organizing issues.

To this end, the Institute decided it would conduct other periodic educational activities in large sessions that brought organizers from all affiliates together, in order to encourage more interaction and build a sense of solidarity.

These sessions have been held on a variety of topics, such as:

- processing employment standards complaints;
- developing comprehensive campaign strategies;
- utilizing campaign specific polling and survey tools;
- demonstrating organizing software packages; and
- understanding recent labour law developments.

In the fall of 2005, the Institute plans to hold its first communications workshop for experienced organizers.

Additionally, the Institute periodically holds "round-tables" for senior organizers. The two day roundtable sessions have been a forum for sharing new information and ideas through presentations and moderated discussions, and for identifying the needs of affiliates so the Institute program can be adjusted to respond to these needs.

Internet technologies have also been applied to build and maintain the organizer network. In 2001, the Institute launched an e-mail discussion list for organizers. The list is used to rapidly disseminate research and news to more than 200 activists. It also allows individual organizers to seek advice and assistance from their peers.

Leadership education

Many of today's union leaders have limited recruitment organizing experience, and need support to help promote and manage organizing within their union. In addition to providing training to novice organizers, the Institute identified the need to provide education to affiliate leaders to assist them in gaining a better understanding of the organizing process, and in managing organizational change in order to increase the resources and attention devoted to organizing. To this end, the Institute delivered a workshop to the Federation's ranking officers on the challenges of moving their union from a servicing model to an organizing model, and addressing the many issues involved in making that transition.

The Institute delivers similar workshops to individual unions at educational sessions, conferences, and conventions. It has also responded to requests for leadership workshops on specific topics of interest, such as increasing volunteerism in the union.

As well, a number of ranking officers have taken the lead-organizer training program—a credit to both their humility and their commitment to moving their union's organizing program forward.

Research and evaluation

Any successful strategy must be underpinned by insightful research and an evaluation of successes and failures. As we reviewed and renewed our organizing effort in B.C., the Institute identified the need to gain a greater understanding of many issues. What techniques were employers using to successfully defeat organizing campaigns? How well were new organizing strategies working? What caused some certification campaigns to succeed, and others to fail? What were the attitudes of B.C.'s non-union workforce regarding work and unions?

While organizers involved in the Institute had many anecdotal and subjective answers to these questions, and some academic research from other jurisdictions, it was clear that we had little research in our own province that could fully inform our organizing strategies and tactics. We needed to answer these and other impor-tant questions in the context of the many variables that influence union organizing in our own locale: public policies, the economy, and provincial demographics.

To this end, the Organizing Institute initiated research projects and shared the results with affiliates so they could use the information to shape organizing tactics, strategies, and programs.

The Institute developed a partnership with Charlotte Yates of McMaster Uni-versity and the Ontario Federation of Labour to conduct a comparative analysis of the strategies and tactics both unions and employers were using in certification campaigns in British Columbia and Ontario. The report gave us more insight into the strengths and weaknesses of our efforts, a first step in improving the effective-ness of campaigns.

In order to promote an understanding of the study's findings, the Institute and Professor Yates presented the research at meetings of the Federation's officers and Executive Council, to meetings of affiliate organizers, and finally to delegates to the following Federation convention. These findings were also incorporated into the organizers' training program.

In addition to academic research, the Institute also sponsored a major survey of British Columbia's non-union employees. This polling work was designed to identify employees' attitudes toward joining a union, gain a perspective on the workplace issues prospective members wanted a union to address, and determine whether the recent weakening of public protection of workers' rights by the pro-vincial Liberal government influenced interest in union organizing.

Again, this information was broadly disseminated to affiliates to help inform their organizing strategies, and incorporated into the training curriculum.

The Institute also focused on helping affiliates make better use of information technology to support organizing. One of these initiatives was evaluation of soft-ware being used to support organizing work—something we discovered was not being utilized significantly, despite its value.

Diversifying the organizer pool

In 1996, similar to other jurisdictions, Federation affiliate organizers in B.C. were predominantly white "boomer"-aged males. This was readily identified as a prob-lem by the Institute for two reasons. First, our research told us that campaigns were more successful if the organizers' personal characteristics were similar to the group of workers attempting to form a union. Second, in a province with more than 100 linguistic groups and high immigration levels, the lack of language skills was an obvious impediment to organizing. A number of initiatives have been taken by the Institute to remedy the situation.

The Institute has actively worked to train a more diverse group of activists. Affiliates are encouraged to seek out candidates from under-represented groups. Organizing Institute training sessions are held in conjunction with the Summer Institute for Union Women.

The Institute also launched a Young Workers' Committee at the Federation, and sponsored the first Federation conference specifically for young workers. Workplace organizing was a key theme of the conference, and a number of attendees later attended the Institute training program.

While these efforts proceeded, the Institute also recognized that no affiliate would likely be able to recruit and retain a sufficiently diverse cadre of trained organizers on an ongoing basis, so it decided to create a pool of organizers who could make themselves available to work on affiliate campaigns. Since 2000, Institute graduates interested in gaining experience outside of their own union's environment have registered in a database identifying their experience, personal characteristics, and language skills. Affiliates seeking an organizer with specific traits can contact the Institute and be provided with candidates who fit their needs for term work on individual campaigns. In some cases, the Institute can arrange the "loan" if requested, but in most cases affiliates work bilaterally to make the arrangements.

Providing information to workers

One of the objectives of the Institute is to provide a central point of contact for information about the process of forming a union. Most non-union workers readily report that they have no information about the process of forming a union, or about their legal rights and protections.

To fill that need, the Institute took several simple steps. A section on organizing was added to the Federation's website. A "Guide to Workers' Rights" was developed in magazine format, providing a primer on legislation protecting workers, but with a specific focus on the process of forming a union. Even the Federation's advertisement in the telephone directory was changed to encourage organizing inquiries.

Tools for improving cooperation

In our early analysis, the Institute recognized that it had to begin its work in a competitive organizing environment. With the decline of union jurisdiction as an organizing principle of the Canadian Labour Congress, otherwise friendly organizations found themselves competing to organize groups of workers in the same sector. Accordingly, the Institute began to develop understandings between affiliates aimed at creating a healthy environment for that competition, and to foster better cooperation.

For example, one barrier to inter-union exchanges and loans of organizing staff was a concern that "visiting" organizers might obtain information that would assist their own union, to the detriment of the host union. In response, the Institute developed a set of ethical guidelines that the dispatching organization, the host union, and the loaned organizer were expected to observe. It obliged the parties to protect the confidentiality of information and organizing leads obtained during the assignment, and required the dispatching union to notify the Organizing Institute if it intended to attempt to organize a workplace that had previously been the target of a certification bid by the host union. It also prohibited involvement by the visiting organizer in the internal affairs of the host organization.

The Institute also promoted the adoption of organizing protocol agreements designed to reduce inter-union conflicts. The first of these came in the growing health care sector, where three public sector affiliates often found themselves in competition to organize the same groups, and provided a structure for ongoing liaison and problem-solving.

However, the most significant agreement was developed in 2002 in response to the newly-elected Liberal government's declared intent to extensively contract out the work of public health care workers. Early evidence indicated that the government intended to eliminate any form of successorship protection for the incumbent unions, and, moreover, that the government would encourage contractors to seek out other Federation affiliates to represent the new employees. This strategy was a means of undermining the solidarity of B.C.'s labour movement, and breaking the union that the Liberals believed to be its most militant opponent: the Hospital Employees' Union (the B.C. health care division of the Canadian Union of Public Employees).

Throughout early 2002 (and concurrent with the development of "Disputes Protocol" by the Canadian Labour Congress), the Institute worked to develop what became known as the "Code of Practice on Organizing Successor Employers." In signing the Code of Practice, Federation affiliates agreed to respect the principle of successorship in organizing workers now performing the "out sourced" work.

The Code of Practice On Successorship Organizing did not give the former union exclusive and unconditional organizing jurisdiction over its former work. Instead, signatories agreed that their respective unions would encourage these workers to seek representation by the previous incumbent union whenever possible, and provide notice to the original union if it had been contacted by an employee (or employer) about representing the new employees. In situations where the employees did not wish to join the prior union, the Code outlined practices for avoiding, mediating and resolving disputes, with the support of the Federation.

By September of 2002, all but two of the Federation's affiliates had formally endorsed the Code of Practice.

Assessing the Impact of the Organizing Institute

Evaluating the effect of the Organizing Institute is a difficult challenge, since many variables affect the rate at which workers decide to form unions. Not unexpectedly, observers look first to the numbers of new members and certifications as a measure of success.

By that measurement, the Organizing Institute could not be pronounced a success. The first years of the Organizing Institute saw increasing numbers of new members and certifications, but this growth was largely sparked by the introduction of sectoral bargaining in B.C.'s health care and social services sectors. Under this system, new certifications in government-funded services could gain coverage by an established industry–wide collective agreement once they had achieved union recognition. This significantly boosted organizing success in these sectors. The Institute may have contributed to the success of those efforts by increasing the capacity of affiliates through its organizer training program, but the system of sectoral agreements was a key factor in this growth.

In the year 2000, the number of new members and new certifications began a significant decline. From a high of approximately 12,000 members recruited through organizing in 1998, organizing success declined precipitously after 2000, and has hovered in the 2,500-to-3,000 range annually since 2002.

This initial downward trend was not unique to British Columbia, and was reflected in other parts of Canada and in the United States. But it was accelerated by the incoming Liberal government's changes to the B.C. Labour Relations Code in 2001, removing certification based solely on membership card evidence and weakening restraints on employer interference in union organizing.

Similarly, the ensuing success or failure of Code of Practice on Organizing Successor Employers might be judged solely by its highly visible failure—the conflict between the Hospital Employees' Union (HEU) and the Industrial Wood and Allied Workers (IWA). The latter refused to endorse the Code of Practice and entered into voluntary recognition agreements with the new contractors.

On the other side of the scale, however, the Code of Practice resulted in every other Federation affiliate encouraging contractor employees to return to the HEU, despite offers of voluntary recognition agreements from the contractors. As a result, the HEU was able to organize successfully and regain representation rights for many workers in health care support work that had been contracted out. Affiliate support for the Code of Practice is credited as a significant factor in minimizing the harm to B.C.'s labour solidarity and defeating the Liberals on one of their key political objectives in the privatization process.

Other measures indicate the positive impact of the Institute. One of these is the number of unions that have become more actively involved in organizing. Since 1997, a number of Federation affiliates have introduced or expanded organizing programs, with the Institute providing support for these initiatives.

Perhaps the key benefit of the Organizing Institute has been the impact on the culture of organizing. At the time the institute began its work, organizers tended to be insular, rarely working together, and often seeing themselves as rivals. The development of a cross-union network of activists who are supportive of organizing, are willing to help other organizations develop their programs, and readily share information that used to be very closely held, is a significant change. This has helped reduce the frequency and severity of organizing disputes between unions in British Columbia.

The Organizing Institute has contributed to developing a new generation of organizers with a greater commitment to solidarity, and appears to have a positive effect on the development and morale of individual organizers, especially those in smaller unions which may lack sufficient internal resources to support and mentor the progress of organizers.

Many unions place a high value on participating in the Institute's joint training in developing their organizing capability. At an average training session, activists from 10 or 12 different unions share the experiences of the seven instructors, who are chosen to reflect a mix of sectors and organizing environments. This "cross-fertilization" helps not only the students, but also the instructor/organizers, to incorporate ideas and strategies they might not otherwise be exposed to working in isolation.

While it may be difficult to evaluate British Columbia's Organizing Institute thorough an empirical cost/benefit analysis, the subjective evaluation of most of the union activists and leaders in B.C. who have been involved with the Institute has been positive.

Conclusion

There are many steps today's union movement must take to attract a greater portion of the workforce to join its ranks. If organizing is considered so central to the future of unions, we need to look at the potential contribution every group, structure, and individual can make to improving our organizing success.

The B.C. Federation of Labour's Organizing Institute is an attempt to fulfill that potential.

Notes

1. The question of whether these services are truly in the sphere of private business, since they continue to be provided to the public at public expense, prompts me to use the term cautiously.

Chapter 18
Union Education, Union Leadership and Union Renewal: The Role of PEL

JOHANNA WESTSTAR

Introduction

The past few decades have seen substantial changes in the economic, social, and political realities facing the Canadian labour movement. These changes have disrupted traditional labour-management relationships and created more diversified and fragmented union memberships. Downsizing and the increased use of flexible, part-time work have reduced union membership and created precarious environments for many workers. As well, to achieve economic streamlining and increased competitiveness, employers have become more aggressive in demanding concessions and restructuring. Faced with these realities, unions are striving to improve the services to their members and maintain the gains of past bargaining. While aggregate union membership is stable, union density has been declining, and many workers are resorting to individual solutions to combat social and economic challenges. As workers become more demoralized and individualized, unions are struggling to develop a pro-active agenda to revitalize the labour movement.

To develop such an agenda, unions have been re-evaluating their role in the workplace and society, as well as their relationship with their membership and employers. As a result of this critical analysis, there appears to be a general consensus that unions must re-invigorate and engage activists on broad social and economic issues while also addressing the specific role of unions in workplace change and reorganization. Key components of this agenda involve strategies which focus on increasing the mobilization of rank-and-file members, organizing in non-traditional workplaces, aligning the struggles of labour with those of community groups, and developing pro-active tactics toward workplace change (Yates 1998; Frost 2000; Kumar and Murray 2003; Baccaro et al. 2003; Ferge and Kelly 2003; Hurd et al. 2003).

An important vehicle to achieve this rebuilding is union education. Throughout the history of the labour movement, union education has been used to strengthen union leadership, mobilize the rank and file, and build bridges of understanding and support among union members and among various social groups (Waldie et al. 1985; Martin 1995; Taylor 2001, Burke et al. 2002; Delp et al. 2002). This chapter profiles the Paid Education Leave (PEL) programme of the Canadian Auto Workers' Union (CAW), arguably the most developed union education program in North America, and assesses the degree to which PEL fosters union renewal and the development of union leaders and activists.

The first section contains a contextual background regarding the development and evolution of PEL, its funding, and courses and key aspects of the core program's structure and curriculum. The second section details the evaluation methodology of interviews, survey data, participant observation, and review of curriculum. The third section highlights the impact of the PEL program in the key areas of activism, solidarity, and diversity. The fourth section discusses the challenges that still remain in achieving the full effectiveness of the PEL program, and the last section details subsequent research that has been conducted on PEL and resultant changes that the CAW has made to the PEL program.

Contextual background

Development and Evolution of PEL

The International Labour Organization (ILO) passed Convention No. 140 for paid education leave in 1974. It stipulates leave granted within working hours with adequate financial entitlement provided for, "training at any level, general, social and civic education and trade union education" (ILO 2003). In 1976, the leadership of the Canadian Region of the International United Automobile, Aerospace and Agricultural Implements Workers of American (UAW, now the CAW) made paid education leave a top priority (White 1988; Gindin 1995) and achieved a permanent paid education leave provision through collective bargaining in the small auto parts plant of Rockwell International in 1977 (CAW 2002). PEL was solidified and truly established in the union by 1979 when the "Big Three" auto assemblers (Ford, General Motors and Chrysler) also signed-off on PEL provisions.

At the time, the CAW was the only union to negotiate PEL, and has since been able to achieve provisions throughout the union of considerable breadth and depth (Gindin 1995; Taylor 2001). For each CAW member employed by the Big Three auto companies, the union now receives 5 cents per hour per employee. As reported by the CAW, although the recent Canadian Labour Congress (CLC) review of 1,000 major collective agreements across Canada showed that almost one-quarter of the workers surveyed were covered by a clause providing funding for union education, the incidence of *employer-paid* union education was still quite rare (CAW 2003c; CLC 1997, 1999).

The CAW accounts for 41% of the 88 contracts with paid education leave clauses across all sectors. Fourteen other unions were identified by the CLC review as having at least one paid education leave clause, with the Canadian Union of Public Employees (CUPE) accounting for 11% of the total, the United Steelworkers of America (USWA) and the United Food and Commercial Workers (UFCW) 8% each, and the Teamsters 5% of all contracts with PEL clauses (CAW 2003c). Though not indicated in the CAW summary, the Canadian Union of Postal Workers (CUPW) also offers a significant Union Education Program paid for by the employer at 3 cents per worker per hour (CLC 1997, 1999; CUPW 2003).

Funding and Courses

In the CAW, PEL provisions are negotiated between the local bargaining unit and the employer, and the contributions are placed in a central Trust Fund. An account is kept of the contributions of each bargaining unit which represent a certain number of entitlements to the one-, two- or four-week programs. These entitlements include the price of room and board, travel, and lost time from work. The interest earned on moneys in the central fund is set up as a subsidy fund to support the participation of smaller bargaining units.

The CAW offers a variety of educational programming under the banner of PEL in the form of one-, two- and four-week residential programs at its education facility.[1] The four-week program is the core PEL program. It is the original course and carries a different message from the one- and two-week programs. Whereas one or two week programs are 'tool' courses in orientation—'how-to' courses that teach a certain skill or set of skills—the four-week PEL has an ideological focus and strives to create broad awareness about the world and society from a worker's perspective. It is the program of study for this research. Since the PEL program graduated 88 students from its first four-week session in fall 1978, the program has grown and expanded. At the end of 2002, 14,246 people had graduated from PEL programs, with 5,614 or 40% from the core four-week PEL. As well, more than 450 workers have been trained as instructors (CAW n.d.).

Core Structure and Curriculum

PEL is a residential program with the four weeks spent at the CAW Family Education Centre in Port Elgin each separated by several weeks back in the workplace. The program is prefaced by an introductory weekend session that is not compensated by lost-time wages and includes the participant's spouse or partner. The principle behind this session is to gain a commitment from the participants, introduce them to the structure of the program, and solicit the support and interest of the participant's partner, who will be required to "hold the fort" alone at home when the program is in session (Kryzaniwsky 2003).

Since the first 1978 session, the program has been revamped on a regular basis.[2] At present, the curriculum attempts to reflect popular education and adult education theories by breaking down the expert model of lecturing, focusing on hands-on group activities, and introducing a co-facilitator model for discussion leaders. A stringent curriculum was written to provide a consistent message across classrooms and across PEL sessions, reinforcing the premise of facilitating activism and critical thinking (Discussion Leaders 2003; Phillips 2003; Rosenfeld 2003).

The curriculum tackles issues from five over-arching perspectives: the workplace, the union, politics, economics, and human rights (social identity). Each week different aspects of these themes are explored through small group activities, classroom discussions and plenary sessions, with the expectations of analysis deepening as the topics progress over the four weeks (Rosenfeld 2003). The program also includes many activities outside of the classroom. Participants form committees on various topics and run events over the four weeks. A communications section focuses on public speaking. A project is required to be completed between weeks three and four, and a mock convention concludes the program (CAW 2003a).

Evaluation methodology

To some degree, an evaluation of internal union education programs such as PEL is inherently biased, as the information and perceptions which temper this analysis are gathered from CAW members who are closely tied to the program, and to the CAW Education Department in general. Notwithstanding, care was taken to include informants with varying degrees of separation from PEL and the Education Department. To this end, interviews were conducted with members of the Education Department, other national staff, past and current Education Directors, a retired CAW senior staff member, an experienced union educator not affiliated with the CAW, and four core PEL discussion leaders who hail from various locals across Canada. As well, many informal conversations were held with other discussion leaders and PEL participants during the spring 2003 session. A survey was also administered to the entire class of the Spring 2003 core PEL session (N=78). The response rate for this survey was 56 out of 78, or approximately 72%. Copies of the course curriculum, complete with discussion leader notes, were also closely reviewed and the researcher attended week three of the program as a participant observer.

Impact and scope of PEL

PEL is a leadership training course and focuses on mobilizing, encouraging critical analysis skills in the leadership, fostering equity, and providing a democratic and participatory forum to explore issues. In this way, PEL is seen by all interviewees as a program to develop leadership, build a cadre of activists, inspire people about issues, and take that excitement home to their families, communities, and locals. The following sections outline how PEL builds leadership around the issues of activism, solidarity, and diversity.

Building Activism

Interviewees reported that the purpose of PEL is not to create headstrong activists who return to their locals and depose their elected leadership. Instead, PEL provides foundations of knowledge and practical experience, and encourages individuals to become active on a range of levels. For example, though anecdotal evidence indicates that many PEL graduates go on to become elected officials or Canadian Council delegates,[3] most simply participate more at rallies, attend a demonstration, join a community group, sign a petition, or generally stand up for issues on the workplace floor. In essence, PEL imparts information, provides a safe forum for open discussion and debate, and builds the confidence to join such debates on many levels.

In addition, PEL provides an opportunity for new members to begin to relate to the union. The curriculum is designed to show the role of labour and the history

Table 1: Activity Levels Before and After PEL

	YES Prior to PEL	NO Prior to PEL	MORE LIKELY After PEL	NOT MORE LIKELY After PEL
Steward or Committee Member	49.1%	50.9%	40.4%	59.6%
Involved in Collective Bargaining	8.8%	91.2%	33.3%	66.7%
Attend Union Meetings	75.4%	24.6%	77.2%	22.8%
Attend Union Education	64.9%	35.1%	87.7%	12.3%
Engage in Union Discussion with Friends, Family or Co-Workers	77.2%	22.8%	73.7%	26.3%
Attend Union Organized Events	64.9%	35.1%	70.2%	29.8%
Active in Community	50.0%★	50.0%★	66.7%	33.3%
Interested in Politics	43.8%★	56.2%★	63.2%	36.8%
Attend Education Outside the Union	N/A†	N/A†	42.1%	57.9%
Teach Union Education	N/A†	N/A†	49.1%	50.9%

★   Numbers obtained from different question format where 'fairly' and 'very' active translate to 'Yes' and 'not' and 'somewhat' active translate to 'No'
†   Questions were not asked regarding prior activity in these areas

of labour struggles in the context of society. For new members or new activists, this historical context provides ample opportunity for connection and resonance, which in turn fosters the desire to become active. As two interviewees mentioned, PEL is a place of renewal because it is often the first time that people can discuss other alternatives, share views and strategies with 100 or more brothers and sisters, and think about hope (Discussion Leaders 2003; Phillips 2003).

Undeniably, people associated with the delivery of PEL feel that it builds awareness, interest, confidence, and therefore activism, and that aspects of the curriculum directly foster this development (CAW 2003a). Survey responses from PEL participants also indicate that, regardless of the level of activity prior to attending, PEL does have a positive influence on the intention to become active. Though 59.7% of the spring 2003 participants already considered themselves to be fairly or very active in their union before attending, 91.2% responded that PEL either increased or greatly increased their interest level in the union. As well, over 90% indicated that PEL increased or greatly increased their motivation to take one- or two-week PEL courses or other union education. PEL influenced the intention of participants to become more active on a range of levels (see Table 1).

In particular, respondents indicate that PEL has greatly increased their likelihood of attending union meetings, enrolling in other union education courses, becoming vocal about union-related issues, and participating in union organized events. The survey responses further reveal that, to a lesser extent, PEL has also influenced respondents' level of activity in their community and their interest in political affairs.

Responses to a set of questions regarding self-confidence showed that 77.2% of respondents believed that their self-confidence has increased or greatly increased as a result of PEL, with 66.7% of respondents being more likely to speak at union meetings. With reference to critical thinking, the majority of participants stated

Figure 1: Percentage of PEL Participants More Likely to Question the Decisions Made by Various Sources

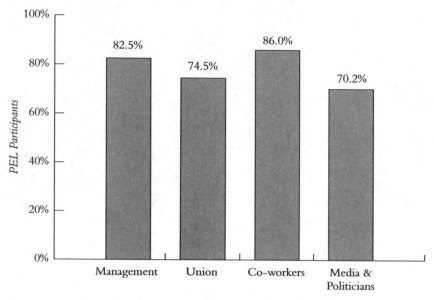

Information Source

that they were more likely to question management decisions, union decisions, the views of fellow workers, and media and political commentary (see Figure 1).

Survey responses also indicate that PEL participants do discuss issues and talk about their experiences at Port Elgin, both formally and informally, upon return to their workplace, family, and community. A majority of survey respondents (52.6%) reported reading PEL resources outside of class, and sharing those resources with family (52.6%), friends (56.1%), and co-workers (80.7%). In addition, 80.7% of the respondents suggested that they speak informally with co-workers about their experiences at PEL often or regularly. Two-thirds, or 66.7%, expressed their intention to speak formally about PEL experiences through union meetings, teaching courses, or writing articles in union or other publications.

When interpreting the survey data, it is important to note that this survey was administered to PEL participants at Port Elgin nearing the end of their third week of the course. It reflects their attitudes and intentions at that time. Indeed, the dynamics and atmosphere of PEL and Port Elgin for inspiring action is much more conducive than the routine of every day life. For this reason, the survey responses, particularly those answers which pledge future action, must be considered through the appropriate and potentially rose-tinted lens. Despite this caveat, however, many responses were overwhelmingly indicative of an increased commitment to the union, increased confidence in one's self, and increased desire to apply PEL experiences and become more active.

Table 2: The Impact of PEL on Feelings of Solidarity toward Various Groups

	Co-worker	Local Union	National Union	Can. Mov't	Int'l Mov't	Com-munity	Political Party	Prev. Union
Greatly Decr.	3.5%	0.0%	0.0%	1.8%	1.8%	0.0%	7.1%	0.0%
Decr.	1.8%	0.0%	0.0%	0.0%	0.0%	1.8%	1.8%	0.0%
No Chg.	42.1%	29.9%	19.3%	29.8%	42.1%	33.3%	57.1%	84.2%
Incr.	42.1%	56.1%	47.4%	50.9%	43.8%	47.4%	26.8%	10.5%
Greatly Incr.	10.5%	14.0%	33.3%	17.5%	12.3%	17.5%	7.2%	5.3%
≥ Incr.	52.6%	70.1%	80.7%	68.4%	56.1%	64.9%	34.0%	15.8%

Fostering Solidarity and Diversity

When asked whether PEL acts to foster solidarity among participants, interviewees refer immediately to the residential nature of the program. Over the time spent at Port Elgin, participants quickly and visibly develop a unifying bond. The act of living together, eating together, running events together, and tackling hard issues together in and out of class develops the feelings of trust, understanding, and support on which solidarity is built. This solidarity of being the "Class of Spring 2003" is extended to foster other levels of acceptance, as well.

PEL participants arrive at Port Elgin from workplaces across Canada; they come from jobs in different industries, jobs with different organizational structures; they are people of diverse gender, sexual orientation, race and ethnicity. In the context of PEL and within the safer environment of Port Elgin, these workers can discuss and share experiences where they may never have been directly exposed to such situations before.

Class activities include discussions, videos, and information sessions about other private sector unions, about public sector unions, about the struggle for public services, about community action and universal movements such as the environment, homelessness, and international human rights. Through its basic tenet of looking at the world from a worker's perspective, PEL emphasizes the common bonds that all workers share and the common struggles that all workers face. As with activism, where being more aware of issues increases the inclination to form opinions and take action, with solidarity, increased awareness of other people's struggles and how they relate to your own creates room for empathy and commonality.

Though one interviewee commented that education alone on issues such as homophobia, racism, sexism, and ageism is unlikely to change a person's consciousness, the solidarity experienced at PEL plants a seed that can be further nurtured by reinforcing experiences (Martin 2003). This seed or introductory step toward identifying common bonds between workers, rather than isolating differences, is demonstrated in survey responses. The responses presented in Table 2 suggest that PEL has increased or greatly increased participant feelings of solidarity to the majority of listed groups. Most notably, respondents indicate increased or greatly increased solidarity towards their national union (80.7%), their local (70.1%), the

Figure 2: The Impact of PEL on Awareness Regarding Diversity in the CAW

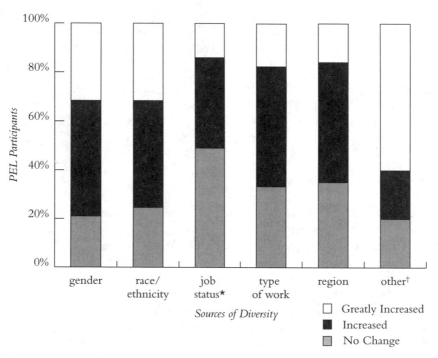

Sources of Diversity

☐ Greatly Increased
■ Increased
▨ No Change

★ Job Status was defined on the survey with the clarification 'i.e. full-time, part-time, etc.'
† Responses for other included: sexual orientation which received 83.3% of the responses, disabilities at 16.7% and family status at 16.7%

Canadian labour movement (68.4%), their communities (64.9%), and the international labour movement (56.1%).

Figure 2 shows that PEL has a great impact on diversity awareness based on social identity factors such as gender and race with 79.0% and 75.4% responding that their awareness of these topics was increased or greatly increased. Somewhat less impact is seen on factors associated with changes in the CAW structure such as job status (50.9%), type of work/industry (66.6%) and regions/geography (64.9%). These areas seem to be more overlooked in the curriculum and classroom where examples, exercises and participant demographics and input tend to be more homogeneously centered on full-time, manufacturing (auto), workplaces in Ontario.

Challenges for PEL

PEL is undeniably a feat in terms of labour education programming. Despite its success, however, several barriers do hamper its ability to sustain leadership development and contribute to union renewal.

PEL Coverage

It is up to local leadership to put PEL on the bargaining table, select who attends the program, and be responsible for returning graduates. As such, there appears to be a decrease in the priority placed on PEL at the bargaining table. The most recent CAW report indicates that 73% of all CAW members are currently covered by PEL clauses that represent approximately 850 bargaining units, 45% of the total (CAW 2003b). However, this coverage is not uniform, and several inequalities exist depending on bargaining unit size, industrial sector, and region (see Figures 3-5).

In general, units without PEL are smaller. The PEL coverage is low where bargaining units were formed following merger activity (services) and in areas outside of Ontario. Consequently, much of the local leadership and national staff who have more recently joined the CAW have neither had the history nor the experience of PEL that is so deeply rooted in the CAW's ideology (Bellefeuille 2003; Kryzaniwsky 2003). The development of a common bond and fostering of collective identity as workers and CAW members which occurs at PEL is therefore not available to these new "fringe" groups.

Figure 3: PEL Coverage by Bargaining Unit Size

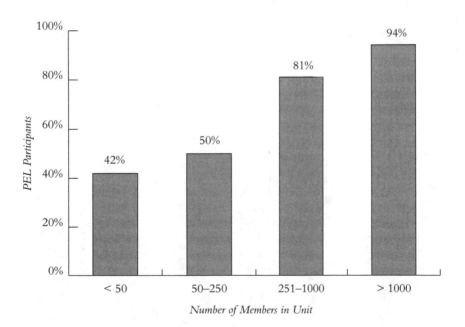

Figure 4: PEL Coverage by Sector

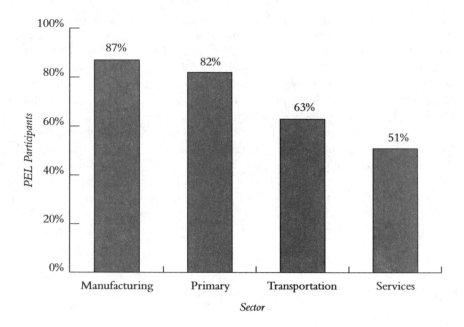

Figure 5: PEL Coverage by Region

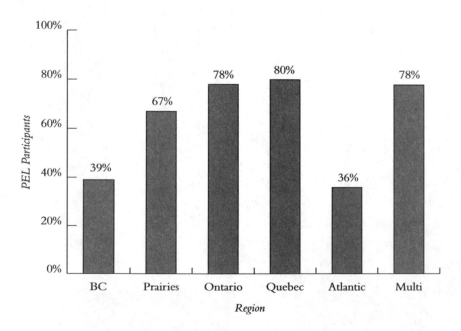

Source: Internal document on PEL coverage. CAW, 2003b.

Selection Process

A second challenge stems from the lack of a union-wide conception of the scope and purpose of PEL and involves applicant selection as well as curriculum development. Currently, there is considerable deviance in the process of selecting PEL participants across locals. Many use a committee to screen applications and base selection upon the applicant's previous demonstrations of activism or commitment to the union (Bellefeuille 2003; Gindin 2003). Some locals fill entitlements first with people of local leadership and then turn to the rank and file, while other locals have already sent a majority of leadership or committee people and consequently send a large majority of rank-and-file members. Still others base decisions on the skill development required at that time, or perhaps use a combination of these methods (Bellefeuille 2003; Discussion Leaders 2003; Kryzaniwsky 2003). As well, informal conversation with many PEL participants indicated a degree of politicking surrounding the encouragement and selection of PEL applicants.

This uneven selection process creates a challenge for PEL in two ways. First, potential applicants may become turned off or may feel intimidated to apply if selection is seen to be undemocratic or élitist. This would manifest most strongly in people not readily associated with the dominant group in the workplace and perhaps contribute to the difficulty in attracting women, visible minorities, youth, or other targeted groups to the program. Second, in having no concrete agenda on selecting workers in leadership positions or rank and file, the composition at PEL represents a broad range of activism and experience with the union. Though this is undeniably an asset in many ways, as more experiential diversity allows for more extraneous sharing, learning and mentoring, the mix creates challenges for the curriculum and classroom learning.

With the infusion of rank-and-file participants (40% of the spring 2003 class deemed themselves inactive or only somewhat active in the union), new demands and strains are being placed on curriculum developers and peer educators as the interests and experiences of the entire group need to be addressed and incorporated. In the classroom, this tension plays out in the time balance between delivery of content and free discussion, the pacing of material, the depth of analysis, and the relationships among the participants and the peer educators.

Debate exists in the union as to the best model for the core PEL program and whether it should have remained a groundwork for preparing leadership rather than moving into the rank and file (Gindin 2003). Sound arguments support the participatory nature of education, the benefit to rank-and-filers to get off the job and have the space and time to reflect, and education's ability to develop future leaders. As well, once PEL had become established in the locals, the majority of the leadership, aside from new recruits, had already attended and rank-and-filers were the next obvious pool of participants. However, with the rapid addition of units unfamiliar with the CAW and in a time when the labour movement is increasingly demoralized and fragmented, local leadership may be in a better position to benefit from and apply PEL experiences. They have more opportunity to reinvigorate their locals from a stable elected platform than a small group of rank-and-filers returning to their jobs (Gindin 2003).

PEL Graduates

The notion of rank-and-file PEL graduates returning to the workplace opens another area where the impact of PEL is hindered. While the environment at PEL is relatively accepting and participants can flex new activist muscles, the same atmosphere does not exist in the workplace. Invigorated PEL graduates returning to the workplace ready to challenge the world are not necessarily welcomed by an established leadership who see them as a threat to their position, or by co-workers who see them returning from a "holiday." In some cases the transition is smooth and the PEL activist can easily "plug-in" to a cause in the workplace. Many locals sit down with applicants before they leave for PEL to get a sense of what they would like to be involved in when they return. Others meet after the four weeks and assist the graduate in connecting with a group or struggle of interest. However, in most cases, PEL graduates are left on their own to find outlets for their activism. This poses several challenges and problems.

First, each day back into the routine of everyday life makes sustaining activist energy and the lessons learned at PEL more difficult. Many potential activists are lost through this process of time and isolation. Second, there are only a limited number of positions available in the local leadership, and these are often contested. As well, in larger locals many committees or action groups have elected memberships or contain only a certain number of members. This limitation turns graduates away from formal union activism or workplace-situated struggles to community organizations or other social action groups. Though this is no doubt a positive experience for the activist and a welcome addition for the group s/he joins, the opportunity to build a direct link or bridge between the union/workplace and the external group is lost. In fostering a sense of activism and social consciousness, the intent is to bring groups of struggle together with labour as a common core. When activists join these groups of struggle as individuals and not as organized representatives of the CAW or labour more generally, no networks are created and these social actors continue to operate in isolation.

PEL Agenda

This notion also surfaces in the debate over whether a concrete struggle or agenda for action is necessary for the success of educational programming as a tool for union renewal. Though the vision of PEL undeniably has an underlying agenda to develop activists and to present issues from a worker's perspective, in current times, an overall union message or struggle is not emphasized. The curriculum is broad and dense, and covers areas of struggle that are not always directly related to the union or the workplace.

This topic raised differing views among interviewees. Some educators felt that PEL's broad issues-based and general approach to developing activism was an asset as graduates learn general strategies and could apply them to any struggle. They focus on the development of each individual and the prospering of many activist tendencies and projects. They feel that PEL acts as an incubator while labour is in transition (Discussion Leaders 2003; Martin 2003).

Conversely, several interviewees indicated that the development of broad and general activists is not fruitful to union renewal (Gindin 2003; Rosenfeld 2003). They argue that activists without a specific purpose may attempt to tackle large issues on their own and burn out, or they may develop groups of struggle and work in a multitude of areas isolated from the labour movement or each other. Without the development of concrete labour-situated action groups in these areas, the worker activists cannot build bridges between the labour movement and community groups, and therefore groups of struggle remain isolated and disjointed. Here union leadership must create the agendas and create the structures for budding activists to join.

Core PEL versus Tool Courses

Another challenge relates to the choices local leadership make in filling PEL entitlements. The one-week program requires much fewer entitlements than the four-week program, and many locals choose to send workers to the shorter PEL courses to benefit the maximum number of people. While this is positive in terms of the number of workers experiencing education at Port Elgin, it has a negative impact on the core PEL program. Discussion leaders assert that all PEL programming contains segments which encourage activism, but the tool courses do not contain the systematic building of leadership and activist tendencies seen in the core PEL.

Similarly, though all students at Port Elgin benefit from the camaraderie, solidarity, and sharing of experiences, notions of change strategies, social identity issues, and broad solidarity are not emphasized in the tool courses as they are in the core PEL. The core PEL is the only program which allows for holistic development of a worker's critical consciousness rather than a strict set of skills. Analysis of per-session breakdown of PEL graduates indicates that classes contained 100 or more workers 85% of the time in the 1980s, 74% of the time in the 1990s, and stand at 60% of the time in the period 2000-2002 (CAW n.d.). The spring 2003 class contained 78 participants, further indicating a trend away from the core PEL program. Given the vision and importance placed on PEL as a developer of social actors, a trend away from the core PEL program toward tunneled skill development would be a detriment to the union.

Diversity

A last challenge exists with respect to uniting the diverse groups of the union. Although the union actively manages the selection of PEL applicants to include representatives from non-dominant groups, the numbers do not reflect the composition of the CAW membership. Despite the subsidy fund, smaller or newer units cannot send a group of workers, but must send one at a time. This individual worker, and other workers from identified minorities, cannot help but feel different and isolated, despite the rhetoric at PEL which focuses on the common bond of all workers.

Also, for many women, particularly women of colour, leaving their home and community for a week at a time is not a feasible option. Thus, despite representing some diversity and thoroughly discussing social identity issues and the importance of common bonds, the composition of PEL and the resulting classroom discussions reinforce an outdated union image.

Conclusion

The statement on the back of the CAW name cards given to students attending PEL at Port Elgin exemplifies the vision that the CAW leadership holds for PEL and union education:

> We can only remain a strong, articulate union if we have an informed and active membership from which to develop the dynamic leaders required to meet head on the challenges of tomorrow. We can only develop those leaders through education.

It can be concluded from this research that the core four-week PEL does strengthen the membership and build leadership. Participants become invigorated and develop activist tendencies in a multitude of areas, both within and outside the workplace. They develop close bonds with each other and also feel increased solidarity toward other workers and their communities. PEL unites people from across Canada and delves deeply into issues of social identity, diversity, and the importance of finding commonality among workers. PEL also provides ample opportunity for student participation and allows workers to share experiences and strategies about workplace change and other workplace issues.

However, despite the success of PEL in planting the seeds of activism and solidarity, these tendencies and teachings are not adequately supported following return to the workplace. If the union is to maximize PEL's ability to generate workers ready to re-invent and re-invigorate the labour movement and incorporate it into broader struggles, the union must develop a clearer agenda on the use and purpose of PEL graduates. To maintain the enthusiasm, motivation, and knowledge generated at Port Elgin, local unions must have concrete struggles, tasks, and agendas in which to "plug-in" returning workers. The union must also continuously strive to meet the equity and diversity needs of its membership.

Future Research

Some research has already been conducted as a more specific follow-up to this assessment of PEL. Based on interviews, as well as participant and graduate surveys, Ruth María Cáceres (2004) takes a closer look at how eight tool courses and the core program can be used to promote equality and diversity in the CAW. She also comments more fully on the levels of activity of PEL graduates and their support structures back in the workplace. In line with the current research, Cáceres recommends further studies that would include a longitudinal survey of PEL participants to garner a true sense of their activity levels before and after the PEL program, a more complete assessment of local union selection procedures, and a continual attempt to increase access and applicability for minority or equity-seeking groups, whether this be based on race, gender, ethnicity, bargaining unit size, region, type of industry, or other diversifying characteristics.

Recent Program Changes

Since this research was completed and presented to the CAW in late 2003, the Education Department has undergone a careful review of the core PEL program and made some significant changes. These changes include: 1) $100,000 subsidies awarded annually to members from equity-seeking groups and/or from non-auto affiliated bargaining units; 2) an LGBT (lesbian, gay, bisexual, and transgendered) workers' caucus in every PEL program at the adjournment of the first day; 3) offerings of PEL courses outside of the Port Elgin education facility to increase access for members of non-auto and non-Ontario affiliated bargaining units; 4) increased offerings of on-site child care for one- and two-week programs; 5) provisions for sign language interpretation; 6) increased tracking of youth participants in core PEL versus tool courses (to augment current tracking of women and workers of colour); and 7) the launch of an updated core program scheduled for the fall of 2005 which will reflect, among other things, "our commitment to be more forward-looking (how we're going to build the union vs how we built the union) ... our commitment to include more examples and analysis from industries other than auto, including public sector workplaces ... and our commitment to increase content with respect to Aboriginal issues" (CAW 2004, 1-3).

These changes are noteworthy not only because of the significant improvements that they will make to the PEL program (both core and tool), but also because they highlight the considerable receptivity of the CAW. Such a commitment to continual improvement and openness to advice and recommendations from all forums is critical as unions forge new ground and renew themselves in today's industrial relations landscape.

Notes

1. Other one-day local 'Area Schools' and the summer 'Family Education Programme' at Port Elgin are funded by general revenue at 3% of membership dues.

2. Subsequent to this research the PEL programme was reviewed by members of the Education Department and significant changes were made. These changes are discussed briefly at the end of this chapter.

3. The Council consists of representatives from CAW locals and acts as the rank and file interim decision-making structure or 'parliament' of the union. The National President reports to the Council and Council executive board members sit on the National Executive Board of the CAW.

References

Baccaro, Lucio, et al. 2003. The Politics of Labour Movement Revitalization: The Need for a Revitalized Perspective. *European Journal of Industrial Relations* 9 (1): 119-133.

Bellefeuille, Pete. 2003. National Representative, CAW Education Department; former Director, CAW Education Department. Interviewed in May.

Burke, Bev, et al. 2002. *Education for Changing Unions*. Toronto: Between the Lines.

Canadian Auto Workers Union (CAW). 2002. Chapter Twelve: Education and Training. Presented at Collective Bargaining and Political Action Convention, Toronto, May 7-10.

————. 2003a. Discussion Leader binders for Core PEL Program weeks 1-4.

————. 2003b. Internal document on PEL coverage. Completed May 29; updated June 4.

————. 2003c. Focus on Union Education Leave. CAW-TCA News. Available at http://www.caw. ca/news/allCAWnewsletters/atthetable/atthetableno1.asp (accessed January 5, 2003).

————. 2004. Report to the National Executive Board. Prepared by the Education Department. November 15.

————. N.d. Internal document on PEL graduates 1978-2002.

Canadian Labour Congress (CLC). 1997. Canadian Labour Education at a Glance. Presented at Educ-Action: Union Building for the 21st Century Conference, Toronto.

————. 1999. Labour Education at a Glance. Presented at Making a Difference with Union Education Conference. September 16-19.

Canadian Union of Postal Workers (CUPW). 2003. Available at http://www.cupw.ca/main_pages/ edu_eng.php (accessed June 28, 2003).

Cáceres, Ruth María. 2004. Promoting Diversity and Equity in the CAW Through Paid Education Leave. Unpublished paper prepared for the Planning Department, University of Toronto.

Delp, Linda, et al. (eds). 2002. *Teaching for Change: Popular Education and the Labour Movement.* Los Angeles: UCLA Center for Labor Research and Education.

Discussion Leaders. 2003. Four Core PEL Discussion Leaders. Interviewed in May.

Ferge, Carola, and John Kelly. 2003. Union Revitalization Strategies in Comparative Perspective. *European Journal of Industrial Relations* 9 (1): 7-24.

Frost, Ann. 2000. Explaining Variation in Workplace Restructuring: The Role of Local Union Capabilities. *Industrial and Labor Relations Review* 53 (4): 559-578.

Gindin, Sam. 1995. *The Canadian Auto Workers: The Birth and Transformation of a Union.* Toronto: James Lorimer & Company.

————. 2003. Retired CAW National Representative. Interviewed in June.

Hurd, Richard, et al. 2003. Reviving the American Labour Movement: Institutions and Mobilization. *European Journal of Industrial Relations* 9 (1): 99-117.

International Labour Organization (ILO). 2003. Convention No. 140: Paid Education Leave. Available at http://www.ilo.org/ilolex/english/convdisp2.htm (accessed June 24, 2003).

Kryzaniwsky, Cheryl. 2003. Director, CAW Education Department. Interviewed in May.

Kumar, Pradeep and Gregor Murray. 2003. Strategic Dilemma: The State of Union Renewal in Canada. In *Trade Unions in Renewal: A Comparative Study,* ed. Peter Fairbrother and Charlotte Yates. London, U.K.: Continuum.

Martin, D'Arcy. 1995. *Thinking Union.* Toronto: Between the Lines.

————. 2003. Union Educator and Coordinator, Centre for the Study of Education and Work (CSEW), Ontario Institute for Studies in Education (OISE). Interviewed in June.

Phillips, Carol. 2003. Director, CAW International Department; former Director, CAW Education Department. Interviewed in May.

Rosenfeld, Herman. 2003. National Representative, CAW Education Department. Interviewed in May.

Taylor, Jeffery. 2001. *Union Learning: Canadian Labour Education in the Twentieth Century.* Toronto: Thompson Educational Publishing.

Waldie, Brennan, et al. 1985. *Labour Education in Canada: The Impact and Value of the Labour Education Program.* Report for Labour Canada. Kingston and Toronto: Waldie, Brennan and Associates.

White, Robert. 1988. *Hard Bargains: My Life on the Line.* Toronto: McClelland and Stewart.

Yates, Charlotte. 1998. Unity and Diversity: Challenges to an Expanding Canadian Autoworkers' Union. *Canadian Review of Sociology and Anthropology* 35 (1): 93-118.

Index

Aboriginal communities, 153
Aboriginal workers, 46, 54, 150–51, 159, 163, 165
  forestry and mining, 281
  young, 198
academic-support positions, 71, 225, 281
accommodation sector, 75–76, 201, 281
  hotel workers, 23, 124, 201–5, 208, 212, 214, 239
  new hotel development campaigns, 212–16
  organizing campaigns, 217
  Quebec, 224
  racial and gender division of labour, 202
  union density, 204
ACCOR, 205
ACSESS, 244
activism, 22, 107, 151
  community, 251, 255
  local, 132–36, 140
  social, 166
  women, 111
activist servicing, 19, 91, 99
AFL-CIO, 38–39, 178, 216–17, 298
  Organizing Institute, 297
Air Canada, 167
AL-CAN, 232
Alberta, 187–88, 195–96
  private hospitals, 274
  union density, 50, 68–69
Alberta Federation of Labour, 109
Aluminum, Brick and Glass Workers Union (ABG), 225
Amalgamated Association of Iron, Steel and Tin Workers, 222
Amalgamated Meat Cutter and Butcher Workmen of North America, 191
American labour movement. See U.S. labour movement
American unions. See U.S. unions
anti-sweatshop campaigns, 117
anti-war demonstrations, 172
Asia-Pacific Economic Cooperation (APEC), Vancouver, 171
Assemblée législative du Québec, 194
audiology, 263
Australia, 37, 48–49
  organizing institutes, 53
  union decline, 15, 61
  union organizing, 106
Australian Council of Trade Unions "Organizing Works" program, 297
auto industry, 115, 161

Big Three, 167, 169, 172, 308
autonomous workers' organizations, 237

'Bad Boss Bus Tour,' 246
"Bad Boss" campaign, 245–46
bad bosses, 257
Bain, Peter, 278–79
balance of power. See power
Ballantyne, Morna, 11, 20
banks, 281
bargaining power, 164–65
  decrease in, 115
B.C., 19, 83, 104, 106–8, 195–96, 281
  Campbell's Liberal government, 138–40, 157, 303
  community services workers, 64
  labour legislation, 47, 130
  NDP, 130, 296
  polarized political environment, 295
  political rallies, 174
  private hospitals, 274
  private sector union density, 68
  sectoral bargaining, 53
  Social Credit, 130, 180, 296
  union density, 295–96
  union organization rate, 66
  women organizers, 108–9
B.C. Federation of Labour (BCFL), 104, 109
B.C. Ferries, 138
B.C. Government and Service Employees Union (BCGEU), 11, 20, 22, 107, 114, 296
  "Building for the Future," 22, 130
  Campbell's Liberal government attack, 138–41
  fightback campaign, 139
  history, 129–30
  local authority, 134, 141
  local initiative and action, 140
  members' ownership, 132
  membership education, 133
  need for union renewal, 131
  Operation Solidarity, 130
  pilot projects, 132–38, 142
  political power, 130, 140
  present profile, 131
  staff, 131, 133, 135–36, 141
  structure, 129, 140
  Temporary Staff Rep program, 130–31
  Train the Trainers program, 130–31
  union renewal, 136–37, 141–42
B.C. Human Rights Commission, 139
B.C. Hydro, 138

B.C. Nurses' Union (BCNU), 107
B.C. Organizing Institute (B.C.O.I.). *See*
    Organizing Institute
B.C. Rail, 138
B.C. World Fair (Expo '86), 296
B.C Labour Relations Code, 296
BCGEU. *See* B.C. Government and Service
    Employees Union (BCGEU)
best practices, 16, 19, 79–80, 100
Bickerton, Geoff, 11, 24
"Big 3+1," 207–8, 210
Big Three auto-makers, 167, 169, 172, 308
bipartite and tripartite industry committees, 86,
    98, 124
Black, Chicano/Latino and Asian Americans, 240
Bloc Québécois, 194
blue-collar category, 76. *See under* men
Blue Heron Casino, 169
Boisbriand GM factory, 118
Bombardier, 167
boycotts, 224
Brazil, 48, 222
Britain. *See* U.K.
British Columbia. *See* B.C.
Bronfenbrenner, Kate, 80, 104, 283
    Organizing to Win, 38
Brooks, Alberta, 192
building cleaning industries, 244
"Building for the Future," 22, 130
business-funded think tanks, 261
business unionism, 33, 81–83, 86, 88, 97

Cáceres, Ruth María, 320
Calgary, 69
call centres, 24–25
    "call centre ready" policy, 279
    "feminized" and poorly paid, 279
    mobility, 280, 287
    "new economy" of information and
        communication services, 278
    "off-shoring," 280
    Omega Direct, 24, 277–90
    Ontario, 279, 281
    technology-based work arrangement, 279
    union avoidance strategies, 280
    wages, 279–80
Canada, 32, 37, 44, 48, 222
    company unionism, 32
    immigration policies, 240
    inter-union tensions, 45–46, 111
    labour legislation, 47, 51
    neoliberal public policies, 51
    sector-wide union organization, 64
    social union perspective, 45, 82
    tradition of labour education, 43
    traditions of social unionism, 171
    trend towards general unionism, 45
    union density, 16, 61
    union leadership/membership mismatch, 46
    union losses, 15
    union renewal, 50–55

universal public health care, 52
waves of union organizing, 64
women's equality, 52
workplace-by-workplace organizing, 43–44
Canada Health Act, 265, 271–72, 274
Canada Pension Plan, 159
Canadian Auto Workers (CAW), 16, 20–21, 25, 46,
    161–83, 227, 255, 258, 269, 307–8
    break away, 161, 165
    building alliances with social movements,
        171–72
    Collective Bargaining Conventions, 163, 167
    Days of Action, 171, 179, 183
    education programs, 25, 29, 163, 308–21
    generational renewal, 170
    growth, 161
    history, 161
    internal democracy, 168
    international solidarity, 172–73
    Kentucky Fried Chicken outlets, 111
    membership composition, 162
    membership involvement, 169–70
    membership level, 163–65
    National Executive Board (NEB), 161
    Paid Education Leave program, 25, 29, 308–21
    Social Justice Fund, 163, 166, 172
    social unionism, 170–71
    Statement of Principles, 168, 170–71
    Task Force on Working Class Politics, 163,
        166, 181
    union culture, 174
    union renewal, 161, 163, 166, 174
Canadian Auto Workers (CAW) Council, 161,
    163, 165
Canadian Auto Workers (CAW) National
    Executive Board, 165
Canadian beef industry, 192
Canadian Council for Public Private Partnerships,
    155
"Canadian experience," 237–38
Canadian Federation of Labour, 82
Canadian Food and Allied Workers, 191
Canadian Health Coalition, 268
Canadian International Development Agency
    (CIDA), 221, 227–28
Canadian Labour Congress (CLC), 15–16, 18, 46,
    51, 52, 54, 81–82, 87, 146, 158, 168, 181,
    194, 227, 239, 268–69, 295, 302–3
    Women's Symposium (2002), 247
Canadian labour movement, 47
    social and political agenda, 88
Canadian Manufacturers Association, 189
Canadian Paperworkers Union, 186
Canadian Union of Postal Workers (CUPW), 21,
    24, 252–53, 255, 257–59
    literary project, 254
    Union Education Program, 308
Canadian Union of Public Employees (CUPE).
    See CUPE
Canadian unions
    approach to servicing, 90–91

areas of change, 89
culture and philosophies, 97
declining influence on state policies, 84
inclusiveness strategies, 92–93
individualized services to members, 92
membership engagement, 88
organizational culture and philosophies, 84–86
organizational innovations, 88
organizing, 66, 89, 93–95
political action, 84, 88, 97–98
risk of marginalization, 62
social orientation, 83
staff profile, 92–93
traditional bases of strength, 75
use of new technologies, 89–90
capacity to mobilize, 163–66, 173
capital mobility, 43, 206
capitalism, 167
card check agreements, 213
Casselman, George, 281–82, 284, 289
casual and seasonal labour (accommodation
    sector), 207
CAW. See Canadian Auto Workers (CAW)
CAW and Politics (paper), 168
Central Hotel Group, 206–7, 209
central labour bodies, 295
centralized collective bargaining, 147
CEP. See Communications, Energy and
    Paperworkers' Union (CEP)
child care, 71, 124, 146, 159
Chile, 22, 48–49, 222, 229
    bargaining contexts, 230–31
    labour code, 230
    mining boom, 221, 228
    mining unions, 222
Chilean Confederation of Mining, 228–29, 231
China, 192–93
China. See China Minmetals Corp.
China Minmetals Corp., 232
chiropody, 263
Chow, Olivia, 214
Chretien, Jean, 261, 264
CIBC–VISA, 280
civil society coalitions, 84–85, 88. See also
    community coalitions
Clair Commission, 265
class inequalities, 237, 242–43
Clawson, Dan, 247, 284
    Next Labour Upsurge, The, 47
CLC. See Canadian Labour Congress (CLC)
Clean Clothes Campaign, 239
Clifford, Paul, 208
coalition building, 36, 40–41, 49, 89. See also civil
    society coalitions; community coalitions
    extra-parliamentary, 84
Coalition For A Living Wage campaign, 172
Coalition for Fair Wages and Working Conditions
    for Homeworkers, 239
"Code of Practice on Organizing Successor
    Employers," 303
Cohen, Larry, 287
collective bargaining, 30, 33

bargaining power, 115
centralized, 147
co-ordinated, 124
coverage, 48–49
industry-wide, 64, 241
international pattern bargaining, 211
making gains in bargaining, 166–67
master bargaining (hotel sector), 206, 211, 217
sectoral bargaining, 53
in tough times, 167
Cominco, 229
Cominco-Tek, 227
Commission of Inquiry on Corporate Conduct in
    the Americas, 222
Common Frontiers, 229
Commons, John R., 32
communications, 74, 185, 225
Communications, Energy and Paperworkers'
    Union (CEP), 20–23, 153, 227, 258, 269
    Energy Policy, 185, 187–88
    environmental campaigns, 188
    environmental issues, 186
    formation of, 185
    hours of work, 186
    membership, 185–86
    opposition to export of natural gas, 190
    pattern bargaining, 186
    pay equity, 186
    rank-and-file involvement, 185
    women members, 186
community activism, 251, 255
community campaigns, 269–70
community care systems, 263
community coalitions, 30, 37, 55, 87, 261. See also
    civil society coalitions
community groups, 123, 271, 307
community organizing, 155, 241, 258
    community development model, 240–42
    community outreach, 107, 153
    community solidarity, 88
    community/union relationship, 270
community unionism, 23–24, 55, 242, 251, 259
    conceptualizing, 240
    labour movement renewal, 237–38
    pre-union associations, 239
    self-organizing model, 243
community work, 98
Companhia Vale do Rio Doce (CVRD) SA, 232
company relocation to low-wage jurisdictions,
    206, 221, 225, 227–29
company unionism, 32
competitiveness
    corporate agenda of, 34
    low wages and, 117
concessions, 15, 113, 115, 227, 307
Confederation of Industrial Unions (CIO), 223
Confederation of Nurses' Union, 269
conflict of interest (unions and employers), 17, 33
construction, 238
    non-union workers, 76
construction unions, 107

consumer and citizen pressures, 117
consumer unionism, 31
continental economic integration, 61. *See also* free
    trade
    American, 51
continental free-trade agreements, 83
contingent and precarious workforce. *See*
    precarious employment
contracting-out, 68, 138, 157–58
Cornfield, Daniel, *Labour Revitalization*, 48
corporate anti-unionism, 51. *See also* employer
    hostility to unions
corporate restructuring, 15, 35, 43
Council of Canadians, 24, 253, 270
courier workers, 254–55, 257–58
Cranford, Cynthia, 11, 23
credit collection, 279
crisis in social democracy, 163, 166
cross-border and international coordination, 41,
    89. *See also* international solidarity
CSQ, 81, 86, 119, 122, 124
Cuba-Canada Solidarity Network, 255
CUPE, 20–21, 71, 145–59, 227, 258, 265–66, 269
    affirmative action hiring program, 150
    background on, 145–46
    collective agreements, 147
    Commission on Structure and Services,
        147–48, 150, 157
    coordinated bargaining, 149
    education program, 149, 152
    Equal Opportunities Department, 150
    gender parity, 152
    Global Justice Fund, 154
    human rights committees, 151
    human rights training, 150, 152
    impact on broader public policy, 149
    internal and external solidarity, 153, 155, 157
    local union autonomy, 146–47
    maternity leave provisions, 147
    member activist/staff divisions, 152
    membership, 145–46
    National Executive Board (NEP), 148, 150
    opposition to privatization, 153–54, 157
    organizing strategy, 155–56
    Organizing the Organized policy, 152–53
    PELCUPE, 308
    Provincial Divisions, 149
    Provincial legislation and, 146, 149
    Rainbow Committee, 150
    staff, 150, 152, 158–59
    structural change, 147
    union renewal, 147, 151, 157, 158–59
    women's participation, 159
    work stoppages, 153
"CUPE into the 1990s" (policy paper), 147

Dallaire, Denis, 282, 284–90
DANA, 232
day care. *See* child care
day labour, 240
de-industrialization, 64

de-skilled clerical work, 238
de-unionization initiatives, 138
deep community outreach, 271–73
Delivery Drivers Alliance of Manitoba (DDAM),
    255, 257
Delta Chelsea, 206
democracy, 17, 20–21, 47–48, 51, 106, 119–23,
    125, 145, 165–68, 284
Denmark, 49
department stores, 75, 169
deregulation, 35, 64, 68, 74
    of care standards, 264
disadvantaged workers, 54, 55
    disabled, 46–47, 54, 92, 151
"Disputes Protocol," 303
domestic workers, 240
downsizing, 15, 35, 42–43, 113, 307
Downtown Temp Workers' Committee, 243–44
Duplessis, Maurice, 121
Dyck, Harold, 254–56
Dynamex, 258
Dynamex v. Mamona, 257

Early, Steve, 284
Eco Mafia, 255
economic restructuring. *See also* corporate
    restructuring
    loss of union jobs, 61
education, 33, 36, 43, 65, 69, 71, 131, 182, 194. *See
    also* union educational programs
    privatization, 154
    union coverage, 68
education assistants, 146
Eiro-line, 48
"electronic sweatshops," 280
Elementary Teachers Federation of Ontario
    (ETFO), 21, 269
employer hostility to unions, 37, 43–44, 68, 74–75,
    157, 217, 296
employer intimidation, 212, 214–15
employment insurance, 159
employment standards, 246, 252, 255–56
Employment Standards Act, 240, 243, 245
energy, 185
Energy and Chemical Workers Union, 186
environmental issues, 31, 186, 188
equality, 65, 98, 150
equity-seeking groups, 152, 320
Ethiopia, 226
ethnic minorities, 37, 44
Europe
    strengthening partnerships between labour,
        business and the state, 49
    union cooperation across national borders, 173
    union losses, 15
European Foundation for Improvement in Living
    and Working Conditions, 48
European Trade Union Confederation, 41
European Works Councils, 41
"Everybody's Union" theme, 225, 281
"the evolutionary theories of trade unionism," 31

Extendicare, 265
external solidarity, 20, 119–20, 123–25, 145

"Facing Global Management," 227
Fairbrother, Peter, 30
    Trade Unions In Renewal, 48
Fairmont, 202, 210
Fairness For Whom? (Short), 256
faith communities, 270–71
Falconbridge-Noranda workers, 233
family doctor shortage, 263
Fantasia, Rick, 283
fashion and clothing firms, 115
fast-food workers, 245
Fatigue Kills trucking campaign, 172
federal transfers, 262, 271–72
Fédération des syndicats de l'enseignement (FSE),
    116
Fédération des travailleurs et travailleuses du
    Québec (FTQ), 116, 118–19, 122, 124, 194
Fédération du Comerce of the Confédération des
    syndicats nationaux (CSN), 81, 116, 119,
    122
Female Majority Workplaces (FMW), 104, 106,
    109–10
    attempts to organize, 107–8
Filipinos, 238
financial and business services, 68
Fine, Janice, 247
Finland, 49
flexible, part-time work, 53, 238, 307
flight attendants, 145
Flint, Michigan strike
    impact in Canada and Mexico, 117
"following the work," 156, 296
Fondation de la CSN, 86, 122, 124
Fonds de solidarité de la FTQ, 86, 122, 124
for-hire call centre industry, 280
for-profit drug industry, 264
forest products, 185
Fort McMurray, 188
Fotomat, 224
Four Seasons, 211
France, 173
    industrial relations trends, 115
Fraser, Michael, 193–94, 196–97
Fraser, Wayne, 282, 290
Fraser Institute, 273
free trade, 15, 68, 74, 87, 225, 227
    industrial restructuring in response to, 74
    international trade agreements, 153–54, 173,
        228
    NAFTA, 154, 173, 189, 221, 227–28
Free Trade Agreement of the Americas (FTAA),
    173
Frege, Carola, *Varieties of Unionism*, 48
Friesen, John, 258
FTQ, 119
FTQ-CLC affiliated organizations, 122
FTQ-CROP study, 116, 118, 124
FTQ Solidarity Fund, 86, 117, 122, 124

Fyke Commission in Saskatchewan, 265

Garcia-Orgales, Jorge, 11, 22, 24
garment industry model, 238, 244
garment workers, 239–40, 245
gays, lesbians, bisexual and transgendered
    members, 92, 151, 163, 165
Gellatly, Mary, 11, 23
gender and ethnic mis-matches, 46–47
gender and racial equality, 97
    promotion of, 85
gender bias
    union organizing, 103–4, 108
gender inequalities, 237, 242–43
gendered pattern of union growth, 19, 75
General Strike Bus Tour, 253
general unionism, 45, 87
generational renewal, 166
Georgetti, Ken, 297
Gerdau, 232–33
Germany, 44, 48
Ghana, 48
Gildan Activewear, 117
global firms. *See* multinational corporations
"global" hotel workforce, 202
Global Justice CareVan Project, 239
Global Justice Fund, 154
global production or value chains, 114
global social solidarity, 226
global solidarity. *See* international solidarity
Global Union Federations, 233
globalization, 15, 22, 34–35, 44, 48, 68, 79, 87, 222
    developing local union power in, 114, 117, 119
    effect on union power, 119
    global alliance of workers, 226 (*See also*
        international solidarity)
    global incapacitation thesis, 114
    labour-management collaboration and, 118
    opportunities for union action, 113
    power and, 113–14, 117, 119
    stereotypical view of, 125
    union opportunities in, 125
    weakening link between unions and their
        members, 116
Grass Roots Women, 251, 253
grassroots education and action, 36, 39, 153,
    214–15
grocery stores, 75
Guard, Julie, 11, 24
"Guide to Workers' Rights, 302

Hargrove, Buzz, 22, 174, 177
    on union renewal, 174, 181
Harper, Stephen, 274
Harris, Mike, 273–74
Harris government in Ontario, 179, 262
Hartman, Grace, 150
health, 71, 131
    privatization, 154
    union coverage, 68
health accord, 272

health and community social services workers, 71
health and social services, 145
health care horror stories, 263
health care services, 146, 161–62, 169, 191
health insurance privatization, 271
health service delivery
    privatization, 263, 274
health system
    privatization, 264
HERE, 111, 210, 216
    organizing strategy, 106
Hickey, Robert, 38
high performance work systems, 31
hiring into unionized workplaces, 67
home care, 71
home workers, 240
homecare sector
    "market competition," 263
homophobia, 55
Hospital Employees' Union, 302
hospital worker positions, 263
hospitality sector, 131, 161–62
hospitality unionism, 201
hospitals, 147
hostile environment, 18, 80
Hotel Employees and Restaurant Employees
    (HERE), 20
Hotel Employers Group of Toronto, 206
hotel workers, 23, 124, 201, 239
    employer intimidation, 212
    gender, ethnic and income segmentation,
        202–3
    increased visibility in the community, 202
    multiple unions, 204–5
    organizing strategies, 214
    solidarity, 203, 212
    vulnerability, 212
Human Resource and Skills Development
    Canada, 80
    union survey, 81
Human Resources Development Canada, 19, 54
human rights, 252, 255
Humanities Fund, 22
Hurd, Richard, 31, 287
hydro workers, 145

IBEW, 21, 107
Ifill, Louis, 253
immigrant workers, 23, 54–55, 204, 217, 241–43
Immigrant Workers Centre/Centre des Travailleurs
    et Travalleuses Immigrant (IWC/CTI), 240
immigration problems, 255
inclusiveness, 55, 99
independent contractors, 244
India, 48–49
individualism, 43, 169, 181
industrial relations trends, 115
industrial unionism, 87, 240–41
Industrial Wood and Allied Workers (IWA), 225,
    227, 269, 281
Industrial Workers of the World (IWW), 255

industry-wide collective bargaining, 64, 241
information and communication services
    "new economy" of, 278
information technology workers, 245
innovations and change in labour organizations in
    Canada, 19, 79–81, 99–100
inside organizers. See rank-and-file organizers
institutional isomorphism, 80
inter-union competition, 45–46, 122
inter-union cooperation, 36, 41, 295
    barriers to, 111
inter-union solidarity, 122, 124
INTERCEDE, 240
Intercontinental Hotel, 204
internal solidarity or democracy, 20, 119–23, 125,
    145, 165
International Association of Machinists (IAM),
    269
International Brotherhood of Electrical Workers
    (IBEW), 21, 107
International Brotherhood of Teamsters (IBT), 21
International Carnival (Caribana), 207
International Confederation of Free Trade Unions,
    41
international framework agreements, 206, 233
International Labour Organization (ILO), 308
international pattern bargaining, 211
international solidarity, 22, 41, 85, 124, 154–55,
    166, 172, 222, 226–27, 232–33
    union cooperation across national borders, 173
international trade agreements, 153–54, 228. See
    also free trade
International Transport Workers' Federation
    Womens' Conference, 172
international worker solidarity centres (CISO),
    124
internationalization of labour, 41
Internet technology, 300
Irwin Toy, 224
Israel, 48
Italy, 48
IWA, 225, 227, 269, 281

Jackson, Andrew, 11, 19
Jackson, Jesse, 208
janitors, 64, 239
Japan, 48–49
job market
    changing occupational structure, 69
job security, 111, 115–16, 158
Johnson Controls, 169
Jonquière, Québec, 117, 193
Jose, A.V., Organized Labour in the 21st Century, 48
"Jumping-scales," 211, 217
Juravich, Tom, 283
Just the Beginning, Walking the Union Walk, 186
Just Transition, policy of, 186, 188–89
Justice for Janitors campaigns, 64
Justicia for Migrant Workers, 239

Kelly, John, 48

Kentucky Fried Chicken, 53, 111
King, Mackenzie, 32
Kirby, Michael, 265, 271
Klein, Ralph, 265, 273–74
"knowledge-based economy," 65, 70
knowledge intensive strategies, 213, 215, 217
　unions access to expertise, 124
Korea, 48
Kumar, Pradeep, 11, 16, 19, 121
Kyoto Protocol, 185, 187–90

Laborers' International Union (LIUNA), 21
labour boards, 241
labour central body, 297
labour force. See workforce
Labour International Development Committee
　(LIDC), 227
labour legislation, 23, 40, 43, 47–48, 51, 66, 138,
　173, 237, 243, 257
　Canada, 47, 51
　Quebec, 122
labour-management cooperation, 32
labour-management partnerships, 31, 33–34, 36,
　42. See also partnerships or mutual gains
　form of unionism
labour movement. See also union movement
　changing face of, 66
　divisions, 84
labour movement renewal, 237–38. See also union
　renewal
Labour Revitalization (Cornfield), 48
labour screen, 228
labour standards. See employment standards
labourers, 74
Labrador, 50, 69
Labrana, Moises, 228
Ladd, Deena, 11, 23
Lajoie, Don, 255
Lakeside Packers, 192–93
Las Vegas, 47, 64
Layton, Jack, 214
leadership development, 16, 25, 42–43
leadership training and education, 91, 243, 300
legislative reform, 239, 241
lesbian-gay-bisexual-transgender members, 92,
　152, 163, 165
"level playing field," 35
Lévesque, Christian, 11, 19
Levi Strauss plants, 192
　move to China, 193
Lewenza, Ken, 174, 179–80
　on union renewal, 176, 182
light manufacturing, 238
Lithuania, 48
Little Steel Strike, 223
Liu, Anna, 11, 22
lobbying and policy work, 33, 228
local accountability, 137
local activists, 132–36, 140
local government, 145
local unions

authority and accountability, 132, 137, 141
　autonomy, 146
　power resources, 125
　and trans-national firms, 115
long-term care, 71, 146–47, 264, 273
Los Angeles, 47
Los Angeles Manufacturing Action Project, 297
Low Income Intermediary Project (LIIP), 254–56
low-paid and insecure jobs, 64, 224, 237

machine operators, 74, 245
Magna, 169
MAI, 227
male blue-collar unionism, 69, 75–76
　loss of jobs, 68
　union density, 71, 74
male industrial working-class, 64, 241
Male Majority Workplaces (MMW), 104, 106–10
"managerial theory of union renewal," 31
Manitoba, 83, 145, 187
　call centres, 281
　labour legislation, 47
　union density, 69
　youth committees, 196
Manitoba Employment Standards Code, 256–57
Manitoba Federation of Labour, 195
Manitoba Government Employees Union, 92
Manitoba Human Rights Commission, 256
Manitoba Workers' Compensation Board, 258
Manning, Preston, 273–74
manufacture of chemicals, 185
manufacturing sector, 67, 168–69, 191
　decline, 43, 201
　organizing drives, 110
　union density, 74
Maquila Solidarity Network, 117
marches, 173
market-oriented public policy, 35, 37, 51
Marriott, 202
Marriott Eaton Centre hotel, 204
Marshall, Judith, 11, 22
Martin, D'Arcy, 11, 24
Martin, Paul, 262
mass actions, 173
master bargaining (hotel sector), 206, 211, 217
Mayworks, 251, 253
Mazankowski, Don, 265, 271
McCammon, Holly, 48
McConnell, Pam, 214
media, 17, 178, 185, 207, 209, 245
Medicare, 24, 159, 271
　anti-Medicare forces, 262
　contracting out, 139
　privatized hospitals (P3s), 274
Medicare campaign, 261, 270–71, 273
　door-to-door campaign, 266–68
　ethnic and cultural groups, 270
　faith communities, 270
　for-profit lobby, 264
　Korean Canadian Association, 270
　Rallies of Portuguese and Spanish women, 270

seniors' organizations, 270
Mehra, Natalie, 11, 24
membership identification with union, 97, 118,
    121, 123
membership involvement, 19, 21–23, 30, 47,
    49–50, 85, 88, 98–99, 132, 166
    activism, 32, 107
    BCGEU, 130
    in occupational health and safety education,
    131
men
    blue-collar unionism, 68–69, 71, 74–76
    industrial working class, 64–65, 241
    Male Majority Workplaces (MMW), 104, 106,
    109–10
    in professional or highly skilled occupations,
    69–70
    support for unions, 74
    union density among, 67
Mennonite Council for International
    Cooperation, 255
Mexico, 48–49, 125, 173, 222
Michalchuk, Glen, 253
Migrant Agricultural Workers Support Centre, 239
migrant farm workers, 239
Milkman, Ruth, 17, 283
    Rebuilding Labour, 38
Ministers Employment Standards Action Group,
    246
minority or equity-seeking groups, 54, 65, 320
mobilization of rank-and-file members, 139, 307
Montreal, 54, 187
    hotel workers, 124
Mulroney, Brian, 225
multinational corporations, 35, 114, 117, 210, 217,
    222, 227, 230
    from Canada, 231
    locus of power, 115
    opposition to unions, 202
    strategic vulnerability, 117
multiple sub-contracting chains, 237
municipal services, 154
Muñoz, Nestor, 233
Murnighan, Bill, 11, 21, 174
Murray, Gregor, 11, 16, 19, 121, 281
mutual aids/social capital view, 33–34

NAFTA, 154, 173, 189, 221, 227–28
Nash, Peggy, 174, 178
    on union renewal, 175, 181
National Action Committee on the Status of
    Women, 150
National Association of Public Employees
    (NAPE), 146
National Energy Board (NEB), 190
National Union of Public and General Employees
    (NUPGE), 20–21, 71, 146, 269
National Youth Conference, 197
natural gas exports
    CEP opposition to, 185
Navistar, 167

Naylor, Karen, 255
NDP, 64, 66, 83, 87, 132, 194, 296
neo-liberal policies, 15, 34, 44, 51, 167, 218
neoliberal ideology, 44, 48
Netherlands, 48
neutrality agreements (new hotels), 215–16
New Brunswick, 190
    provincial collective agreements, 147
    solidarity pacts, 157
"new economy," 18, 70, 278, 281
new hotel development campaigns, 212, 215–16
    knowledge intensive, 213
    leverage points, 213
    neutrality agreements, 214–16
    top-down orchestration, 214–15
new leadership, 30
new organizing, 19
new technologies, 16, 19, 35, 44, 98, 116
new unionism, 31
New Unity Partnership (NUP), 39, 216–17
"new" workforce, 49, 168
New Zealand, 37, 48–49
    union decline, 61
    union organizing, 106
Newfoundland, 187
    union density, 50, 69
Newman, Keith, 11, 23
Next Labour Upsurge, The (Clawson), 47
NIKE, 115
9/11, 172, 216
NO WAR coalition, 251, 255
non-standard employment, 35
non-union employees
    construction workers, 76
    profile of, 77
non-union private service sector, 19
Noranda, 227, 232–33
North Africans, 238
North American economic integration, 51
North American Free Trade Agreement (NAFTA),
    154, 173, 189, 221, 227–28
North Battleford, Saskatchewan
    Wal-Mart organizing drive, 198
Nova Scotia, 190
    labour legislation, 47
Novotel airport hotel, 205
nurses, 71, 263
nursing and retirement homes, 281

O'Halloran, Chris, 12, 22
oil and gas exports, 185, 189
oil and gas reserves, 188
Omega Direct Response, 24, 277–79
    "electronic sweatshop," 280
    inside committee, 289
    organizing drive, 281–90
Omega Direct Response managers, 287
    abuse of workers, 289
    anti-union activities, 288, 290
"On the front line locally and globally (Policy
    Statement), 154–55

One Big Union, 241
Ontario, 19, 21, 83, 104, 106–8, 145, 171, 187, 195, 261
    call centres, 279, 281
    employer aggression, 110
    funding for hospitals, 262–63
    inter-union tensions, 111
    labour legislation, 47, 110
    private hospitals, 274
    rate of unionization, 116
    union density, 50, 68–69
    union organization rate, 66
    women organizers, 108
Ontario Federation of Labour (OFL), 15, 104, 266, 270, 301
Ontario Health Coalition (OHC), 24, 265–66, 268. *See also* Medicare campaign
Ontario Hydro, 153
Ontario Labour Relations Board, 288
    certification practices, 213
Ontario Ministry of Labour, 243
Ontario Nurses' Assn (ONA), 21, 269
Ontario Public Services Employees Union (OPSEU), 269
Ontario Secondary School Teachers Federations (OSSTF), 21, 269
Operation Solidarity, 22, 130
Organization of American States (OAS), 171
organizational change, 16, 54
organizational restructuring, 36
Organized Labour in the 21ˢᵗ Century (Jose), 48
organizers
    "boomer"-aged males, 301
    gender differences, 109
    manufacturing sector, 110
    members of colour, 156
    Omega, 282
    seasoned or professional, 284
    women, 108, 111–12, 151
organizing, 61, 93–97, 155, 166, 168–69, 240, 258, 295
    gender bias, 19, 103–4, 108
    gender differences, 109
    new strategies, 30
    in non-traditional workplaces, 307
    strategies, 107
Organizing Advisory Committee (OAC), 297–98
"Organizing Call Centres from the Workers' Perspective" (Conference), 278
Organizing Institute (AFL-CIO), 38
Organizing Institute (B.C.O.I.), 15, 53, 109, 111–12, 295, 298
    Code of Practice, 304
    impact of, 303
    leadership education, 300
    organizer network, 299
    organizing protocol agreements, 303
    origins of, 295–96
    providing information to workers, 302
    research and evaluation, 300
    training program, 298

organizing model of unionism, 33, 37
Organizing the Organized policy statement, 151, 154
organizing the unorganized, 36–37, 106, 148, 169, 252
Organizing to Win (Bronfenbrenner), 38
outsourcing, 35, 42–43, 113, 123, 303

PACE (Paper, Allied-Industrial, Chemical and Energy Workers International), 226, 233, 281
Paid Education Leave (PEL) program, 25, 312
    Aboriginal issues, 321
    building activism, 309–11
    core PEL *vs.* tool courses, 319
    coverage, 315–16
    development and evolution, 308–9
    diversity, 319–20
    fostering solidarity, 313
    impact on diversity awareness, 314
    leadership training, 310
    minority or equity-seeking groups, 320
    public speaking, 310
    rank-and-file participants, 317
    selective process, 317
    union renewal, 307, 318
    women, 319
Parkdale Community and Legal Services, 245
part-time temporary work, 238
part-time workers
    in CAW, 161
    union density, 76
Parti Québécois, 83
partnerships or mutual gains form of unionism, 31, 33–34, 36, 42, 49, 86, 98
PATCO example, 181
PEL. *See* Paid Education Leave (PEL) program
PELCUPE
    paid education leave clause, 308
pension plans, 163
people of colour, 46, 55, 202, 217, 237
    as organizers, 156
people with disabilities, 46–47, 54, 92
People's Summit, Argentina, 233
People's Summit, Quebec City, 172, 222, 229
personal contact, 285, 288
personal empowerment, 242
Peru, 22, 221–22, 231
Petro-Canada, 190
Pharmacare, 139
pharmacare program, 272
physiotherapy, 263
pink-collar jobs, 69
Placer Dome, 227, 229
plant closures and moves, 192–93, 221. *See also* company relocation
Platz, John, 205
policing of labour unrest, 218
political action, 30, 39–40, 87, 97–98, 166
    importance in Canadian union activity, 84
political alliances, 106

political cynicism, 168
political influence, 163–65
political power, 140
political rallies, 173
politics, 19
"post-industrial" economy, 64
power, 114. *See also* union power resources
    balance of, 17
    importance of, 113
    privatization, 153, 155
precarious employment, 237, 240, 242, 244, 279, 287
    erosion of standards for all workers, 243
    "flexible" work, 53, 238, 307
    low-paid and insecure jobs, 64, 224, 237
    temporary, part-time, 35, 238
press. *See* media
primary industries, 74
private health industry, 261–62, 265
private health insurance industry, 264
private sector, 19–20, 111
    organizing tactics, 110
    union density, 68, 74, 108
    unionization rate, 201
private services sector, 68–69, 105, 201
    increased importance of, 64
    organizing, 168
    rise of, 65
    union coverage, 75
privatization, 35, 64, 68, 87, 113, 138, 155, 158, 180, 261, 264
    anti-privatization fight, 274 (*See also* Medicare)
    CUPE opposition, 153–54, 157
    of delivery systems, 272
    "following the work," 156, 296
    global nature of, 153–54
    of Petro-Canada, 190
    of public space, 218
    support services, 272
privatization strategy (Bennett and Vander Zalm), 296
privatized hospitals (P3s), 274
production of goods and services
    strategic uncertainty, 119
professional and skilled jobs, 76
    in natural and applied sciences, 70
professional and technical "knowledge-based" jobs, 64
professional/managerial jobs
    union coverage, 70
professional organizers, 287, 289
provincial governments
    cuts to hospitals, 262
provincial jurisdictions, 43
public administration
    union coverage, 68
public and social service jobs, 701
    union coverage, 71
public campaigns, 224
public health care. *See also* Medicare
    popular support for, 274

public health insurance system, 24, 261, 264
public holiday campaign, 243–44
public policy, 35–37, 51, 66
public private partnerships, 153, 158, 274
    CUPE opposition to, 155
public-public partnerships, 155
public sector, 67, 171
    unionization rate, 71
public sector unions, 20, 71, 82, 107, 272, 296
    organizing tactics, 110
Public Service Alliance of Canada (PSAC), 21, 269
pulp and paper, 185

Quebec, 20, 81, 145, 158, 187, 190, 196
    anti-war marches, 174
    Bloc Québécois, 194
    Clair Commission, 265
    common front bargaining, 147
    industrial relations trends, 115
    inter-union competition, 122
    labour legislation, 47
    manufacturing sector, 115
    pension fund, 124
    private hospitals, 274
    private sector union density, 68
    provincial collective agreements, 147
    rate of unionization, 116
    security guards, 64
    union density, 50, 69
    union involvement in work organization, 118
    union organization rate, 66
    union renewal, 16, 19, 114, 118
    unionization rate, 118
Quebec Labour Code, 122
Quebec Teaching Congress (CEQ), 21
Quebec unions, 83, 113, 119, 123–24
    social projects, 121
    support for sovereignty, 121
Quebrada Blanca mine, 229–30, 233

race to the bottom, 222
racism, 55, 202, 237, 242–43
radical unions, 241
Radio Shack, 224
Rae, Kyle, 214
rail, 161–62
rank-and-file, 36, 87
rank-and-file activism, 30–33, 42, 208, 215
rank-and-file communication, 91
rank-and-file involvement, 37
rank-and-file organizers, 277–78, 283, 287, 289
rank-and-file participation, 49, 284–85, 291
"rat unions," 297
Reagan, Ronald, 181, 224
Rebuilding Labour (Milkman), 38
recent immigrants, 168, 202, 237–38, 245, 284
recession (1981-82), 224
recession (1990-91), 225
Red Boine Metis Local, 255
Red River local (courier drivers), 258–59
rehabilitation services, 263

reservations, 279
resource industries, 226
restaurants, 75
Retail Clerks International Union, 191
retail workers, 161–62, 169
retirees, 92, 170, 281
right-wing ideology, 87, 169
Ritz Carlton project, 213
Riverview Hospital, 135
    local activists, 134
Robertson, David, 12, 21, 174, 180
    on union renewal, 176–77, 183
Romanow Commission, 24, 261–62, 264–66,
    271–74
    rallies, 268–69
Royal York, 207, 209
Ruel, Len, 298
Ryan, Sid, 265

Saanich Indian School Board, 135
Saint-Hyacinthe, Quebec, 193
Saskatchewan, 83, 195
    labour legislation, 47
    union density, 69
    youth committees, 195–96
Saskatchewan Labour Relations Board, 198
Saskatoon and District Labour Council, 195
Schenk, Chris, 12, 284
school boards, 147
sectoral bargaining, 53
security guards, 111, 191
security officers, 224
"self-employed," 244
"self-employed" contractors, 238, 242
Self-Employed Women's Association in India, 242
self-organizing, 245
Service Employees International Union (SEIU),
    21, 204, 216, 269–70
    "corporate organizing," 156
service industries
    USWA representation, 224
service model, 33
service sector, 226, 281
service unionism, 23, 33
servicing/business/value-added unionism, 33
servicing or business unionism, 32–33, 132
sexism, 55, 290
Sheraton Centre, 206
shipbuilding, 162
Short, Jay, *Fairness For Whom?*, 256
short-term contracts, 237
single mothers, 284
small group meetings, 285
small workplaces, 53, 105, 111, 241
    union density, 76
Social Affairs Federation (FAS/CSN), 21
social assistance, 159
social capital unionism, 33–34
social change, 33, 174
Social Credit, 130, 133
social justice, 121, 174, 255

Social Justice Fund, 163, 172
social movement unionism, 32–33, 37, 45, 47,
    49–50, 81, 83–84, 87–88, 97, 239
social movements, 172
    alliances with, 22, 166
social services, 69, 71, 131, 147
    union coverage, 68
social transformation, 168
social unionism, 21, 23, 81–82, 84, 86–88, 97–98,
    130, 166, 170–71, 284, 289
    CAW commitment to, 163
social workers, 71
sociology of organizational change, 80
Sodexho, 156
solidarity, 25, 32, 35–36, 47, 54–55, 82, 155–56,
    174, 253–54
    accommodation sector, 203
    across lines of gender and skill, 76
    broader forms, 85, 99
    external solidarity, 20, 119–20, 123–25, 145
    hotel workers, 212
    inter-union, 85, 97, 122, 124
    union-community, 24
Solidarity Fund, 87
solidarity pacts, 157
South Africa, 48–49
South African Municipal Workers Union
    (SAMWU), 155
South Asians, 238
Spain, 48–49
speech pathology, 263
Sri Lankan Tamil women, 243
Stand UP: CUPE's Action Plan for Jobs and
    Services (Policy Paper), 153
Starbucks, 53
Statistics Canada, 46, 75, 105, 238, 279
Stearns, Catherine, 12, 24
Steedman, Mercedes, 12, 24
Steel Workers' Organizing Committee (SWOC),
    222–23
Steelworkers' Humanities Fund, 221–22, 226–28
    education and worker exchanges, 227–28
    lobbying and policy work, 228
    worker exchanges and global alliances, 229–31,
    233
Steeves, Gary, 12, 22
Stelco, 232
Sterling Truck, 169
Stinson, Jane, 12, 20
strategic capacity to develop vision or agenda,
    119–21, 125, 164–65
strategic planning, 47
Strieb, Lee, 212
strikes, 157, 173, 207, 212, 224
Structured Movement Against Capitalism
    (SMAC), 255
struggle, 83, 183
Studies in Political Economy, 16
Sudbury, 24
    union consciousness, 277–78, 286
Summer Institute for Union Women, 302

supplier neutrality agreements, 169
Supreme Court of Canada, 257–58
Sutton Place, 211
Sweden, 48–49
  industry-wide collective bargaining, 64
Sweeny, John, 217
  "New Voice" campaign, 38
Switzerland, 49

Talking Union program, 196
Tamil Temp Workers' Committee, 243–44
Tascona, Bruce, 254
Task Force on Reconstructing America's Labour
  Market Institutions, 34
teachers, 71
technological change, 68
telecommunications, 244
telemarketing, 279–80
temporary agency workers, 238, 240–42, 244
temporary employment agencies, 237
tenants' rights, 255
"Thinking North South," 227
TOFFE, 23, 237, 242–46
  employer-specific committees, 245
  public holiday campaign, 243–44
  self-organizing activities, 244
Toronto, 23, 55, 201–2, 216
  accommodation sector, 201, 205
  union density, 69
Toronto Hilton, 206
Toronto Labour Council
  Organizing Institute, 109
Toronto Organizing for Fair Employment. See
  TOFFE
Trade Unions in Renewal (Fairbrother), 48
trans-national firms. See multinational
  corporations
transfer payments, 262, 271–72
transport-equipment operators, 74
transportation, 74, 162, 225
Transportation Communications International
  Union, 225
Trump, Donald, 213
Tufts, Steven, 12, 23
Turkey, 49
two-tier health system, 264–65, 271, 274

UFCW. See United Food and Commercial
  Workers (UFCW)
UFWA, 239
U.K., 37, 48–49
  Private Finance Initiative (PFI), 155
  union decline, 15, 61
  union leaders, 52
  union organizing, 106
unfair labour practices, 237
union advantage, 63, 66
union-busting consultants, 202, 205
Union Cities Program, 38
union-community alliances, 23, 253. See also
  community groups; community outreach

union cooperation across national borders. See
  international solidarity
union coverage
  geographical trends, 69
  longer-term trends in, 66–69
  private services sector, 75
  professional/managerial jobs, 70
  public and social service jobs, 71
  women vs. men, 68
union decline, 34, 44
  U.S., 38
union density, 19, 35, 49–50, 67, 76, 145, 155, 164,
  307
  Canada, 16
  changes in, 65, 72–73
  as factor in union renewal, 48
  importance of, 62–64
  power and, 64
union educational programs, 22, 25, 42, 55, 107,
  135–37, 145, 227–28, 307, 320. See also Paid
  Education Leave (PEL)
  CUPW, 308
  leadership training and education, 91, 243, 300
Union in Politics Committees (UPCs), 163
union innovation, 99
union internationalism, 172–73. See also
  international solidarity
union involvement in work organization, 118
union leadership, 47. See also leadership
  development
  demographic makeup, 46
"union life" program, 122
union losses
  Australia, 15
  Britain, 15
  Canada, 15
  Europe, 15
  job losses in union plants, 61, 74
  U.S., 15
union mergers, 36–37, 161–62, 185–86, 191, 216,
  223, 225–26, 281
  CUPE, 148–49
union movement. See also labour movement
  increasing precariousness, 29, 34
union movement in Canada
  declining influence on political agenda, 83
Union of National Defense Employees (UNDE),
  269
Union of Needle Trades, Industrial and Textile
  Employees' Union (UNITE), 20
union power resources, 19, 120–21, 123, 125,
  163–65
  reconfiguration, 119
  traditional sources of, 114
union renewal, 29, 32, 49–50, 108, 118, 165, 209,
  217, 222, 239, 261, 282, 285, 307
  Buzz Hargrove on, 174, 181
  in Canada, 15–16
  Dave Robertson on, 176–77, 183
  debates on, 79
  decision-makers at top and, 283

definitions, 145
in a global context, 113–14, 201
Ken Lewenza on, 176, 182
managerial theory of, 31
meaning, 30–32
obstacles to, 43–46
Peggy Nash on, 175
professional organizers and, 283
Quebec, 16
rationale of, 34–35
strategies, 36
thesis of, 35–36
women's potential contribution, 103
union resistance, 166
Union Resistance and Union Renewal (Policy
    Paper), 21, 164, 174
Union Summer Program, 38
unionization rates, 15, 29
women *vs.* men, 46
unions
bad press, 17, 35
competitive relationships, 211
culture and philosophy, 100, 143
global exchanges and alliances, 222
in global workplaces, 118
importance of, 17
participative forms of management, 116
relations with political parties, 40, 82, 87, 97,
    259
role in workplace change, 119
as social and political actors, 66
UNITE, 192, 216
UNITE-HERE, 20–21, 23, 156, 202, 212, 216
international sectoral unionism, 205
master agreement, 206–7, 209–11
multiple and integrated tactics, 201, 205–7,
    216–17
pattern bargaining, 209–10
pre-union associations, 239
rallies and demonstrations, 209
trusteeship, 201, 205
United Auto Workers (UAW), 161
United Brotherhood of Carpenters and Joiners
    (UBC), 21
United Food and Commercial Workers (UFCW),
    20–22, 107, 204, 211, 217, 239, 258, 269–70,
    303
formation, 191
local union youth committees, 195–96
membership by gender, 191
Wal-Mart, 192–93
youth conferences, 196–98
youth internship program, 191, 194–95
youth programs, 191–99
United Mine Workers, 222
United Rubber, Cork, Linoleum & Plastic
    Workers of America (URW), 225
United Steelworkers of America (USWA), 107,
    204, 211, 223
bargaining for security guards, 111
paid education leave clause, 308

United Steelworkers (USW), 20–22, 226, 233,
    269–70
call centres, 277, 280–81
campaign to organize Omega, 281, 283
history, 222–23
Humanities Fund, 221–22, 226–31
membership diversity, 224–26, 281
new organizing model, 281
organizing, 225
organizing strategies, 225, 277
rebuilding, 224
response to corporate-led globalization, 226
service sector workers, 281
union renewal, 226
working women in Ontario, 225
University of Toronto, 225
University of Victoria Student Society employees,
    225
Upholsterers' International Union, 225
U.S., 32, 37–38, 40, 44, 48–49, 52, 125
community-based labour organizing, 239
company unionism, 32
private for-profit health industry, 275
trend towards general unionism, 45
union decline, 15, 38, 61, 179
union leadership/membership mismatch, 46
union organizing, 80, 106
values-based right-wing movement, 179
U.S. labour movement, 38
tensions within, 39
U.S. "right to work," 213
U.S. unions, 32, 38, 171
"card check" and "neutrality" agreements, 212
losses, 145
USW. *See* United Steelworkers (USW)
utilities, 74

vacation and holiday pay, 257
"value-added" or "mutual gains" model of
    unionism, 32, 34
Vancouver, 55
Vargas, Cinthya, 253
Varieties of Unionism (Frege), 48
Venezuela, 48
Victims' Services, 139
visible minorities, 202
vision and goals, 119–21, 125, 145, 164–65
Vosko, Leah, 12, 23
Voss, Kim, 17, 283
Voss, Rebuilding Labour (Milkman), 38

Wal-Mart, 112, 115, 193, 197–98
anti-union tactics, 193
closure of unionized Jonquière plant, 117, 193
influence in the manufacturing industry, 192
water privatization, 153–55
Webb, Beatrice and Sidney, 79
Weir, John, 12, 25
welfare and charity activities, 85
welfare issues, 256
"We're Building a Future Together," 21, 161

West Asians, 238
Westin Harbour Castle, 211
Wetstar, Johanna, 12, 25
White Spot restaurants, 53
wholesale, 162, 169
"Why Do Workers Join Unions?", 257
Wilhelm, John, 217
Wills, Jane, 205
Winners department store, Saskatoon, 195
Winnipeg, 24, 259
Winnipeg Free Press, 256
Winnipeg General Strike, 161, 251
"Wisconsin School," 32
Wobblies, 240
women, 19, 37, 44, 46–47, 54–55, 61, 63–66, 92,
    163, 165, 168, 186, 202, 217, 237–38, 241,
    279, 281, 284, 287. *See also* gender bias
  activists, 111
  barriers to, 111
  in CAW, 161
  in CUPE, 145, 159
  equality, 153
  Female Majority Workplaces, 104–10
  Grass Roots Women, 251, 253
  health, education and social services jobs, 69
  immigrant, 23, 242–43
  initiative to organize, 108
  interest in joining unions, 105–6
  International Transport Workers' Federation
      Womens' Conference, 172
  labour force participation, 105
  leadership role in unions, 46
  leadership training, 110
  National Action Committee on the Status of
      Women, 150
  PEL program, 319
  pink-collar jobs, 69
  poor wages and working conditions, 105, 224
  professional jobs, 69–71
  public and social services, 64, 68, 70, 75, 105
  rate of unionization, 46, 105
  role in union renewal, 16
  as source of new membership, 103
  in Steelworkers, 225
  Summer Institute for Union Women, 302
  support for unions, 65, 76, 110
  union density among, 67
women organizers, 108, 111–12, 151
women's groups, 84, 97
women's shelters, 146
Wong, Kent, 283
WORC
  model of union–community solidarity and
      cooperation, 259
work–life–balance issues, 65
worker ambivalence, 44
worker as citizen, 82
worker conservatism, 50
worker empowerment, 240
worker exchanges and global alliances, 227–31,
    233

worker investment funds, 86–87
worker mobilization, 31, 215
worker resistance, 35, 43
worker support for right-wing political parties, 87
worker-to-worker education techniques, 122
Workers' Action Centre (WAC), 23, 243, 246
Workers' Compensation Board, 254
Workers' Information Centre (W.I.C.), 23, 243–46
  employer-specific committees, 245
workers of colour, 54, 63, 65–66, 92, 150–51, 153,
    159, 161, 163, 165, 168, 204, 281
  union density among, 75
Workers of Colour Support Network, 251, 253
Workers' Organizing and Resource Centre
    (WORC), 24, 240, 251–59
  cross-sectoral solidarity, 255
  mandate, 252
  mission statement, 251
  public advocacy, 257
  referrals to unions, 257
  staff, 251
workers with disabilities, 46–47, 54, 92, 151
workforce
  changing composition of, 65, 69, 79
  diverse, 36
  diversity, 35, 54
  increased polarization, 76
working class resistance, 241
Working Ventures, 86
Workplace Leadership Program
  Campbell attack and, 139–40
  problems with, 141
World Youth Day, 207, 209
WTO, 227

Yates, Charlotte, 12, 18–19, 48, 80, 283, 301
"Yes! National Public Medicare," 267–68
Yoe, Marion, 253
young immigrants, 198
young workers, 37, 44, 53–55, 63, 92, 107, 151,
    168, 245, 256, 279, 281, 284, 290
  Aboriginal, 198
  of colour, 198
  National Youth Conference, 197
  as organizers, 156
  support for unions, 65
  union density, 76
Young Workers' Committee, 302
youth conferences, 169, 195–98
youth internship program, 22, 191, 194–95
youth initiatives, 23
youth outreach, 252

Zambia, 49
Zimbabwe, 49